Authority

READINGS IN SOCIAL AND POLITICAL THEORY
Edited by William Connolly and Steven Lukes

Authority *edited by Joseph Raz*
Feminism and Equality *edited by Anne Phillips*
Interpreting Politics *edited by Michael T. Gibbons*
Language and Politics *edited by Michael J. Shapiro*
Legitimacy and the State *edited by William Connolly*
Liberalism and Its Critics *edited by Michael J. Sandel*
Power *edited by Steven Lukes*
Rational Choice *edited by Jon Elster*
Social Contract Theory *edited by Michael Lessnoff*

Authority

Edited by JOSEPH RAZ

NEW YORK UNIVERSITY PRESS
Washington Square, New York

Copyright Selection and editorial material © Joseph Raz 1990

First published in the U.S.A. in 1990 by NEW YORK UNIVERSITY PRESS
Washington Square
New York, NY 10003

All rights reserved.

Library of Congress Cataloging-in-Publiication Data

Authority/edited by Joseph Raz.
p. cm. — (Readings in social and political theory)
ISBN 0-8147-7414-8 ISBN 0-8147-7415-6 (pbk.)
1. Authority. 2. Authority—Moral and ethical aspects.
3. Legitimacy of governments. I. Raz, Joseph. II. Series.
JC 571. A84 1990
303.3'6—dc20   90-32844
                                                                    CIP

Typeset in Sabon on 10/11 pt.
by Setrite Typesetters Limited
Printed in Great Britain by Billing & Sons Ltd, Worcester

Contents

Acknowledgements		vi
Introduction *Joseph Raz*		1
1	The Conflict between Authority and Autonomy *R. P. Wolff*	20
2	In Defense of a Hobbesian Conception of Law *R. Ladenson*	32
3	On the Concept of Authority in Political Philosophy *R. B. Friedman*	56
4	Commands and Authoritative Legal Reasons *H. L. A. Hart*	92
5	Authority and Justification *J. Raz*	115
6	On the Source of the Authority of the State *G. E. M. Anscombe*	142
7	Authority *J. M. Finnis*	174
8	Perspectives on Authority *S. Lukes*	203
9	Obligations of Community *R. M. Dworkin*	218
10	Commitment and Community *L. Green*	240
11	Promissory Obligation: The Theme of Social Contract *K. Greenawalt*	268
12	Moral Conflict and Political Legitimacy *T. Nagel*	300
Index		325

Acknowledgements

The sources of the readings in this book are as follows, in order of appearance:

R. P. Wolff, 'The Conflict between Authority and Autonomy', from *In Defense of Anarchy*, by Robert Paul Wolff. Copyright © 1970 by Robert Paul Wolff. Reprinted by permission of Harper & Row, Publishers, Inc.

R. Ladenson, 'In Defense of a Hobbesian Conception of Law', from *Philosophy and Public Affairs*, Vol. 9, No. 2. Copyright © 1980 by Princeton University Press.

R. B. Friedman, 'On the Concept of Authority in Political Philosophy', from *Concepts in Social and Political Philosophy*, edited by R. E. Flatham. Copyright © 1973 by R. B. Friedman. Reprinted by permission of Macmillan, Ltd.

H. L. A. Hart, 'Commands and Authoritative Legal Reasons', reprinted from *Essays on Bentham*, by H. L. A. Hart (1982) by permission of Oxford University Press. Copyright © John Finnis 1980.

J. Raz, 'Authority and Justification', from *Philosophy and Public Affairs*, Vol. 14, No. 1, Winter 1985. Copyright © 1985 by Princeton University Press.

G. E. M. Anscombe, 'On the Source of the Authority of the State', from *Ratio*, 1978, Vol. 20. Copyright © 1978 by Basil Blackwell.

J. M. Finnis, 'Authority', reprinted from *Natural Law and Natural Rights*, by John Finnis. Copyright © John Finnis 1980.

S. Lukes, 'Perspectives on Authority', reprinted by permission of New York University Press from *Authority Revisited: NOMOS XXIX*, edited by J. Roland Pennock and John W. Chapman. Copyright © 1987 by New York University.

R. M. Dworkin, 'Obligations of Community', from *Law's Empire*, by R. M. Dworkin. Copyright © 1986 by R. M. Dworkin. Reprinted by permission of Harvard University Press.

L. Green, 'Commitment and Community', reprinted from *The Authority of the State*, by Leslie Green (1988) by permission of Oxford University Press. Copyright © Leslie Green 1988.

K. Greenawalt, 'Promissory Obligation: The Theme of Social Contract', from *Conflicts of Law and Morality*, by Kent Greenawalt. Copyright © 1987 by Oxford University Press, Inc. Reprinted by permission.

T. Nagel, 'Moral Conflict and Political Legitimacy', from *Philosophy and Public Affairs*, Vol 16, No. 3. Copyright © 1987 by Princeton University Press.

Introduction

JOSEPH RAZ

Authority is a central topic in political studies. It can be and is examined from different points of view and with different aims in mind. Some studies are primarily explanatory-sociological, exploring the conditions and causes of the emergence of authority, its development and disintegration, its causal relations with various political, cultural and economic factors, and the like. The works assembled here represent a different perspective, which is predominantly normative or moral. The focus of attention is on the question of justification, on the question of the considerations, if any, which justify the existence of authority; and determine who is subject to it and who is entitled to hold it, and whether there are any general moral limits to authority. Some of the articles concentrate more on the very idea of authority generally, or of political authority in particular. Others address the moral-justificatory issue more directly. Their juxtaposition here indicates a belief that the conceptual-clarificatory and the moral-justificatory issues are inextricably intertwined. My aim in the following pages is to raise some of the problems which a normative theory of political authority must contend with. The selection will indicate a point of view. On some issues I will briefly argue for certain conclusions. But on the fundamental issues I have nothing to offer but questions.

LOCATING THE ISSUE

Sometimes things are referred to as authoritative simply to indicate that they are binding, perhaps because they can be trusted to guide one correctly, they are dependable. 'The authority of reason' is perhaps used in this way. It means that Reason rather than revelation and the Word of God should be one's guide. This, however, is an extended and watered down use of 'authoritative'. In its central meaning the authoritative is what was made binding or reliable by an authority.[1] An authoritative edition of a poet's work, or the authoritative text of his poems, or the authoritative version of it, are those which were prepared by authorities on his work, and are therefore to be relied upon to represent his intention, or to replicate the original manuscript correctly, etc. Notice that the original manuscript is not an authoritative manuscript. It is simply the original manuscript. In such contexts the 'authoritative' connotes the intervention of an authority which vouches that its works (text, book, translation, etc.) are true to some original. These two elements are very much in evidence when one turns to scientific authorities, and to theoretical authorities generally. An authority on medieval coins, or on Chinese eleventh-century porcelain, or on quantum mechanics, or on the aerodynamic properties of some new materials: these are all people who are expert in their fields, i.e. who are good at stating how things are. Their judgement is a particularly reliable guide as to how things are independently of that judgement.

But not everyone who has authority can make something authoritative, not everyone can make something bind. If I have authority to read mail addressed to my boss I am simply permitted to (and therefore have a right to) do so, by someone who has authority to issue such permissions. This someone need not be my boss. He can be his or her secretary, or his or her superior. So we have at least three uses of 'authority'. To have authority is, sometimes, (1) to have (a right created by a) permission to do something (which is generally prohibited). It is also (2) to have the right to grant such permissions, and finally, it is (3) to be an expert who can vouch for the reliability of particular information.[2] This authority of the expert can be called theoretical authority, for it is an authority about what to believe. Where does political authority belong? At first sight it belongs to none of these. It is a right to command. Perhaps 'command' is too narrow a term here. What we really have in mind is a right to make laws and regulations, to judge and to punish for failing to conform to certain standards, or to order some redress for the victims of such violations, as well as a right to command. If we generalize 'a right to rule' to include the right to make laws, regulations, etc., the expansion is broadened to include our second sense above – having a right to give permissions – as a special case, for the right to make laws and regulations includes the right to grant permissions.

We seem to end with three central uses of authority. Having authority may mean having permission, or having the right to rule, or being an expert who can vouch for the reliability of information, or for the authenticity of a text.

All this may be far from the experience of many for whom political authority just means state power. All the writers represented in this volume agree that neither brute force by itself nor any amount of influence or power are sufficient to constitute any person or body as an authority. We often distinguish between legitimate authorities and those which are merely *de facto*. Legitimate authorities are there by right. They have the right to act as authorities. Mere *de facto* authorities do not, but they claim such right. Here lies the difference between naked power and *de facto* authority. *De facto* authority comes under a mantle of legitimacy. It claims the right of an authority. This leaves open the question of whether political authority must have real power to qualify. This book does not go into the question. All the articles in it share the common ground that only those who have real power can, in normal circumstances, have legitimate political authority. The reasons for this are not always obvious. Most of the succeeding articles give an account of the conditions under which an authority is legitimate. An examination of these conditions shows that they cannot be fulfilled unless the authority possesses *de facto* power.

THE CHALLENGE OF PHILOSOPHICAL ANARCHISM

Back then to the question of political authority. The notion of a right to rule is deeply disturbing. No one has brought out the problematic aspect of authority better than Robert Paul Wolff in his *In Defense of Anarchy*.[3] Most people are puzzled by the idea that one person should have a right to rule another. A conventional cliché says that democracies constitute self-rule. In them the people rule themselves. Whatever the truth of this statement, it does not meet the challenge. Even if it is true that in democracies the people rule themselves, I do not rule myself, not even in a democracy. One more sophisticated answer is that in a democracy each voter has as much political power over himself and over everyone else as is consistent with a like power to others. In this way democracies dissolve the paradox of how anyone can have a right to rule.[4] Clearly this claim in favour of democracy is factually false for all known countries. In all of them disparities of economic power, and other disparities translate into inequality of political power. But even if it were true it would have missed the real puzzle about authority. Even if democratic power is the most extensive power over myself and others I can have, without claiming for myself more than others can have, it is not the most extensive power I can have over myself. It still involves submission to the will of others. Can I not have absolute right to decide my own action while conceding an equal right to all? That is anarchy. But it may be that only anarchy avoids the problem with authority.

Wolff's insight was to see that the problem is not in the right to rule directly, but in the duty to obey the ruler which it brings in its wake. The duty to obey conveys an abdication of autonomy, that is, of the right and duty to be responsible for one's action and to conduct oneself in the best light of reason. If there is an authority which is legitimate, then its subjects are duty bound to obey it whether they agree with it or not. Such a duty is inconsistent with autonomy, with the right and the duty to act responsibly, in the light of reason. Hence, Wolff's denial of the moral possibility of legitimate authority. This is the challenge of philosophical anarchism. Much of the debate about authority in the last two decades is best understood as so many replies to this challenge, even though the authors did not always conceive of the problem in this way.

The most common route followed to avoid the anarchist's challenge consists in attempting to assimilate authority as a right to rule with authority in one of its other uses.[5] Ladenson's essay in this volume is a sophisticated attempt to argue that a right to rule is really like a right to read the boss's mail. To have it is no more than to be authorized, i.e. allowed, to do something. In the case of political authorities that something is the use of coercion in circumstances in which it is usually forbidden. If a right to rule means no more than an authorization to use coercion, then it involves no duty of obedience. Without a duty of obedience the anarchist's problem does not arise.

It is doubtful, however, whether Ladenson's account, which denies that citizens have a duty to obey the law of a legitimate government, matches our understanding of political authority. In my essay in this volume I try to show that it does not, and that a right to rule is not to be understood as a permission to use coercion. Most of the other writers represented in this collection choose the other route. Their ways of understanding political authority point to similarities between political authority and theoretical authority, the authority of the experts. None of them goes so far as to say that political authority is just a species of theoretical authority.[6] But they all show that the two types of authority are closely related.

Indeed a close connection between theoretical and political

authority is presupposed by the philosophical anarchist's challenge. What after all is disturbing in the case of authority? It is not the fact that one person complies with the will of another. If when I walk the street I realize that someone wants to find the gate to my college I will, other things being equal, help him do so. That person's desire to find the gate is my reason. You may think me misguided, but there is no denial of autonomy in my action. Whatever the inadequacies of utilitarianism, no one could think that it requires the abdication of one's autonomy just because it claims that one should act to satisfy other people's preferences.

The special problem with authority is not that it requires one to regard the will of another as one's reason for action, but that it requires one to let authoritative directives pre-empt one's own judgement. One should comply with them whether or not one agrees with them. This feature, analysed in the present volume in the essays by Friedman, Hart and myself, depends on the special function of authority. As the essays by Anscombe and Finnis make clear, authorities are justified in terms of a task they have to fulfil. The right to rule is the result of a need to be ruled, a need arising from the needs of the community and its members, and from the community's interest in developing common facilities and services and in improving the life of its members. Authority is only justified to the extent that it serves these needs and interests. We are duty bound to obey a legitimate authority because doing so is meant to serve best the needs and interests which authorities are there to serve. Unlike the ordinary 'utilitarian' reason to satisfy people's preferences, which takes that satisfaction as good in itself, regardless of the grounds which led people to have these preferences, the directives of legitimate authorities are to be complied with not because this would satisfy the wishes of the authorities but because complying with them is a way of serving other interests and needs, for example, the interests and needs of members of the community subject to that authority.

We can see now the way in which political authority resembles theoretical authority. Just as the word of a theoretical authority is a reason for belief because it attests to the fact that there are other reasons (other than that word) for such a belief, so the directive of a legitimate political authority is a reason for action because it attests to the fact that such action would serve interests and needs we have independent (i.e. independent of that directive) reason to serve.

Perhaps surprisingly, this feature, which appears to make submission to authority more palatable than a utilitarian deference to the will of others, turns out on examination to make it more problematic. Instead of abating the anarchist challenge, the similarity between political and theoretical authority stokes its fire. The reason is simple. While utilitarian reasons for acceding to someone's will are independent reasons, which add to the balance of reasons for action which confront the agent, the reason one has to comply with the directives of a legitimate authority is a dependent reason: it depends on the fact that compliance is the best way of acting in accordance with those reasons which are reflected in the authoritative directives. Therefore, the reason to comply with authority, being dependent on those background reasons, is not to be added to them. Rather it pre-empts them. The subjects of legitimate authority are to comply with its directive as the best way of conforming to those background reasons. This, however, means that they yielded to the authority the right to determine how to comply with (those background) reasons. And here lies the paradox. In obeying the authority they abdicated their autonomy, says the philosophical anarchist, they abdicated their responsibility to decide on the balance of reasons themselves.

AUTHORITY AND COORDINATION

One response to the anarchist challenge is to minimize the significance of authority. This dissolves the challenge by arguing that legitimate political authorities are to be understood in analogy with theoretical authorities. Like the latter, they do not impose obligations and there is no obligation to obey them, and therefore no surrender of autonomy. It has the advantage over Ladenson's position in that it allows that authorities set standards for action which one has reason to follow. They are not merely (legitimately) coercive agents, as they are according to Ladenson. I will simplify this response to make its consideration here possible.[7] I believe that the primary arguments in support of political authority rely on its expertise (or that of its policy-making advisers) and on its ability to secure social coordination. The first is seen most clearly in consumer-protection legislation, the regulation of the pharmaceutical industry, laws to secure safety at work or on the roads, etc. The latter is most evident in the provision of public goods.[8] But both are present in greater or lesser degree in most cases of justified governmental action. Let us concentrate on its coordinative function.

According to the game-theoretical analysis of coordination

problems[9] these problems arise when there are several courses of action available such that each person will be best off if he pursues any of them provided that all (or the vast majority of) the others do the same. Given that everyone wants to do what the others will do the problem is to break the circle and mark one course of action as the one which all will follow confidently expecting all others to do the same. This is the problem of generating salience, of marking one of the alternatives as the one to follow. Governments can secure salience. Statutes and regulations which direct people to follow a certain course of action give that course of action salience and indicate to everyone that everyone is likely to prefer that action to its alternatives. It thus becomes the course which everyone has reason to follow. But, and here is the crux, that reason is not a reason to obey the authority. The authority's directive is simply an indication that one particular course of action is the best one to follow, for it will secure the coordination which everyone desires for independent reasons. Thus the coordinative function of authorities is discharged without anyone having any reason to obey them, let alone to abdicate autonomy in doing so.

The shortcoming of this argument is that it is addressed to a narrow and limited notion of coordination, as analysed in game theory. While there have been arguments to the effect that the authority of law can be explained in such terms, I think that such an attempt is doomed to failure. When I expressed (above) the view that the need to secure coordination is one of the main arguments for political authority I did not have in mind coordination in this rather narrow and technical sense, but I was using the ordinary notion of coordination.[10] Securing coordination means just that. It means getting people to act in ways which are sensitive to the way others are guided, or are likely, to act, so that benefits can be expected which are less likely if they act without coordinating their efforts, i.e. without basing their own actions on a view as to how others should or are likely to act. Coordination presupposes that people are not trying to foil each other. Rather they are trying to secure goals which are agreed to by all, or perhaps just goals that all should have. But coordination does not presuppose that every participant will improve his position by coordinating. People can coordinate in attempting to rescue the victims of a natural disaster, though they do so at a great cost to themselves. The prospect that coordinative practices will automatically emerge, which is held out by game theory, is less than compelling given that the need to secure coordination is not the same as the need to solve recurring game-theoretical multi-person coordination problems.

Let me comment briefly on the reasons which can establish the desirability of social coordination in this wider sense. They arise from two sources. First, without a coordinated effort some good, which can in principle be secured at an acceptable cost, will be lost. Second, sometimes the good need not be lost; it can be secured through the contribution of a smaller number of people, but it would be unjust to impose the full burden of securing the good on those people rather than on a larger group. This last point may suggest to some that I am confusing coordination problems with the free rider problem in the provision of public goods. But remember that I do not have in mind only what game theory dubs coordination problems. Nor do I have in mind only the provision of public goods. Coordination may be necessary to secure the protection of an endangered species, or of a natural wilderness. Their protection need not be thought of as a good to anyone. It may be a good in itself. But the need for a coordinated effort arises out of the two reasons I mentioned. Without the coordination either the goal will not be achieved, or if achieved it will be secured through some individuals carrying more than their fair share of the burden, while others contribute nothing or less than they should, or even stand in the way of the goal by their behaviour which may positively increase the threat to the endangered species or the environment.

The common ways of defining coordination problems in game theory can be adapted to include cases in which people have non-self-interested reasons for securing goals which require coordination with others. But they cannot be extended to encompass another way in which our ordinary notion of a coordination problem differs from the game-theoretical one. The game-theoretical notion is essentially subjective. That is, for a coordination problem to exist it is not enough that people's reasons indicate that there are several courses of action each of which will be the best if adopted by all others. A coordination problem exists only if people generally are (1) aware of the structure of their reasons; (2) aware of the courses of action which, if generally followed, will lead to the desired result; (3) aware that the same is true of other people's reasons; and (4) aware that it is generally known that all three conditions (i.e. the previous two and this one) are met. In common parlance coordination problems are objectively understood. They exist whenever the structure of reasons of individuals is as described above. The subjective conditions are not part of the problem, but commonly, part of its solution. That is, the problem is to get people to realize that they are confronting a coordination problem and, once this is achieved, to get them to realize that it is common knowledge that there is a coordination problem, and that it is common knowledge that it is common knowledge.

Needless to say, the fact that coordination problems arise not only when people can best satisfy their own preferences by coordinating with others, but also when they can only secure the morally best outcome by coordinating with others increases considerably the possibility that they will fail to realize that they face a coordination problem, and if they do that they will doubt whether this understanding is common. But quite apart from this consideration there is a big gap between the existence of a coordination problem in the common (objective) sense and the existence of a coordination problem in the game-theoretical (subjective) sense. Once the subjective conditions are met the most difficult part of solving the problem is over. Indeed on many occasions once the subjective conditions are met there is no remaining problem. On many occasions there is only one course of action which will, if generally followed, secure the desired result. Barring irrationality, forgetfulness, etc., it will be followed if the subjective conditions are met. To salvage a problem out of its definition game theory includes a further condition in the definition of a coordination problem. There is such a problem only if there are several possible equilibria points, i.e. several different courses of action each of which will be best if generally followed. This identifies the only problem that game theory sees as a coordination problem, i.e. which course of conduct should one follow under those conditions.

Our common understanding of coordination and its attendant problems, while recognizing that this problem can be real enough, does not regard it as a necessary condition of a coordination problem. The most difficult problem is not that, but the problem of finding a way of satisfying the four subjective conditions which are necessary to secure coordination. I hope that it is now plain how authorities can play a crucial role in securing coordination, and how this role is vital in establishing the legitimacy of political authorities.

Knowing the limits of my knowledge and understanding, and being aware of the danger that my judgement will be affected by bias, and my performance by the weakness of my resolve, I am aware of the possibility that another person, or organization, might be better able to judge when there are strong or sufficient reasons for social coordination in which I should participate. This may be the case if the person or organization is less likely to be biased than I am and if they have greater expertise than I have on the goods and social needs for which coordination may be required, and the ways of achieving them.[11] In such a case I should adopt a rule to follow the instructions of such a person or body, to regard them as authorities, within certain specified bounds. The rule will be vindicated by the fact that following it will lead me to participate in justified coordinated social behaviour more often than if I should try to decide for myself when the conditions of a coordination problem exist, and when I should follow a certain course of conduct as a way of participating in a justified coordinative practice.[12]

So far I have been assuming that all the conditions for a coordinating practice, barring (when it is a condition for the existence of the practice) my participation, exist. The authority I recognize is an authority on (some) existing coordinative practices. It can instruct me better than I can myself when they are justified and how I should contribute to them.[13] But often I should take a further step. I should recognize that other people are in my position and that if we all adopt a coordinating practice to follow the directives of a certain body within certain limits then we will all be able to establish and preserve justified coordinative practices which would otherwise evade our grasp. The reason is that by sharing the knowledge that we all assigned to this body the power to decide for us when coordination problems (in the objective sense) exist and the responsibility to make generally known its proposed solutions, we solve the problem of making sure that the subjective conditions are met. We know that they are met whenever the body whose authority we recognize issues one of its directives.[14]

In other words, there can be justified (second order) coordinative practices setting a person or body as a coordinative authority, i.e. as capable of authoritatively determining when there is a coordination problem and what to do about it, and such practices may be justified. Such practices are rules which justify the legitimacy of an authority (within proper bounds).[15] They make all of us able to solve coordination problems better than we might do when we try to judge for ourselves whether there is a coordination problem and whether the subjective conditions for its solution are met.

Again we encounter the paradox that this vindication of the importance of political authorities in securing valuable social coordination reinstates the anarchist challenge. For the whole argument of this section has demonstrated how, to achieve coordination,

Introduction

citizens must let the authorities decide for them what is to be done. Only if one does not try to act on one's independent judgement but subjects oneself to the judgement of the authority can its advantages in securing coordination be achieved. Does this mean that authorities can only be had at the cost of one's autonomy as the philosophical anarchist claims?

CONSENT AND THE LIMITS OF AUTHORITY

A familiar attempt to answer the anarchist is to claim that there is no violation of one's autonomy in an authority whose legitimacy derives from the consent of each one of the governed, in an original social contract, to be so governed.[16] Why should consent make a difference? One kind of answer alludes to the benefits of consent. If the authority of governments depends on the consent of the governed, governments are more likely to be responsible and responsive, and the governed less likely to be alienated and embittered, etc. Such arguments cannot answer the anarchist challenge. First, unless heavily qualified they are unconvincing in their own terms. There are reasons to think that in modern industrialized mass societies, indirect democracy, i.e. periodic elections by one or other of the familiar election systems, is better able to secure responsible and responsive government and a high level of welfare than contractarian consent, which gives everyone veto power once in their lives, and no power later on (unless people use their veto to impose a requirement of further consent). Second, the philosophical anarchist is not claiming that governments disadvantage the governed. His claim is that they deny the autonomy of the governed by running their lives for them. To answer this charge the consent theorist points to the fact that once the authority of governments derives from consent they are running their subjects' lives for them on their behalf. But how good is this answer? Can a person who sold himself into slavery be said to be autonomous? The rational or moral requirement for responsibility for one's own life cannot be discharged once and for all by a decision to choose a master who will take over from now on. It is a requirement of continuous responsibility for one's actions which persists throughout one's life.

Some, including R. P. Wolff,[17] conclude that only consent to every single act of the government can be consistent with responsibility for one's own life. This is the total denial of the possibility of legitimate authority. But it seems to be going too far. The same reasoning would condemn those who let their doctor decide for them whether to undergo an operation or not, those who buy property or bonds and hire an agent to handle them, etc. Surely responsibility for one's life does not require continuously deciding for oneself on every aspect of one's affairs. A person may with unimpeachable propriety decide to hand all his tax affairs to his accountant, accept the authority of his trade union in all matters of employment, follow, without inquiring to satisfy himself of its soundness, the advice of the teacher regarding all issues concerning the education of his children, accept the right of one of his friends to determine the programme of a group holiday, and the division of duties among its participants, etc. We recognize that responsibility for one's life is consistent with handing power over to someone else, to be better able to concentrate on those aspects of one's life for which one has better aptitude.

At this point things become messy. One-off decisions abdicating responsibility for large stretches of one's life are abdications of responsibility. Some handing over of power over one's affairs to others is not only sensible, but, due to the circumstances of their lives, may be essential for a satisfactory life for many people. We need an account of the considerations which should guide us in the matter and we do not have any decent account of the kind, at least I do not know of one. Still, one or two conclusions can be safely drawn from the preceding considerations. First, the anarchist challenge is exaggerated. If it is good against all governmental authority then it holds against the possibility of granting authority to a doctor, a teacher, an accountant, or a tour organizer. If their limited authority can be legitimate one can in principle have legitimate governmental authority. Many of the government's functions differ little from those of the above. Second, no unlimited authority can be legitimate. If an autonomous person must keep continuous responsibility for his life he cannot abandon responsibility altogether, or give an authority *carte blanche* to do what it thinks best in any matter whatsoever. Only limited government can be legitimate.

It follows from the above that consent by itself cannot be a sufficient foundation for legitimate authority. We need a doctrine of limited government, i.e. of the principled limitations on the possible scope of governmental authority. Consent can legitimize an authority only within the bounds of, or subject to the limitations articulated by, that doctrine. Consent to the power of government beyond these limits would fail to legitimize it. It seems reasonable to suppose that a doctrine of limited government would have two parts. One would simply say that it does not have authority to do what it cannot do efficiently. The other would set limits to what it is in principle authorized to do, i.e. it would exclude from its jurisdiction certain matters even if it can handle them efficiently. Both parts of the doctrine of the limits of authority, in their abstract formulation, would be sensitive to varying social, technological and cultural circumstances which affect not only the ability of governments to achieve certain goals, but the significance and the moral import of their actions as well.

In recent years some liberal political theorists have promoted the idea that the state should be neutral between different conceptions of the good. Nagel's article, reproduced in this volume, attempts to articulate and defend that idea, connecting it firmly to a theory of authority. His is one view of one limit to the power of legitimate authority.[18] Dworkin's discussion of the obligation to obey the law in this volume suggests other ideas for a doctrine of limited government. In my own contribution to the volume I have put forward another idea in the same direction. My idea is based on the thought that whereas normally there is a case for an authority where compliance with its directives would lead its subjects better to comply with reason than if they were not to be guided in their action by that authority, this general rule has an important exception. It consists of all those matters regarding which it is more important to act independently than to succeed in doing the best. I feel the need for a substantive account of this category.

I have stated that the power of authorities cannot extend to matters which they are incompetent to deal with as if this were a matter of course. But it presupposes a fundamentally instrumental approach to authority. The basis of legitimacy is relative success in getting people to conform to right reason. This perspective seems to me to be necessary to answer the philosophical anarchist. The anarchist's challenge derives part of its appeal from a reaction against the idea that some people can have a right to rule others. That they can have such a right only when this is necessary to enable people better to conduct themselves in the light of considerations which apply to them anyway is not the only reply that can be made. An alternative line of exploration seeks to show that there is inherent value in conforming to communal authorities just because in doing so one recognizes the good of community, or recognizes the duty one owes to one's community, or to one's rulers. Dworkin's essay represents this brand of thought in the present volume. L. Green's chapter included here considers critically though sympathetically so-called 'communitarian' arguments of this kind.[19]

The possibility that instrumental considerations play a role in justifying authority brings us back to the issue of consent. According to such instrumental justifications of authority its function is to enable people to achieve goals, and to act in ways which they have reason to follow in any case. As mentioned above, one major source of legitimacy lies in the ability of authorities to achieve desirable social coordination, which people should pursue, but are unable to achieve at all, or are less likely to achieve as efficiently, unaided by authority. The question can be asked whether it is right to impose a *coercive* authority over people to pursue such goals. If they fail to act in the required way they are, let us assume, to blame, but it does not follow that they may be required by authority to act as they should and be coerced into doing so or be penalized if they do not. One popular view is that authorities can impose coercive requirements only with the consent of the governed. Of the writers here represented this view has been explicitly endorsed by L. Green.

We face two problems here, not one. First, can an authority not consented to by its subjects have the right to impose authoritative requirements on them? Second, can such an authority have the right to use coercive means to secure compliance? The first question is itself problematic. All we are considering here is whether it is justified to hold that people have a duty to obey an authority to the authority of which they did not consent but compliance with which will ensure that they stand a better chance of discharging their moral obligations, and generally will better achieve what they ought to achieve. Since people can have obligations which they did not consent to,[20] why should it be problematic that they should have this obligation (the obligation to obey) independently of consent, given that it depends on those other obligations? This is not to deny that there can be an argument for a limited role for consent in certain areas. For example, one may argue that whereas the legitimacy of an authority put in charge of directing people towards performing their duties to others need not be based on consent, no authority may impose paternalistic duties aimed to protect its subjects against themselves without the consent of each and every one of them. Such considerations belong to the doctrine of limited government mentioned above. Supporters of the 'Harm to Others' principle may well object that authorities do not have the right to impose directly paternalistic duties at all, not even with consent. Others may wish to draw distinctions between matters whose rightful regulation depends on consent, those whose rightful regulation depends on the weaker condition of consensus, and those which must remain outside the legitimate power of any government.[21]

It has to be admitted that most discussions of these issues concentrate on the coercive nature of the law.[22] Many writers view the problem of the legitimacy of political authority as a problem of the justification of coercion. Others, while accepting that political authorities do regularly resort to coercion, and perhaps even that this is their defining feature, seek to find the authoritative quality of their directives elsewhere, i.e. in their moral right to impose duties. Following H. Kelsen and H. L. A. Hart, I have argued elsewhere[23] that the question of coercion is a separate issue. Political authority has coercive powers, but its authority extends beyond its use of those powers. It appeals to people's recognition of their moral and civic duties, while being ready, in many or even most cases, to use coercion if the appeal fails. Two questions have to be confronted: first, has the authority the right to impose duties on certain people regarding certain matters, and second, has it the right to use coercion to secure compliance with duties it (legitimately) imposed or with other duties which apply to its subjects.

The two questions are interconnected in that the answer to the first may depend on the answer to the second: that is, in certain circumstances, authorities do not have a right to require action of their subjects in matters regarding which they cannot legitimately assure the conscientious citizen of general compliance. Regarding some matters it is unfair and unjust to require some people to act in certain ways at a time when many others do not. If others are unlikely to behave in the desirable way unless put under threat of coercion then the authority has no right to require such action unless it has the right and the ability to enforce its directive through the use or the threat of coercion. These remarks recall the earlier discussion of coordination, which is one prime example of the dependence of the right to command on the right to coerce which we are considering. Coordination achieves its goal only if the bulk of the relevant population participates. Both efficiency and fairness may be involved. Coordination may fail altogether if it does not enjoy a sufficient level of cooperation, and those who cooperate may face greater burdens than would be otherwise required because some people prefer to free ride. In such cases it may be that the right to command depends on the right to coerce which is necessary to assure all of compliance by all (or nearly so).

Closely related the issues of authority and coercion may be; nevertheless they are both conceptually and practically distinct. Nor do I find reason to think that coercion can only be justified by the consent of the coerced. There is no doubt that on many occasions making the right to command or coerce depend on revocable consent is an important protection against the abuse of power. But regarding general political issues such protection is sufficiently met by democratic accountability. There is no general argument of principle that I am aware of which would require consent.

So far I have ignored one aspect of authority relations which distinguishes them from most other moral duties. Many moral duties arise out of circumstances, including those created by human action. But they are not deliberately imposed by one human being on another with the aim of subjecting that other to a duty. I have been treating the issue of authority as a problem of action in accordance with right reason, disregarding the fact that it involves this dimension of subjugation. It has been implicitly assumed by writers such as Anscombe and Finnis that where the authority is successfully guided by objectively valid considerations the problem of subjugation does not arise. The problem of subjugation is assumed to arise only when one person is made to serve the interest of his superior, or is subjected to his arbitrary will. This is a misperception. While arbitrary use of power makes things much worse, there is a problem in submitting to the rule even of an enlightened and benevolent other. This is not Wolff's problem. It is not the problem of abdicating one's responsibility for one's actions, of forgoing one's autonomy. It is a problem of the relations between one person and another. We have views of what interpersonal relations are morally acceptable. They involve mutual respect, reciprocity, etc. One-sided submission to the will of an authority seems to violate these precepts. Some may object that our moral notions of proper relationships apply between individuals, and do not concern institutions such as governments. But this seems too sweeping, if for no other reason than because of the fact that in our relations to governmental institutions we deal with people in positions of power. We experience the relationship as a relationship with the people we interact with, and our public culture contributes to this by its tendency to personalize political issues. Besides, if anything, submission to an anonymous, bureaucratic big brother seems to present worse problems and to raise more objections than submission to an individual.

It is true, though, that institutions differ from individuals, and while institutions raise the spectre of bureaucratic insensitivity, they also offer the prospect of membership. We saw earlier how ideas of self-rule through consent were deployed, ultimately unsuccessfully, to reconcile authority and autonomy. Similar ideas have been invoked to describe the way in which submission to authority can be squared with our notions of a proper relationship between people. The aim is to develop a doctrine of political authority which makes its legitimacy conditional on the existence of a population which regards the government as its representative, and in which people identify with the common interest, so that they regard its pursuit as their business and the law as their law. Here too, consent by itself, actual consent to a social contract, cannot solve the problem. But a theory of participatory government in a society in which conditions exist that enable each to see his own well-being as tied up with the prosperity of others can do so. The development of such a theory has been the aim of political philosophy since Rousseau. Its achievement is eagerly awaited.

NOTES

1 'Authoritative' also refers to what has the appearance, or bearing of authority. But throughout this book the use of 'authority' to indicate a style or a manner is disregarded.
2 I mention these distinctions because they are relevant to the argument of this book. By and large both the introduction and the articles in the present volume are not concerned with the large number of important liguistic distinctions between types of authority, between being an authority, having authority, being in authority, acting authoritatively, etc., as these do not affect the main thrust of the analysis and justification of political authorities.
3 R. P. Wolff, *In Defense of Anarchy* (Harper, New York, 1970). Chapter one of the book is reproduced in this volume.
4 See for the claim, and its qualifications, Peter Singer, *Democracy and Disobedience* (OUP, Oxford, 1973).
5 An interesting and challenging exception is H. L. A. Hart's analysis included in this collection. For him legal, and therefore presumably also political, authority is not inconsistent with autonomy as Wolff thinks because it does not enjoy moral status. While both moral issues and legal issues are discussed in the same normative terms, they represent different usages of the language which do not conflict. While the law may be making legal claims to obedience these are not moral claims. Judges who decide that people have certain duties, and

enforce these decisions, decide that that is what people ought-legally to do, and it does not follow that people ought-morally so to act. Accepting the authority of the courts and of other political institutions does not import any moral view, and therefore does not contradict one's moral autonomy.

6 The only recent argument to that effect that I know of is by Heidi Hurd, *Yale Law Journal*, (forthcoming).
7 I am here relying on and adapting to the present purpose the arguments of L. Green and D. Regan. See L. Green, 'Authority and Convention' *Philosophical Quarterly* 35 (1985) 329 and his *The Authority of the State* (OUP, Oxford, 1988): and D. Regan 'Law's Halo' in J. Coleman and E. F. Paul (eds), *Philosophy and Law* (Basil Blackwell, Oxford, 1987): and also his 'Authority and value: Joseph Raz and the practice of law', 62 *Southern California Law Review* 995 (1989).
8 On the coordinative function of authorities see, e.g. J. M. Finnis, in this collection; and Eerik Lagerspetz, 'A conventionalist theory of institutions', *Acta Philosophica Fennica*, vol. 44, 1989.
9 See for example the classic analysis of D. Lewis, *Convention* (Harvard University Press, Cambridge Mass., 1969).
10 The discussion in the following eight paragraphs borrows from my 'Facing up', 62 *Southern California Law Review* 1153 (1989).
11 It is sufficient if that person or body is advised by people with such expertise, and tends to follow such advice.
12 The full story requires much refinement. I may regard the authority's directives as sufficient to indicate that reasons for coordination, within the specified limits, require certain conduct of me, without regarding its directives as a necessary condition for such a conclusion. This seems to be the common attitude, though there are cases in which the authority's directives are regarded, perhaps justifiably, as necessary conditions.
13 There is a further advantage to having such an authority. By making the matter public, and involving other people in it, it can strengthen me against weakness of the will.
14 This is again too simple. I am assuming that the authority is limited to solving coordination problems only. In the normal case in which it has other powers as well, all we know is that if its directive is meant to solve a coordination problem then (1) there is likely to be such a problem, (2) the directive is likely to point to a best solution to the problem, and (3) the subjective conditions are met. We also know that if the directive is not based on the need to solve a coordination problem (but falls within the jurisdiction of the authority) then it is likely to be justified on other grounds.
15 And they do so in accordance with the normal justification thesis, which is explained in my contribution to the present volume.
16 I refer here exclusively to actual consent. Hypothetical consent is irrelevant to a challenge based on the duty of people to take responsibility for and to run (actually, not hypothetically) their own lives.

17 R. P. Wolff, *In Defense of Anarchy*, ch. 3.
18 I have criticized Nagel's arguments in 'Facing diversity: the case of epistemic abstinence', *Philosophy and Public Affairs*, (1990) p.1.
19 An original and interesting variant of a noninstrumental argument for authority has been offered by P. Soper, *A Theory of Law* (Harvard University Press, Cambridge, 1984). For my own reflections see J. Raz, *The Authority of Law* (OUP, Oxford, 1979), ch. 13.
20 Modern contractarians base morality not on consent but on what rational people would consent to, i.e. on what on certain assumptions people ought to consent to.
21 For my own attempt to develop an autonomy-based principle of the limits of political authority see J. Raz, *The Morality of Freedom* (OUP, Oxford, 1986), ch. 15.
22 This is true of J. S. Mill's original advocacy of the Harm Principle in *On Liberty*, as well as of almost all the contemporary discussions of it. See, e.g., H. L. A. Hart, *Law, Liberty and Morality* (OUP, Oxford, 1961); Joel Feinberg, *The Moral Limits of the Criminal Law* (OUP, New York, 1984–8); and for a useful collection of essays on paternalism R. Sartorius (ed.), *Paternalism* (University of Minnesota Press, Minneapolis, 1983).
23 Especially in *Practical Reason and Norms* 2nd edn. (Princeton University Press, Princeton, New Jersey, 1990), and in 'Law, Authority and Morality' *The Monist* 1985.

1
The Conflict between Authority and Autonomy

R. P. WOLFF

THE CONCEPT OF AUTHORITY

Politics is the exercise of the power of the state, or the attempt to influence that exercise. Political philosophy is therefore, strictly speaking, the philosophy of the state. If we are to determine the content of political philosophy, and whether indeed it exists, we must begin with the concept of the state.

The state is a group of persons who have and exercise supreme authority within a given territory. Strictly, we should say that a state is a group of persons who have supreme authority within a given territory *or over a certain population*. A nomadic tribe may exhibit the authority structure of a state, so long as its subjects do not fall under the superior authority of a territorial state.[1] The state may include all the persons who fall under its authority, as does the democratic state according to its theorists; it may also consist of a single individual to whom all the rest are subject. We may doubt whether the one-person state has ever actually existed, although Louis XIV evidently thought so when he announced, "L'état, c'est moi." The distinctive characteristic of the state is supreme authority, or what political philosophers used to call "sovereignty." Thus one speaks of "popular sovereignty," which is the doctrine that the people are the state, and of course the use of "sovereign" to mean "king" reflects the supposed concentration of supreme authority in a monarchy.

Authority is the right to command, and correlatively, the right to be obeyed. It must be distinguished from power, which is the ability to compel compliance, either through the use or the threat of force. When I turn over my wallet to a thief who is holding me at gunpoint, I do so because the fate with which he threatens me is worse than the loss of money which I am made to suffer. I grant that he has power over me, but I would hardly suppose that he has *authority*, that is, that he has a right to demand my money and that I have an obligation to give it to him. When the government presents me with a bill for taxes, on the other hand, I pay it (normally) even though I do not wish to, and even if I think I can get away with not paying. It is, after all, the duly constituted government, and hence it has a *right* to tax me. It has *authority* over me. Sometimes, of course, I cheat the government, but even so, I acknowledge its authority, for who would speak of "cheating" a thief?

To *claim* authority is to claim the right to be obeyed. To *have* authority is then — what? It may mean to have that right, or it may mean to have one's claim acknowledged and accepted by those at whom it is directed. The term "authority" is ambiguous, having both a descriptive and a normative sense. Even the descriptive sense refers to norms or obligations, of course, but it does so by *describing* what men believe they ought to do rather than by *asserting* that they ought to do it.

Corresponding to the two senses of authority, there are two concepts of the state. Descriptively, the state may be defined as a group of persons who are *acknowledged* to have supreme authority within a territory — acknowledged, that is, by those over whom the authority is asserted. The study of the forms, characteristics, institutions, and functioning of *de facto* states, as we may call them, is the province of political science. If we take the term in its prescriptive signification, the state is a group of persons who have the *right* to exercise supreme authority within a territory. The discovery, analysis, and demonstration of the forms and principles of legitimate authority — of the right to rule — is called political philosophy.

What is meant by *supreme* authority? Some political philosophers, speaking of authority in the normative sense, have held that the true state has ultimate authority over all matters whatsoever that occur within its venue. Jean-Jacques Rousseau, for example, asserted that the social contract by which a just political community is formed 'gives to the body politic absolute command over the members of which it is formed; and it is this power, when directed by the general will, that bears ... the name of "sovereignty."' John Locke, on the other hand, held that the supreme authority of the just state extends only to those matters which it is proper for a state to control. The state is, to be sure, the highest authority, but its right to command is less than absolute. One of the questions which political philosophy must answer is whether there is any limit to the range of affairs over which a just state has authority.

An authoritative command must also be distinguished from a

persuasive argument. When I am commanded to do something, I may choose to comply even though I am not being threatened, because I am brought to believe that it is something which I ought to do. If that is the case, then I am not, strictly speaking, obeying a command, but rather acknowledging the force of an argument or the rightness of a prescription. The person who issues the "command" functions merely as the *occasion* for my becoming aware of my duty, and his role might in other instances be filled by an admonishing friend, or even by my own conscience. I might, by an extension of the term, say that the prescription has authority over me, meaning simply that I ought to act in accordance with it. But the person himself has no authority – or, to be more precise, my complying with his command does not constitute an acknowledgment on my part of any such authority. Thus authority resides in persons; they possess it – if indeed they do at all – by virtue of who they are and not by virtue of what they command. My duty to obey is a duty owed to them, not to the moral law or to the beneficiaries of the actions I may be commanded to perform.

There are, of course, many reasons why men actually acknowledge claims of authority. The most common, taking the whole of human history, is simply the prescriptive force of tradition. The fact that something has always been done in a certain way strikes most men as a perfectly adequate reason for doing it that way again. Why should we submit to a king? Because we have always submitted to kings. But why should the oldest son of the king become king in turn? Because oldest sons have always been heirs to the throne. The force of the traditional is engraved so deeply on men's minds that even a study of the violent and haphazard origins of a ruling family will not weaken its authority in the eyes of its subjects.

Some men acquire the aura of authority by virtue of their own extraordinary characteristics, either as great military leaders, as men of saintly character, or as forceful personalities. Such men gather followers and disciples around them who willingly obey without consideration of personal interest or even against its dictates. The followers believe that the leader has a *right to command*, which is to say, *authority*.

Most commonly today, in a world of bureaucratic armies and institutionalized religions, when kings are few in number and the line of prophets has run out, authority is granted to those who occupy official positions. As Weber has pointed out, these positions appear authoritative in the minds of most men because they are defined by certain sorts of bureaucratic regulations having the

The Conflict between Authority and Autonomy

virtues of publicity, generality, predictability, and so forth. We become conditioned to respond to the visible signs of officiality, such as printed forms and badges. Sometimes we may have clearly in mind the justification for a legalistic claim to authority, as when we comply with a command because its author is an *elected* official. More often the mere sight of a uniform is enough to make us feel that the man inside it has a right to be obeyed.

That men accede to claims of supreme authority is plain. That men *ought* to accede to claims of supreme authority is not so obvious. Our first question must therefore be; under what conditions and for what reasons does one man have supreme authority over another? The same question can be restated; under what conditions can a state (understood normatively) exist?

Kant has given us a convenient title for this sort of investigation. He called it a "deduction," meaning by the term not a proof of one proposition from another, but a demonstration of the legitimacy of a concept. When a concept is empirical, its deduction is accomplished merely by pointing to instances of its objects. For example, the deduction of the concept of a horse consists in exhibiting a horse. Since there are horses, it must be legitimate to employ the concept. Similarly, a deduction of the descriptive concept of a state consists simply in pointing to the innumerable examples of human communities in which some men claim supreme authority over the rest and are obeyed. But when the concept in question is nonempirical, its deduction must proceed in a different manner. All normative concepts are nonempirical, for they refer to what ought to be rather than to what is. Hence, we cannot justify the use of the concept of (normative) supreme authority by presenting instances.[2] We must demonstrate by an *a priori* argument that there can be forms of human community in which some men have a moral right to rule. In short, the fundamental task of political philosophy is to provide a *deduction of the concept of the state*.

To complete this deduction, it is not enough to show that there are circumstances in which men have an obligation to do what the *de facto* authorities command. Even under the most unjust of governments there are frequently good reasons for obedience rather than defiance. It may be that the government has commanded its subjects to do what in fact they already have an independent obligation to do; or it may be that the evil consequences of defiance far outweigh the indignity of submission. A government's commands may promise beneficent effects, either intentionally or not. For these reasons, and for reasons of prudence as well, a man may be right to comply with the commands of the government under whose *de facto* authority he finds himself. But none of this settles the question of legitimate authority. That is a matter of the *right* to command, and of the correlative obligation *to obey the person who issues the command*.

The point of the last paragraph cannot be too strongly stressed. Obedience is not a matter of doing what someone tells you to do. It is a matter of doing what he tells you to do *because he tells you to do it*. Legitimate, or *de jure*, authority thus concerns the grounds and sources of moral obligation.

Since it is indisputable that there are men who believe that others have authority over them, it might be thought that we could use that fact to prove that somewhere, at some time or other, there must have been men who really did possess legitimate authority. We might think, that is to say, that although some claims to authority might be wrong, it could not be that *all* such claims were wrong, since then we never would have had the concept of legitimate authority at all. By a similar argument, some philosophers have tried to show that not all our experiences are dreams, or more generally that in experience not everything is mere appearance rather than reality. The point is that terms like "dream" and "appearance" are defined by contrast with "waking experience" or "reality." Hence we could only have developed a use for them by being presented with situations in which some experiences were dreams and others not, or some things mere appearance and others reality.

Whatever the force of that argument in general, it cannot be applied to the case of *de facto* versus *de jure* authority, for the key component of both concepts, namely "right," is imported into the discussion from the realm of moral philosophy generally. Insofar as we concern ourselves with the possibility of a just state, we *assume* that moral discourse is meaningful and that adequate deductions have been given of concepts like "right," "duty," and "obligation."[3]

What can be inferred from the existence of *de facto* states is that men *believe* in the existence of legitimate authority, for of course a *de facto* state is simply a state whose subjects believe it to be legitimate (i.e., really to have the authority which it claims for itself). They may be wrong. Indeed, *all* beliefs in authority may be wrong — there may be not a single state in the history of mankind which has now or ever has had a right to be obeyed. It might even be impossible for such a state to exist; that is the question we must try to settle. But so long as men believe in the authority of states, we can conclude that they possess the concept of *de jure* authority.[4]

The normative concept of the state as the human community which possesses rightful authority within a territory thus defines the subject matter of political philosophy proper. However, even if it should prove impossible to present a deduction of the concept — if, that is, there can be no *de jure* state — still a large number of moral questions can be raised concerning the individual's relationship with *de facto* states. We may ask, for example, whether there are any moral principles which ought to guide the state in its lawmaking, such as the principle of utilitarianism, and under what conditions it is right for the individual to obey the laws. We may explore the social ideals of equality and achievement, or the principles of punishment, or the justifications for war. All such investigations are essentially applications of general moral principles to the particular phenomena of (*de facto*) politics. Hence, it would be appropriate to reclaim a word which has fallen on bad days, and call that branch of the study of politics *casuistical politics*. Since there are men who acknowledge claims to authority, there are *de facto* states. Assuming that moral discourse in general is legitimate, there must be moral questions which arise in regard to such states. Hence, casuistical politics as a branch of ethics does exist. It remains to be decided whether political philosophy proper exists.

THE CONCEPT OF AUTONOMY

The fundamental assumption of moral philosophy is that men are responsible for their actions. From this assumption it follows necessarily, as Kant pointed out, that men are metaphysically free, which is to say that in some sense they are capable of choosing how they shall act. Being able to choose how he acts makes a man responsible, but merely choosing is not in itself enough to constitute *taking* responsibility for one's actions. Taking responsibility involves attempting to determine what one ought to do, and that, as philosophers since Aristotle have recognized, lays upon one the additional burdens of gaining knowledge, reflecting on motives, predicting outcomes, criticizing principles, and so forth.

The obligation to take responsibility for one's actions does not derive from man's freedom of will alone, for more is required in taking responsibility than freedom of choice. Only because man has the capacity to reason about his choices can he be said to stand under a continuing obligation to take responsibility for them. It is quite appropriate that moral philosophers should group together children and madmen as beings not fully responsible for their actions, for as madmen are thought to lack freedom of choice, so children do not yet possess the power of reason in a developed form. It is even just that we should assign a greater degree of responsibility to children, for madmen, by virtue of their lack of free will, are completely without responsibility, while children, insofar as they possess reason in a partially developed form, can be held responsible (i.e., can be required to take responsibility) to a corresponding degree.

Every man who possesses both free will and reason has an obligation to take responsibility for his actions, even though he may not be actively engaged in a continuing process of reflection, investigation, and deliberation about how he ought to act. A man will sometimes announce his willingness to take responsibility for the consequences of his actions, even though he has not deliberated about them, or does not intend to do so in the future. Such a declaration is, of course, an advance over the refusal to take responsibility; it at least acknowledges the existence of the obligation. But it does not relieve the man of the duty to engage in the reflective process which he has thus far shunned. It goes without saying that a man may take responsibility for his actions and yet act wrongly. When we describe someone as a responsible individual, we do not imply that he always does what is right, but only that he does not neglect the duty of attempting to ascertain what is right.

The responsible man is not capricious or anarchic, for he does acknowledge himself bound by moral constraints. But he insists that he alone is the judge of those constraints. He may listen to the advice of others, but he makes it his own by determining for himself whether it is good advice. He may learn from others about his moral obligations, but only in the sense that a mathematician learns from other mathematicians – namely by hearing from them arguments whose validity he recognizes even though he did not think of them himself. He does not learn in the sense that one learns from an explorer, by accepting as true his accounts of things one cannot see for oneself.

Since the responsible man arrives at moral decisions which he expresses to himself in the form of imperatives, we may say that he gives laws to himself, or is self-legislating. In short, he is *autonomous*. As Kant argued, moral autonomy is a combination of freedom and responsibility; it is a submission to laws which one has made for oneself. The autonomous man, insofar as he is autonomous, is not subject to the will of another. He may do

The Conflict between Authority and Autonomy

what another tells him, but not *because* he has been told to do it. He is therefore, in the political sense of the word, *free*.

Since man's responsibility for his actions is a consequence of his capacity for choice, he cannot give it up or put it aside. He can refuse to acknowledge it, however, either deliberately or by simply failing to recognize his moral condition. All men refuse to take responsibility for their actions at some time or other during their lives, and some men so consistently shirk their duty that they present more the appearance of overgrown children than of adults. Inasmuch as moral autonomy is simply the condition of taking full responsibility for one's actions, it follows that men can forfeit their autonomy at will. That is to say, a man can decide to obey the commands of another without making any attempt to determine for himself whether what is commanded is good or wise.

This is an important point, and it should not be confused with the false assertion that a man can give up responsibility for his actions. Even after he has subjected himself to the will of another, an individual remains responsible for what he does. But by refusing to engage in moral deliberation, by accepting as final the commands of the others, he forfeits his autonomy. Rousseau is therefore right when he says that a man cannot become a slave even through his own choice, if he means that even slaves are morally responsible for their acts. But he is wrong if he means that men cannot place themselves voluntarily in a position of servitude and mindless obedience.

There are many forms and degrees of forfeiture of autonomy. A man can give up his independence of judgment with regard to a single question, or in respect of a single type of question. For example, when I place myself in the hands of my doctor, I commit myself to whatever course of treatment he prescribes, but only in regard to my health. I do not make him my legal counselor as well. A man may forfeit autonomy on some or all questions for a specific period of time, or during his entire life. He may submit himself to all commands, whatever they may be, save for some specified acts (such as killing) which he refuses to perform. From the example of the doctor, it is obvious that there are at least some situations in which it is reasonable to give up one's autonomy. Indeed, we may wonder whether, in a complex world of technical expertise, it is ever reasonable *not* to do so!

Since the concept of taking and forfeiting responsibility is central to the discussion which follows, it is worth devoting a bit more space to clarifying it. Taking responsibility for one's actions means making the final decisions about what one should do. For the autonomous man, there is no such thing, strictly speaking, as a *command*. If someone in my environment is issuing what are intended as commands, and if he or others expect those commands to be obeyed, that fact will be taken account of in my deliberations. I may decide that I ought to do what the person is commanding me to do, and it may even be that his issuing the command is the factor in the situation which makes it desirable for me to do so. For example, if I am on a sinking ship and the captain is giving orders for manning the lifeboats, and if everyone else is obeying the captain *because he is the captain*, I may decide that under the circumstances I had better do what he says, since the confusion caused by disobeying him would be generally harmful. But insofar as I make such a decision, I am not *obeying his command*; that is, I am not acknowledging him as having authority over me. I would make the same decision, for exactly the same reasons, if one of the passengers had started to issue "orders" and had, in the confusion, come to be obeyed.

In politics, as in life generally, men frequently forfeit their autonomy. There are a number of causes for this fact, and also a number of arguments which have been offered to justify it. Most men, as we have already noted, feel so strongly the force of tradition or bureaucracy that they accept unthinkingly the claims to authority which are made by their nominal rulers. It is the rare individual in the history of the race who rises even to the level of questioning the right of his masters to command and the duty of himself and his fellows to obey. Once the dangerous question has been started, however, a variety of arguments can be brought forward to demonstrate the authority of the rulers. Among the most ancient is Plato's assertion that men should submit to the authority of those with superior knowledge, wisdom, or insight. A sophisticated modern version has it that the educated portion of a democratic population is more likely to be politically active, and that it is just as well for the ill-informed segment of the electorate to remain passive, since its entrance into the political arena only supports the efforts of demagogues and extremists. A number of American political scientists have gone so far as to claim that the apathy of the American masses is a cause of stability and hence a good thing.

The moral condition demands that we acknowledge responsibility and achieve autonomy wherever and whenever possible. Sometimes this involves moral deliberation and reflection; at other times, the gathering of special, even technical, information. The contemporary American citizen, for example, has an obligation to master enough modern science to enable him to follow debates about nuclear policy and come to an independent conclusion.[5] There are great, perhaps insurmountable, obstacles to the achievement of a complete and rational autonomy in the modern world. Nevertheless, so long as we recognize our responsibility for our actions, and acknowledge the power of reason within us, we must acknowledge as well the continuing obligation to make ourselves the authors of such commands as we may obey. The paradox of man's condition in the modern world is that the more fully he recognizes his right and duty to be his own master, the more completely he becomes the passive object of a technology and bureaucracy whose complexities he cannot hope to understand. It is only several hundred years since a reasonably well-educated man could claim to understand the major issues of government as well as his king or parliament. Ironically, the high school graduate of today, who cannot master the issues of foreign and domestic policy on which he is asked to vote, could quite easily have grasped the problems of eighteenth-century statecraft.

THE CONFLICT BETWEEN AUTHORITY AND AUTONOMY

The defining mark of the state is authority, the right to rule. The primary obligation of man is autonomy, the refusal to be ruled. It would seem, then, that there can be no resolution of the conflict between the autonomy of the individual and the putative authority of the state. Insofar as a man fulfills his obligation to make himself the author of his decisions, he will resist the state's claim to have authority over him. That is to say, he will deny that he has a duty to obey the laws of the state *simply because they are the laws*. In that sense, it would seem that anarchism is the only political doctrine consistent with the virtue of autonomy.

Now, of course, an anarchist may grant the necessity of *complying* with the law under certain circumstances or for the time being. He may even doubt that there is any real prospect of eliminating the state as a human institution. But he will never view the commands of the state as *legitimate*, as having a binding moral force. In a sense, we might characterize the anarchist as a man without a country, for despite the ties which bind him to the land of his childhood, he stands in precisely the same moral relationship to "his" government as he does to the government of any other country in which he might happen to be staying for a time. When I take a vacation in Great Britain, I obey its laws, both because of prudential self-interest and because of the obvious moral considerations concerning the value of order, the general good consequences of preserving a system of property, and so forth. On my return to the United States, I have a sense of reentering *my* country, and if I think about the matter at all, I imagine myself to stand in a different and more intimate relation to American laws. They have been promulgated by *my* government, and I therefore have a special obligation to obey them. But the anarchist tells me that my feeling is purely sentimental and has no objective moral basis. All authority is equally illegitimate, although of course not therefore equally worthy or unworthy of support, and my obedience to American laws, if I am to be morally autonomous, must proceed from the same considerations which determine me abroad.

The dilemma which we have posed can be succinctly expressed in terms of the concept of a *de jure* state. If all men have a continuing obligation to achieve the highest degree of autonomy possible, then there would appear to be no state whose subjects have a moral obligation to obey its commands. Hence, the concept of a *de jure* legitimate state would appear to be vacuous, and philosophical anarchism would seem to be the only reasonable political belief for an enlightened man.

NOTES

1 For a similar definition of "state," see Max Weber, *Politics as a Vocation*. Weber emphasizes the means – force – by which the will of the state is imposed, but a careful analysis of his definition shows that it also bases itself on the notion of authority ("imperative coordination").
2 For each time we offered an example of legitimate authority, we would have to attach to it a nonempirical argument proving the legitimacy.
3 Thus, political philosophy is a dependent or derivative discipline, just as the philosophy of science is dependent upon the general theory of knowledge and on the branches of metaphysics which concern themselves with the reality and nature of the physical world.
4 This point is so simple that it may seem unworthy of such emphasis. Nevertheless, a number of political philosophers, including Hobbes and John Austin, have supposed that *the concept* as well as the principles of authority could be derived from the concepts of power or utility. For example, Austin defines a command as a signification of desire, uttered by someone who will visit evil on those who do not comply with it (*The Providence of Jurisprudence Determined*, Lecture I).
5 This is not quite so difficult as it sounds, since policy very rarely turns on disputes over technical or theoretical details. Still, the citizen who, for example, does not understand the nature of atomic radiation cannot

The Conflict between Authority and Autonomy

even pretend to have an opinion on the feasibility of bomb shelters; and since the momentous choice between first-strike and second-strike nuclear strategies depends on the possibility of a successful shelter system, the uninformed citizen will be as completely at the mercy of his "representatives" as the lowliest slave.

2
In Defense of a Hobbesian Conception of Law

R. LADENSON

> The civil laws are the commands of him who hath the chief authority in the city for direction of the future actions of his citizens.[1]
>
> *Thomas Hobbes*

I contend that despite widely accepted criticism, a Hobbesian conception of law remains the most philosophically illuminating analysis of its kind. The first three sections of this essay deal with H. L. A. Hart's objections to such an analysis. The fourth section provides an additional reason for preferring a Hobbesian conception of law to Hart's views. Insofar as Hart points to certain important legal phenomena which he believes cannot be accounted for by a Hobbesian conception, a more plausible and sophisticated version of this approach emerges from meeting his objections. Since the analysis to be proposed will differ in some important respects from Hobbes' actual thoughts about law, as expressed in his various writings, I refrain from referring to it as Hobbes' conception of law. Nonetheless, being both consistent with, and based upon his fundamental ideas, the analysis can be appropriately described as Hobbesian.

GOVERNMENTAL AUTHORITY AND A HOBBESIAN THEORY

Hart begins chapter 4 of *The Concept of Law*, entitled "Sovereign and Subject," with a perspicuous statement of the central feature of a Hobbesian theory of law. Referring to this feature as the Doctrine of Sovereignty he writes:

> The doctrine asserts that in every human society, where there is law, there is ultimately to be found latent beneath the

In Defense of a Hobbesian Conception of Law   33

variety of political forms, in a democracy as much as in an absolute monarchy, [the] simple relationship between subjects rendering habitual obedience and a sovereign who renders habitual obedience to no one. This vertical structure composed of a sovereign and subject is, according to the theory, as essential a part of a society which possesses law as a backbone is of a man. Where it is present we speak of the society, together with its sovereign as a single independent state, and we may speak of its law. Where it is not present, we can apply none of these expressions, for the relation of sovereign and subject forms, according to this theory, part of their very meaning.[2]

Hart then briefly alludes to, but does not press, an objection to the above theory advanced at greater length in an earlier chapter, namely that in his opinion it crudely and implausibly takes "sovereignty" to mean nothing more than "being in a position to issue orders backed by credible threats."[3] The same objection is voiced succinctly by Ronald Dworkin in the context of an attack upon Austin's jurisprudential theory:

> We make an important distinction between law and even the general orders of a gangster. We feel that the law's strictures – and its sanctions – are different in that they are obligatory in a way that the outlaw's commands are not ... (The view that laws are essentially rules laid down and upheld by the sovereign) ... has no place for any such distinction, because it defines an obligation as subjection to the threat of force, and so founds the authority of law entirely on the sovereign's ability and will to harm those who disobey ... [But] a rule differs from an order, among other ways by being normative, by setting a standard of behavior that has a call on its subject beyond the threat that may enforce it. A rule can never be binding just because some person with physical power wants it to be so. He must have authority to issue the rule or it is no rule, and such authority can only come from another rule which is already binding on those to whom he speaks. That is the difference between a valid law and the orders of a gunman.[4]

Dworkin's explicit target in the above passage is Austin's definition of sovereignty as the possession of vastly greater power than anyone else in a particular social group. Likewise, the sections of Hart's *The Concept of Law* in which similar points are made focus exclusively on Austin's definition. Accordingly, the foregoing criticism does not apply to a theory such as Hobbes' which, while identifying laws with rules that issue forth from the sovereign, conceives of sovereignty in a way that on its face appears to incorporate satisfactorily the normative element cited by Dworkin. That is to say, Hobbes defines "the sovereign" not only as someone with substantially more power than anyone else in a given social group, but also as the possessor of governmental authority.[5] One can thus distinguish between Austinian and Hobbesian conceptions of law, only one of which, Austin's, clearly involves a crudely reductionistic account of sovereignty.

If, however, the notion of governmental authority itself turns out in the end to presuppose that of legal rules, then a Hobbesian conception of law would be inadequate on grounds of circularity. That is, one cannot characterize laws informatively as rules laid down and upheld by the sovereign if (a) one conceives of the sovereign as someone with both governmental power and authority, and (b) such a conception in turn necessarily reduces to the notion of a person with legal entitlement to make rules for others. While neither Hart nor Dworkin explicitly press this criticism there are nonetheless some grounds for thinking that they both would agree with it.[6] Accordingly, I want to suggest a Hobbesian analysis of the notion of governmental authority which, while highly plausible, in no way involves the notion of legal rules.

To begin with, the concepts of governmental power and governmental authority must be distinguished. Power over another person is the ability to make that person do what one wishes. The governmental power can be defined as power with respect to the members of a particular social group sufficient to maintain peaceful relations among them and to protect the group from outside invasion. The notion of governmental authority involves two basic elements. First, to have such authority is to have governmental power, the exercise of which is effectively uncontested. Given human nature, governmental power and this first aspect of governmental authority always go together. That is, most human beings desire a modicum of stability in their lives. Thus they are fearful of the consequences that attend contesting power of the magnitude necessary for maintaining peace within a social group, and will neither actively nor passively resist its exercise. A subject, or citizen, can be defined as someone granted certain kinds of social freedoms in virtue of not contesting exercise of the governmental power by those who possess it, the nature of such freedoms varying from commonwealth to commonwealth.[7]

Second, a plausible conception of governmental authority must incorporate the notion of the right to rule. As ordinarily conceived, a sovereign has not only effectively uncontested governmental power but also the right to exercise it. The possession of such a right by persons acting under governmental authority presumably differentiates coercive actions on their part from such actions by private individuals. In analyzing the concept of the right to rule, one must first distinguish two kinds of rights — those which Joel Feinberg has termed claim-rights and those which can be termed justification-rights.[8] To assert a claim-right is to press a demand with respect to something or other against another individual. Such a right presupposes an institutional background which includes rules to which individuals appeal in order to validate their demands, authoritative procedures for assessing demands with respect to the rules, and effective arrangements for satisfying demands that can be validated. Claim-rights necessarily correlate with duties because when one asserts such a right under the appropriate rules, one makes a claim to certain performances or forbearances by others. That is, if the appropriate rules uphold someone's assertion of a claim-right, then necessarily they imply certain required behavior on the part of others.

As the name implies, when one asserts a justification-right in a particular situation, one does not press a claim against others but rather responds to demands for justification of one's behavior. Such rights then have an altogether different conceptual structure from claim-rights and accordingly differ from them in neither presupposing any institutional background nor correlating with duties.

In one important kind of case, people endeavor to morally or legally justify their actions by standing upon justification-rights. They acknowledge their actions to involve the violation of moral or legal rules, but nonetheless insist that they were justified in virtue of the presence of justificatory considerations. Self-defense paradigmatically exemplifies a right appealed to for this purpose. Other examples are defense of others, consent, necessity, justified paternalism, and parental authority. In another closely related kind of case, one invokes justification-rights not to defend oneself from the charge of having violated a moral or legal rule but rather to rebut the assumption that one's behavior stands in need of justification. Asserting a justification-right in this kind of case amounts to contending that what one did was all right. To cite Judith Thompson's by now classic example, a contention that one must indefinitely submit to having one's kidneys connected to those of a famous violinist in order to keep him alive might be countered by the contention of a right in the circumstances to disconnect oneself from him.[9] Regardless of context, however, people invoke justification-rights as a response to the demand for justification of their behavior and not to press demands against others, as they do by invoking claim-rights.[10]

The right to rule is such a justification right. That is to say, strong reasons can be advanced for holding that possession of the governmental power and acceptance by those one presumes to govern of its exercise jointly constitute as justification for coercive acts which would otherwise be immoral. To explain why, however, one must first focus upon a more general issue of moral theory: what makes factors such as self defense, consent, necessity, and so forth *justificatory* consideration? According to the Rational Contractor Theory of Morality, as developed recently by writers such as John Rawls and Bernard Gert, valid moral rules and principles are exclusively those that would be unanimously advocated by all rational people if they were somehow brought together under conditions of equality and directed to reach agreement among themselves about the supreme rules and principles respectively governing interpersonal conduct and the basic structure of social institutions.[11] Since such conditions of equality in reality cannot be attained, the theory invites us to reason about what choices would be made if, contrary to fact, this were possible by imagining a representative group of rational people deliberating about moral rules and principles when placed under a veil of ignorance that prevents them from knowing facts about themselves, such as their respective sexes, races, incomes, skills, and so forth, that could tempt them to base their respective choices of rules on the desire to promote their own interests to the disadvantage of others.

The Rational Contractor Theory takes valid moral rules and principles to be those that would be unanimously advocated by all rational people under the above described hypothetical condition. Similarly, according to this view, moral justifications (very roughly) are considerations such that no rational person placed under the veil of ignorance would object to the violation of a moral rule if these considerations obtained. How does one provide a theoretically illuminating explanation of why considerations such as self-defense are moral justifications for conduct that would otherwise be immoral? By setting out a plausible account of a line of reasoning that would lead all rational people under the veil of ignorance not to object to the violation of a moral rule if the consideration in question obtained.

The right to rule can be thought of as a justification-right because one can set out a plausible account of a line of reasoning that would lead all rational people under the veil of ignorance not to object to coercion when genuinely carried out by governmental authority. In this connection one need only recount chapter 13 of *Leviathan* in which Hobbes points out that human beings tend to have certain characteristics which continually draw them into mutually destructive conflict with one another and, as far as we can tell, the only way to cope with such a situation is through the institution of the state. In other words, given their general knowledge of human nature and their desire to avoid mutually destructive conflict, all rational people under the veil of ignorance would acknowledge the necessity of the state, and thus would not object to the exercise of coercive power by those people who act in its name.

Two important subsidiary points, however, must be made in connection with the foregoing suggestion. First, to hold that governmental authority is a moral justification for coercion does not thereby commit one to the position that the mere claim of having acted under governmental authority always serves as a blanket justification for anything a governmental official might do. Governmental authority, like the other justificatory considerations, has its limitations and exceptions. That is, for example, just as self-defense can pass into retaliation, necessity can pass into negligence, and parental authority can be exceeded, so also justificatory claims on the basis of governmental authority can be invalid from a moral point of view. Clarifying the limitations upon and exceptions to governmental authority as a justificatory consideration, or for that matter clarifying these matters with respect to all the other justificatory considerations, is an important task for moral philosophers that has not yet been fully addressed. It suffices here, however, simply to note that on any reasonable account of justificatory considerations, valid claims of governmental authority have limitations and exceptions. Thus, merely claiming a justification for one's actions on grounds of governmental authority is not the same thing as having such a justification.

Second, the claim that governmental authority constitutes a moral justification for coercion by itself implies nothing about either the subject's duties of allegiance to the state or of compliance with the law. This is because the right to rule, being a justification-right rather than a claim-right, entails no correlative duties. Thus no neat logical connection holds between the right to rule and the duties of subjects with regard to allegiance to the state and compliance with the law. To be sure, some of the points that figure crucially in an analysis of the one may also loom large in an analysis of the other. Such, however, is very different from inferring from an account of the sovereign's right to rule that a subject has a duty not to resist the power of the sovereign or to obey the law.

According to a Hobbesian analysis, then, the two elements constitutive of sovereignty – the governmental power and governmental authority, although conceptually distinct – can be thought of as always going together given certain reasonable assumptions about human nature and moral theory. In addition, the foregoing accounts of these notions both accord well with common sense. In general, the governmental power can be distinguished from interpersonal power most easily by conceiving of it basically as an ability to maintain the social peace and to protect a social group from outside invasion through the use of force. The above account of governmental authority likewise seems plausible. The most straightforward way of taking the question of who has such authority in a given area – let us say, as asked by Marco Polo in the course of his travels – is, in part, as a request to be informed of who has effectively uncontested governmental power in that region. Similarly, it makes good sense intuitively to analyze the notion of a right to rule, which figures in the idea of governmental authority, in terms of the concept of justification-rights rather than claim-rights. The moral force of an admonition that only the authorities have the right to punish – for example, as addressed to a vigilante committee – most naturally strikes one as a reminder to them that the authorities, and the authorities alone, are morally justified in visiting evil upon individuals who perpetrate acts of a kind that tend to disrupt the social peace.

As an additional point worth noting, the foregoing analysis can be applied to a serious problem plaguing any theory that introduces normative elements into the definition of sovereignty, namely, how to reconcile the existence of thoroughly evil regimes with the notion that sovereignty necessarily involves having a right to rule. Consider for example the case of Nazi Germany. On the one hand, most poeple would agree that the Nazis were sovereign in Germany from say 1933 to 1944; and yet on the other hand, the notion that they had a right to rule seems on its face to morally condone them, clearly from any reasonable standpoint an unacceptable point of view.[12]

Resolution of this problem lies in recognizing that, according to the foregoing analysis, possessing the right to rule amounts to having a particular kind of justification for the exercise of certain

In Defense of a Hobbesian Conception of Law 39

types of coercion. That is, the analysis holds that having governmental authority is a consideration that can justify otherwise morally unjustifiable coercive behavior. Now as mentioned earlier, all justificatory considerations have limitations beyond which they do not apply. Nonetheless, even if one exceeds these limitations in particular circumstances, one does not thereby cause the justificatory consideration in question to cease to apply to oneself regardless of circumstances. Thus, suppose that in defending himself a person X applies force in excess of that justified by the right to self-defense. We can say of such a case that in the circumstances X can no longer appeal to the right of self-defense to justify his actions, and that the other party Y can now invoke the right himself as a justification for the further use of force. We cannot say, however, that by virtue of using excessive force, X forfeits the right to self-defense — that is, he can never again in any circumstances invoke it.

By the same token, even though the Nazis abused the right to rule, thereby making resistance justifiable, this did not cause it to be the case that they no longer had such a right. That is, just as a person still has a right to self-defense even if he or she exceeds the degree of force allowed by that right in a given situation, so also a sovereign's right to rule is not voided when abused. Although one might well emotionally resist conceding the Nazis a right to rule, it must be reemphasized that according to the Hobbesian analysis here proposed the notion of having such a right is compatible with abusing it in particular circumstances and with that of a (justification) right to resist on the part of those individuals subject to the power of an oppressive sovereign. *Indeed, conceding someone the right to rule, according to the above view, is logically compatible with believing that the particular governmental institutions under which he or she acts ought not to exist at all.* Acknowledging such a right simply amounts to holding that so long as the governmental institutions in question exist, then individuals acting under their authority have a right to engage in certain kinds of coercive behavior that is morally impermissable for private citizens.[13]

Such a view I think accords with common sense. One can, for example, believe that German citizens had a right to resist the Nazis and that German traffic police on the *Autobahn* had a right to detain speeding motorists which private citizens did not have. This latter right stemmed simply from the Nazi government's power and general acceptance, not from the moral worth of its ideological foundations.[14] It goes without saying, however, that while issuing traffic tickets constituted a valid exercise of the right to exercise power over others under governmental authority, placing people in death camps did not.[15]

The foregoing Hobbesian account of sovereignty thus has two noteworthy characteristics: first, it in no way presupposes the concept of legal rules; second, it has substantial intuitive plausibility, appearing to apply in cases where we would unquestionably ascribe (or withhold ascription of) sovereignty to certain individuals, and to provide an illuminating framework for the analysis of problematic situations. It seems then that a Hobbesian conception of law can include an account of sovereignty that accords the notion of governmental authority its proper place.

PERSISTENCE AND CONTINUITY

Hart's second set of objections concern two important phenomena that typify legal systems; first, the persistence of law – that is, the fact that laws enacted centuries ago may still be laws today – and second, the continuity of law-making power – that is, the common tendency of legal systems to contain rules, securing the uninterrupted succession from one lawmaker to another. Hart adduces a number of arguments endeavoring to show that a Hobbesian theory of law cannot account for either of these two typical features of legal systems.

The prima facie difficulty for a Habbesian conception posed by the persistence of law can be stated succinctly: if law necessarily emanates from the sovereign then how can laws made by an earlier legislator who is long dead still be law under a different regime? Hobbes' answer was that in cases such as this "the legislator is he not by whose authority the laws were first made, but by whose authority they continue to be law."[16] In other words, Hobbes argued that though as a matter of history the origin of some archaic law was the legislative operation of a past sovereign, its current status as law stems from its recognition as such by the present sovereign. Hart finds this apparently straightforward, Hobbesian response unsatisfactory, but for a curious reason. He rejects it as unacceptably counterintuitive on grounds of entailing that a given statute enacted under a past regime does not acquire its status as law until actually applied by present day courts at which time it becomes law in virtue of the sovereign's tacit acquiesence.[17] Hart never explains, however, why he takes a Hobbesian account of the persistence of law to have such an

In Defense of a Hobbesian Conception of Law   41

entailment. Tacitly accepting an archaic law by letting its current application in courts go uncontested is not the only way a sovereign can indicate recognition of it. Such could be thought of as stemming from a general policy that any laws enacted under a previous sovereign will continue to have legal effect until explicitly overturned.

Hart adduces two arguments for holding that a Hobbesian conception of law cannot account for the continuity of lawmaking power. First, he invites us to imagine a country ruled long and peacefully by a monarch named Rex I who dies and, in accordance with prevailing rules of succession, is followed to the throne by his son, Rex II. Hart objects that insofar as one cannot say at the outset with absolute certainty whether Rex II will be accepted as sovereign by Rex I's former subjects, it follows that according to a Hobbesian conception of law one also cannot say of Rex II's first command, as could be said of Rex I's last, that it was given by a person who was sovereign and therefore was law. That is, Hart objects that if we follow a Hobbesian approach then there is nothing to make Rex II sovereign from the start. Such strikes Hart at least in some instances as counter-intuitive.[18]

The foregoing objection, however, admits of a straightforward response. A Hobbesian can hold that, indeed, Rex II is not monarch unless accepted as such by those people over whom he presumes to rule. However, such acceptance may well be forthcoming immediately upon Rex I's death owing to deeply engrained traditions pertaining to the succession of sovereignty. If in fact this occurs, then Rex II will inherit both the governmental power and acquiesence in his exercise of it by Rex I's former subjects. While in this kind of case one cannot say with absolute certainty that Rex II's commands will be obeyed, one can nonetheless often be as confident about it as is possible in regard to almost anything. By the same token, if such confidence is unwarranted then genuine doubts are possible as to whether a designated successor may be thought of plausibly as having attained sovereign status immediately upon the termination of his predecessor's reign. Admittedly a Hobbesian analysis of law *per se* cannot account for why the above kinds of traditions should exist in certain circumstances. But this problem falls more appropriately within the province of the sociology of law than analytical jurisprudence.

Hart, however, has a second objection to a Hobbesian analysis of law that deals with the continuity of lawmaking power. Rex II's immediate accession to the throne upon Rex I's death, Hart contends, does not stem simply from inheriting both the governmental power and acceptance as sovereign by Rex I's former subjects. Also, and equally significant, it stems from his having a right to make law grounded in the rule of succession which dictates that upon Rex I's death the crown shall pass to him.[19] According to Hart, a Hobbesian analysis cannot account for the notion of such a right.

The rejoinder here, however, is that according to our analysis of the right to rule articulated earlier, Hart simply errs in supposing that this right stems from rules of succession in regard to sovereignty. As emphasized in the previous section, while the notion of sovereignty clearly includes that of governmental authority, and thus also of a right to rule, this last notion is better understood in terms of the concept of a justification-right than of a claim-right. In other words, having a right to rule constitutes a moral justification for the exercise of coercive power available to anyone who possesses both the governmental power and acquiesence in its exercise by those he or she presumes to govern. If Rex II immediately inherits both of these things then *ipso facto* he has such a right. Prevailing rules of succession do not enter into the matter at all.

Against the above rejoinder one might object that for centuries in Europe, those who claimed to be legitimate monarchs defended themselves by invoking traditional rules of succession in regard to the passing of the crown. While admittedly a Hobbesian cannot explain away the fact that these claims were frequently made, he or she can take the bull by the horns and simply deny that the notion of legitimacy they presupposed was coherent. If a person Z claims to be the legitimate bearer of the crown solely upon the basis that it passed to him or her from its previous bearer Y in accordance with valid rules of succession, this raises the question of whether Y bore it legitimately. But such must then also be asked about Y's predecessor X, and so on down to the first bearer of the crown A. Fatal difficulties, however, attend any attempt to explain the primal acquisition of sovereignty. On the one hand, the proposal that it stemmed from a voluntary agreement of some kind or other runs up against the unanswerable question of how such an agreement could bind future generations. On the other hand, the attempt to account for it in other ways seems to lead one directly into the theory of divine right of kings.

At this point one might feel that although the foregoing discussion satisfactorily addresses Hart's specific objections to a Hobbesian analysis because of its presumed inability to account for the persistence and continuity of law, it does not address the following problem, which these objections implicitly suggest. If one holds

In Defense of a Hobbesian Conception of Law

that laws are essentially rules laid down and upheld by the sovereign, then one cannot maintain that rules of succession are *legal* rules, for by their very nature these rules cannot be upheld by the current sovereign. In some cases, however, such rules clearly seem to carry with them the force of law – for example, the provisions of the United States Constitution specifying the manner of selecting the president, the justices of the Supreme Court, and the members of Congress.

In dealing with this problem a distinction first must be drawn between those governments in which sovereignty is divided, and those where it resides in a single head of power. In the former case the various fundamental sovereign powers – for example, to make laws, to adjudicate disputes, to tax, to appoint counselors and administrators – are divided among various individuals or bodies, while in the latter case such powers all inhere in a single person, natural or artificial.

Now in the case of divided sovereignty, a Hobbesian can maintain that since those currently holding sovereign power are always in a position to uphold the prevailing rules of succession, such rules can be regarded as legal in character. The argument in support of this contention, however, must be deferred temporarily because it presupposes a Hobbesian analysis of the notion of the separation of governmental powers which, for reason of convenience in regard to exposition, is best addressed in the next section.[20] As for governments where all sovereign powers reside in a single head, one can plausibly deny that the conventions in regard to succession of sovereignty are legal rules at all.[21] If they were, then we should expect one or the other of the following two modes of thought to prevail widely. First, we should expect that a distinction be drawn between "legal" sovereigns – those who accede to sovereignty in accordance with prevailing rules of successions – and "illegal" sovereigns – those who do not. Alternatively, we should expect that "legality," in the sense of acquiring governmental power through regular means, enters into the very definition of sovereignty, so that one simply cannot be thought of as having it unless it was acquired in the manner prescribed by prevailing rules of succession.

As a matter of fact, however, neither of the above two modes of thought play any role in the way sovereignty is generally conceived. Alexander the Great, Julius Caesar, Napoleon, the Communist party in the Soviet Union, and Fidel Castro, to name a few holders of sovereign power, all acquired it in ways that entailed departures from the prevailing rules of succession. Nonetheless, one does not distinguish their respective situations as holding sovereign power from those of individuals like Henry VIII, Peter the Great, or Louis XIV, in each of whose cases the normal practices in regard to succession were followed. To suggest, for example, that Napoleon was not a genuine sovereign but that Louis XIV was, or that the Communist party in the Soviet Union holds power illegally but that Peter the Great held it legally, surely have a counter-intuitive feel to them.

As an additional point in this regard, it is instructive to consider one aspect of our attitudinal reactions toward the perpetrators of serious insurrection which plunges a society into protracted civil war. The rebels generally cease to be regarded as subjects or citizens of the government they oppose, but rather as more or less equal contenders for sovereignty. In the same way, if the rebels succeed then one generally does not describe them as having seized power illegally. By contrast, such a description seems to be reserved for the actions of individuals who perpetrate a relatively sudden *coup d'état* in circumstances where one can doubt whether they will be capable of ultimately holding onto the governmental power.[22] Thus, rather than being entailed by the notion of sovereignty as ordinarily conceived, the view that rules of succession in cases of undivided sovereignty are legal rules actually involves a significant departure from it.

One might object that the reason we draw no distinction between legal and illegal, or genuine and false, sovereigns with respect to the above kinds of cases is that where conquest or revolution occurs, the prevailing rules of succession simply cease to exist and are replaced by others. Accordingly, so this response would have it, the failure to draw these distinctions when considering a pair of sovereigns such as Napoleon and Louis XIV, or the Soviet Communist party and Peter the Great, does not imply that in all cases it would be pointless to do so.

Whether Hart can embrace such a response, however, is doubtful. Upon pressing the question of why prevailing rules of succession cease to exist in the case of conquest or revolution one might conclude most naturally that it happens simply because a new sovereign comes to power who bears no relationship to the previous one in terms of heretofore prevailing rules of succession. But such an answer cannot be given by someone who holds as a general thesis that having sovereign power necessarily requires that it be acceded to in accordance with precisely those kinds of rules. There may be another plausible account of why such rules pass out of existence as a result of conquest or revolution, but, so far as I can see, Hart does not supply it.

In Defense of a Hobbesian Conception of Law

LEGAL LIMITATIONS UPON SOVEREIGN POWER

Hart's third set of objectives to a Hobbesian conception of law has to do with legal limitations upon legislative power. The notion that laws essentially are rules laid down and upheld by the sovereign, he maintains, cannot account for situations where a written constitution restricts the competence of a legislature by excluding altogether the consideration of certain matters from its scope. That is, on the one hand, such constitutional provisions – for example, the First Amendment to the United States Constitution – clearly count as laws; but on the other hand, it would seem that insofar as they specify legal limits upon the exercise of power by a legislature, they cannot be thought of as rules laid down and upheld by it.

Hart notes that recognition of theoretical problems posed by legal limitations upon legislative power has led some writers to embark upon a search for "the sovereign behind the legislature." According to Hart, however, the search is futile because if, as is generally done in this regard, one identifies such a sovereign with the public then the distinction between sovereign and subject, essential to a Hobbesian theory, collapses. Hart points out further that the above problem cannot be evaded by distinguishing between the public and the electorate, for the latter body is constituted by legal rules. Hence, so Hart argues, if one considers the electorate sovereign then a definition of law in terms of sovereignty will be circular. He concludes that legal limitations upon legislative authority consist not of duties imposed on the legislator to obey some superior legislator, but of disabilities contained in rules which qualify him or her to legislate.[23]

The foregoing arguments comprise Hart's most powerful criticism of a Hobbesian conception of law. Nonetheless, a response to them can be articulated which, while not immediately obvious, provides an analysis of constitutional provisions imposing legal limitations upon legislative power that is both consistent with the fundamental ideas of a Hobbesian conception of law and attractive in its own right. As a prelude to the analysis it will be useful to consider briefly the conclusion that Hart draws from his discussion, namely that the constitutional provisions in question consist of disabilities in regard to putative legislation rather than rules imposed upon the legislature by yet another sovereign. In this regard Hart distinguishes between rules specifying conditions whose presence voids otherwise duly enacted legislation, and rules which require a legislature to follow certain prescribed courses of conduct.

Now while he rightly points out that constitutional provisions imposing limitations upon legislative power fall into the former category rather than the latter one, Hart fails to press the question of what features must characterize a legal system in which disabling conditions for legislation exist. It would seem essential in this connection that there be a body which decides when the provisions of the constitution specifying such conditions in fact apply, and which has the power and authority to insure that its decisions will prevent putative legislative enactments from being implemented. Without such a body, constitutional provisions purporting to impose legal restrictions upon legislative power are merely hortatory. Hart himself implicitly acknowledges the above point because his entire discussion presupposes that these kinds of provisions operate primarily through decisions by courts.[24]

This, however, raises the issue of whether a convincing Hobbesian gloss can be put upon the idea of a sovereign legislature that is subject to the rulings of a court. More generally it poses the question of how Hobbesians might account for the separation of governmental powers. Consideration of this issue will provide the key to meeting criticism of a Hobbesian analysis in regard to legal limitations upon sovereign power.

As a preliminary to articulating a Hobbesian account of the separation of powers let us imagine the constitutional convention of some newly emerging nation which, after protracted discussion, adopts a governmental plan with the following characteristics.[25] First, the constitution calls for the creation of several governmental institutions such as a legislature, an executive department, and courts, each of which will have as its primary responsibility the carrying out of one or more important governmental functions. Such functions are articulated in broad terms but with enough specificity to be distinguishable in most cases. The constitutional provisions pertaining to these functions thus stipulate an important kind of limitation of power with respect to the various branches of government.

Second, in order to protect the citizens' basic liberties the constitution imposes certain general conditions upon the way in which the branches can carry out their respective functions; it stipulates, among other things, that the legislature cannot pass any law abridging freedom of expression. Third, the document locates the responsibility for seeing that the above-mentioned limitations and conditions are adhered to by a given branch in one or more of the other branches. According to this scheme each branch checks the exercise of power by one or more of the others, and in turn is so checked by them. However, as a fourth feature, the constitution

In Defense of a Hobbesian Conception of Law 47

stipulates that so long as a branch exercises power in accordance with the constitutionally prescribed limitations and conditions it need not defer to the judgment of any other branch in the carrying out of its functions.

The foregoing plan then dictates that each branch of government have sovereignty in regard to carrying out its functions but stand subject to the sovereignty of the other branches insofar as they carry out their own. Moreover, the plan calls for each branch to be liable to the imposition of sanctions by one or more of the others if it oversteps the limitations and conditions attending its constitutional mandate. According to a Hobbesian conception of law, however, the plan is not realized at the moment of its adoption by the constitutional convention. Instead, the government envisaged by it will come into existence only if each contemplated governmental branch can actually acquire the requisite power to carry out its prescribed functions. Many situations could well arise which might cause the government that eventually emerges to deviate from the plan in substantial respects. A bitter disagreement might arise between two governmental branches over their respective proper spheres of power which, in turn, might lead to a struggle that results in one of them taking over certain powers that the original plan contemplated would be exercised by the other.[26] Or, in attempting to establish its sovereignty a given branch might damage itself by moving too swiftly. That is, the branch might attempt to exercise more power than the public will accept, and thus become permanently weakened as a consequence of overreaching its grasp.[27] Also in this regard, general conditions of social conflict can always produce civil strife that results in the emergence of a fundamentally different governmental system altogether.

Nonetheless, given propitious institutional design and historical circumstances, each branch may succeed in acquiring both the power to carry out its various functions and to resist encroachment upon its constitutionally mandated domain by the other branches. If this occurs then the branches will all attain sovereign status as it is understood according to a Hobbesian analysis. The governmental power, it may be recalled, is definable by Hobbesians as power with respect to the members of a social group sufficient to maintain peaceful relations among them and to protect the group from outside invasion. Such power is divisible into a variety of more specific ones – to make laws, to adjudicate disputes, to tax, to enforce laws – each of which can be called a power of government, and the totality of which can be referred to in the singular as the governmental power.[28] Accordingly, insofar as each branch possesses several powers of government it has a share in the governmental power. Furthermore, a Hobbesian analysis suggests that, in light of certain plausible assumptions about human nature and moral theory, anyone with the governmental power will also have governmental authority. It follows that the branches all possess such authority in regard to carrying out their respective functions. Thus, since governmental power and authority are both ascribable to the various branches, they can all be thought of as having sovereign status in regard to their respective proper domains. The fact that each of them in turn is subject to the sovereignty of the other branches outside of its proper domain does not affect its own sovereign status.

The foregoing account of the separation of powers makes it possible to address Hart's objections to a Hobbesian analysis for its alleged inability to account for legal limitations with respect to legislative power. Constitutionally imposed conditions upon a legislature in the exercise of its sovereign functions, such as the First Amendment to the United States Constitution, can be thought of by a Hobbesian as rules that are upheld *vis-à-vis* the legislature by another branch of government, namely the judiciary. Such a view implies than the latter is sovereign over the former in this particular regard but not that it stands superior to it in all others. Indeed the constitutional plan might call for the legislature to uphold similar kinds of conditions upon the exercise of power by the judiciary, for example, through impeachment of judges who disregard the fundamental rights of litigants.

Similarly, limitations of scope upon the functions of a given branch of government can be thought of as rules upheld against that branch by the others. Thus, for example, the constitution might invest the legislature with power to create, abolish, and alter the jurisdiction of courts so that, relatively speaking, the judiciary cannot exercise too much independent initiative in the matter of creating social policy.[29] Indeed, under a governmental scheme that provides for the separation of powers the very constitutive rules defining basic offices and positions within a particular branch of government can also be conceived of as upheld by the other branches. In this regard, matters such as a person's eligibility to run for office, to succeed himself or herself in office, to accede to an office or position – for example, given charges that he or she violated campaign laws, may all be conclusively adjudicated by a branch of government other than the one of which the office or position in question is part. Hence, as mentioned in the previous section, where separation of powers exists a Hobbesian can regard

In Defense of a Hobbesian Conception of Law 49

rules of succession in regard to sovereignty as themselves legal rules.

As a final point in this connection, it should be noted that the foregoing account of legal limitations upon legislative power obviates the need to search for a sovereign behind the legislature. According to a Hobbesian conception of the separation of powers, the sovereign who upholds such legal limitations does not stand behind the legislature, but rather alongside of it. A question remains, however, of where the electorate fits into a Hobbesian model of the separation of powers. One can say here that it shares sovereignty along with the various branches of government. That is, the electorate resembles these branches in two key respects: first, it has governmental power and authority in regard to certain important functions – in its case, the selection of political leaders; second, like the governmental branches, the electorate is not completely sovereign. Holding it to be so would imply that it carries out all the basic functions of government itself. Such, however, is not the case. The electorate plays one very important independent role along with the other heads of governmental power.

AN ADDITIONAL CONSIDERATION

If the foregoing arguments are sound, then two objectives have been accomplished: first, Hart's specific criticisms of a Hobbesian analysis of law have been answered; and second, insofar as this discussion includes plausible accounts of governmental authority, the continuity and persistence of law, and legal limitations upon sovereign power, it also constitutes positive support for a Hobbesian view. In addition, however, at least one other important reason for preferring such a view to Hart's basic ideas, as developed in *The Concept of Law*, should be mentioned. A crucial desirability condition of philosophical analyses of concepts generally is that they explicate concepts that are felt to be problematic for one reason or another in terms of others that seem less so. Such analyses thus strive for what might be termed reductive elucidation, that is to say, reduction of the puzzling to the better understood. Hart's well-known analysis of the nature of law in terms of primary and secondary rules, however illuminating in other respects, does not provide such reductive elucidation.

A brief summary of his approach brings out why this is so. Hart takes a legal system to be essentially the union of two kinds of rules, which he terms respectively primary and secondary. Primary rules grant rights or impose obligations upon members of the community, while secondary rules stipulate how and by whom such primary rules may be formed, recognized, modified, or extinguished. According to Hart, primitive communities have only primary rules and these are binding because of practices of acceptance. Such communities cannot be said to have law, he argues, because their legal rules are indistinguishable from their other social rules. When, however, a community has developed a fundamental secondary rule that stipulates how legal rules are to be identified, the idea of a distinct set of legal rules, and thus of law, emerges. Hart calls this kind of rule a "rule of recognition."[30]

Primary and secondary rules alike thus derive their status as law, according to Hart, in virtue of validation in terms of a rule of recognition. But how, in turn, is this kind of rule identified? Hart says in this regard that rules of recognition may be relatively simple or very complex. Being the ultimate criteria of law they are the only rules in a legal system whose binding force depends upon their acceptance. Hart asserts further that if we want to know what rules of recognition a particular community has adopted or follows we must observe how its citizens, and particularly its officials behave. We must observe what arguments they ultimately accept as showing the legal validity of a particular rule and what arguments they use to criticize legal officials and institutions.[31]

The above suggestions, however, pose a problem for Hart. On the one hand, he wants to analyze the concept of law in terms of the notion of rules of recognition; but on the other hand, he elucidates this latter notion primarily in terms of the concept of law. That is, Hart's approach to the issue of how to identify rules of recognition implies they should be thought of as the rules that everyone in a given society, but particularly people who hold offices and positions *defined by law* ultimately appeal to in *legal* argument. Now admittedly legal arguments appear to involve, or presuppose, rules of recognition in Hart's sense; and it is a great merit of his account that it illuminates so well this important aspect of law. One cannot, however, conclude from this that the notion of such rules can be taken as fundamental in a philosophical analysis of the concept of law, for as the above considerations should indicate, the former notion presupposes the latter. Thus, whatever other virtues can be ascribed to Hart's account, and certainly there are very many, it does not provide a philosophically illuminating reductive elucidation of the concept of law.

By contrast, a Hobbesian analysis, according to which laws are essentially rules laid down and upheld by the sovereign, provides

In Defense of a Hobbesian Conception of Law 51

us with the desired kind of reductive account. The grounds for making this claim stem in large measure from the arguments of the preceding three sections, for all these arguments in one way or another have endeavored to illustrate the possibility of articulating a plausible conception of sovereignty that does not presuppose the concept of law. If the arguments are sound then a Hobbesian approach, widely believed to have been all but completely discredited, still provides the most philosophically illuminating elucidation of the concept of law.

NOTES

This paper was written while I was in residence at the University of Chicago Law School as a Visiting Fellow during the 1977-8 academic year. I gratefully acknowledge the generous support of the law school and the helpful comments of Gerhard Casper, Arthur Flemming, Bernard Gert, Anthony Kronman, Bernard Meltzer, Fay Sawyier, and F. Patrick Hubbard. I also received valuable criticism from the members of the Philosophy Department at the University of Wisconsin-Parkside at whose colloquium I presented the first section of this paper. Responsibility for the content of the paper, of course, is my own.

1 Thomas Hobbes, *The Citizen* in *Man and Citizen*, ed. Bernard Gert (New York: Doubleday, 1972), p. 178. (Hereafter cited as *The Citizen*.)
2 Hart, *The Concept of Law* (London: Oxford University Press, 1961), p. 49.
3 Hart, *The Concept of Law*, p. 50.
4 Ronald Dworkin, "The Model of Rules," in *Philosophy of Law*, ed. Joel Feinberg and Hyman Gross (Encino, CA: Dickenson, 1975), p. 74. While Dworkin, of course, differs from Hart on other important matters of jurisprudential theory, evidently he concurs with Hart in regard to the inadequacy of a Hobbesian analysis of law for its alleged failure to deal satisfactorily with the normative elements in the concept of sovereignty.
5 See *The Citizen*, p. 188 and *Leviathan*, p. 132.
6 In the passage quoted above, Dworkin distinguishes a valid law from the orders of a gunman on the ground that the former, unlike the latter, issues forth from someone who had authority to make rules grounded in "another rule which is already binding on those to whom he speaks." Given that Dworkin aims here to differentiate valid laws from threats that do not have the force of law, it is natural to suppose that he takes the rule, binding those to whom the person with lawmaking authority issues rules, to be legally binding. Hart, in one passage, states that the rules conferring legal authority upon individuals generally are known in detail only by a society's legal authorities and experts. See Hart, *The Concept of Law*, pp. 59-60.

7 See *Leviathan*, pp. 151–5.
8 The following brief account of claim-rights differs from that advanced by Feinberg in his paper, "The Nature and Value of Rights" *The Journal of Value Inquiry* 4 (Winter 1970): 243–57, in that it insists that such rights presuppose the kind of institutional background described below. I have developed this account of claim-rights more fully in a paper entitled "Two Kinds of Rights," *Journal of Value Inquiry*.
9 See Judith Jarvis Thompson, "A Defense of Abortion," *Philosophy and Public Affairs* 1, no. 1 (Fall 1971): 47–66.
10 When standing upon justification-rights in other contexts besides the moral and legal, one frequently seeks to justify attitudes rather than behavior. Thus, for example, on varying occasions, a person might stand respectively upon a right to be angry with someone, to be concerned about a situation, or to put one's trust in another individual. The point of invoking the above kinds of rights is not to assert that one's anger, concern, trust, and so on are morally (or legally) justified, but rather to assert that they are justified in the sense of being reasonable in the circumstances.
11 The most important works in this regard are John Rawls, *A Theory of Justice* (Cambridge: Harvard University Press, 1971), and Bernard Gert, *The Moral Rules* (New York: Harper & Row, 1970).
12 The above problem I think underlies the tendency of many people to be pulled both ways in the debate between Hart and Lon L. Fuller about natural law. See H. L. A. Hart "Positivism and the Separation of Law and Morals," *Harvard Law Review* 71, no. 4 (1958): 593–629 and Lon L. Fuller, "Positivism and Fidelity to Law," *Harvard Law Review*: 630–72. On the one hand, Hart contends that application of the criteria of validity for law in a particular case does not involve substantive moral judgment about either the law in question or the regime which enacted it. Such a view seems intuitively plausible. On the other hand, if, as Hart asserts in *The Concept of Law*, being sovereign entails having a right to rule, then how, one might ask, can such moral evaluation be avoided? This consideration, in turn, inclines one, at least in some measure, toward Fuller's view that seemingly law-like rules can be so immoral as not to be law. The analysis to follow should be helpful in resolving this dilemma.
13 The above approach is suggested by the following remark by Hobbes about the marks of sovereign authority: " ..... if there be any man who by right can do some one action which is not lawful for any citizen or citizens to do beside himself, that man hath obtained the suspreme power. For those things which by right may not be done by any one or many citizens, the city itself can only do. He therefore that doth those things useth the city's right; which is the supreme power." See *The Citizen*, p. 188. Since Hobbes speaks of the above right as belonging to the city and since he holds that the city cannot be legally bound, it would appear that he did not conceive of this right as being

In Defense of a Hobbesian Conception of Law   53

legal in nature. Rather it seems that he thought of it as a justification-right.

14 Something very much like the above way of conceiving regimes which one objects to strongly on moral grounds appears to have been at work in several interesting court cases. One might suppose that after the American Civil War, all measures enacted under the presumed authority of the various Confederate state legislatures would have been deemed to have no force and effect. However, to avoid potential chaos the Federal Courts adopted the principle of distinguishing between those laws of the rebellious states which were directed toward the ordinary affairs of life and those which had been passed with the object of furthering secession and rebellion. Thus, after the Civil War, American courts gave effect to legislative and administrative measures enacted by a government whose existence was at least officially regarded as fundamentally unjustifiable, provided such measures were not hostile in their objects to the purposes of the national government, and did not infringe the rights of citizens under the Constitution. In this regard, see Texas v. White (1867) 7 Wall 700. See also Geoffrey Marshall, *Constitutional Theory* (London: Oxford University Press, 1970) p. 67.

A line of reasoning similar to the above was adopted by the High Court of Rhodesia in an action brought in 1966 which directly challenged the legality of the Smith regime. At issue was the validity of detention orders made under the government's emergency regulations. The court first held that insofar as the government's unilateral declaration of independence in 1965 violated the provisions of the 1961 Rhodesian Constitution, the Smith regime was an illegal organization acting without authority. Secondly, however, the court declared that since *de jure* government was suspended, regulations made by those in *de facto* control should be upheld to the extent that they were necessary to maintain peace and order. In this regard it was decided further that effect should be given to such measures as could lawfully have been taken by authorities under the 1961 Constitution. By this test the detention orders were upheld since they were made under an act which, although passed in 1966, could have been made under the 1961 Constitution. In this regard, see Judgement GD/CIV/23/26. See also Marshall, *Constitutional Theory*, p. 65.

The Rhodesian case poses the problem of how the court could consistently declare the Smith government to be acting without authority, and yet, at the same time, uphold one of its enactments. That this enactment could have been made by a legitimate government does not explain how it could have the force of law although issuing forth, in fact, from a source without legal authority. I would suggest that the best way to make sense of the Rhodesian High Court's decision is to conceive of it as inchoately relying upon the above account of how an immoral regime can have the right to rule. That is, in effect the court held that even though, in virtue of its origins, one could question whether the Smith regime deserved to wield governmental power, nonetheless, the fact that it had such power gave the Smith regime the (justification) right to exercise it for the maintenance of peace and order.

15 It should be pointed out here that given Hobbes' account of the sovereign–subject relationship, described at note 13 above, the European Jews were not citizens of the Nazi government, but rather its captives. That is to say, for Hobbes, a subject or citizen is someone who enjoys certain liberties – for example, corporal liberty and being subject to the rule of law – in return, as it were, for not contesting the sovereign's power. Accordingly, since the Jews eventually came to have no such liberties they stood in a slave–master, rather than a citizen–sovereign relationship with respect to the Nazis.
16 See *Leviathan*, p. 200.
17 Hart, *The Concept of Law*, pp. 63, 64.
18 Hart, *The Concept of Law*, p. 52.
19 Hart, *The Concept of Law*, p. 53.
20 See discussion below at note 26.
21 A. V. Dicey adopted this point of view in *Introduction to the Study of the Law of the Constitution* (London: MacMillan, 1889), p. 31.
22 Noting that serious insurrection severs the bonds between sovereign and subject, Hobbes contended that if such an insurrection fails then the sovereign deals with rebel forces as enemies rather than as subjects. That is to say, Hobbes held that the sovereign's justification for visiting harm upon defeated rebels does not stem, as in ordinary cases involving violations of the criminal law, from his or her governmental authority; rather it emanates from the natural right of all individuals to take whatever measures they regard as appropriate with respect to people whom they perceive as posing a threat to their security. See *The Citizen*, p. 287.

An interesting application of this Hobbesian reasoning can be found, of all places, in legal proceedings that concerned the issue of whether, after the Civil War, Jefferson Davis would be brought to trial for treason. See Case of Jefferson Davis, 7 Fed. Cas. 63, 100 No. 3621a (C.C.D. Va. 1867). In this case Davis's attorney first distinguished a rebellion that is put down quickly from one where the rebel forces attain the status of a recognized belligerent. He then argued with regard to the latter case, in almost perfect Hobbesian terms, that a leader of rebel forces cannot in all propriety be charged with violating the law. Davis's attorney acknowledged that in such a situation the "law of the victor over the vanquished" applies, and hence, in the case at hand the United States could indeed do what it wished with Jefferson Davis. He hastened to add, however, that surely so great a country as the United States would be magnanimous in victory, and so killing Davis would be unthinkable. Since eventually the Federal government declined to prosecute, the courts never had a chance to render a judgment in regard to this interesting argument.
23 Hart, *The Concept of Law*, p. 69.

In Defense of a Hobbesian Conception of Law 55

24 Hart, *The Concept of Law*, pp. 67, 68.
25 The account of the separation of powers that follows is the only part of the Hobbesian conception of law proposed here that diverges significantly from Hobbes' expressed views. See *The Citizen*, pp. 194, 248, and *Leviathan*, p. 240. Nonetheless, while Hobbes denied the possibility of dividing the governmental power, his grounds for this denial do not involve any propositions central to his political philosophy. In *Leviathan* Hobbes asserts unqualifiedly that "powers divided mutually destroy each other." Such, however, cannot be inferred from his theories of human nature and society. These theories, to be sure, entail that serious dangers attend any set of arrangements for the division of powers among individuals in virtue of its inherent instability. Hobbes' views about human nature and society, however, do not imply that such arrangements are absolutely doomed. Favorable circumstances conceivably could facilitate their flourishing for a considerable period of time. In this regard one can usefully compare division of the governmental power with a business partnership. Insofar as this latter kind of association calls for division of power among the partners, it has a built-in source of serious instability; and, to be sure, many business partnerships dissolve precisely because of conflict between partners. Notwithstanding this fact, however, under favorable conditions many partnerships manage to continue in existence for very considerable periods of time. Hobbes's theories of human nature and society no more imply the absolutely inevitable demise of regimes where the governmental power is divided than they imply that all business partnerships must necessarily consume themselves in flames of conflagration.
26 Geoffrey Marshall, *Parliamentary Sovereignty and the Commonwealth* (London: Oxford University Press, 1957) contains a valuable extended summary of such a struggle in South Africa arising out of the case of Harris v. Donges (1952) 1 T.L.R. in which petitioners proposed to test the constitutionality of apartheid laws in regard to the suffrage.
27 The brilliantly calculated way, à la Machiavelli, in which John Marshall endeavored to increase the power of the Supreme Court through judiciously stated claims of jurisdiction in his various opinions is described in Robert McCloskey, *The American Supreme Court* (Chicago: University of Chicago Press, 1960), pp. 26–44.
28 Hobbes enumerates these powers in *Leviathan*, p. 134, and *The Citizen*, p. 173.
29 Citing the American governmental scheme as an example in this regard, Felix Frankfurter's repeated calls for judicial restraint no doubt were, at least in some measure, motivated by his perception of the dire consequences in terms of congressionally applied sanctions that might attend overindulgence by the Supreme Court in the exercise of power.
30 Hart, *The Concept of Law*, pp. 77–97.
31 Hart, *The Concept of Law*, pp. 59–60, 98–107.

3
On the Concept of Authority in Political Philosophy

R. B. FRIEDMAN

The concept of authority is one of the rare ideas that has remained stubbornly central both to political philosophy and to empirical social science in spite of their divergence in the twentieth century. The highly self-conscious interest that political philosophy has in authority is obvious. For authority is a notion intimately bound up with most, if not all, of the central questions of political philosophy, especially the so-called problem of political obligation. And as for social science, the heavy intellectual burden placed on the notion of authority may be seen in the preeminent role played by the concepts of legitimacy and legitimate power in the study and definition of such "subjects" as the stability of political systems, the transition from traditional to modern society, organizational behavior, political socialization, etc.

At the same time, the "meaning" of authority has been the subject of ceaseless and acrimonious controversy in both political philosophy and social science. This controversy is invariably cast in the form of a dispute over the relation between the notions of authority, power, and legitimacy; and a large variety of approaches to authority have been forged out of these elements.[1] Moreover, since Weber, this controversy has come to effect the very question of what politics is and what the field and the scope of political study consists in. In addition to all this, there is also the peculiar but interesting and important claim that the very concept of authority has been corrupted or even lost in the modern world, and that it is this loss of understanding that lies behind the confusion over authority prevailing in contemporary thought. This is an opinion frequently expressed in some of the most well-known discussions of authority in recent years,[2] though in fact it first became something like a common view during the great debate over the dissolution of traditional authority in early nineteenth-century European thought. Kierkegaard expressed a view that may be found among most critics of "modern" society, when he spoke of the "confusion involved in the fact that the concept of authority has been entirely forgotten in our confused age."[3]

Authority, then, has proved to be an elusive concept, as well as an indispensable one, and perhaps there is no single view of authority that can serve as the model for understanding all the different uses to which it is put. But rather than attempt to survey the various different views of authority that may be found in contemporary thought, I propose to set out in a series of brief remarks what I take to be the main elements of the concept of authority. This procedure will perhaps obscure some of the subtleties and may seem to neglect some of the larger problems traditionally coupled with the examination of authority. But, one hopes it will make clear the main lines of interpretation.

THE SCOPE OF THE CONCEPT OF AUTHORITY: BELIEF AND ACTION

Discussions of authority, especially by political scientists and legal philosophers, often deal exclusively with authority over conduct. But the scope of the concept as it is actually used is in fact a good deal broader. For although a man who exercises authority does indeed influence other men, this influence may be over beliefs as well as conduct. Thus, the *Oxford English Dictionary* gives for "authority" not only the "right to command" and "power to influence action," but also "power over the opinions of others," "intellectual influence," "power to inspire belief," and "title to be believed." Concomitantly, a person may be said to "have authority" in two distinct senses. For one, he may be said to be "in authority," meaning that he occupies some office, position, or status which entitles him to make decisions about how other people should behave. But, secondly, a person may be said to be "an authority" on something, meaning that his views or utterances are entitled to be believed (including, to complicate matters, beliefs about the right and wrong way of doing things). And so we speak of teachers, priests, parents, and experts (of various kinds) as having authority over beliefs as well as of legislators, judges, and generals having authority over conduct.

Now the broad scope of the concept of authority is closely connected to the central and controversial role it plays in political philosophy. For the concept of authority has been characteristically invoked in political philosophy to help define the nature of the cohesion or unity characteristic of human societies. Neither coercion nor rational argument, nor both together, seem capable of accounting for the coordination of wills required for a society to exist. Additional concepts appear to be required for this task, and authority has been preeminent among these other concepts. But, in this connection, it is possible to distinguish two very different approaches to the way in which the concept of authority has entered into the attempt to conceive the unity of a human society. One approach concentrates on the nature and role of authoritative beliefs, maintaining that society cannot exist in the absence of a consensus of authoritative beliefs about the meaning of human life and the ends of human conduct. "Without common belief," Tocqueville claims, "no society can exist," and he makes quite clear in an extended discussion of this matter that he means beliefs held on the "principle of authority," that is, "on trust and without discussion."[4] On this view, the notions of "authority" and "legitimacy" have a derivative application in politics. Political institutions are said to have "authority" or "legitimacy" to the extent to which the members of society regard those institutions as reflecting, embodying, or promoting their shared beliefs; and the dominant theme of this approach is that, although a common set of authoritative beliefs is consititutive of the social order, the weakening or dissolution of those beliefs is bound to generate destructive acts directed against the values and practices of the established social order and even ultimately against the self, for example, suicide, madness. It is usually some version of this approach to authority — in terms of shared beliefs — that those writers have had in mind who claim that the notion of authority has been lost or distorted in modern times.

The second approach, by contrast, concentrates on the authoritative regulation of conduct by the state. Its central theme is that social life is impossible in the absence of the authority of the state. It is political authority that is needed just because men are "individuals" who do not share the same values or, what is the same thing, who conceive themselves to have different and often conflicting purposes in life, so that no social order whatever could be maintained among such individuals if each were to insist that government reflect his "values," as a condition of acknowledging the duty of obedience to government. All men, then, must submit to common rules, regardless of their own "private" opinions as to the worth of those rules: the authority necessary to the existence of society is not conceived in terms of common beliefs, but in terms of a common framework of rules of conduct, within which the individuals can then pursue their own ends. On this view, then, the authority required for social cohesion is defined against the background of the absence or loss of shared beliefs, and so appears as a kind of compensation for that absence or loss.[5]

Now these two approaches to authority have been mentioned at the outset of this paper for two reasons. First of all, to point out what I take to be, in rough outline, the general character of the debate which has provided the intellectual context of the discussion of authority at least in modern political philosophy since, say, Hobbes, and especially in the last two centuries. It is hard to think of a significant discussion of authority in modern times that has not been inspired by the confrontation of these two approaches. But, in the second place, I have called attention to them in order to indicate, perhaps in an overly dramatic manner, the scope of philosophical inquiry into the idea of authority. I am suggesting, in other words, that it would be a gratuitous limitation on the proper scope of inquiry to restrict analysis in advance to authority over conduct, or, on the other hand, to assume that a modern system of legal authority constitutes the paradigm for understanding all forms of authority. Even if legal authority is made the principal focus of inquiry, that particular form of authority can, I suggest, be fully understood only by way of contrast with a system of authoritative belief. Indeed, the elimination of any element of authoritative belief from our present conception of political and legal authority needs to be seen as a historical achievement profoundly tied up with the work of certain modern political philosophers – if indeed it can now be taken for granted. To call attention to these two approaches should at least serve as a precaution against an unduly narrow restriction on the scope of inquiry.[6]

AUTHORITY AND "LEGITIMATE POWER"

However, the broad scope of the concept of authority is not the only thing that has made that notion so intricate and controversial. For political philosophy and social science have both been preoccupied with the problem of the difference between authority and other forms of influence. Indeed, it is now commonplace in political philosophy as well as in social science to assume that the notion of authority belongs to a network of concepts having to do with the various ways in which some men get other men to do what they wish, such as power, domination, coercion, force, manipulation, persuasion, etc. Authority thus appears as a species of the genus "social control" or "influence" and hence as a concept coordinate with, yet distinct from, say, coercion or persuasion through rational argument. From this perspective, then, an account of the nature of authority must be cast in the form of an exploration of the relationship between authority and the other notions forming this network of influence-terms, and the main task of analysis thus becomes that of exhibiting the distinctive type of influence involved in the idea of authority.[7]

In keeping with this general program of analysis, the dominant approach to authority in contemporary social science has been to construe authority in terms of the notion of "legitimacy" and, accordingly, to define authority as "power that is legitimized."[8] Here again, what has been at issue is the use of "authority" to help come to terms with political and social cohesion. For modern social science has been especially concerned with the maintenance of cohesion not simply by force, but by the sense of "legitimacy" attached to power, and this has led to the development of the view of authority as "legitimate power" or, as Weber put it in initiating this development, the "legitimate use of physical force" or even "legitimate violence."[9] Given this approach, it is not surprising to be told that: "The principal analytical problem is to clarify the relationship between political authority and coercion."[10]

To forestall confusion over the relation between the concepts of authority and coercive power that might be introduced into my discussion of authority by the dominance of the Weberian approach in modern social science, it is necessary to observe a familiar distinction between two uses of the word "authority" in everyday political discourse. For there is still another distinction embedded in the notion of a person's having authority, besides that between being "in authority" and being "an authority." In the first place, when we state that a particular person has authority, we often mean that he has the right, or is entitled, to issue commands, make decisions, enforce obedience, etc. This is to use the word "authority" in the *de jure* sense, and it presupposes some sort of legal conventions, system of rules, or method of entitlement, whereby it may be determined who shall have this particular right. It is in this sense that Justice Frankfurter, for example, used the term "authority" when he denied that the presidency had the right to seize the steel industry: "Absence of authority in the president to deal with a crisis does not imply want of power in government." Hobbes was defining authority in this *de jure* sense when he said in a famous passage of *Leviathan*: "and as the right of possession, is called dominion; so the right of doing any action is called

AUTHORITY. So that by authority, is always understood a right of doing any act; and *done by authority*, done by commission, or license, from him whose right it is."[11] "Authority" used in this fashion characteristically forms part of a judgment, and it is a judgment passed on the *source* of a man's claim to act (or to speak), not on the *content* of his action. Thus, to concede or to deny that some particular person has the authority to perform some action is not precisely to approve or to disapprove of that action itself, but rather to affirm or reject his warrant (his "authorization") to be the one entitled to do such a thing.

However, in the second place, the statement that a person has authority is also used in a *de facto* sense, to indicate that that person is quite capable of eliciting a distinctive kind of obedience, allegiance, or belief, involving (let us say roughly and provisionally) deference or respect or trust. Here the term "authority" is being used to call attention to the peculiar type of influence or control or sway that one person does in fact exert over others, and the term "authority" thus serves the purpose of distinguishing that mode of influence from such other modes of procuring compliance as the threat of punishment or the offer of reward. However, this particular type of influence is not identical with authority in the *de jure* sense, nor is it even necessarily the consequence of the recognition of that authority. Thus, a man may receive deference from others because they recognize and respect his legal right to govern or instead because of his "personal" qualities. So James Mill wrote to Brougham, "You already hold such a station in the minds of men, that office can add nothing to your dignity." And de Gaulle, it was said, had *de facto* authority in the Fifth Republic partly because his *de jure* authority was acknowledged and respected and partly because he was a man *of* authority able to stimulate deference on his own account. (This is, of course, part of the point Weber is making when he contrasts charismatic authority with legal-rational authority.)

Now it should be noticed that to say that a person has authority in the *de jure* sense of the right to rule does not imply that his will is necessarily effective, nor even if it is, why it is. To be more specific, the fact that a person has the right to rule does not mean that those under his jurisdiction acknowledge his title to ascendancy over them, so that his commands may be either ignored (in which case he lacks influence of any sort) or else obeyed, but out of fear, prudence, hope of reward, etc. (in which case he lacks authority in the *de facto* sense).[12] Likewise, a person who holds a position which entitles him to use force to secure compliance with his decisions may be obeyed because he is recognized to be entitled to command or for the very different reason that he exercises the force he rightfully possesses. That a person possesses the authority to use force does not alter the fact that if he does use force to exact obedience, his subjects are not then obeying him out of respect for his authority. That force is rightfully or lawfully exercised does not alter the cause of obedience, though it may *justify* the use of coercion.

Essentially the same point may be made about the notion of legitimate power. For the use of that notion exhibits an ambiguity parallel to the one already pointed out in the use of the term "authority." Thus, to introduce the idea of legitimate power as a way of explaining the fact the X obeys Y sometimes means that X obeys because he regards Y as legitimately in command; but at other times it means that X gets Y to obey by exercising coercive power although the use of coercion is regarded as legitimate (by X himself or by some third party).[13] In the first case, obedience is voluntary, and the term "legitimacy" serves the function of pointing to the reason why the subject obeys; in the second case, obedience is compelled, and the term "legitimacy" serves the very different function of pointing to the fact that the use of compulsion is regarded with approval. Thus, the term "legitimate power" sometimes serves to point to the operation of a type of influence distinct from coercion, sometimes to the fact that it is precisely coercive influence that is operating, though with the approval of at least some of the people involved.

The basic difficulty here is that the word "authority" is, or has come to be (confusingly), used in ordinary political discourse to mark a pair of quite different distinctions. First, it is used to distinguish between the legitimate and illegitimate use of coercion. Second, it is used to distinguish between coerced obedience (whether legitimately imposed or not) and noncoerced deferential obedience. Take, for example, the statement that, "the authority of the government has broken down." This may mean that respect, trust, deference for the government has collapsed, although people may still be obeying as a result of fear of punishment, self-interest, bargaining, apathy, cynical resignation, etc. Or it may mean that those "in authority," who are legally entitled to maintain order, cannot do so, even by the exercise of force and the threat of punishment. Thus, the word "authority" is used both to refer to the rightful use of force in order to procure obedience and to characterize a particular mode of submission or subordination that excludes compulsion. The criterion for the correct application of the term

On the Concept of Authority in Political Philosophy 63

"authority" in the first case is the legal status of the person who uses force, and the legal standing of his actions (for example, whether or not they are *ultra vires*); whereas, in the second case, the criterion is the type of allegiance accorded rulers by their subjects. Depending, then, on which sense of the word "authority" is employed, it can be correct usage either to affirm or to deny that authority is exhibited in one and the same activity of compelling obedience. The point, then, is not that it is somehow improper to use the word "authority" to mean "legitimate power" or "legitimate use of force," but rather that it is essential to distinguish between the two very different explanations of why people obey that are embedded confusingly in our current terminology.

AUTHORITY, REASON, AND THE "SURRENDER OF PRIVATE JUDGMENT"

The preceding section was not intended to suggest that the general program of analyzing authority as a distinctive mode of influence was itself necessarily misguided. In fact, the word "authority" is frequently used to point to a special kind of influence that some persons exert over others in contrast to other kinds of influence; and, on this score, I believe a useful point of departure for further analysis may be found in a position adopted by several recent writers on authority. R. S. Peters writes:

> Maybe the term "authority" is necessary for describing those situations where conformity is brought about *without* recourse to force, bribes, incentives or propaganda and *without* a lot of argument and discussion ... we describe such situations by saying that an order is obeyed or a decision is accepted *simply because X* gave it or made it ... The use of authority, in other words, is a manner of regulating human behaviour which is an intermediary between moral argument and the use of force ... The main function of the term "authority" in the analysis of a social situation is to stress ... ways of regulating behaviour by certain types of utterance in contrast to the other ways of regulating behaviour.[14]

Hannah Arendt states that "if authority is to be defined at all, then, it must be in contradistinction to both coercion by force and persuasion through argument." And elsewhere she goes on to supply the following vivid example:

> Its hallmark is unquestioning recognition by those who are asked to obey; neither coercion nor persuasion is needed. (A

father can lose his authority either by beating his child or by starting to argue with him, that is, either by behaving to him like a tyrant or by treating him as an equal.)[15]

On this view, authority is distinguished from coercion as a mode of influence because it involves some sort of "recognition" on the part of the subject that the person to whom he submits is "entitled" to obedience and it is distinguished from persuasion in that obedience is not procured by "argument." Now this view seems to me correct as far as it goes, but susceptible of further development and explication: and to bring out most sharply what is involved in this approach to authority, it is necessary, first of all, to reintroduce an idea that had traditionally been regarded as absolutely central to the understanding of authority by political philosophers. This is what used to be called "deference" or (better) the "surrender of private judgment" or "individual judgment" in discussions of authority up until quite recently. To take a single example, the following passage from Mill's essay on Tocqueville provides an exemplary statement of this understanding of authority.

> The Americans, according to M. de Tocqueville ... carry into practice the habit of mind which has been so often inculcated as the one sufficient security against mental slavery — the rejection of authority, and the assertion of the right of private judgement ... They are not accustomed to look for guidance either to the wisdom of ancestors, or to eminent contemporary wisdom, but require that the grounds on which they act shall be made level to their own comprehension.[16]

The idea being conveyed by such notions as the surrender of private judgment or individual judgment is that in obeying, say, a command simply because it comes from someone accorded the right to rule, the subject does not make his obedience *conditional* on his own personal examination and evaluation of the thing he is being asked to do. Rather, he accepts as a sufficient reason for following a prescription the fact that it is prescribed by someone acknowledged by him as entitled to rule. The man who accepts authority is thus said to surrender his private or individual judgment because he does not insist that reasons be given that he can grasp and that satisfy him, as a condition of his obedience.

Conversely, to have authority is not to have to offer reasons in behalf of what one has prescribed as a condition of being paid obedience. In this sense, obedience to a command "simply because X gave it" (Peters) entails abdication of one's own judgment as to

On the Concept of Authority in Political Philosophy 65

the particular act in question and the adoption in its place of the judgment of someone else as guiding one's conduct.[17]

This view of authority may be briefly illustrated by considering one especially significant kind of authoritative utterance – a command. What is the difference between a prescription coming from someone acknowledged to have authority and a prescription coming from, say, a friend? If your friend tells you to stop smoking you may well listen to his reasons, think his advice good, and so take it; but there is nothing in this that makes it obligatory. His prescription is a piece of advice; acquiescence is conditional on your own judgment of the contents of the prescription. By contrast, the point of claiming that an imperative comes from authority is to put a person under an obligation to obey it, and what this involves is that the subject is supposed to obey it apart from his own opinion of its merits. The point of claiming that a prescription comes from authority is to waive the requirement of justifying it, as a condition of its being something that ought to be followed, and instead to offer as sufficient "reason" for following the prescription the fact that it comes from a certain person. Hobbes draws the distinction between command and advice as follows:

> counsel is a precept, in which the reason of my obeying it is taken from the thing itself which is advised; but command is a precept, in which the cause of my obedience depends on the will of the commander. For it is not properly said ... I command, except the will stands for reason. Now when obedience is yielded to the laws, not for the thing itself, but by reason of the advisor's will, the law is not a counsel but a command.[18]

This quote from Hobbes brings out the basic difference between command and counsel upon which the element of authority involved in a command depends for its distinctive meaning. In the case of advice or counsel, the "reason" for going along with the prescription depends on the content of the prescription. To explain why one did an act advised by another person is to show one's reasons for doing *this* particular act rather than some other act. One's explanation remains at the level of the action itself. But a command carries weight not because of what is said, but because of the fact that what is said is an order given by a particular person. To explain why one did the act is to show that one falls under the jurisdiction of the person who prescribed it at least as regards the act in question, and if that explanation is challenged, then the next step in explanation is to show the importance of submitting to his authority. But in either case, and however far one's explanation goes, the explanation does not take place on the level of the particular act itself: the point of this conception of authority is precisely to bypass the action itself in giving "reasons" for doing it. The "reason" for doing the act is thus transferred from the "thing itself" to the "will" of the person who prescribes the act so that, as Hobbes put it, the "will stands for the reason"; and this in turn makes it possible for the person who submits to authority to abdicate his own judgment of the merits of the prescription as a condition of obedience. What is therefore essential to the concept of an authoritative command is the opening up of a distinction between the person who prescribes and what he prescribes, so that the content of the prescription becomes irrelevant, and the person becomes the factor that endows the prescription with its distinctive appeal.

At this point, the question arises whether the command is to be taken as the model for all types of authoritative utterance. In particular, what about the case of believing someone who is an "authority"? Is the command–obedience relationship to be taken as the model for understanding the relationship between the believer and the authority he believes? Now far from denying that there are crucial differences between authority over belief and authority over conduct, I shall in fact lay a great deal of stress on the differences. Indeed, the distinction between these two forms of authority seems to me absolutely critical for understanding political authority, and I shall take up this matter further on. Nevertheless, it seems to me that both forms of authority share in common the feature so far emphasized in this discussion, namely, the surrender of private judgment. In the case of a command obeyed on authority, the subject complies without making his conduct dependent on his own judgment of the act commanded. When a person accepts a belief on authority, he is to be understood to be abdicating his own judgment as to the basis of the belief, i.e., the grounds on which it is supposed to rest, out of deference to the judgment of someone else. In his *Essay on the Influence of Authority in Matters of Opinion* (1849), G. C. Lewis supplies the following useful definition:

> When any one forms an opinion on a question either of speculation of practice, without any appropriate process of reasoning really or apparently leading to that conclusion, and without compulsion or inducement of interest, but simply because some other persons, whom he believes to be competent judges on the matter, entertain that opinion, he is said to

have formed his opinion on authority ... The principle of authority ... [is] the principle of adopting the belief of others, on a matter of opinion without reference to the particular grounds on which that belief may rest.[19]

In authoritative belief, then, the same two features reappear once again as paramount: on the one hand, it is some particular person rather than his utterance itself that determines assent; on the other hand, the subject does not make his assent conditional on his own private judgment of the proposal. This analysis is scarcely new. Aquinas says, in discussing authoritative belief, that the "decisive factor is who it is whose statement is assented to; by comparison the subject matter which is assented to is in a certain sense secondary."[20]

To defer to authority, then, is to refrain from insisting on a personal examination and acceptance of the thing one is being asked to do (or to believe) as a necessary condition of doing it (or believing it). And what I am claiming, therefore, is that we have to see the notion of authority in connection with the idea of a very special sort of reason for action (or belief). To cite authority as a reason for doing an act (or believing an opinion) is to put a stop to the demand for reasons at the level of the act itself, and to transfer one's reason to another person's "will" or judgment. From this standpoint, then, it is the contrast between authority and persuasion through rational argument (rather than the contrast between authority and coercive power) that is essential to the delineation of the distinctive kind of dependence on the will or the judgment of another person involved in an authority relationship. That is, the crucial contrast is between the case in which one man influences another to adopt some course of action by helping him to see the merits of that particular action and the case in which no reasons have to be given to a person to gain his compliance with a prescription because he "accepts" the person who prescribes it. In what we might conceive as the pure or ideal case of persuasion through rational argument, only the substance of the argument matters. Who the speaker is – his social status, position, office, or "personality" – is in principle strictly irrelevant to the agent's reasons for adopting the action. In an authority relation, by contrast, it is precisely the status of the speaker which is decisive. We might think of it in this way. To the extent to which the social identity or "personality" of the individual who prescribes an act becomes incidental to the reason for complying with it, the relationship between the parties moves away from the case of authoritative influence; to the extent to which the content of the prescription becomes incidental, the relationship moves away from the case of persuasion through rational argument. Kierkegaard brings out the central point succinctly: "To ask whether the king is a genius, with the implication that in such a case he is to be obeyed, is really *lèse-majesté*, for the question contains a doubt concerning subjection to authority."[21]

THE "MARK" OF AUTHORITY

The authority relation, however, has another dimension besides that special and distinctive kind of dependence on the will or judgment of another so well conveyed by the notion of a "surrender of private judgment." It also involves a certain kind of "recognition" that the person to whom one defers is entitled to this sort of submission. In the vocabulary of discourse about authority, a number of different terms are used on this score, such as "recognition," "acceptance," and "acknowledgment"; and in contemporary social science it has become a stock practice to speak of the "belief" in the "legitimacy" of the person accorded authority, a phrase intended to express the so-called subjective element of opinion that goes along with the "objective" element of "behavior" to make up the authority relation. This "subjective" element of "belief" or "recognition" has been the subject of a good deal of analysis and classification; and it has proved easy to become confused about it. In a recent discussion of authority, it has been contended that:

> Authority ... always implies a belief as to right; and we need to add that this belief may be either one in the correctness of someone's view on a matter of fact or theory or, alternatively, one in the correctness of someone's practical judgement or advice. Any account of authority must cover both kinds of case and it seems to me that this can only be done by bringing out the general dependence of the concept on beliefs as to right in general.[22]

The difficulty with this view is that it obscures the distinction between two quite distinct types of belief involved in the authority relation – the belief that a person is entitled to rule and the belief in the correctness of his commands or utterances. To confound these two beliefs is to fail to recognize that belief can enter into the authority relation at two distinct points and can be directed on

On the Concept of Authority in Political Philosophy 69

two distinct objects, the source of the authoritative utterance and the content.[23] But, furthermore, the failure to distinguish these two beliefs tends to obscure the more serious problem as to whether every form of authority must involve belief in the correctness of the utterances of authority: in the section on the concept of being "in authority" in this paper, the argument will be made that it is a definitive feature of the commands of someone "in authority" to be dissociated from any claim to belief in their correctness, as contrasted with the claim merely to external conformity.

To bring out the precise character and role played by the element of "recognition" or "belief" that a person is entitled to rule (or to speak) within the authority relation, it is necessary to observe that that relationship must possess another feature in addition to the element of deference or "surrender of private judgment" so far stressed. And this is that there must be some public way of identifying the person whose utterances are to be taken as authoritative. In legal systems, this is often explicitly provided for by formal conventions or what H. L. A. Hart calls "rules of recognition." But the point I wish to make is that some public way of identifying authority is a *logical* requirement of deferential obedience wherever it is to be found in society. I can explain what I mean as follows. Since in an authority relationship a command is obeyed, a pronouncement accepted, etc., on account of who it comes from, rather than as a result of an evaluation of its merits, there must be some way of identifying the person who has authority apart from an evaluation of his utterances. For if there is no way of telling whether an utterance is authoritative, except by evaluating its contents to see whether it deserves to be accepted in its own right, then the distinction between an authoritative utterance and advice or rational persuasion will have collapsed. The appeal of the utterance will lie in such rationality as it may be seen to possess in its own right, rather than in its derivation from some particular person. In that event, the subject's reason for accepting the utterance may well be more secure, but his confidence will now be placed in his own independent judgment of the merits of the utterance. What is therefore essential to an authority relationship is a distinction between statement and speaker such that the latter can endow the former with its appeal. And for this, the speaker must be capable of somehow being known as "having authority" apart from a personal assessment of the merits of his utterances. So there must be some way of identifying authority that is independent of the act of inspecting his proposals in their own right.

In an interesting paper on authority, the social psychologist Milton Rokeach states that:

> every communication received from an external authority source contains two kinds of information. It contains information of a substantive nature and it contains information about the authority source itself. Substantive information is typically obtained from the sheer content of the message. The prestige aspects of the source are obtained from the expressive and evaluative aspects of the message.[24]

What I am arguing is that these two elements of an authoritative communication are not a contingent, empirical feature of the authority relationship, but rather part of the very meaning of the concept of authority. It is essential that an authoritative communication transmit both the substantive proposal the subject is supposed to follow and information about the communicator himself by virtue of which he can somehow be identified as entitled to speak. In the absence of some means of identifying authority apart from an assessment of the content of his commands, the notion of authority would be dissipated, being reduced to a kind of advice which could only be accepted or rejected on the basis of a judgment of its merits.

Now, historically, this means of identification was usually called the "mark" of authority. (Alternatively it was referred to as the "sign," "symbol," "certificate," or "credentials" of authority.) As Hobbes put it, there must be "marks, whereby a man may discern in what man, or assembly of men, the sovereign power is placed and resideth."[25] Or, in Bentham's words, there must be a "common signal ... notorious and visible to all."[26] Of course, many different things have been viewed by human beings as "marks" of authority: office, social station, property, "great" power, pedigree, religious claims, "miracles" (Augustine),[27] etc. In formal legal systems, there are often explicit rules or conventions defining the conditions that must be satisfied in order for the declarations of a man or body of men to count as authoritative. But throughout social life there are less explicitly formulated but nonetheless established marks of authority, such as Bagehot's "wealth and rank," "tradition and custom" which, according to the author of *The English Constitution*, did in fact identify authority and "excite reverence" in nineteenth-century England.[28] The "mark" of authority may then be understood as the criteria that men do in fact accept as designating who is to have authority, that is, whose judgment is to be deferred to.

The concept of authority can thus have an application only within the context of certain socially accepted criteria which serve to identify the person(s) whose utterances are to count as authoritative. For it is logically possible for a man to take as his "reason" for doing an act the fact that it was prescribed by another person, bypassing the question of the merits of the act itself, only if the person who prescribes is somehow "recognized" as entitled to this sort of ascendancy. The act of deferring to authority contains as an essential part of its meaning for the actor, a recognition of what went before as an order issued by some particular person. From this perspective, then, the authority relation may be depicted as a complex structure consisting of two tiers: at the first level, there is the special kind of influence one person is exerting over another person, at the second level, there is the recognition and acceptance of certain criteria for designating who is to possess this kind of influence.[29] But now it may be noticed that this analysis has a direct bearing on the widespread view of authority as an "influence" concept. For it follows that to use the concept of authority to explain the influence one man has over another always implies that there exists between those persons something more than that the one is "influencing" the other. It implies that there exists some mutually recognized normative relationship giving the one the right to command or speak and the other the duty to obey. Authority thus involves a form of influence that can only be exercised from within a certain kind of normative arrangement accepted by both parties. Therefore to explain how one man can exercise authoritative influence over another always calls for an explanation of the existence (acceptance) of the arrangement within which the parties conceive themselves to be embraced. However, this does not necessarily imply that this arrangement itself exists because of the exercise of influence by the authority over his subject. We should not jump to the conclusion that because the exercise of authority is the exercise of influence, it follows that the structure within which this kind of influence can alone be exercised itself exists (i.e., is accepted) because of the exercise of influence. It is this consideration that calls into question the attempt in so much contemporary political science to construe authority relations on the model of individualist-power relations which are wholly reducible without remainder to a matter of influence, that is, reducible to the capacity of some individuals to work their wills over other individuals.[30]

"TRADITIONAL AUTHORITY"

In this discussion I have laid a great deal of stress on the notion of a surrender of private judgment. But this key idea covers several possibilities which now call for discrimination.

In the first place, many writers on authority speak indiscriminately of "unthinking submission" (Bergson), "unquestioning recognition" (Arendt), "uncritical acceptance," and the like.[31] And indeed the notion of authority is often popularly associated with the idea of "blind obedience." It should therefore be made clear that the notion of a surrender of private judgment covers two separate possibilities. For there is a difference between the case in which a person submits to authoritative utterances without evaluating them at all because he automatically concedes them an unchallengeable normative validity and the case in which a person does judge, but submits anyway, irrespective of his own judgment. In the former case, what is surrendered is judgment itself: the subject does not judge but simply obeys. In the latter case, what is suspended is not judgment but choice: the subject desists from acting on his own judgment, even though he may "privately" dissent from the authoritative utterance. Here the authority relationship is characterized by what Oakeshott, in discussing Hobbes, calls the "will not to will."

Now it should be observed that this same distinction does *not* apply to authority over beliefs. For it seems contradictory to speak of a person believing some opinion on authority irrespective of his own judgment of its validity or regardless of the fact that he dissents from that opinion. Belief on authority calls for internal assent, whereas the notion of acting in conformity to the commands of authority allows for the dissociation of thought and action. It is necessary, then, to recognize that the authority relationship can involve different sorts of submission which should not all be lumped together under the category of "blind obedience," although the key issue for political philosophy in this respect has been whether it is necessary for specifically political authority to claim unquestioning obedience and internal assent, or only external conformity. Both Hobbes and Spinoza, for example, were deeply concerned with this issue, and they were able to arrive at the conclusion that political authority need not require internal assent only as a result of a comprehensive critique and reconstruction of received views of political authority in which the element of authoritative belief had remained central.[32]

These remarks point to a form of authority that has been the subject of prolonged inquiry in political philosophy. So far, the authority relationship has been specified as a relation in which the subject *refrains* from demanding a satisfactory justification of the proposal he is being asked to accept, as a condition of his acceptance. Authority thus involves the absence of justification (at the level of the particular action or belief in question). But the point is that justification may be absent not because the subject desists from demanding one, but because it does not occur to him that he is capable of evaluating the demands authority makes on him. That is, he may not conceive the possibility that he could stand back from the established ways of society and make up his own mind whether or not those ways are deserving of his allegiance. The grip that the established authority structure has over a person's mind may be so complete that it does not occur to him that that structure could be judged in the light of any standards external to it, for example, natural rights. The authority relationship will then be characterized not by the deliberate abstention from acting on one's own judgment, but by the absence of the recognition that one has the capacity to judge. From this perspective, then, the point is not that "private judgment" or "individual judgment" is surrendered or suppressed, but that it has not appeared because the experience in which it can gain a foothold has not appeared, namely, the recognition of alternatives and the experience of tension and conflict between established practices and independent moral standards. It is in this sense that Hegel speaks of a certain "objective" or preautonomous stage of human consciousness in which men are unaware of their own capacity for moral judgment and choice, and unquestioningly concede to established social arrangements an unconditional validity to which they are not conscious of making any contributions of their own.[33] Again, it is in this sense that Mill, in the opening pages of *On Liberty*, speaks of a "customary" or "traditional" morality in which "The rules which obtain among themselves appear to them self-evident and self-justifying ... because the subject is one on which it is not generally considered necessary that reasons should be given either by one person to others or by each to himself."[34] Here, then, roughly, is a type of authority in which justification is absent for a very different reason than that men somehow recognize the point in certain circumstances of deliberately abstaining from requiring a justification acceptable to them.

I think it is undeniable that something like this conception of "traditional" authority has always been of central concern to political philosophy. It has been especially important to those political philosophers who have set their treatments of authority within the context of the decay of traditional beliefs and the rise of a self-conscious mode of morality to fill the vacuum. Nevertheless, I shall not discuss this type of authority any further in this paper.[35] It raises difficult and intricate questions that require extended treatment in their own right. I have mentioned it only in order to clarify the preceding account of authority and to point to a topic that would have to be developed in any comprehensive examination of authority.

AUTHORITY AND "AUCTORITAS"

Recently a number of political philosophers working on the topic of authority have devoted a considerable amount of attention to the Latin origins of the term "authority." Indeed, Peters speaks of "auctoritas as the key to authority," a view expressed in several other recent discussions of authority.[36] It is worth pausing briefly at this juncture to consider this matter as it bears on the view of authority being developed in this paper.

The word "authority" and its cognates, such as "authorize," "author," "authentic," stem from the Latin "auctoritas" and "auctor."[37] "Auctoritas" was the legal term for a surety in a transaction, the testimony of a witness or the means for the verification of some fact, for example, a document. It apparently then came to mean the respect or dignity or weight attached to the person or document involved; and later yet, the Roman Senate was said to have the "authority" to be heard, though not the "power" to govern which was held by the "people." The word "auctor" apparently derives from the lost verb "augere": to augment, increase, enrich, tell about. An "auctor" was "he that brings about the existence of any object, or promotes the increase or prosperity of it, whether he first originates it, or by his efforts gives greater permanence or continuance to it," and thus according to the different objects brought about or augmented, an auctor could be, on the one hand, a creator, inventor, producer, founder, etc., or on the other hand, the "author of a writing, a writer ... in general one that gives an account of something, a narrator, reporter, informant."[38] The Latin "auctor" thus points to both senses of the English "author": (1) a writer, and (2) an actor in the sense of the person responsible for an action or for starting a line of action. Now, in this connection, what has been selected for emphasis in contemporary philosophical discussions of authority, that look back to the Roman notion of an "auctor" for insight into our idea of authority, is the notion of an "auctor" in the second sense of an actor who originates, begins, founds, etc. From this perspective, a person with authority has been understood to be someone to whom a decision or opinion can be traced back as the source of that decision or opinion or else as someone who carries forward into the present, continues or "augments" some founding act or line of action started in the past. However, it is equally important not to ignore the notion of an "auctor" in the first sense of a writer, witness, or someone who gives an account of something. The significance of this aspect of an "auctor" for our concept of authority is brought out in the following passage from what is the best discussion of the relation between authority and "auctor" that I have come across. This discussion is by none other than William Gladstone and was part of a prolonged debate over authority in Victorian England started by John Auston's original lectures on jurisprudence (1829). As Gladstone's own contribution to this debate, as well as the debate itself, are almost completely forgotten today, it is especially worth quoting at length from the key passage:

> The proper idea (of "auctor") is that of one who *adds*. In strictness, this must be adding to what existed before, as a witness adds to the thing his testimony about the thing ... From this original form the meaning passes on to a gradual creation, the creation of something that receives successive increment ... the use of the word author for writer is strictly correct, and belongs to the original sense. An "author" comes between us and the facts or ideas, and adds to them a ... ground of belief, in his own assurance to us respecting them ... And hence perhaps we obtain the largest and clearest idea of "authority," as that which comes between us and an object, and in relation to us adds something to the object which is extrinsic to it, which is apart from any examination of it by ourselves, but which forms a motive, of greater or lesser weight as the case may be, for belief or action respectively in their several spheres.[39]

In speaking of the "idea of authority" in this fashion, the examples Gladstone offered were those of an authority in religion in the sense of a witness to some unique historical event or revelation, such that others are in the position of being dependent on his testimony about that occurrence; or a scientific authority whose views must be taken on trust by laymen insofar as they cannot comprehend the reasoning which supports those views. In both cases of authority, there is dependence on the "account" of another person, and it is this special kind of dependence that, on Gladstone's analysis, links our idea of authority to the notion of an "auctor" in the sense of a writer whose "words" or report about some thing others must rely on for their own (vicarious) knowledge of that thing.[40] On Gladstone's scheme, then, an authority is an intermediary between the thing he is an authority on and the persons who accept him as an authority on that thing. He has access to it and they have access to his augmentation of or testimony about that thing. Authority in this sense always involves differentiated access: direct, personal access, on the one hand, and vicarious, mediated access, on the other hand. Authority and author thus share in common the notion of a special type of reliance of one person on another, whereby one person is dependent of his experience or knowledge of some thing upon the account of the person who has direct access to or knowledge of it. Gladstone's discussion thus brings out the connection between the Roman notion of an "auctor" and the modern concept of authority as involving the surrender of one's own judgment and the adoption in its place of the judgment of someone else.

Now, while the preceding remarks need not be regarded as anything more than a heuristic suggestion for thinking further about authority, they do require qualification in one crucial respect. For the above analysis does not fit all forms of authority, at least in the modern world, but only some. The idea that to have authority is to be *interposed* between something on which one speaks and the persons who accept that speech as credible is retained in our concept of being "an authority." It is above all in the idea of believing an authority that the central element of an intermediary is retained. In the notions of a religious authority or a scientific authority (Gladstone's two examples), there are still preserved the essential element of differentiated access, which makes one person dependent on another for his knowledge or experience of the thing in question. However, not everyone who has authority is said to be "an authority" on something. A person may rather be "in authority," and this notion does not necessarily imply an authoritative interpretation of some antecedent experience, but only an authoritative *decision*. Someone who is "in authority" need not derive his claim to deference from having access to something from which his subject is debarred. Nevertheless, he does claim deference; he does claim obedience that is not conditional on an examination of the merits of his commands – and so a certain residue of the Roman notion of an "auctor" as involving dependence on the "word" of another is still preserved even in the notion of being "in authority."[41]

These brief remarks on the terms "auctoritas" and the contrast they point up between the notions of "in authority" and "an authority" may, then, constitute a preface to what follows.

THE CONCEPT OF BEING "IN AUTHORITY"

I have so far presented the authority relation as a complex structure in which a person desists from demanding a justification of the thing he is being asked to do (or to believe) as a condition of his doing it (or believing it). However, this does not mean that the entire authority relation is incapable of justification. It only means that the form assumed by an argument for authority must possess a special character, and to make a beginning on this matter, I now want to show the importance of distinguishing between the kind of entitlement or justification implied in being "in authority" from that implied in being "an authority" *on* something. These two types of authority, and their respective justifications, should not be confused with one another. Each rests on a different pattern of argument, and so far from either one being a necessary condition of the other, they involve conflicting presuppositions.

To begin with, it should be observed that the justification or point of having someone "in authority" is to be discovered by considering the predicament it is designed to remedy. This predicament occurs whenever men cannot agree on what is to be done, so that, to avoid chaos, there must be agreement about who is to decide what is to be done. That is, the predicament occurs whenever there is a situation in which a collection of individuals wish to engage in some common activity requiring a certain degree of coordinated action but they are unable to agree on what the substance of their common behavior should be. And because they cannot agree, it follows that if each insists on following his own views, the common activity will be made impossible. Since the cost of insisting on following one's own judgment is chaos, it may then appear reasonable for each man to sacrifice his own judgment as the basis of (some part of) his behavior and also to forego pressing his own views on all the others, even though he regards his own views as fully justified and theirs as mistaken; and instead accept someone to make binding decisions for all, or to establish some procedure, such as election lottery or hereditary lineage, designed to define who is to have the right to make binding decisions upon all. In other words, to a rational man, despairing of agreement at the substantive level, it may appear reasonable to step up to the procedural level in order to reach agreement on who is to be obeyed, on whose utterances are to count as authoritative. However, this move will be reasonable for a man to adopt only on two conditions. First, the coordination of activity achieved by the abandonment of one's own judgment must be more important than the values thereby sacrificed, including the value of being free to pursue one's views and to try to win other men over them. (For Hobbes and Spinoza, it is the existence of society itself which depends on the acceptance of authority, and since the security provided by a social order is a necessary condition of the freedom to pursue one's values, whatever they may be, it is always a rational sacrifice to accept such an authority.) Second, it must be sufficiently unlikely or even impossible for consensus to be brought about at the substantive level, whereby no one will have to sacrifice his own judgment because each will have come to concur with all the others. If it is held that people really do agree at some deep, unapparent level, and that disagreement is merely a superficial surface phenomenon that can be supplanted by consensus brought about through persuasion, education, or an historical transformation, then the establishment of a system of authority of this sort will have lost its point because the desired coordination of activity can be achieved without the sacrifice of individual judgment. (This is why the criticism of this type of authority in the history of political theory has always taken the form of an argument that there really is underlying consensus among men — whether that consensus is conceived to be "natural," though concealed from men's eyes by corrupt institutions and superstitious beliefs, as in certain strains of eighteenth-century thought, or "social," though obliterated by "individualism," as in certain strains of nineteenth-century thought.)[42]

So the point of having someone "in authority" is to be discovered by considering what would happen if each person insisted on making up his own mind as a condition of coordinating his actions with his fellows. From this perspective, the authority relationship will then appear as an elaborate contrivance designed to achieve agreement at the procedural level in the face of disagreement at the substantive level — by defining whose judgment is to count as "public" and whose judgment is to be deemed "private." In this connection, it is worth noting the meaning acquired by the term "private" within the framework of this type of system of authority.

On the Concept of Authority in Political Philosophy 79

"Private judgment" is *not* a judgment exercised on private matters such as family life or business affairs; it is not a privatized or apolitical judgment. It is rather a nonauthoritative judgment, which may be highly political in content but which is nevertheless not entitled to prescribe behavior. Indeed, it is precisely because of the highly contentious public character of human opinions that from the standpoint of this view of authority it becomes necessary to have a public definition of whose judgment is to be designated as merely private. It is therefore a serious though common misunderstanding of this type of system of authority to assume that it presupposes a type of person who restricts himself to a nonpolitical existence: the privatized, apolitical character that has so often been given a central role in nineteenth- and twentieth-century criticisms of "liberalism" constitutes an inversion of the original premises of the individualistic theory of authority.

From this standpoint, then, the basis of the claim to obedience made by a person "in authority" is of a very special kind. This claim does not derive from any special personal characteristics of the person invested with authority, such as superior powers of judgment or special knowledge (as in the case of being "an authority"). His claim to be obeyed is simply that he has been put "in authority" according to established procedure, rather than that his decisions are, on independent grounds, sound, meritorious, or superior decisions. What makes an act obligatory is that it has been declared obligatory by the person invested with authority over that class of actions. (We might well wish to consider the view, therefore, that there is a "performative" element involved in this conception of authority, which is no part of the concept of "an authority.")[43] The merits and demerits of the actual decisions are strictly irrelevant to the "obligation" to obey, and therefore the claim to obedience is not compromised by showing that it is inferior to some other decision that might have been taken. Indeed, the whole point of setting up this sort of authority is to dissociate the claim to obedience from the question of the merits of the particular decisions one is being asked to accept. For as long as the claim to obedience is left contingent on a judgment of merits, the disagreement among men at the substantive level is bound to reintroduce the chaos the system of authority was set up to avoid in the first place. At the same time, it is not contradictory to defer to the decisions of this sort of authority and yet also to disapprove of those decisions. For if a person's private judgment has become irrelevant to his duty to obey, it is also the case that his internal assent is also irrelevant. This type of authority produces a decision to be followed, not a statement to be believed.[44] Belief is both unjustified (since no decision can make something true, but only obligatory) and unnecessary (since it is common action not common opinion that constitutes the purpose behind the establishment of this type of authority).[45]

THE CONCEPT OF BEING "AN AUTHORITY"

I now turn to the very different kind of title to authority implied in being "an authority." Here the justification for deferring to some person is that he is thought to have special knowledge, wisdom, or insight or to be the recipient of a revelation or unique experience not available to other men. What is essential to this sort of authority is that something be accessible to one person that is inaccessible or less accessible to others, whether this special access involves expertise, learning, singular experience or skill, revelation, etc. It is this special knowledge that constitutes the vindication of the layman's deferential acceptance of the authority's utterances even though he does not or even cannot comprehend the grounds on which those utterances rest. Examples of this sort of authority are plentiful, ranging from rather mundane cases drawn from everyday life to extraordinary religious and political examples. So we speak of an authority on ancient history, modern physics, and economic problems of employment as well as such extraordinary cases as Weber's charismatic leader whose authority rests on the "normative patterns or order revealed by him."[46] Perhaps, however, the exemplary case of this type of authority for Western political philosophy has been that of religious authority, whether of priests or prophets. Ullmann states that the concept of *auctoritas* was rather swiftly taken over from Roman thought in order to define the special ascendancy claimed for the papacy:

> What is evil and what is not evil in a Christian world ... can clearly enough be pronounced only by those who are in a special sense qualified to pronounce upon this crucial issue. It was here that the concept of the papal *auctoritas sacrata* played its decisive role ... The king so it was held, had not sufficient *scientia* to enable him to state authoritatively what was, and what was not, evil, what was, and what was not, sinful.[47]

This example brings out the basic elements of the concept of "an authority": on the one hand, the special knowledge or "scientia" claimed by one man; on the other hand, the contention that other men are debarred from this special knowledge, so that they are dependent on those who do possess the knowledge in question, if they are not to be left in ignorance. Thus the basic purpose of this sort of authority is to substitute the knowledge of one person for the ignorance or lesser knowledge of another person, although what the person who defers thereby comes to possess as a surrogate for his ignorance is not knowledge, but "true belief" in the sense of belief that is indeed justified, though the believer knows not why.

The justification of this sort of authority must, then, always be cast in the form that X knows something that Y does not know: for if X does not know, Y has no reason to defer; whereas if Y knows also, there is no need to defer. Moreover, it is precisely the particular ground on which the claim to authority rests in this case, namely, superior knowledge or insight, that makes belief, and not merely external conformity, the appropriate response to authority. Here what is produced is not merely a decision to be followed, but a statement to be believed. The claim that a person makes to authority in this case is not, then, based on the bare fact that he has been put "in authority" in accordance with an established procedure, but on his being qualified to speak because of certain special personal characteristics that set him apart from other men. Accordingly, his claim to be deferred to is logically independent of his "having authority," and this amounts to a fundamental difference from the case of being "in authority." In the latter case, a person claims that his decisions should be deferred to because he has authority: if he does not have authority, there is no reason to defer to him. By contrast, in the case of being "an authority," the person claims he should have authority because of his special capacities: if people do not acknowledge his authority, it remains the case that they ought to, since his special knowledge does not cease just because he lacks acknowledgment.[48]

In the former case, the system of authority is logically prior to the person; in the latter case, the person is prior to the system.[49] (Presumably, this is the logical basis of the distinction Weber draws between charismatic authority, which is personal, and legal-rational authority, which is based on rules. The typical expression of the charismatic authority is, according to Weber, "It is written that ... But I say unto you ... ")[50]

The concept of "an authority" can thus be recognized to rest on two connected presuppositions. The first presupposition is inequality. One person defers to another on some matter because he lacks the knowledge or insight that he assumes the other possesses. Believing an authority thus presupposes a recognized inequality between the parties, and it is this that provides the justification for the abdication of judgment. The assumption always is, in Mill's words, that "some are wise, and some are otherwise." However, the key consideration is that this recognized inequality is *logically* prior to the authority relationship itself. It is *because* of the superior insight of some person that he should be acknowledged as "an authority" by others: the deference relation is thus supposed to reflect the antecedent concrete "personal" differences between the parties. In this respect, there is a fundamental difference between the concept of "an authority" and the concept of "in authority." In the latter case, there is certainly inequality too, for every authority relation involves (by definition) the direct inequality of command and obedience, someone influencing and someone being influenced. However, it is only in this limited sense that it is correct to say that every authority relation is "hierarchical."[51] For the fact that one person is "in authority," whereas the other obeys, does not imply an inequality antecedent to the authority relation itself. On the contrary, what it does imply is a particular sort of equality, recognized by all parties. For as we saw in discussing the notion of being "in authority," it is precisely in the context in which men cannot agree on what is to be done that it can be rational for them to accept someone to decide what is to be done. But this will appear as a rational solution to their predicament only if each is prepared to acknowledge the impossibility of producing consensus at the substantive level by somehow winning others over to his own views. If, for instance, one of them can somehow get himself recognized as "an authority" on the basis of, say, religious charisma, then consensus becomes possible on a very different basis. The equality assumption involved in the concept of being "in authority" is, therefore, of a subtle order. The assumption is not that nobody actually knows any more than anyone else, that no one is wiser, better or superior; but rather that no one can "persuade" the others that his judgment is superior, such as to justify deference. The equality involved here, therefore, is the equal abandonment by each person of the presumption that a consensus can be produced in conformity to his own individual views. Each must thus recognize his own opinions as merely "private," and the claim that they are more as a conceit.[52]

The key point is, then, that it is only one particular type of authority that necessarily presupposes a recognized antecedent inequality or hierarchy: there is a second type of authority that presupposes that men acknowledge one another as equals in precisely the respect in which the first type of authority demands acknowledgment of inequality.

The second presupposition is what I shall call the "epistemological" presupposition. For the claim that a person should defer to the superior knowledge or insight of another person presupposes that such knowledge or insight is in principle available – at least to some humans. And, in turn, the person who defers must share with his authority this same "epistemological" framework which defines what sorts of things are accessible to the human mind or to human experience, even though he is himself debarred from that knowledge or experience through lack of the requisite learning, wisdom, grace, revelation, opportunity, etc. The first-order claim to be an authority on some matter implies the second-order claim that the matter in question belongs to the class of things capable of being known, and the acceptance of the first-order claim implies acceptance of the second-order claim. Thus, between the person who is an authority on some matter and the person who accepts his statements as credible, there is a double system of belief: belief in the utterances of authority and belief that the mind of man can have contact with the reality on which that authority speaks. Thus, to revert to the example from Ullmann on papal authority, it is the assumption of a "Christian world" in which knowledge or understanding of "evil" and "sin" is possible, that makes it intelligible to think of some person as being an authority on such matters. Again, in his illuminating discussion of authority in *Secularization and Moral Change*, Alasdair MacIntyre writes:

> In our society the notion of moral authority is no longer a viable one. For the notion of authority can only find application in a community and in areas of life in which there is an agreed way of doing things according to accepted rules. There being an agreed right way of doing things is logically prior to the acceptance of authority as to how to do things. It is possible for there to be people who can function as authorities upon chess either in saying what the rules are which define the game, or what the most effective ways to play chess are, only because the game of chess exists as a set of established and agreed practices, both in respect of following the rules and in respect of legislating about them. Were it not for this prior social agreement the notion of an authority in chess would be a vacuous one. What is true of chess is also true of morality; unless there is an established

and right way of doing things, so that we have social agreement on how to follow the rules and how to legislate about them, the notion of authority in morals is empty.[53]

MacIntyre is here concerned with the way in which the concept of "moral authority" becomes vacuous, and his contention is that this occurs when the "prior social agreement" on which that authority rests breaks down, so that fundamental moral principles no longer appear to belong to the class of things capable of being known, but are instead viewed as relative to human choices and desires (as, say, Hobbes regarded them).[54] However, what I especially wish to point out about MacIntyre's argument as to the dissolution of moral authority is that it applies strictly to the case of being "an authority" because it is here only that authority need be a spokesman or interpreter of a prior system of beliefs. But someone who is "in authority" is not necessarily an authority *on* anything: his decisions do not have to be presented as authoritative expressions, deliverances, or interpretations of logically prior beliefs or principles. On the contrary, it is precisely the key point about the concept of "in authority" to be *dissociated* from any background of shared beliefs. It is, then, in those circumstances in which a society has lost the sense of a common framework of substantive moral beliefs and has grown sceptical of the idea of a homogenous moral community, that the notion of being "in authority" may present itself as the appropriate form of authority for defining the general rules all men must conform to. But this does not imply that there is no "social agreement" lying behind the practice of being "in authority." For as we saw, the establishment or existence of someone "in authority" presupposes a complex *recognition* of dissensus and equality at the substantive level over against which men are prepared to step up to the procedural level and abide by the decisions of the person designated as being "in authority," whether or not those decisions happen to coincide with their "private" opinions. And it is therefore essential to differentiate between the two kinds of "prior social agreement" which lie behind the two kinds of authority.[55]

To sum up, then, the relationship between a person who is "in authority" and the person who defers presupposes a very different sort of context than that presupposed by the relationship between a person who is "an authority" and the person who defers to him. In the latter case, it is a world of common beliefs and the recognition of inequality in the capacity of men to understand those beliefs. In the former case, it is a world of conflicting opinions and the

On the Concept of Authority in Political Philosophy 85

recognition that all opinions are equally "private," no one of them having a claim in its own right to organize society.

NOTES

This is a revised and enlarged version of a paper delivered at the 1971 Annual Meeting of the American Political Science Association. However, it still remains a provisional sketch of ideas that form part of a work in progress. Reprinted by permission of the author.

1. For surveys of various definitions, see John Schaar, "Reflections on Authority," *New American Review*, No. 8 (New American Library, New York, 1970); Young C. Kim, "Authority; Some Conceptual and Empirical Notes," *Western Political Quarterly*, Vol. 19 (June, 1966), 223–34; Robert Peabody, "Authority," *International Encyclopedia of the Social Sciences* (New York, 1968), Vol. I, 473–7.
2. For example, Hannah Arendt, "What Is Authority?" in *Between Past and Future* (Cleveland and New York, 1963); Bertrand de Jouvenel, *Sovereignty* (Chicago, 1957), p. 30; John Schaar, "Reflections on Authority"; Alasdair MacIntyre, *Secularization and Moral Change*, The Riddell Memorial Lectures, 1964 (London, 1967), pp. 50–5.
3. Soren Kierkegaard *On Authority and Revelation: The Book on Adler*, trans. Walter Lowrie (Princeton, 1955), p. XVI.
4. Bradley (ed.), *Democracy in America* (New York, 1955), two volumes, Vol. II, pp. 9–10. See also, for example, Auguste Comte, "Considerations on the Spiritual Power" in *System of Positive Polity* (London, 1877), four volumes, Vol. 4, especially pp. 619–21 and 636–8, and Emile Durkheim, *The Elementary Forms of the Religious Life* (New York, 1965), pp. 236–45. Cf. Parsons: "Without attachment to the constitutive common values the collectivity tends to dissolve ... That the stability of any social system ... is dependent on a degree of such integration may be said to be the fundamental dynamic theorem of sociology." *The Social System* (Glencoe, Illinois, 1951), pp, 41–2.
5. As examples of this view, consider Hobbes, *Leviathan*; Spinoza, *Theologico-Political Treatise*, ch. 16ff.; and Mill, *On Liberty* in connection with Utilitarianism, ch. 5.
6. There has been almost no discussion of authority over beliefs in contemporary philosophy. One illuminating exception is E. Anscombe, "Authority in Morals," in John M. Todd (ed.), *Problems of Authority* (Baltimore, 1962), 179–88. I will return to the discussion of the distinction between being "in authority" and being "an authority" in the last three sections of this paper.
7. This is the approach to authority taken by a wide variety of contemporary political philosophers and social scientists. In this connection, compare, for example, R. S. Peters, "Authority," in Anthony Quinton (ed.), *Political Philosophy* (Oxford, 1967) and Hannah Arendt, *On*

Violence (New York, 1969), pp. 43–7 with Robert Dahl, "Power," *International Encyclopedia of the Social Sciences*, Vol. 12, pp. 405–15 and Dorwin Cartwright, "Influence, Leadership, Control," in James March (ed.), *Handbook of Organizations* (New York, 1965). As different as all these writers may be in other respects, they all share the assumption that authority can only be understood by differentiation from other influence terms. Most of the differences between these writers have to do with the relationship between authority and coercive power. I should add that there is no single agreed-on name for the entire class of concepts in question: "power" (Dahl, "Power") and "social control" (H. L. A. Hart, *The Concept of Law* [Oxford, 1961]) are often used, but it seems to me that "influence" is perhaps less likely to mislead because it does not as readily suggest coercion and hence the deprivation of liberty.

8 G. A. Theodorson and A. G. Theodorson, *A Modern Dictionary of Sociology* (New York, 1969), p. 21. Cf. Dorwin Cartwright, "Influence, Leadership, Control," p. 150.

9 Max Weber, *The Theory of Social and Economic Organization*, trans. Talcott Parsons (New York, 1947), p. 154, and "Politics as a Vocation" in Gerth and Mills (eds), *From Max Weber* (New York, 1958), p. 78.

10 C. W. Cassinelli, "Political Authority: Its Exercise and Possession," *Western Political Quarterly*, XIV (Sept. 1961), pp. 635–46, 637.

11 *Leviathan*, ch. XVI (Oakeshott [ed.], pp. 105–6). Cf. *Luke*, 20, 2 (King James): "Tell us, by what authority doest thou these things? or who is he that gave thee this authority?"

12 On this matter, see the useful discussions of Anthony de Crespigny, "Power and Its Forms," *Political Studies* (1968), pp. 192–205; D. D. Raphael, *Problems of Political Philosophy* (London, 1970), pp. 66–75; John Day, "Authority," *Political Studies* (1963), pp. 257–71.

13 Cf. Terry Nardin, *Violence and the State: A Critique of Empirical Political Theory*, Sage Professional Papers in Comparative Politics (Beverly Hills, California, 1971), pp. 38–40.

14 R. S. Peters, "Authority," p. 92. See also Peters, *Authority, Responsibility and Education* (New York, 1960), p. 15.

15 Arendt, "What is Authority?" p. 93, and Arendt, *On Violence*, p. 45. For this same approach, see also Anthony de Crespigny, "Power and Its Forms"; R. F. Khan, "A Note on the Concept of Authority," in G. Wijeyawardene (ed.), *Leadership and Authority* (Singapore, 1968).

16 Tocqueville on Democracy in America," Vol. II (1840) in Gertrude Himmelfarb (ed.) *Essays on Politics and Culture* (Garden City, New York, 1963), p. 241. Mill is here talking about authority over belief, but the general point applies also to authority over action, as argued below. Compare Tocqueville's own discussion of authority in the opening chapters of Vol. II: this discussion is conducted in terms of the "philosophical method of the Americans" which is "to submit to the private judgement of each man all the objects of his belief."

17 I believe this analysis is what underpins the view, to be found among

many political thinkers, that to be under the sway of authority is to be (literally) unself-determined, because guided by another self in the manner indicated. (On the sense in which authority involves lack of self-guidance, see also sections on "Traditional Authority" and Authority and "Auctoritas".) This is one sense in which freedom and authority have been thought to be opposed: note Mill's use of the imagery of "mental slavery" to bring home not his own view, but that of the Americans. Note also the parallel between authority and coercion in that both involve "reasons" for doing an act extraneous to a direct personal assessment of the merits of the act itself.

18 Hobbes, *De Cive*, 14, 1. Cf. *The Elements of Law*, I, 13, 6 and II, 10, 4.
19 George Cornewall Lewis, *An Essay on the Influence of Authority in Matters of Opinion* (London, 1849), pp. 6–7. Note again the division of influence into basically three types – authority, rational argument, and coercion.
20 *Summa Theologica*, Second Part of the Second Part, II, i. Cf. Newman: "it is not a direct assent to the proposition, still it *is* an assent to the authority which enunciates it." *The Grammar of Assent* (Garden City, New York, 1955), p. 53.
21 Soren Kierkegaard, *On Authority and Revelation The Book on Adler* (Princeton, 1955), p. 113. Cf. "Of the Difference Between a Genius and an Apostle" in Walter Kaufmann (ed.), *The Present Age* (New York, 1962), p. 100.
22 David R. Bell, "Authority" in G. N. A. Vesey (ed.), *The Proper Study*, Royal Institute of Philosophy Lectures, Vol. 3 (London, 1971), p. 197.
23 On the two sorts of belief in relation to authority, see the long discussion by Hobbes of the idea "that in belief are two opinions; one of the saying of the man; the other of his virtue." *Leviathan*, ch. 7 (Oakeshott [ed.], pp. 41–2).
24 Milton Rokeach, "Authority, Authoritarianism, and Conformity," in Irwin A. Berg and Bernard M. Bass (eds), *Conformity and Deviation* (New York, 1961), p. 235.
25 *Leviathan*, ch. 18 (Oakeshott [ed.], p. 118). Cf. "Nor is it enough the law be written, and published; but also that there be manifest signs, that it proceedeth from the will of the sovereign. For private men, when they have, or think they have force enough to secure their unjust designs, and convey them safely to their ambitious ends, may publish for laws what they please, without, or against the legislative authority. There is therefore requisite, not only a declaration of the law, but also sufficient signs of the author and authority. The author, or legislator is supposed in every commonwealth to be evident ..." (ch. 26, p. 178).
26 Wilfrid Harrison (ed.), *A Fragment on Government* (Oxford, 1960), p. 99.
27 *City of God*, XXII, 8.

28 Walter Bagehot, *The English Constitution* (London, 1928), pp. 238–9, 6–7.
29 The authority relation is a two-tiered structure, and this is what makes it possible to conceive the activity of "civil disobedience" (or "conscientious objection") as an activity in which disobedience to a particular law is joined together with some sort of sign on the part of the disobedient person that he does not mean his disobedience to imply a repudiation of the authority whose law it is. This particular notion of civil disobedience at any rate is logically dependent on the structure of the concept of authority, and it is because of this dependence that it has come to seem plausible to maintain that it is not even a necessary condition of the existence (acceptance) of an authority relation for there to be compliance in every instance.
30 It will be readily recognized that there are a number of interlocking issues here, through which political philosophy tends to get entangled with problems now taken up in "philosophy of social science." First, it is at this point that the analysis of authority becomes bound up with the controversy over "methodological individualism," namely, whether (in this case) the kinds of explanation we are able to give to account for the existence (or dissolution) of authority structures are or can be couched wholly in terms of individualist influence concepts, such as force. Secondly, there is the controversy over the character of explanation in social science, in this case, whether explanation in terms of "causes" or "meaning" is possible or appropriate as to the existence/acceptance of authority structures. Cf. Peter Winch: "Authority is not a sort of influence. It is not a kind of *causal* relation between individual wills but an *internal* relation." "Authority" in Quinton (ed.), *Political Philosophy*, p. 98.
31 Henri Bergson, *The Two Sources of Morality and Religion* (Garden City, New York, 1956), pp. 9–26; Hannah Arendt, *On Violence*, p. 45; Compare David Easton's definition of authority: "if *A* sends a message to *B* and *B* adopts this message as the basis of his own behavior without evaluating it in terms of his own standards of what is desirable under the circumstances, we can say that *A* has exercised *authority* over *B*," "The Perception of Authority and Political Change," in Carl J. Friedrich (ed.), *Authority*, Nomos I (Cambridge, Mass., 1958), p. 179.
32 Some facets of this achievement are suggested below in the sections on the concept of being "in authority" and the concept of being "an authority." Hobbes says "by the captivity of our understanding is not meant a submission of the intellectual faculty to the opinion of any other man; but of the will to obedience, where obedience is due." *Leviathan*, ch. 32 (Oakeshott [ed.], p. 243). See also Hobbes, *Elements of Law*, II, 6, 3 and Spinoza, *Theologico-Political Treatise*, ch. 20.
33 For a most illuminating discussion of this side of Hegel's thought, see Frederick A. Olafson, *Principles and Persons an Ethical Interpretation of Existentialism* (Baltimore, 1967), ch. III, from which the above formulation of Hegel's view is taken.

34 *On Liberty* (London, 1910), p. 69. On certain aspects of this notion in Mill's thought, see my article "A New Exploration of Mill's Essay *On Liberty*," *Political Studies*, XIV (October, 1966), pp. 281–304.
35 Especially instructive materials for thinking about this aspect of authority are provided by studies of the dissolution of systems of authoritative belief; see, for example, the discussions of the erosion of "traditional" authority in eighteenth-century Europe by Klaus Epstein, *The Genesis of German Conservatism* (Princeton, 1966) and Bernard Groethuysen, *The Bourgeois Catholicism vs. Capitalism in Eighteenth-Century France* (New York, 1968) and the discussion of the "way of authority" in the "intellectual crisis of the reformation" by Richard H. Popkin, *The History of Scepticism from Erasmus to Descartes* (New York, revised edition, 1968).
36 Peters, "Authority," p. 85. See also C. J. Friedrich, "Authority, Reason, and Discretion," in Friedrich (ed.), *Authority*, Nomos I (Cambridge, Mass., 1958), pp. 29–31; Arendt, "What Is Authority?" pp. 120–8; Schaar, "Reflections on Authority," p. 55.
37 In the following discussion I have relied on C. T. Lewis and C. Short, *A Latin Dictionary* (Oxford, 1966); Henry Nettleship, *Contributions to Latin Lexicography* (Oxford, 1889); J. P. V. D. Balsdon, "Auctoritas, Dignitas, Otium," *The Classical Quarterly*, X (May, 1960), pp. 43–50; R. Heinze, "Auctoritas," *Hermes*, LX (1925), 348–66.
38 Lewis and Short, *A Latin Dictionary*.
39 "On the Influence of Authority in Matters of Opinion," *The Nineteenth Century*, I (March, 1877), pp. 3–4. Among the other participants in the debate were G. C. Lewis, J. F. Stephen, J. S. Mill, and Nasau Senior. On Austin's and Mill's views on authority, see my article, "An Introduction to Mill's Theory of Authority," in J. B. Schneewind (ed.), *Mill: A Collection of Critical Essays*, Modern Studies in Philosophy, (New York, 1968), pp. 379–425.
40 Cf. Hooker's definition: "By a man's authority we here understand the force which his word hath for the assurance of another's mind that buildeth upon it ... For so it is said in St John's Gospel, 'Many of the Samaritans of that city believed in him for the saying of the woman, which testified, He hath told me all things that ever I did.'" *Laws of Ecclesiastical Polity*, II, ch. VII, 2.
41 Note the difference between an "auctor" as someone who writes or testifies about his experience of something he did not himself create and a modern understanding of an "author" as "creative," *ex nihilo*. Then compare the notion of "auctoritas" as involving "augmentation" of a prior foundation through the continuous handing down of the original accounts of that foundation with, say, Hobbes's notion of a sovereign authority as someone who makes law by "will," against the background of natural chaos. The crux of the change in both cases is the disappearance or elimination of the pre-existing thing which the author or authority does not himself create, but only augments or interprets.
42 For the eighteenth-century strain, see, for example, Condorcet, in

S. Hampshire (ed.), *Sketch for an Historical Picture of the Progress of the Human Mind* (New York, 1955), pp. 17–18, 50–3, 109, and Paine, *Age of Reason*, ch. 17; for the nineteenth century, *The Doctrine of Saint-Simon*, 1st sess., and Comte, "Plan of the Scientific Operations Necessary For Reorganizing Society" in *System of Positive Polity* (London, 1875–7), Vol. 4, Appendix.

43 Cf. J. R. Lucas's definition of authority: "A man, or body of men, *has authority* if it follows from his saying 'Let X happen,' that X ought to happen." *The Principles of Politics* (Oxford, 1966), p. 16. See also Max Black, "Notes on the meaning of 'rule,'" *Theoria*, XXIV (1958), pp. 142–4.

44 Cf. John Rawls, "Legal Obligation and the Duty of Fair Play" in Sidney Hook (ed.), *Law and Philosophy: A Symposium* (New York, 1964), pp. 8–9.

45 On this, see especially E. Anscombe, "Authority in Morals."

46 Max Weber, *Theory of Social Economic Organization*, trans. Parsons, p. 301.

47 Walter Ullmann, *Principles of Government and Politics in the Middle Ages* (London, 1961), p. 64; also pp. 67, 272, 257–2n, 305. See also J. M. Cameron, *Images of Authority: A Consideration of the Concepts of "Regnum" and "Sacerdotium"* (New Haven, 1966), pp. 4, 14–15, 36.

48 Cf. Kierkegaard: "the man who is called by a revelation and to whom a doctrine is entrusted, argues from the fact that it is a revelation . . . it remains St Paul's responsibility to see that he produces that impression, whether anybody bows before his authority or not." "Of the Difference Between a Genius and an Apostle," in W. Kaufmann (ed.) *The Present Age* (New York, 1962), p. 93.

49 However, this is oversimplified. For the question remains how someone with special knowledge is to be recognized by those who lack it. Here the notion of publicly accepted "marks" of authority must re-enter the discussion, and with it the difficult concept of "faith in authority." But this is an intricate problem, requiring extended treatment that cannot be undertaken within the confines of this paper. Further, the notion of papal authority must also complicate this analysis because here the claim to "auctoritas" is made to depend on the occupancy of special office. Yet plainly this conception of authority is not based on the Hobbesian predicament which forms the basis of the notion of "in authority"; it rather satisfies the two presuppositions (mentioned in the following paragraph in text) that are always involved in the idea of being entitled to speak authoritatively.

50 Max Weber, *Theory of Social and Economic Organization*, p. 301.

51 For example, Arendt, "What Is Authority?" p. 93.

52 Cf. Hobbes: "If nature therefore have made men equal, that equality is to be acknowledged: or if nature have made men unequal; yet because men that think themselves equal, will not enter into conditions of peace, but upon equal terms, such equality must be admitted . . .

The breach of this precept is pride," *Leviathan*, ch. 15 (Oakeshott [ed.], pp. 100–1). Cf. *Elements of Law*, I, 17, 1. Hence the suppression of a certain kind of intellectual pride becomes a condition for the liberation of the individual's intellect from the requirement of internal assent involved in a system of authoritative belief.
53 Alasdair MacIntyre, *Secularization and Moral Change*, p. 53.
54 For example, *Leviathan*, ch. 4.
55 The passage from MacIntyre is thus misleading to the extent to which it suggests application to authority in general, and not just "an authority." The same error, it seems to me, is committed by Peter Winch when he runs together "in authority" and "an authority," and indiscriminately claims that both involve a "system of ideas" ("Authority" in Quinton [ed.], *Political Philosophy*, pp. 101, 105–6).

4
Commands and Authoritative Legal Reasons

H. L. A. HART

A pervasive theme of some of my other essays on Bentham is that the central concepts of Bentham's imperative theory of law, namely, command and permission, habits of obedience, legality and illegality, are inadequate in the sense that there are important features of law which cannot be successfully analysed in these terms and are distorted by Bentham's attempted analysis of them. These features include legal obligation and duty, legislative power, legally limited government, and the existence of a constitution conferring legislative power and legally limiting its scope, and also the notions of legal validity and invalidity as distinct from what is legally permitted and prohibited. I have argued that to understand these features of law there must be introduced the idea of an authoritative legal reason: that is a consideration (which in simple systems may include the giving of a command) which is recognized by at least the Courts of an effective legal system as constituting a reason for action of a special kind. This kind of reason I call 'content independent and peremptory' and I explain these terms below. In touching on this idea I have expressed the view much disputed by some contemporary writers, that while its introduction into the analysis of the features of law which I have mentioned would certainly involve discarding Bentham's imperative theory of law, it would still be possible to preserve a distinctive 'positivist' part of his theory which insists on a conceptual separation of law and morality. Accordingly in this essay I attempt a threefold task. The first is to examine critically Bentham's account of what a command is and the curious theory of assertion, indeed of meaning, on which his analysis in part rests. The second part is to show that though Bentham's account of what a command is is in various ways defective, he does touch on certain elements embedded in the notion of command out of which the idea of an authoritative legal reason may be illuminatingly constructed. Thirdly and lastly I raise the question (but certainly do not dispose of it here) whether, as I think, it is possible to bring the notion of an authoritative legal reason into the analysis of the relevant legal phenomenon without surrendering the conceptual separation of law and morality.

I

Given the importance which Bentham attributes to the notion of a command, he is surprisingly cavalier about its analysis. He does indeed say important and interesting things. He presents with great originality and clarity the elements of a logic of imperatives in his *Logic of the Will*, exhibiting relationships of compatibility, incompatibility, and necessary connection between the four 'forms of imperation' which he calls command, prohibition, permission, and non-command,[1] and he also correctly identifies a command as a form of rational communication. But what he gives us by way of analysis is open to certain criticisms partly along lines made familiar by contemporary philosophers[2] in their discussion of 'speech acts' and their analysis of meaning. The main criticism which I shall make, though it is consistent with and indeed supported by this modern analysis of meaning, was first suggested to me by Hobbes who said some simple but illuminating things about commands and the similarity and differences between commands and covenants as sources of obligation or as obligation-creating acts. But I do not think I should have seen the full importance of Hobbes's remarks on these topics had I not had the benefit of the work of Joseph Raz[3] on what he terms 'exclusionary reasons' which resembles in many respects the notion which I have taken from Hobbes.

Bentham, in his first simple account of the connection between laws and commands given in his first considerable work *A Fragment on Government*,[4] tells us that statutes passed by legislatures are commands and that commands are the expression of a will of a superior concerning the conduct of others. He does not define here the term 'superior' but seems to treat it as a synonym for 'governors' defined as the person or assembly of persons to whom a number of persons are supposed to be in the habit of paying obedience.[5]

Bentham distinguishes explicit commands (which he calls 'parole expressions of will') where the expression of will is made by words, from what he calls 'fictitious' or 'quasi-commands' where the commander's will is expressed by acts other than speech acts and of these he cites acts of punishment as an example.[6] For Bentham the common law was comprised of such quasi-commands, and his thought was that the judge expresses his will that an act be done by punishing the non-performance of such an act and the sovereign adopts the judge's will as his own by allowing judges thus to punish those who disobey.

In the more elaborate definition of law with which *Of Laws in General*[7] opens Bentham introduces the wider notion of the 'volition' conceived or adopted by the sovereign; this comprises the four aspects of the will distinguished as command, prohibition, and the two forms of permission (non-prohibition and non-command). He then distinguishes the following different constituents of law:

1 a volition which is conceived by the sovereign or if conceived by someone else is adopted by the sovereign concerning the conduct to be observed by other persons who either are or are supposed to be subject to a sovereign's power.
2 words or other signs which are declarative of the volition conceived or adopted by the sovereign.

To this Bentham adds that the legislator must rely upon certain motives if the law which he makes is to produce the effects in terms of obedience at which he aims, and he frequently describes the sovereign as trusting both to what he calls the auxiliary sanction (popular opinion or divine displeasure) and the specifically legal sanctions which will be provided by the legislator himself.[8] The position is complicated because although to modern ears the word 'sanction' suggests punishment, Bentham admits, as a class of possible laws declarative of the sovereign's volition, those which he calls 'praemiary' where the subject is not punished for disobedience but rewarded for obedience. Secondly, Bentham makes use, when he expounds his logic of the will, of a technical or, as he terms it, 'confined' sense of the word 'command' which merely describes the 'decided' aspect of legislator's will without regard to the motive or sanction relied upon for the accomplishment of that will.

I shall for the moment leave aside Bentham's account of sanctions and their part in motivating obedience and also what he has to say about the two forms of permission, and shall consider in the case of command the two elements of the legislator's volition and the declaration of that volition which enters into his analysis.

Bentham gives no explicit account of a volition; he refers to it sometimes as an 'internal state of the will'[9] and contrasts it with belief which is 'a state of the understanding',[10] will and understanding being both 'states of mind'.[11] In the case of the 'decided' aspects of the will (commands and prohibitions) as distinct from the 'undecided' aspects (the two forms of permission) he frequently uses as synonyms for volition the expressions 'wish' or 'inclination of the mind' or 'will towards an act'.[12] Nearly all the examples of the use of these varying expressions suggest that Bentham's meaning may be best rendered by the word 'wish', that is a wish that an act be done by another person.

So much, then, for the psychological component of commands which Bentham calls 'volition'. On this account it is a necessary condition of an utterance constituting a command that the utterer wishes the person to whom the command is directed to do the act commanded. Of course in the case of most commands this necessary condition is satisfied since commands are normally given only when the speaker wishes his hearer to do the act commanded and indeed are normally given to bring this about. But there are a variety of exceptions to this which would have to be taken into account in any full analysis of the notion of a command. Thus, to take a fictional but perhaps not unrealistic example from army life, a sadistic sergeant-major, finding an incompetent and absent-minded recruit whom he delighted in punishing, gave him command after command hoping, as was often the case, that the recruit would forget or fumble over what he was told to do and would thus provide the sergeant with the opportunity which he sought for inflicting punishment. Such cases of what might be called insincere commands include also not only commands given to the counter-suggestible to procure contrary behaviour to that commanded, but more impressive examples of commands given simply to test obedience, as in the case of God giving Abraham a command to sacrifice his son. Of course in such cases it is not true that the commander intended the subject to do the actions commanded (though it is true that he intended the subject to believe that he so intended): yet there seems little doubt that we must speak of him as giving a command or order. Such insincere commands where the speaker does not in fact intend the person to do as he commands him are parasitic on 'normal' commands where the speaker does so intend. For the speaker makes an insincere or deviant use of a distinctive conventional linguistic device such as the grammatical imperative mood which is used to give 'normal' commands. Bentham does not notice this case but on his descriptive analysis of commands explained below, the difference between a sincere and an insincere command would simply be the difference between a true and a false first-person descriptive statement.

I turn now to the second element in Bentham's account of command: the words or other signs which constitute a 'declaration', as he terms it, of the commander's volition. Bentham gives no explicit definition of a declaration[13] but he seems consistently to have thought of commands and prohibitions as assertions or statements of the fact that the speaker has the relevant volition. So command at least includes a statement that the speaker wishes an action to be done, and the form of permission which Bentham calls non-command is a negative statement asserting that it is not the case that the speaker wishes the action to be done. So, too, *mutatis mutandis*, for prohibition and non-prohibition, which last Bentham calls permission.

Though Bentham has much to say of interest on the difference between the indicative or, as he actually calls it, the assertive style of discourse and the imperative and the way in which the former may 'mask' the latter[14] he did not succeed in identifying the radical difference of function in communication which they standardly perform. A command for Bentham was a kind of assertion differing from others only because it was specifically an assertion about the speaker's volition concerning the conduct of others. He did not recognize it as a form of non-assertive discourse. That this is so is not only suggested by his calling the words used in giving a command a 'declaration' of volition, but is made clear by two other observations which he makes. First he quite generally held that to express anything in speech, whether it be the expression of one's will or one's belief, is to assert[15] something about one's will or belief. Secondly, he considered that the ordinary imperative forms of language used for giving commands are essentially elliptical and when expressed at full length would display the fact that they were assertions about the speaker's will. Thus he says the imperative form 'Kill that robber' is an elliptical way of saying 'My will is that you kill the robber'[16] and a law expressed as 'Export no corn' is an elliptical form for the assertion 'It is my pleasure that you do not export any corn'.[17]

If this doctrine, that commands and prohibitions because they are expressions of will are assertions, seems a gross error, it is I think to be remembered that Bentham was not alone in failing to grasp the distinction between what is said or meant by the use of a sentence, whether imperative or indicative, and the state or attitude of mind or will which the utterance of a sentence may express and which accordingly may be implied though not stated by the use of the sentence. When I say 'Shut the door' I imply though I do not state that I wish it to be shut, just as when I say 'The cat is on the mat' I imply though I do not state that I believe this to be the case. Philosophers are no doubt now quite familiar with these distinctions which enable them for any proposition 'p', not mentioning the speaker's belief, to explain the oddity of saying 'p but I do not believe that p' without maintaining that we have here a contradiction or that p means or entails that I believe p. The same is true of course of the relationship between 'Shut the door' and 'I do not want you to shut the door'.

But Bentham, like Hume who seems not to have distinguished between reporting and expressing a 'sentiment', lacked these modern tools for making this kind of distinction, and his doctrine that commands are assertions about the speaker's will was grotesquely paralleled by the doctrine which appears in his early writings that ordinary statements of fact in the indicative mood, like 'The cat is on the mat', are elliptical ways of asserting that the speaker has a certain belief. Bentham even says that the simplest form of proposition is complex. To quote again his own example,[18] 'if I say "Eurybiades struck Themistocles" all I assert and can assert is "It is my opinion that Eurybiades struck Themistocles"'.

I have sketched in the introduction to *Essays on Bentham* the paradoxes which would result if this view were taken and its refutation. Together with the doctrine that the ordinary forms of imperative and indicative sentences are elliptical it is plainly mistaken, and the differences between commands and statements must be sought elsewhere than in a difference between two kinds of statements, one asserting that the speaker believes something, and the other asserting that he wishes something to be done.

More interesting perhaps is the fact that Bentham's logic of the will as he calls his account of the compatibilities and incompatibilities between commands, prohibitions, and permissions seems to reflect a conception of these as statements about the will of the commander and not as forms of non-assertive discourse. Thus he speaks for example, of a prohibition and a permission as being contradictories so that it will always be the case of any action that it is either prohibited or permitted but not both. This could be maintained as an obvious truth if sentences expressing prohibitions and permissions are assimilated to indicatives, and a prohibition identified with the statement that the speaker wishes an action not to be done and a permission to act with a statement that it is not the case that the speaker wishes the act not to be done. So too all the other relationships which Bentham identifies (contraries, contradictories, etc.) could rest on the ordinary formal logic of propositions combined with the assumption that as a matter of the meaning of the verb 'to wish' it is impossible both to wish that an act be done and that it not be done by the same person at the same time. If we abandon this propositional account of commanding and this assumption concerning the meaning of the verb 'to wish', something which Bentham does not give us but which I have attempted to supply in chapter V of *Essays on Bentham* is required to show that commands, prohibitions, and permissions are related to each other in ways sufficiently analagous to the relationships of contrariety and contradiction between statements which have truth values to justify the use of these terms in their case.

However, it may be that something more creditable to Bentham may be said about his account of a command as an assertion. It may I think be taken as a mistaken or clumsy way of putting a point of quite central importance of which contemporary philosophical analysis of meaning has stressed: namely, that a command is a form of human communication and that the way in which its utterance is intended to get the hearer to whom it is addressed to act is very different from the way in which one who says 'Boo' intends his utterance to get a person to jump, and yet it is also very different from the way in which one who says 'Your house is on fire' may intend thereby to get his hearer to go home.

In some sense it is true that one who commands intends his hearer to take what he says as the expression of the speaker's wish that he should do some action and the question is in what sense is this true? Bentham saw that commands as expressions of will belong to a large class of utterances which also include invitations, exhortations, requests, and certain forms of giving advice. He also said correctly that common language has no word for this broad class[19] for which contemporary philosophers sometimes use the general classificatory term 'imperatives'. Bentham also saw that in utterances of this kind the speaker says what he does in order to get his hearer to do an act for certain reasons: their use therefore is a form of communication between rational beings. These utterances have also in common the feature that they make use of a special linguistic device, namely the imperative mood, to discharge the function of communication which they have, though this also may be discharged by other linguistic forms.

Now Bentham's insistence that a command is an assertion elliptically expressed that the speaker wishes the hearer to do an act may be regarded, perhaps somewhat charitably, as a way of putting the point that in such cases the speaker not only speaks with the intention of getting his hearer to act but also intends that the hearer shall recognize that this is the speaker's intention and that this recognition should function as at least part of the hearer's reason for acting. It is this latter feature which differentiates saying 'Please jump' in order to get a person to jump from saying 'Boo' with the same purpose, though this of course is only to give one necessary condition of an utterance being an imperative. What constitute sufficient conditions is still a matter of complex debate between philosophers who broadly accept what may be called the recognition-of-intention analysis of imperative meaning. Bentham was therefore right in thinking that it is part of commanding and the other imperative speech acts which characteristically make use of the imperative mood that the speaker intends his hearer in some way to recognize his wish that he should do the act. Where he went wrong was in not seeing or at any rate in not making clear two things. First that strictly what the commander intends his hearer to recognize is not that he, the commander, merely wishes the act to be done but more specifically that his intention in speaking is to get the hearer to do it through the latter's recognition that the commander has spoken with that intention. In other words, the commander intends his hearer to recognize the giving of a command as a step intentionally taken towards furthering the commander's intention to get his hearer to act. Secondly, the use of the imperative mood is not as Bentham said an elliptical form of assertion: it is not a way of stating that the speaker wishes something to be done, for, when the imperative mood is used, though the speaker mentions the content of his wish or intention, he does not state that he has that wish or intention. So the way in which the commander intends his hearer to recognize that he intends him to do the act is not via a belief that something said by the commander is true, but by way of an inference from the fact that he has said it irrespective of any question of truth or falsity of anything said. If a man says to another 'Leave the room' he intends the hearer to infer the speaker's intention much as he might infer it from his starting to push the hearer towards the door. In both cases the hearer is intended to infer it because what the speaker does by words mentioning the content of the speaker's wish in one case and by the act of pushing him in the other case is recognized as something which people do when they wish others to leave the room and as a step towards securing this. In one case the means used is a conventional linguistic means; in the other it is a natural means.

What I have said up to this point is far from a complete analysis of commands or other imperative speech acts. I have displayed only certain necessary conditions of an utterance constituting a command and I have carried the analysis only so far as is required to focus attention on the fact that where a command is sincere the commander intends the expression of his intention to function as at least part of the hearer's reasons for doing the act in question. But in fact there is something quite distinctive in the case of a command in the way in which the expression of intention is intended to constitute a reason for action, and I shall turn now to Hobbes, who was I think the first to notice this distinctive feature, for he said something, though all too briefly, which illuminates the point.

Hobbes, like Bentham, thought that all laws were commands of a Sovereign but, unlike Bentham, thought the commands were laws only if given to those who were under a prior obligation to obey, and his account of this prior obligation was that it arose from the subject's covenant or contract to obey the commander. So on Hobbes's view the Sovereign in giving his commands which are law is exercising a right arising from the subject's contract. Bentham, however, would have none of this prior obligation to obey nor of the social contract alleged to generate it nor of the idea that in making laws the Sovereign was exercising a right or normative power, so he defined the Sovereign in flatly descriptive non-normative terms as one who is habitually obeyed by his subjects and himself habitually obeys no one. But Hobbes in discussing the general notion of a command and in differentiating it from the mere giving of advice or counsel in imperative form says something not said by Bentham. Hobbes in Chapter XXV of his *Leviathan* says 'Command is when a man saith do this or do not do this yet without expecting any other reason than the will of him that saith it. By this Hobbes meant that the commander characteristically intends his hearer to take the commander's will instead of his own as a guide to action and so to take it in place of any deliberation or reasoning of his own: the expression of a commander's will that an act be done is intended to preclude or cut off any independent deliberation by the hearer of the merits pro and con of doing the act. The commander's expression of will therefore is not intended to function within the hearer's deliberations as a reason for doing the act, not even as the strongest or dominant reason, for that would presuppose that independent deliberation was to go on, whereas the commander intends to cut off or exclude it. This I think is precisely what is meant by speaking of a command as 'requiring' action and calling a command a 'peremptory' form of address. Indeed the word 'peremptory' in fact just means cutting off deliberation, debate, or argument and the word with this meaning came into the English language from Roman law, where it was used to denote certain procedural steps which if taken precluded or ousted further argument. If we remember this we can call the reasons which the commander intends his hearer to have for action 'peremptory' reasons.

Of course the commander may not succeed in getting his hearer to accept the intended peremptory reason as such: the hearer may refuse or have no disposition at all to take the commander's will as a substitute for his own independent deliberation, and it is typical of commanding, therefore, to provide for this failure of the primary peremptory intention by adding further reasons for acting in the form of threats to do something unpleasant to the hearer in the event of disobedience. Now these further reasons are indeed intended to function within the hearer's deliberation as dominant reasons or reasons strong enough to overcome any contrary inclinations. But these secondary reasons are in a sense a *pis aller*: they are secondary provisions for a breakdown in case the primary intended peremptory reasons are not accepted as such. It is, however, important to observe that the concentration on the threats of sanctions which commonly attend the giving of a command obscures the most important feature differentiating commanding from most of the other speech acts which may be performed by use of the imperative mood.

So much then for the peremptory character of the reasons for action involved in the notion of a command. I turn now to pick out a second important feature of the reasons intended to be operative when a command is given. I shall call this feature the 'content-independent' character of such reasons. This is a term which I used many years ago[20] in seeking to differentiate the notion of obligation from the general notion of what morally 'ought' to be done. Content-independence of commands lies in the fact that a commander may issue many different commands to the same or to different people and the actions commanded may have nothing in common, yet in the case of all of them the commander intends his expressions of intention to be taken as a reason for doing them. It is therefore intended to function as a reason independently of the nature or character of the actions to be done. In this course it differs strikingly from the standard paradigmatic cases of reasons for action where between the reason and the action there is a connection of content: there the reason may be some valued or desired consequence to which the action is a means, (my reason for shutting the window was to keep out the cold) or it may be some circumstance given which the action functions as a means to such a desired consequence (my reason for shutting the window was that I felt cold).

It is I think true that reasons with these two characteristics, which I have called peremptory or deliberation-excluding and content-independent are to be found involved in many interpersonal normative transactions besides commands. They are for example both involved in promising: for the giving of a promise is intended to be a reason not merely for the promisor doing the action when the time comes but for excluding normal free deliberation about the merits of doing it. This is I think what is meant by speaking of the promisor as committed in advance to doing the action and any full account of the way in which a promise creates an obligation must I think include the giving of a promise as such a peremptory or deliberation-excluding reason for action. Since we may promise to do very many different sorts of actions in no way related to each other, the giving of a promise regarded as a reason for doing the action promised has also the feature of content-independence. This is true even though the range of possible actions which one may validly promise to do is not unlimited and does not include grossly immoral actions or those intended to be harmful to the promisee.

II

The relevance of the two features of command which I have stressed, namely the peremptory and content-independent character of the reasons for action to legislation and law-making events is the following. It is of course true, as I have said, that a commander's primary peremptory intention may not be realized; the person commanded may not accept the command as a peremptory reason and either may not obey the command at all or if he obeys the command he may obey only out of fear of punishment after full deliberation of the pros and cons. On the other hand, the command may be taken just as the commander intended it to be taken: the command may be accepted as such a peremptory reason so that the hearer obeys without deliberation on the merits from his point of view of what he is commanded to do. More than this, it may be that the commander, before he issues his command, has ample reason for believing that those to whom he addresses his command are generally disposed to recognize in his words (perhaps whatever he commands or perhaps only his commands within some limited field of conduct) as a peremptory reason for doing what is commanded. Such a standing recognition (which may be motivated by any of a variety of ultimate reasons) of a commander's words as generally constituting a content-independent peremptory reason for acting is a distinctive *normative* attitude not a mere 'habit' of obedience, and in my view this is the nucleus of a whole group of related normative phenomena, including not only the general notion of authority, legislation or law-making but many other cases where by words or deeds we are unable to bring into existence or to vary or to distinguish obligations of one sort or another.

If we consider as a model a commander, placed in the setting of a social group where the normative attitude to his commands which I have described is widely shared, that is where there is a general acceptance of the commander's expression of will as a peremptory reason for action or decision, there is room for four kinds of variation. First the commands may be addressed either to individuals and refer to single actions or may be addressed as general commands to classes of person and referring to action types. Secondly those who are disposed to recognize the commander's words as constituting such reasons for action may have very diverse ultimate reasons for being so disposed, though I do not exclude as absurd the possibility that some may have no reason for this attitude beyond a wish to please or a simple satisfaction they find in identifying their wills with that of the commander. Some may have a moral reason, or the well- or ill-founded belief that the commands to be issued would be likely to be in the best interests of all or would co-ordinate the actions of different persons in a generally beneficial way or would be just or fair. Others still may adopt this attitude as part of the tradition in which they have been reared or simply because they wish to do what others do. Others still may adopt this attitude out of fear on the footing that the alternative of calculating each time afresh when the question of obedience comes up the chance of being punished for disobedience is too dangerous, or they may adopt this attitude in the hope of getting rewards.

Thirdly, the commander's words may be taken not only as a peremptory guide to action by those who are themselves commanded to act, but may be taken by them and others also as a standard of evaluation of the conduct of others as correct or incorrect right or wrong (though not necessarily morally right or wrong) and as rendering unobjectionable and permissible what would normally be resented, that is demands for conformity, or various forms of coercive pressure on others to conform, whether or not those others themselves recognize the commands as peremptory reasons for their own actions.

Fourthly, the normative attitude in question recognizing the commander's words as such reasons may be widely spread throughout the group: all or nearly all may share it though for different ulterior reasons. On the other hand it may be narrowly confined and at its narrowest may be shared only by a well-organized or powerful minority able to coerce by threats the majority into acquiescence. Or the majority may conform to the commands given not because they look upon them as reasons for action but simply because the contents of those commands happens to coincide generally with what they are already disposed to do for moral or prudential reasons independently of the giving of the command.

This model of a normative command situation may be regarded as an embryonic form of a society in which a developed legal system is in force. It is merely embryonic because a feature of crucial importance in the development of a system is missing from it and the addition to the model of this feature would transform it in many ways. This missing feature is the existence of effective law-applying and law-enforcing agencies, that is of courts effectively directing the enforcement in particular cases of the commander's commands and applying them in the settlement of disputes. Where courts with these functions exist the normative attitude consisting in the recognition of the commands as content-independent peremptory reasons for action and as standards for the assessment of conduct as right or wrong is itself institutionalized as defining public standards of correct adjudication, and a duty to conform to these standards is attached to the office of judge and assumed by individual judges when they take up that office. I shall discuss later one important way in which this institutionalization of the recognition of a commander's words as peremptory reasons for action transforms the simple embryonic model; but here I wish to stress that even in this embryonic, pre-legal social situation there are present some of the essential elements which constitute practical authority: and show what it is for a person or persons to have authority as distinct from coercive power over others. For to have such authority is to have one's expression of intention as to the actions of others accepted as peremptory content-independent reasons for action. But this same embryonic model also indicates how some of the features of a developed legal system which Bentham's analysis in terms of commands and habits of obedience distorts, are to be understood. Among these features are the idea that a legislator, even a supreme legislator, exercises a legal authority or legal power and not merely a coercive power, the idea that this legal power may be legally limited and not merely ineffective in respect of certain areas of conduct, and thirdly the idea that what a legislator attempts to do by way of legislating may be assessed as valid or invalid and not merely as permitted or prohibited or as successful or unsuccessful in causing men to behave in certain ways.

Thus the general recognition in a society of the commander's words as peremptory reasons for action is equivalent to the existence of a social rule. Regarded in one way as providing a general guide and standard of evaluation for the conduct of the commander's subjects, this rule might be formulated as the rule that the commander is to be obeyed and so would appear as a rule imposing obligations on the subject. Regarded in another way as conferring authority on the commander and providing him with a guide to the scope of manner of exercise it would be formulated as the rule that the commander may by issuing commands create obligations for his subjects and would be regarded as a rule conferring legal powers upon him. The legal limitation of a commander's power to legislate would simply be a reflection of the fact that the sphere of conduct in relation to which his words are recognized as constituting peremptory reasons for action is limited. Thirdly, in this setting of a general recognition of the commander's words as peremptory reasons for action his words are more than commands which may or may not secure obedience or have other natural consequences; for in this setting the issue of a particular command within the scope of the commander's powers will have certain normative consequences, in addition to whatever natural consequences it has. That is, it will make certain actions right and obligatory, and others wrong, a violation of obligation and an offence. If on the other hand the command issued is not within the scope of the commander's powers it will fail to have such normative consequences whatever natural consequences it has, and success or failure in this respect will be shown by the assessment of the commander's words as valid or invalid.

However, as I have said, this model of a command situation is a merely embryonic version of a law-making situation and if it is to approximate to law-making in a developed legal system it must be amplified, but also modified, in a number of different ways, not all of which I can discuss here. However, the first and most important step would be to generalize the notion of a content-independent peremptory reason for action and to free it from any necessary or specific connection with the notion of a command which would then fall into place as one particular variant of the general idea. Indeed in the history of legal theory it has often been pointed out that, except in very simple societies, a simple command is an inappropriate model for legislation since, except in those societies, a definite law-making procedure must be complied with if the legislator's words or deeds are to make law, and if this procedure is complied with then a law is made. For this reason the enactment of a law is very unlike a simple command or expression by an individual of his wishes or intentions as to other persons' conduct, and the habit of speaking of the Sovereign as if he were a single individual is unfortunate just because it may encourage too close an assimilation of law-making to the giving of a command and conceal the need and importance of a recognized procedure, compliance with which is required for the making of the law. Given such a procedure which may include the voting and counting of votes, the reading of a bill, the issue of certificates, etc., law is created by compliance with it and the analogy of a simple command or order expressing the will of an individual is misleading. Perhaps indeed instead of words like 'imperative' or 'prescriptive' which are commonly used to characterize the act of legislation it would be better to use the technical word employed by conveyancing lawyers, namely, 'operative' or the word introduced by J. L. Austin, 'performative'.[21] These do not carry with them any specific connections with a command but would stress illuminatingly the similarity between law-making and other rule or convention governed practices whereby new reasons or guides to action are created. I mean here to refer not only to the things that lawyers are accustomed to call legal transactions altering legal rights and duties such as wills, leases, contracts, and the like, but also to non-legal transactions like the taking of a vow or the giving of a promise where individuals create obligations for themselves and their words are recognized as content-independent peremptory reasons for their own action.

What is crucial for legislation is that certain things said or done by certain persons which can be construed as guiding actions should be recognized by the courts as constituting just such peremptory reasons for actions, and so as law-making events. This generalization of the idea of content-independent peremptory reasons beyond the particular case of commands allows room for something of great importance which Bentham's imperative theory, focused on the idea of a command, fails to accommodate. This is the feature that in most legal systems there are radically different sources of law or ultimate criteria of legal validity recognized by the courts, which are neither forms of legislative actions nor derived from such an action, even if in some systems they may be subordinate to the latter in the sense that in case of conflict the requirements of legislative enactment may prevail over the requirements of law identified by reference to other sources. Thus the fact of customary practices of various sorts (local, commercial) may be recognized by the courts (though no doubt subject to various limiting conditions as to lengths of time, reasonableness, etc.) as itself a peremptory content-independent reason for action falling within the scope of the customary practices and so as rendering them legally obligatory. Similarly, in a system where there is a strict theory of precedent the judge's decision in a particular case or a sufficient line of cases may be recognized as a fact constituting a peremptory reason for deciding similar cases in the same way and so though not itself a command, as creating a general legal rule.

This recognition of content-independent reasons as sources of law, though not derived from statute even if subordinate to statute, eliminates the need for the elaborate and unsuccessful explanation found in Bentham of the status of such sources of law as due to 'tacit' forms of legislative commands. What such sources of law all have in common is not that they are commands but they are recognized as different forms of content-independent peremptory reasons.

More important, it is clear that the notion of a content-independent peremptory reason for action or something closely analogous to it enter into the *general* notion of authority, that is not only authority over persons in matters of conduct, but also authority on scientific or other theoretical matters and so in one sense authority in matters of belief rather than conduct. For where some great scientist for example is regarded as an authority on some subject, say, astrophysics, then within that sphere his saying what he says — 'Aristotle has said it' — is accepted as constituting a reason for believing what he says without an independent assessment of the arguments pro and con, that is without the theoretical deliberation within which the merits or strengths of reasons for believing what he says are considered and assessed. So though the statement of an authority on some subject is not regarded as creating an obligation to believe, the reason for belief constituted by a scientific authority's statement is in a sense peremptory since it is accepted as a reason for belief without independent investigation or assessment of the truth of what is stated. It is also content-independent since its status as a reason is not dependent on the meaning of what is asserted so long as it falls within the area of his special expertise.

III

I now want to use this last case of authority on theoretical matters to enter a caveat against a possible misinterpretation of what I have been saying. I certainly think that a shift from the notion of a command to the notion of a content-independent peremptory reason for action is needed to overcome the deficiencies of Bentham's account of law and law-making and generally to explain the 'normativity' of law. But I do not by any means think that, if we make this shift, we shall also have finally settled the issue concerning the relationship of law and morals raised by the denial that there is any conceptual or necessary connection between them. The point may be illustrated by reference to the concept of authority on theoretical matters in the following way. To be an authority on some subject matter a man must in fact have some superior knowledge, intelligence, or wisdom which makes it reasonable to believe that what he says on that subject is more likely to be true than the results reached by others through their independent investigations, so that it is reasonable for them to accept the authoritative statement without such independent investigation or evaluation of his reasoning. Hence a characterization of the person as being an authority on a certain subject entails that he has the requisite expertise and is not only a matter of how his statements are in fact regarded. Moreover, even to *regard* a person as a scientific authority, however mistakenly, is to believe that he really has the superior knowledge or qualifications which would make it reasonable to believe the statements he makes within the areas of his competence without independent investigation of them. So the idea that the authority is a suitably qualified expert and hence the reasonableness of treating his statements in this way enters into the ideas both of *being* such an authority and of being *regarded* (rightly or wrongly) as such an authority. The statement 'X is a scientific authority' commits the speaker to the belief that X is qualified in the appropriate way, whereas 'X is regarded as a scientific authority' only commits the speaker to the belief that some other persons believe that X is so qualified.

Now against the whole style of positivist jurisprudence, which like Bentham's and my own work denies that there is any conceptual or necessary connection between law and morality, and so attributes to expressions like legal right and legal duty meanings which are not laden with any such connection, it has been urged that there is in fact a strong parallel between being a theoretical authority and having practical, e.g. legislative authority over people which shows the positivist view to be mistaken. The parallel suggested is that just as in the case of a scientist, if he is to rank as an authority on his subject, there must be good reason for accepting his pronouncements as sufficient reason for believing what they state without independent investigation, so in the case of a legislative authority there must be good reason for accepting its enactments as peremptory reasons for action or, at least, it must be believed by some that there are such good reasons. In the case of the theoretical authority the good reasons are provided by his superior expertise and this is prior to the notion of theoretical authority which cannot be explained without reference to it; in the case of legislative authority as in any form of practical authority over people the good reasons must be moral reasons for accepting its enactment of laws as content-independent peremptory reasons for action. So the moral legitimacy of the legislature is prior to its authority over people which cannot be explained without reference to it. The moral legitimacy of a legislator may of course arise in many different ways: for example it may arise from the fact that the composition of the legislature, e.g. in a parliamentary democracy, conforms to morally acceptable principles of government; or it may arise from the fact that whatever the composition of the legislature or its defects, it secures order and co-ordination necessary for a tolerable social life and without it there would be greater evils than any which the government itself perpetrates.

The question whether there is in fact this suggested parallel between theoretical and legislature authority raises issues as to whether there is an essential moral component in the idea of legal obligation, so that statements of legal obligation (at least if they are 'committed' statements in the sense of commitment explained there) are a form of moral judgement. In chapter VI of my *Essays on Bentham*, I distinguished two forms of the theory opposed to the positivist doctrine that legal and moral obligation are not conceptually connected. The first extreme form of this theory claims that a legal obligation actually is a species of moral obligation, while the second moderate form of the theory claims only that for legal obligations to exist there need only be the belief, true or false, that what is legally required is morally obligatory, and that only committed statements of legal obligation carried with them the implication of such a belief. There is a similar possibility (allowed for in my initial description of the suggested parallel) of an extreme and moderate form of the theory that there is a parallel between theoretical and legislative authority. On the extreme view, for a legislative authority to exist there actually must be good objective moral reasons for accepting its enactments as peremptory reasons for action, while on the moderate view there need be only the belief that there are such moral reasons or even, as in Raz's version, only the pretence or show of such belief or readiness to avow it.[22] I will not here discuss the extreme form of this theory since as I have attempted in chapter V of *Essays on Bentham* to demonstrate in the case of Dworkin's account of the conceptual connection between legal and moral rights and obligation, it is clearly incapable of explaining what must be admitted, as Dworkin says, namely, that what is legally right is not always morally right, and there can be morally iniquitous legal systems where the clearly settled law none the less creates legal rights and obligations.

The moderate view, however, that for legislative authority to exist, there need only be belief in its moral legitimacy and in the limiting case such belief may be confined to the courts and officials of the legal system presents a more formidable case for one form of conceptual connection between law and morality. Its main thrust, so far as my exposition in this chapter of the idea of a legal authoritative reason is concerned, is that it was a mistake on my part when speaking of the courts as 'accepting' a legislative command as an authoritative legal reason, not to have included as a constituent of such acceptance belief in the moral legitimacy of the legislature or at least a disposition to avow such a belief. I think the strongest argument supporting this criticism is the one which insists that the notion of the acceptance of some consideration as an authoritative legal reason cannot stand alone. How can an artefact of the human will such as a command, or compliance with a legislative procedure, either in itself be or be believed to be a reason for action? Surely, the critic may urge, such products of the human will could only be such a reason if there were some non-artificial ulterior reason for taking the former as guides to action, and the only kind of ulterior reason which could satisfactorily explain what courts do and say involves their belief in the moral legitimacy of the legislature.

This argument, in my opinion, goes too far and fails at the last step. I agree that it would be extraordinary if judges could give no answer to the question why in their operations as judges they are disposed to accept enactments by the legislature as determining the standards of correct judicial behaviour and so as constituting reasons for applying and enforcing particular enactments. But if all that is required is that judges should have some comprehensible motives for behaving as they do in this respect, this can be easily satisfied by motives which have nothing to do with the belief in the moral legitimacy of the authority whose enactments they identify and apply as law. Thus individual judges may explain or justify their acceptance of the legislator's enactments by saying that they simply wish to continue in an established practice or that they had sworn on taking office to continue it or that they had tacitly agreed to do so by accepting the office of judge. All this would be compatible with judges either having no belief at all concerning the moral legitimacy of the legislature or even with their believing that it had none. Raz, who has given more careful thought than any other writer to this matter, characterizes judicial acceptance of the legislator's authority for such personal reasons as these as a 'weak'[23] form of acceptance, and insists that what is required is either a 'strong' form of acceptance which involves their belief that there are moral reasons for conforming to and enforcing the enactment of the legislature or at least involve the pretence of such belief.

The main argument for this view consists of two points. The first is that when judges accept the authority of a legislature this characteristically is manifested, in the course of applying and enforcing its laws, by their statements that the subjects to whom the laws are applied have a legal obligation or duty to do what such laws require. Secondly since this requirement may be to act in ways which are contrary to the subject's personal interests, desires, or inclinations, such statements of legal duty must be a form of moral judgement. Such a judgement will be sincere if the judge believes in the moral legitimacy of the legislature; insincere or 'pretence', if he does not.

I reject this argument in its general application to an account of legislative authority, because its factual implications seem to me open to question. Of course many judges, when they speak of the subject's legal duties, may believe, as many ordinary citizens may do, in the moral legitimacy of the legislature, and may hold that there are moral reasons for complying with its enactments as such, independently of their specific content. But I do not agree that it must be the case that judges either believe this or pretend to do so, and I see no compelling reason for accepting an interpretation of 'duty' or 'obligation' that leads to this result. Surely, as far as the facts are concerned, there is a third possibility; that at least where the law is clearly settled and determinate, judges, in speaking of the subject's legal duty, may mean to speak in a technically confined way. They speak as judges, from within a legal institution which they are committed as judges to maintain, in order to draw attention to what by way of action is 'owed' by the subject, that is, may legally be demanded or exacted from him. Judges may combine with this, moral judgment and exhortation especially when they approve of the content of specific laws, but this is not a necessary implication of their statements of the subject's legal duty.

Of course if it were the case, as a cognitive account of duty would hold it to be, that the statement that the subject has a legal duty to act in a way contrary to his interests and inclinations entails the statement that there exist reasons which are 'external' or objective, in the sense that they exist independently of his subjective motivation, it would be difficult to deny that legal duty is a form of moral duty. At least this would be so if it is assumed that ordinary non-legal moral judgements of duty are also statements of such objective reasons for action. For in that case, to hold that legal and moral duties were conceptually independent would involve the extravagant hypothesis that there were two independent 'worlds' or sets of objective reasons, one legal and the other moral.

Until the alternative interpretation which I have offered of judicial statements of the subject's legal duty is shown to be absurd or to distort the facts, I do not think it should be excluded. But I am vividly aware that to many it will seem paradoxical, or even a sign of confusion, that at the end of a chapter, a central theme of which is the great importance for the understanding of law of the idea of authoritative reasons for action, I should argue that judicial statements of the subject's legal duties need have nothing directly to do with the subject's reasons for action. I can also see that it may well be objected that if the judge's acceptance of the legislature's authority means only that he accepts its enactments as setting the standards of correct adjudication and law enforcement, so providing the judge with peremptory content-independent reasons for their official action in applying and enforcing the law, this is to whittle down the notion of acceptance of the legislator's enactments as reasons for action to something very different from what I represented it to be when I first introduced it in the model of a simple society whose members accepted a commander's words as content-independent peremptory reasons for doing what he commands them to do.

I do not think I have at present a sufficient grasp of many complexities which I suspect surround this issue to do more than offer the following reply to this last objection. The charge of 'whittling down' is in a sense well taken; but it is something for which I expressly made provision when I said on p. 104 that the introduction into the simple society of specialized law-applying and law-enforcing agencies would mean the institutionalization of the recognition of the commander's authority as now defining public standards of official adjudication and this would transform the situation depicted in the model. Of course except in societies where only the courts and officials accept the authority of the legislature, the rest by and large conforming to the law for other reasons, this institutionalized 'whittled down' form of acceptance will coexist with full-blooded acceptance by many others of enactment by the legislature as reasons for their conforming to what is enacted and for making upon others and accepting from others demands for conformity. But in neither case need there be, though there may often be, belief in the moral legitimacy of the legislature or the pretence of such belief.

I would however in conclusion stress the fact that whoever is right on this larger issue between the legal positivist and his critics, which needs much further discussion, this would not affect the point that the notion of a content-independent peremptory reason for action is required for the understanding of legal authority and law-making. So though it was a mistake and a large one on Bentham's part to attempt to explain legal authority and law-making in terms only of command and obedience to a commander, the mistake is none the less an illuminating one; for buried in the idea of command there are, as I have attempted to show, elements which are crucial to the understanding of law.

NOTES

1 *Of Laws in General* Chap. X ed. H. L. A. Hart in *Collected Works* (The Athlone Press London 1970).
2 For this modern analysis, which is both wider and far more complex than appears from the simple use of a part of it which I make here to elucidate the notion of a command, see the seminal work of H. P. Grice in 'Meaning' in *Philosophical Review* 66 (1967) and a critique of Grice's theory in Schiffer, *Meaning* (OUP 1972).
3 See his *Practical Reason and Norms* (London 1975); *The Authority of Law* (OUP 1979).
4 Bentham, *A Fragment on Government* eds Burns and Hart Chap. I, para. 12, n. o in CW (1977) 429.
5 *Fragment* Chap. I, para. 10 in CW 428, but see *Comment* (Alternative Draft for Chap. I) in CW 275, where Bentham says: 'When I speak of a superior being making laws for me I mean only that he can make my happiness less or greater than it is.' Cf. Austin, *The Province of*

Jurisprudence Determined 24 (The Noonday Press New York 1954): 'Superiority signifies might, the power of affecting others with evil or pain and of forcing them through fear of that evil to fashion their conduct to one's wishes.'

6 *Fragment* Chap. I, para. 12, n. o in *CW* 429.
7 *OLG* 1.
8 *An Introduction to the Principles of Morals and Legislation*, eds Burns and Hart Chap. III para. 12, in *CW* (1970) 37: Chap. XIV, para. 26 in *CW* 172: *OLG* 70, 245, 248.
9 *OLG*, Chap. X, para. 8 in *CW* 97.
10 *PML*, Chap. XVII, para. 29, n. b 2 in *CW* 299.
11 Ibid.
12 *OLG* 93, 94, 298.
13 He uses as synonyms 'manifestation' in *PML*, Chap. XVI, para. 25, n. 2, in *CW* 206, and more frequently 'expression', e.g. *OLG* 94, 99, 298.
14 *OLG* 106, 178–9, 302, 303.
15 *PML* Chap. XVII, para. 29, n. b 2 in *CW* 299–300.
16 Ibid.
17 *OLG* 154.
18 *Essay on Logic, Works* VIII 321.
19 *OLG* 14, n. 1; 298, n. a (299).
20 See my essay on 'Legal and Moral Obligation' in *Essays on Moral Philosophy*, ed. Melden (Seattle 1958).
21 J. L. Austin, *How to Do Things with Words* (2nd edn. OUP 1975).
22 J. Raz, *The Authority of Law* 28.
23 Ibid., 155, n. 13.

5
Authority and Justification

J. RAZ

This article defends a certain conception of the nature of practical authority, that is, authority with power to require action. The explanation proceeds through normative theses of three kinds. One concerns the type of argument required to justify a claim that a certain authority is legitimate. The second states the general character of the considerations which should guide the actions of authorities. The last concerns the way the existence of a binding authoritative directive affects the reasoning of the subjects of the authority. The explanation and defense of the three theses is preceded by an introductory section defending the general approach to the analysis of authority adopted here, and introducing some of the themes which are explored in greater detail later in the article.

AUTHORITY AND REASON

It is common to regard authority over persons as centrally involving a right to rule, where that is understood as correlated with an obligation to obey on the part of those subject to the authority. Robert Ladenson has recently challenged this common view. He agrees that political authority is a right to rule, but denies that it entails an obligation to obey. That political authority is a right to rule means, according to him, that "strong reasons can be advanced for holding that possession of the governmental power and acceptance by those one presumes to govern of its exercise jointly constitute a justification for coercive acts which would otherwise be immoral."[1] Power over a person here is not normative power. It means "the ability to make that person do what one wishes."[2]

It is clear that not every power amounts to an authority. My neighbor can stop me from growing tall trees in my garden by threatening to burn rubbish by my border. He, therefore, has some power over me but no authority. Nor does his power turn into an authority just by the fact that I acquiesce and do not pick a fight with him. An authority, according to Ladenson, has a justification-right to possess and exercise its power. A justification-right is contrasted with a claim-right in not implying any obligations. My neighbor's justification-right to threaten me does not mean that I have a duty to obey him. It merely means that he does no wrong in threatening me and this is compatible with my having a right to resist him.[3]

Let us therefore assume that such threats are in general wrong because they interfere with a person's use of his own property. Let us further assume that my neighbor has nevertheless the right to threaten me either because my growing tall trees will greatly harm his interests, or for whatever other reason seems an acceptable justification, provided it is compatible with our final assumption, that is, that I have the right to resist him (both his and my rights being justification-rights). It seems clear that my neighbor does not have authority over me just because he can affect my behavior and would be justified in doing so. If this is authority, we all have authority over our neighbors. Nor is it clear whether Ladenson would deny that. He adds two further elements to his explanation of political authority. First, it is authority to use coercion. Second, it is justified by the fact that its possessor successfully exercises governmental power with the acquiescence of his subjects. It is tempting to say that these two conditions do not belong to an explanation of authority over persons generally. They simply establish which authorities are political authorities. But perhaps it is wrong to factor out the explanation of political authority into two separate parts, an explanation of authority and of what makes it political. Let us therefore examine the two conditions that Ladenson requires.

It seems plain that the justified use of coercive power is one thing and authority is another. I do not exercise authority over people afflicted with dangerous diseases if I knock them out and lock them up to protect the public, even though I am, in the assumed circumstances, justified in doing so. I have no more authority over them than I have over mad dogs. The exercise of coercive or of any other form of power is no exercise of authority unless it includes an appeal to compliance by the person(s) subject to the authority. That is why authority is typically exercised by giving instructions of one kind or another. But appeal to compliance makes sense precisely because it is an invocation of the duty to obey.

Some, particularly those with Hobbesian sympathies, may think that there is an alternative and a better explanation of the fact that authority is usually exercised by issuing directives. These are, they will say, threats or coercive threats. There can indeed be no doubt that threats are another type of what may be loosely called "appeals to compliance." Nor do I doubt that all political authorities must and do resort to extensive use of and reliance on coercive and other threats. Yet all legal authorities do much more. They claim to impose duties and to confer rights. Courts of law find offenders and violators guilty or liable for wrongdoing. None of these or similar claims have much to do with threatening people. To threaten is not to impose a duty, nor is it to claim that one does. None of this shows that legal authorities have a right to rule, which implies an obligation to obey. But it reminds us of the familiar fact that they claim such a right, that is, they are de facto authorities because they claim a right to rule and because they succeed in establishing and maintaining their rule. They have legitimate authority only if and to the extent that their claim is justified and they are owed a duty of obedience. Ladenson's mistake is to think that since there can be political authority which is not owed a duty of obedience, there can also be one which does not claim that it is owed such a duty.

It should be clear by now that Ladenson's last condition — that the authority has a justification-right to use coercion because it regularly exercises governmental power with the acquiescence of its subjects — cannot retrieve the situation. Acquiescence seems relevant to the explanation of de facto authority rather than to that of legitimate authority. To have effective political control requires, in the circumstances of our world, a high degree of acquiescence. Ladenson's conception of authority amounts to a claim that all de facto authorities are legitimate. It is a familiar Hobbesian view which will be challenged in the next section. But can it really be claimed to be faithful to the main features of the notion of political authority prevalent in our culture?

To test it, try to imagine a situation in which the political authorities of a country do not claim that the inhabitants are bound to obey them, but in which the population does acquiesce to their rule. We are to imagine courts imprisoning people without finding them guilty of any offense. Damages are ordered, but no one has a duty to pay them. The legislature never claims to impose duties of care or of contribution to common services. It merely pronounces that people who behave in certain ways will be made to suffer. And it is not merely ordinary people who are not subjected to duties by the legislature; courts, policemen, civil servants, and other public officials are not subjected by it to any duties in the exercise of their official functions either.

Two things stand out when contemplating a political system of this kind. First, it is unlikely that any such society ever existed. Societies we know about invariably are subject to institutions claiming a right to bind their subjects, and when they survive, this is in part because at least some of their subjects accept their claim. Second, if such a society were to exist we would not regard it as being governed by authority. It is too unlike the political institutions we normally regard as authorities.

The two points are related. The second is a conceptual point. But we have the concept of authority that we do because in our world societies are governed by institutions claiming and being acknowledged to have the right to bind their subjects. Ladenson's analysis is not merely not an analysis of the concept of authority which is part of our cultural tradition. It is an analysis of a concept that does not have much use in our world.

To conclude: Ladenson offers an explanation of legitimate authority in terms of de facto authority. It is justified de facto authority. De facto authority is then understood as some form of power over people. The analysis fails because the notion of a de facto authority cannot be understood except by reference to legitimate authority. Having de facto authority is not just having an ability to influence people. It is coupled with a claim that those people are bound to obey.

How is authority to be related to the nebulous notion of a valid requirement for the obedience of one's subjects? As Richard Flathman disapprovingly remarked. "There has been a remarkable coalescence of opinion around the proposition that authority and authority relations involve some species of 'surrender of judgment' on the part of those who accept, submit or subscribe to the authority of persons or a set of rules and offices. From anarchist opponents of authority such as William Godwin and Robert Paul Wolff through moderate supporters such as John Rawls and Joseph Raz and on to enthusiasts such as Hobbes, Hannah Arendt and Michael Oakeshott, a considerable chorus of students have echoed the refrain that the directives ... of authority are to be obeyed by B irrespective of B's judgments of their merits."[4]

But what is "a surrender of judgment"? H. L. A. Hart, who has recently added his voice in support of this kind of analysis, provides the following explanation. "The commander characteristically intends his hearer to take the commander's will instead of his own as a guide to action and so to take it in place of any deliberation or reasoning of his own: the expression of the commander's will . . . is intended to preclude or cut off any independent deliberation by the hearer of the merits pro and con of doing the act."[5] This explanation is, however, implausible. Surely what counts, from the point of view of the person in authority, is not what the subject thinks but how he acts. I do all that the law requires of me if my actions comply with it. There is nothing wrong with my considering the merits of the law or of action in accord with it. Reflection on the merits of actions required by authority is not automatically prohibited by any authoritative directive, though possibly it could be prohibited by a special directive to that effect.

Richard Friedman offers an explanation aimed at the same target which avoids this objection:

> The idea being conveyed by such notions as the surrender of private judgment . . . is that in obeying, say, a command simply because it comes from someone accorded the right to rule, the subject does not make his obedience *conditional* on his own personal examination and evaluation of the thing he is being asked to do. Rather, he accepts as a sufficient reason for following a prescription the fact that it is prescribed by someone acknowledged by him as entitled to rule. The man who accepts authority is thus said to surrender his private or individual judgment because he does not insist that reasons be given that he can grasp and that satisfy him, as a condition of his obedience.[6]

Is this conception of authority correct? One point to remember (it is consistent with Friedman's account) is that a person may have limited authority (for instance, in matters concerning football only, or in military affairs, but not in the conduct of the economy). It should be noted that Friedman's explanation shows how misleading the metaphor of "surrendering one's judgment" can be. Unlike Hart's, Friedman's explanation shifts the emphasis from the subjects' deliberations to their actions. The subjects accept that someone has authority over them only if their willingness to do his bidding is not conditional on their agreement on the merits of performing the actions required by the authority.

This condition is open to two interpretations. The minimalist interpretation maintains that they are willing to obey if they have no judgment of their own on the merits of performing the required action. They will not then defer decision until they form their own judgment. The maximalist interpretation claims that the subjects accept that they should obey even if their personal belief is that the balance of reasons on the merits is against performing the required act.

The minimalist interpretation is too weak since it assumes that people are never bound by authority regarding issues on which they have firm views. The maximalist interpretation is more promising, and the views to be argued for in the rest of this article explore and develop it. Either way, no surrender of judgment in the sense of refraining from forming a judgment is involved. For there is no objection to people forming their own judgment on any issue they like. Nor does one surrender one's judgment if that means acting against one's judgment. For an authority is legitimate only if there are sufficient reasons to accept it, that is, sufficient reasons to follow its directives regardless of the balance of reasons on the merits of such action.

There are more ways than one in which a metaphor can mislead. It can sometimes mislead people who perceive clearly the fallacies the metaphor invites and therefore reject it altogether, turning a blind eye to the true insight it encapsulates. This happened to the many theorists who thought they had a simple explanation for the confusion of thought which led to the surrender of judgment metaphor. According to them, to accept the legitimacy of an authority is simply to accept that whatever other reasons there may be for a certain action, its being required by the authority is an additional reason for its performance. Inasmuch as that additional reason may tip the balance, one can perhaps overdramatize the situation by saying that an authoritative requirement is a reason to act against the balance of reasons on the merits of the case. This means no more than that the authoritative requirement is an additional factor. Much the same can be said of any reason for action. The fact that it will rain tomorrow, for example, may mean that I should not go to London, even though the balance of reasons on the merits of my going (that is, all the reasons pro and con but the rain) suggests that I should go.

This description of the relevance of authority to practical reasoning is profoundly misguided. It is wrong not in what it says, but in what it leaves out and implicitly denies. To be sure, if a person accepts the legitimacy of an authority then its instructions are accepted by him as reason for conforming action. But until we understand how and why the instructions are such reasons and how they differ from ordinary reasons, we will not begin to understand the nature of authority. Perhaps the point can be best

Authority and Justification

brought out by considering authority first as it functions in one, not untypical, context.

Consider the case of two people who refer their dispute to an arbitrator. He has authority to settle the dispute for they have agreed to abide by his decision. Two features stand out. First, the arbitrator's decision is for the disputants a reason for action. They ought to do as he says because he says so. But this reason is related to the other reasons which apply to the case. It is not (like the rain in the example of my going to London) just another reason to be added to the others, a reason to stand alongside the others when one reckons which way is better supported by reason. The arbitrator's decision is meant to be based on the other reasons, to sum them up and to reflect their outcome. He has reason to act so that his decision will reflect the reasons which apply to the litigants. I shall call reasons of this character dependent reasons. I shall also refer to his decision as a dependent reason for the litigants. Notice that in this second sense a dependent reason is not one which does in fact reflect the balance of reasons on which it is based. It is one which is meant to do so.

This leads directly to the second distinguishing feature of the example. The arbitrator's decision is also meant to replace the reasons on which it depends. In agreeing to obey his decision they agreed to follow his judgment of the balance of reasons rather than their own. Henceforth, his decision will settle for them what to do. Lawyers say that the original reasons merge into the decision of the arbitrator or the judgment of a court, which, if binding, become *res judicata*. This means that the original cause of action can no longer be relied upon for any purpose. I shall call a reason which displaces others a preemptive reason.[7]

It is not that the arbitrator's word is an absolute reason which has to be obeyed come what may. It can be challenged and justifiably refused in certain circumstances. If, for example, the arbitrator was bribed, or was drunk while considering the case, or if new evidence of great importance unexpectedly turns up, each party may ignore the decision. The point is that reasons that could have been relied upon to justify action before his decision cannot be relied upon once the decision is given. Note that there is no reason for anyone to restrain their thoughts or their reflections on the reasons which apply to the case, nor are they necessarily debarred from criticizing the arbitrator for having ignored certain reasons or for having been mistaken about their significance. It is merely action for some of these reasons which is excluded.

The two features, dependence and preemptiveness, are intimately connected. Because the arbitrator is meant to decide on the basis of certain reasons, the disputants are excluded from later relying on them. They handed over to him the task of evaluating those reasons. If the disputants do not then reject these reasons as possible bases for their own action, they defeat the very point and purpose of the arbitration. The only proper way to acknowledge the arbitrator's authority is to take it to be a reason for action which replaces the reasons on the basis of which he was meant to decide.

THE DEPENDENCE THESIS

The crucial question is whether the arbitrator's is a typical authority, or whether the two features picked out above are peculiar to it and perhaps a few others, but are not characteristic of authorities in general. It might be thought, for example, that the arbitrator is typical of adjudicative authorities, and that what might be called legislative authorities differ from them in precisely these respects. Adjudicative authorities, one might say, are precisely those in which the role of the authority is to judge what reasons apply to its subjects and decide accordingly, that is, their decisions are merely meant to declare what ought to be done in any case.

A legislative authority on the other hand is one whose job is to create new reasons for its subjects, reasons which are new not merely in the sense of replacing other reasons on which they depend, but in not purporting to replace any reasons at all. If we understand "legislative" and "adjudicative" broadly, so the objection continues, all practical authorities belong to at least one of these kinds.[8] It will be conceded, of course, that legislative authorities act for reasons. But theirs are reasons which apply to them and which do not depend on, that is, which are not meant to reflect, reasons which apply to their subjects. A military commander should order his troops in the way best calculated to achieve victory at a minimal cost. If he wisely orders his men to occupy a certain hill, it does not follow that they had reason to occupy that hill even before they were ordered to do so. Parliament is to distribute the burden of taxation in an equitable way, but it does not follow that the citizens had any reason to pay tax before the passing of the (just) tax law.

These are telling points. But the argument is by no means over. First, even if not all legislative authorities share the characteristics of dependence and preemptiveness we found in the arbitrator's

Authority and Justification

case, it is plain that some do. Consider, for example, an act of Parliament imposing on parents a duty to maintain their young children. Parents have such a duty independently of this act, and only because they have it is the act justified. Parliament, of course, is not limited to the enactment of laws where there is a prior obligation on the subjects to behave in the required way. But there can be, and perhaps there are authorities which are so limited. Note that the decrees of such a body will be binding even if they in fact err as to what people's obligations are. The arbitrator's decision is binding even if mistaken and so are the decrees of our imagined legislator. Both are meant to decide on the basis of dependent reasons and therefore their decisions are preemptive.

The example shows that the objector's neat distinction between adjudicative and legislative authorities is mistaken. The mark of the adjudicator is simply that he is called upon to decide what parties in dispute should have done or should do in the circumstances of a particular case. Nevertheless, the objector may well remain convinced that many legislative authorities are not meant to act on dependent reasons and that their directives are not preemptive. So let us consider his examples with some care.

One simplifying assumption has to be explained before we proceed. We have been concerned with the authoritative imposition of duties. But authorities, even practical authorities, do much else besides. They can declare that a certain day shall be a national holiday, that a certain organization shall have legal personality, that a person shall be granted citizenship or shall be divorced or excommunicated, that certain land shall be dedicated to the public, or that some people shall have certain rights, and much else.

Concentration on the imposition of duties does not, however, distort our understanding of authority since all the other functions authorities may have are ultimately explained by reference to the imposition of duties. The possession of citizenship, for instance, is important because it confers rights (such as the right to vote in general elections) and duties (such as the duty of loyalty). Rights themselves are grounds for holding others to be duty-bound to protect or promote certain interests of the right-holder. Legal personality is the capacity to have rights and duties. In every case the explanation of the normative effect of the exercise of authority leads back, sometimes through very circuitous routes, to the imposition of duties either by the authority itself or by some other persons. It is therefore possible to explain "authority" by explaining the sense in which authorities can impose duties.

One difficulty is that prising apart the imposition of duties from other effects of the exercise of authority is far from straightforward. Consider a tax law again. It not only imposes a duty to pay, but also sets up (not necessarily in the same statute) the machinery for collecting and distributing the money. When the imagined objector said that there was no reason to pay the money now due as tax before the tax law was passed, he was of course right. But is this because there was then no machinery for collecting and distributing the money or because there was no authority-imposed duty to pay it?

For the first two years of World War I there was no conscription in Britain, but there was machinery to recruit volunteers. So this may be the sort of case we are looking for, a case in which the effect of the duty can be separated from the effect of other aspects of authoritative action. In this case, at any rate, the conclusion is clear. By and large, those who approved of conscription when it came did so because they believed that everyone had a duty to serve in the armed forces in any case, or at least that everyone ought to have done so. They would have denied that the conscription law had imposed a completely new duty. It merely declared what people ought to have done. Because the doubters were bound by the fact that they acknowledged the authority of Parliament to follow Parliament's judgment as to what their duties were, its act is not merely dependent on those duties but also preempts them.

We are to imagine a situation in which the state provides all the services it currently provides, let us say roads and a sewerage system, free education and a free health service, social security and unemployment benefits, and the like. They are provided by raising money from the public for a state-run charity, contributions to which are voluntary, but which publishes guidelines for self-assessment for those who wish to use them. I hope it will be agreed that those who think that the tax law is justified do so partly because they believe that there is in the circumstances imagined a reason to contribute voluntarily a sum which is equivalent to a just tax.

Let us take stock of the argument so far. I am arguing for one main thesis claiming that authoritative reasons are preemptive: *The fact that an authority requires performance of an action is a reason for its performance which is not to be added to all other relevant reasons when assessing what to do, but should exclude and take the place of some of them.* It will be remembered that the thesis is only about legitimate authority. It is relevant for the explanation of de facto authorities because every de facto authority claims or is acknowledged by others to be a legitimate authority.

But since not every authority is legitimate, not every authoritative directive is a reason for action.

Furthermore, authoritative directives are not beyond challenge. First, they may be designed not to determine finally what is to be done in certain circumstances but merely to determine what is to be done on the basis of certain considerations. For example, a directive may determine that from the economic point of view a certain action is required. It will then replace economic considerations but no others. Or the authority may direct that the final decision must be based on economic considerations only, thus replacing all but the economic factors. Even where an authoritative decision is meant to settle finally what is to be done, it may be open to challenge on certain grounds, for example, if an emergency occurs, or if the directive violates fundamental human rights, or if the authority acted arbitrarily. The nonexcluded reasons and the grounds of challenging an authority's directives vary from case to case. They determine the conditions of legitimacy of the authority and the limits of its rightful power.

This point is worth emphasizing not only because of its importance in the developing argument to follow, but also because it marks the way in which my use of "the limit of an authority's rightful power" differs from some common uses (though it conforms with others including the legal usage). Sometimes authorities are understood to be limited by the kinds of acts they can or cannot regulate (given some restrictive ways of classifying acts). In this article authorities are said to be limited also by the kinds of reason on which they may or may not rely in making decisions and issuing directives, and by the kinds of reasons their decisions can preempt.

The argument for the preemption thesis proceeds from another, which I shall call the dependence thesis. It says: *All authoritative directives should be based, in the main, on reasons which already independently apply to the subjects of the directives and are relevant to their action in the circumstances covered by the directive.* Such reasons I termed above "dependent reasons." The examples of conscription and taxation were intended to give the dependence thesis some plausibility, and in particular to disprove the suggestion that dependence is the mark of adjudication. But doubts are bound to linger and further clarifications are required to dispel them.

A few preliminary points. The dependence thesis does not claim that authorities always act for dependent reasons, but merely that they should do so. Ours is an attempt to explain the notion of legitimate authority through describing what one might call an ideal exercise of authority. Reality has a way of falling short of the ideal. We saw this regarding de facto authorities which are not legitimate. But naturally not even legitimate authorities always succeed, nor do they always try to live up to the ideal. It is nevertheless through their ideal functioning that they must be understood. For that is how they are supposed to function, that is how they publicly claim that they attempt to function, and, as we shall see below, that is the normal way to justify their authority (that is, not by assuming that they always succeed in acting in the ideal way, but on the ground that they do so often enough to justify their power), and naturally authorities are judged and their performance evaluated by comparing them to the ideal.

Remember also that the thesis is not that authoritative determinations are binding only if they correctly reflect the reasons on which they depend. On the contrary, there is no point in having authorities unless their determinations are binding even if mistaken (though some mistakes may disqualify them). The whole point and purpose of authorities, I shall argue below, is to preempt individual judgment on the merits, and this will not be achieved if in order to establish whether the authoritative determination is binding individuals have to rely on their own judgment of the merits.

Nor does the thesis claim that authorities should always act in the interests of their subjects. Its claim is that they should act for reasons which apply also to their subjects, but these need not be reasons advancing their interests. A military commander, for example, should put the defense of his country above the interests of his soldiers. He may therefore order them to act against their own interests. But then soldiers are supposed to put their country above their personal interests, and only because of this should they obey their commander.

Much of the resistance to the dependence thesis comes from confusing it with a claim about what authorities do in fact, or with the view that requires authorities to act only in the interests of their subjects. But the most common confusion is between the dependence thesis and another which can be called *the no-difference thesis*, which asserts that *the exercise of authority should make no difference to what its subjects ought to do*, for it ought to direct them to do what they ought to do in any event.[9] It may appear that the dependence thesis entails the no-difference thesis. But this is not the case. There are at least four ways in which authority acting correctly may make a difference to what its subjects ought to do, which are all consistent with the dependence thesis.

Authority and Justification

First, the dependence thesis does not exclude the authority from acting for additional reasons which apply to it alone, and not to its subjects. All it requires is that it shall act primarily for dependent reasons. The force of the qualification and the role other reasons are allowed to have will be explained below. Typical examples of considerations which affect authoritative decisions but do not apply to individuals acting on their own are considerations arising out of the needs and limitations of bureaucracies. They have to be considered alongside substantive considerations which do apply to the individual subjects of the law or any other authority. The intrusion of the bureaucratic considerations is likely to require a solution which differs from the one an individual should have adopted if left to himself. But since the right authoritative solution is also, we assume, based on some dependent reasons, it conforms to the dependence thesis.

Second, many aspects of every action we perform for a reason are not uniquely determined by reasons. I have a reason to buy a loaf of bread but, let us assume, no reason to prefer a sliced loaf to an unsliced one or vice versa. Since I have a reason to buy a loaf of bread, I have a reason to buy a sliced loaf, as well as a reason to buy an unsliced one. But I have no reason to get one rather than the other. Since there is no other kind of bread, inevitably if I do as I have reason to and buy a loaf, I will buy one or the other. That is, in acting for the best reasons I will also inevitably transcend reason and take a deliberate decision (for example, to buy a sliced loaf) concerning some aspects of which reason is undetermined.

The same general considerations apply to directives issued by authorities. The legislator, for example, has reason to impose a certain tax. There are reasons showing that it is better to require that the tax be paid either in quarterly or in monthly payments. These intervals are superior to all others. But while some reasons favor monthly payments and others favor quarterly ones, neither is sufficient to establish the superiority of doing it one way rather than the other. In this situation the authority may leave the choice to individuals, but sometimes there are decisive reasons against doing so. Then the authority has to decide on one of the two or more acceptable options.[10] When this happens the authoritative directive does make a difference. Without it individuals would have had a choice of which of the acceptable solutions to adopt. The authority quite properly denies them the choice and exercises it itself.

Third, one important function of authoritative directives is to establish and help sustain conventions. Conventions are here understood in a narrow sense in which they are solutions to coordination problems, that is, to situations in which the vast majority have sufficient reason to prefer to take that action which is (likely to be) taken by the vast majority. Where there is a coordination problem the issuing of an authoritative directive can supply the missing link in the argument. It makes it likely that a convention will be established to follow the authoritatively designated act. It is often the proper job of authorities to issue directives for this purpose. Such authoritative directives provide the subjects with reasons which they did not have before. They therefore make a difference to their practical deliberations, and serve to refute the no-difference thesis.

These cases are not only common (though they hardly ever occur in the much oversimplified form we have considered), but are also of some theoretical interest. Once the directive is issued, individuals have reasons to take the action it requires which they did not have before because now there is ground to expect that a convention will be formed. But while this shows that the directive made a difference, it does not refute the dependence thesis. The authority took the action in order to help generate a convention. In so doing it acted for a dependent reason, for the assumption is that individuals have reason to wish for a convention and hence reason to take action to help form one. Every person in the group concerned has, before the directive is issued, a reason both to form a convention and to follow it once formed. This is the reason for which the legislation is adopted and it is, for the legislator, a dependent reason.

Fourth, prisoner's-dilemma type situations are another class of cases where authorities make a difference while conforming with the dependence thesis.[11] In these cases while people have reason to act in a certain way given the situation they are in, they also have reason to change the situation. It is this feature, shared by cases where there are coordination problems, which enables authorities to make a difference while acting on dependent reasons. It should be remembered that many moral theories may land their adherents in prisoner's-dilemma type situations. The problem does not arise merely through lack of moral fiber.[12]

The considerations adumbrated above do not prove the dependence thesis. They adduce support for it mainly by removing misunderstanding and a few possible objections. Implicitly the argument appeals to our common understanding of the way authority should be exercised. The argument gains much strength by considering the case of theoretical authority, that is, authority for believing in certain propositions. Nowadays it is not the fashion to talk of authorities in this context. Instead we have experts. But the notions are very similar, at least in all that matters to our concerns.

There is likely to be ready agreement that experts of all varieties are to give advice based on the very same reasons which should sway ordinary people who wish to form their minds independently. The experts' advantage is in their easy access to the evidence and in their better ability to grasp its significance. But the evidence on which they should base their advice to me is the same evidence on which it would have been appropriate for me to form my own judgment. It is possible that practical and theoretical authorities have little in common. But it is more likely that, while they provide reasons for different things, they share the same basic structure. If so, the fact that a dependence thesis is true of theoretical authorities is strong evidence to suppose that it holds for practical authorities as well.

THE JUSTIFICATION OF AUTHORITY

The dependence thesis, it will be remembered, is a moral thesis about the way authorities should use their powers. It is closely connected with a second moral thesis about the type of argument which could be used to establish the legitimacy of an authority. I shall call it the *"normal justification thesis."* It claims that *the normal and primary way to establish that a person should be acknowledged to have authority over another person involves showing that the alleged subject is likely better to comply with reasons which apply to him (other than the alleged authoritative directives) if he accepts the directives of the alleged authority as authoritatively binding and tries to follow them, rather than by trying to follow the reasons which apply to him directly.*

This way of justifying a claim that someone has legitimate authority, that is, that those subject to his authority should acknowledge the authoritative force of his directives, is not the only one. It is, however, the normal and primary one. Consider the case of a person whose reason for accepting his friend's advice is that the friend will be hurt if he does not. This may well be a perfectly good reason for accepting advice, but it is not the normal reason. It is regrettable that the friend will be hurt if his advice is not followed after it was given due consideration, or at least it is regrettable that he will be hurt to a degree which justifies this reaction. The friend himself does not intend his advice to be accepted for that reason, and is likely to be doubly hurt if he finds out that his advice was judged mistaken on the merits but was followed in order not to hurt him. The friend will be hurt because even when this is a good reason to accept advice, it is not a reason to accept it as a piece of advice. It is a reason to accept it as a way of being kind to a friend.

The normal reason for accepting a piece of advice is that it is likely to be sound advice. The normal reason to offer advice is the very same. It will be clear that these judgments of normality are normative. But we can understand the very nature of advice only if we understand in what spirit it is meant to be offered and for what reasons it is meant to be taken. The explanation must leave room for deviant cases, for their existence is undeniable. But it must also draw the distinction between the deviant and the normal, for otherwise the very reason why the "institution" exists and why deviant cases take the special form they do remains inexplicable.

The example of advice is close to the case of authority. Indeed some, though not all, advice is authoritative advice. It is, for example, sometimes justifiable to accept someone's authority in order not to hurt his feelings. Many grown-up people feel obliged by such considerations to continue to acknowledge the authority of their parents over them. But just as in the case of advice, and for the very same reasons, such grounds for recognizing the authority of another, even though sometimes good, are always deviant grounds.

Slightly different considerations show that some reasons for recognizing the authority of another are secondary. To call them secondary means that they are valid reasons which are, in normal cases, sufficient only in combination with the primary reasons (whereas deviant reasons may validly replace the normal reasons). Accepting the authority of a person or an institution is, for example, a way of defining one's own identity as a member of a nation or some other group, though needless to say it is unlikely to be the only way any person will express his identification with such a group. Such a reason can be perfectly valid, but only (according to the normal justification thesis) if the normal and primary justification applies to the same case as well. The secondary justification serves to lower the burden of proof required to establish the primary justification, that is, they may suffice in conjunction in circumstances in which the primary justification will not by itself be enough to establish the legitimacy of an authority. But reasons of identification and self-definition cannot by themselves establish the legitimacy of an authority.

Identification is a common and often proper ground for accepting authority. It is therefore important to establish the reasons why it is no more than a secondary justification dependent on the availability, at least to a certain degree, of another justification. Acceptance of an authority can be an act of identification with a group because it can be naturally regarded as expressing trust in the person or institution in authority and a willingness to share the fortunes of the group which are to a large extent determined by the authority. But trust in an authority is trust that the authority is likely to discharge its duties properly. It therefore presupposes a principle which should govern its activities. Accepting the authority as a way of identifying with a group is justified only if the trust is not altogether misplaced. Otherwise the odd situation may result that a person will quite properly express his identification with a group by supporting an institution which grossly betrays its duties to the group. For the same reasons one cannot properly express one's willingness to share the fortunes of a group by submitting to an authority which grossly betrays the trust it owes to the group. Identification with the group in such circumstances calls for the rejection of that authority.

The dependence and the normal justification theses are mutually reinforcing. If the normal and primary way of justifying the legitimacy of an authority is that it is more likely to act successfully on the reasons which apply to its subjects, then it is hard to resist the dependence thesis. It merely claims that authorities should do that which they were appointed to do. Conversely, if the independence thesis is accepted, then the case for the normal justification thesis becomes very strong. It merely states that the normal and primary justification of any authority has to establish that it is qualified to follow with some degree of success the moral principle which should govern the decisions of all authorities. Together the two theses present a comprehensive view of the nature and role of legitimate authority. They articulate the service conception of the function of authorities, that is, the view that their role and primary normal function is to serve the governed. This, to repeat a point made earlier, does not mean that their only role must be to further the interest of each or of all of their subjects. It is to help them act on reasons which bind them.

The service conception, that is, the two theses taken together, clarifies one point which the dependence thesis itself left vague. As we saw, the thesis requires authorities to act primarily for dependent reasons. But it left unexplained the place and possible importance of the others. The justification thesis, which explains that acting for the dependent reasons is the normal function of authorities, explains the point. Sometimes one has to act for nondependent reasons. Bureaucracies, for example, are almost invariably forced to embrace a *de minimis* rule in order to be able to achieve their tasks where it really matters. The justification thesis, in other words, establishes the subservience of the nondependent reasons which should guide authoritative action to the dependent ones.

It will be both noticed that the normal justification thesis identifies the case that must normally be established to show that a person has authority. It is not a matter of showing that he is entitled to have authority, but that he has it, that he is an authority, with all the consequences which follow from this fact. The main objection to this point revolves around the feeling that a person can have authority, be an authority or in authority, only if his authority is recognized by some people whose identity varies with the nature of the authority. The difficulty in assessing this point is that in most cases the normal justification cannot be established unless the putative authority enjoys some measure of recognition and exercises power over its subjects. There is a strong case for holding that no political authority can be legitimate unless it is also a de facto authority. The case for the legitimacy of any political authority rests to a large extent on its ability to solve coordination problems and extricate the population from prisoner's-dilemma type situations.

These considerations explain why to say of someone that he is entitled to have authority means that he should be in a position of real power, for then he will have legitimate authority. They may be sufficient to account for the feeling that as a matter of meaning, recognition is a condition of possessing legitimate authority. If I am right, then this is not a matter of meaning but of normative justification.

The normal justification thesis allows for deviant and secondary reasons. Apart from these it is meant to account for the reasons there can be for accepting authorities. But a complete justification of authority has to do more than provide valid reasons for its acceptance. It also has to establish that there are no reasons against its acceptance which defeat the reasons for the authority. Because the reasons against the acceptance of authority vary, it is not possible to discover in advance how strong the reasons for acceptance of the authority need be to be sufficient.

Some reasons against the acceptance of authority pertain, with

Authority and Justification

varying force, to many situations. One recurring kind of reason against accepting the authority of one person or institution is that there is another person or institution with a better claim to be recognized as an authority. The claim of the second is a reason against accepting the claim of the first only when the two authorities are incompatible, as are the claims of two governments to be legitimate governments of one country. Sometimes there are two compatible authorities whose powers overlap, as is the case with the authority of both parents over their children.

Another cluster of recurring considerations concerns the intrinsic desirability of people conducting their lives by their own lights. This obviously applies to some areas of life more than to others, to choice of friends more than to choice of legal argument in a court case. The case for the validity of a claim to authority must include justificatory considerations sufficient to outweigh such counterreasons. That is one reason why the case is hard to make. But if anarchists are right to think that it can never be made, this is for contingent reasons and not because of any inconsistency in the notion of a rational justification for authority, nor in the notion of authority over moral agents.

THE PREEMPTIVE THESIS

From the dependence and normal justification theses it is but a short step to the preemption thesis. It turns on the general relation between the justification for a binding directive and its status as a reason for action, and more generally the relation between rules as reasons for action and their justification. Consider the rule that when being with one person and meeting another, one should introduce them to each other. The fact that this is a sound, valid, or sensible rule is a reason for anyone to act in accordance with it. It is a sound rule because it facilitates social contact. But the fact that introducing people to each other in those circumstances facilitates social contacts is itself a reason for doing so. Do we then have two independent reasons for introducing people? Clearly not. When considering the weight or strength of the reasons for an action, the reasons for the rule cannot be added to the rule itself as additional reasons. We must count one or the other, but not both. Authoritative directives are often rules, and even when they are not because they lack the required generality, the same reasoning applies to them. Either the directive or the reasons for holding it to be binding should be counted, but not both. To do otherwise is to be guilty of double-counting.

This fact is a reflection of the role of rules in practical concrete decisions. They provide an intermediate level of reasons to which one appeals in normal cases where a need for a decision arises. Reasons of that level can themselves be justified by reference to the deeper concerns on which they are based. The advantage of normally proceeding through the mediation of rules is enormous. It enables a person to consider and form an opinion on the general aspects of recurrent situations in advance of their occurrence. It enables a person to achieve results which can be attained only through an advance commitment to a whole series of actions, rather than by case-to-case examination.

Most importantly, the practice allows the creation of a pluralistic culture. For it enables people to unite in support of some "low or medium level" generalizations despite profound disagreements concerning their ultimate foundations which some seek in religion, others in Marxism or in Liberalism, and the like. I am not suggesting that the differences in the foundations do not lead to differences in practice. The point is that an orderly community can exist only if it shares many practices and that in all modern pluralistic societies a great measure of toleration of vastly differing outlooks is made possible by the fact that many of them enable the vast majority of the population to accept common standards of conduct.

More directly relevant to our case is the fact that through the acceptance of rules which set up authorities, people can entrust judgment to another person or institution which will then be bound, in accordance with the dependence thesis, to exercise its best judgment primarily on the basis of the dependent reasons appropriate to the case. Thus the mediation of authorities may, where justified, improve people's compliance with practical and moral principles. This often enables them better to achieve the benefits that rules may bring as explained above, and other benefits besides.

These reflections on the mediating role of authoritative directives and of rules generally explain why they are reasons for actions. Ultimately, however, directives and rules derive their force from the considerations which justify them, that is, they do not add further weight to their justifying considerations. In any case in which one penetrates beyond the directives or the rules to their underlying justifications one has to discount the independent weight of the rule or the directive as a reason for action. Whatever force they have is completely exhausted by those underlying consider-

Authority and Justification

ations. Contrariwise, whenever one takes a rule or a directive as a reason one cannot add to it as additional independent factors the reasons which justify it.

Hence the preemption thesis. Since the justification of the binding force of authoritative directives rests on dependent reasons, the reasons on which they depend are (to the extent that the directives are regarded simply as authoritative) replaced rather than added to by those directives. The service conception leads to the preemption thesis. Because authorities do not have the right to impose completely independent duties on people, because their directives should reflect dependent reasons which are binding on those people in any case, they should have the right to replace people's own judgment on the merits of the case. Their directives preempt the force of at least some of the reasons which otherwise should have guided the actions of those people.[13]

The preemption thesis will be readily accepted inasmuch as it concerns successful authoritative directives, that is, those which correctly reflect the balance of reasons on which they depend. But, a common objection goes, the thesis cannot justify preempting reasons which the authority was meant to reflect correctly and failed to do so. Successfully reflected reasons are those which show that the directive is valid. They are the justification for its binding force. Therefore, either they or the directive should be relied upon, but not both, that is not if relying on both means adding the weight of the directive to the force of the reasons justifying it when assessing the weight of the case for the directed action. Reasons that should have determined the authority's directive but failed to do so cannot be thought to belong to the justification of the directive. On the contrary they tell against it. They are reasons for holding that it is not binding. The preemption thesis is wrong in claiming that they too are preempted.

So much for the objection. It fails because its premise is false. Reasons which authoritative directives should but fail to reflect are nonetheless among the reasons which justify holding the directives binding. An authority is justified, according to the normal justification thesis, if it is more likely than its subjects to act correctly. That is how the subjects' reasons figure in the justification, both when they are correctly reflected in a particular directive and when they are not. If every time a directive is mistaken, that is, every time it fails to reflect reason correctly, it were open to challenge as mistaken, the advantage gained by accepting the authority as a more reliable and successful guide to right reason would disappear. In trying to establish whether or not the directive correctly reflects right reason the subjects will be relying on their own judgments rather than on that of the authority, which, we are assuming, is more reliable.

These reflections suggest another objection to the preemption thesis. It says[14] that in every case authoritative directives can be overridden or disregarded if they deviate much from the reasons which they are meant to reflect. It would not do, the objection continues, to say that the legitimate power of every authority is limited, and that one of the limitations is that it may not err much. For such a limitation defeats the preemption thesis since it requires every person in every instance to consider the merits of the case before he can decide to accept an authoritative instruction.

The objection does not formally challenge the preemption thesis. It does not claim that the reasons which are supposed to be displaced by authoritative instructions are not replaced by them but should count as additional independent reasons alongside the instructions. Its effect is to deny that authoritative instructions can serve the mediating role assigned them above. That role is to enable people to act on nonultimate reasons. It is to save them the need to refer to the very foundations of morality and practical reasoning generally in every case. But as the directives are binding only if they do not deviate much from right reason and as we should act on them only if they are binding, we always have to go back to fundamentals. We have to examine the reasons for and against the directive and judge whether it is justified in order to decide whether its mistake, if it is not justified, is large or small. The mediating role is unobtainable.

The failure of this objection stems from its confusion of a great mistake with a clear one. Consider a long addition of, say, some thirty numbers. One can make a very small yet clear mistake as when the sum is an integer whereas one and only one of the added numbers is a fraction. On the other hand, the sum may be off by several thousands without the mistake being detectable except by laboriously going over the addition step by step. Even if legitimate authority is limited by the condition that its directives are not binding if clearly wrong, and I wish to express no opinion on whether it is so limited, it can play its mediating role. Establishing that something is clearly wrong does not require going through the underlying reasoning. It is not the case that the legitimate power of authorities is generally limited by the condition that it is defeated by significant mistakes which are not clear.

The preemption thesis depends on a distinction between jurisdictional and other mistakes. Most, if not all, authorities have limited powers. Mistakes which they make about factors which determine the limits of their jurisdiction render their decisions void. They are not binding as authoritative directives, though the circumstances of the case may require giving them some weight if, for example, others innocently relied on them. Other mistakes do not affect the binding force of the directives. The preemption thesis claims that the factors about which the authority was wrong, and which are not jurisdictional factors, are preempted by the directive. The theses would be pointless if most mistakes were jurisdictional or if in most cases it were particularly controversial and difficult to establish which are and which are not. But if this were so, then most other accounts of authority would come to grief.

OBJECTIONS

I will conclude this article by considering a few objections to the account of authority suggested above which challenge its general orientation.

Three theses were presented as part of an explanation of the concept of authority. They are supposed to advance our understanding of the concept by showing how authoritative action plays a special role in people's practical reasoning. But the theses are also normative ones. They instruct people how to take binding directives. The service conception is a normative doctrine about the conditions under which authority is legitimate and the manner in which authorities should conduct themselves. Is that not a confusion of conceptual analysis and normative argument? The answer is that there is an interdependence between conceptual and normative argument.

The philosophical explanation of authority is not an attempt to state the meaning of a word. It is a discussion of a concept which is deeply embedded in the philosophical and political traditions of our culture. The concept serves as an integral part of a whole mesh of ideas and beliefs, leading from one part of the net to another. There is no, nor has there ever been, complete agreement on all aspects of the concept's place and its connection with other concepts. But there is, as part of our common culture, a good measure of agreement between any two people on many, though frequently not the same, points. Accounts of "authority" attempt a double task. They are part of an attempt to make explicit elements of our common traditions, a highly prized activity in a culture which values self-awareness. At the same time such accounts take a position in the traditional debate about the precise connections between that and other concepts. They are partisan accounts furthering the cause of certain strands in the common tradition, by developing and producing new or newly recast arguments in their favor. The very activity is also an expression of faith in the tradition, of a willingness to understand oneself and the world on its terms and to carry on the argument, which in the area with which we are concerned is inescapably a normative argument, within the general framework defining the tradition. Faithfulness to the shape of common concepts is itself an act of normative significance.

How can the account of authority offered here be thought to represent important strands in Western thought? As John Bell pointed out to me, if there is a common theme to liberal political theorizing on authority it is that the legitimacy of authority rests on the duty to support and uphold just institutions, as, following Rawls, the duty is now usually called. But that duty is of course dependent on a prior understanding of which institutions are just. The account here offered is meant as a beginning of an answer to that question. Or rather it contributes by setting the question in a certain way. One has a duty to uphold and support authorities if they meet the conditions of the service conception as explained above.

To the extent that legitimate authorities have power over us, the preemption thesis governs our right attitude to them. The duty to uphold and support just institutions does not come into play. It is primarily an other-regarding duty. I have a duty to support just governments in foreign countries, even though they have no legitimate power over me and I have reason to support the authority of my neighbors over their children. In other words, the duty to uphold and support just institutions comes into play when the conditions of legitimacy implied by the service conception of authority are satisfied. It then supplements the preemption thesis by showing that we should be concerned not merely to have the proper attitudes to those in authority over us, but also to those in authority over others.

Finally, let us return to our starting point. What is wrong with regarding an authoritative directive as one additional prima facie reason for the action it directs, which supplements, rather than supplants, the other reasons for and against that action? The service conception established that the point of having authorities is that they are better at complying with the dependent reasons.

Take a simplified situation. I regularly confront a decision whether or not to sell certain shares of stock in varying circumstances. Suppose that it is known that a financial expert reaches the "right" decision (whatever that may be) in twenty percent more cases than I do when I do not rely on his advice. Should I not, when confronting such decisions, carry on as before but take his advice as a factor counting in favor of the decision he recommends?

Perhaps I should always take the case for his solution as being twenty percent stronger than it would otherwise appear to me to be. Perhaps some other, more complicated formula should be worked out. In any case would not the right course require to give his advice prima facie rather than preemptive force? The answer is that it would not. In cases about which I know only that his performance is better than mine, letting his advice tilt the balance in favor of his solution will sometimes, depending on my rate of mistakes and the formula used, improve my performance. But I will continue to do less well than he does unless I let his judgment preempt mine.

This way of reasoning is unrealistically simple even in the relatively straightforward circumstances of simple stock-selling decisions. But it helps to illustrate the general lesson. If another's reasoning is usually better than mine, then comparing on each occasion our two sets of arguments may help me to detect my mistake and mend my reasoning. It may help me more indirectly by alerting me to the fact that I may be wrong, and forcing me to reason again to double-check my conclusion. But if neither is sufficient to bring my performance up to the level of the other person, then my optimific course is to give his decision preemptive force. So long as this is done where improving the outcome is more important than deciding for oneself, this surrender of judgment and acceptance of authority, far from being either irrational or an abdication of moral responsibility, is in fact the most rational course and the right way to discharge one's responsibilities.

NOTES

I am grateful to R. M. Dworkin, J. M. Finnis, K. Kress, D. Miller, and to the editors of *Philosophy and Public Affairs* for helpful comments on earlier drafts of this article.

1 R. Ladenson, "In Defense of a Hobbesian Conception of Law," *Philosophy and Public Affairs* 9, no. 2 (Winter 1980): 139.
2 Ibid., p. 137.

3 If I understood his meaning, Ladenson regards "having a justification right to do A" as meaning being justified in doing A. This is to confuse "having a right to do A" with "doing A is alright." But my argument does not depend on rejecting Ladenson's conception of rights.
4 R. E. Flathman, *The Practice of Political Authority* (Chicago: University of Chicago Press, 1980), p. 90.
5 H. L. A. Hart, *Essays on Bentham* (Oxford: Oxford University Press, 1982), p. 253. I used to hold a similar view. See my comment on Chisholm in *Practical Reasoning*, ed. S. Korner (Oxford: Basil Blackwell, 1974).
6 R. B. Friedman, "On the Concept of Authority in Political Philosophy," in *Concepts in Social and Political Philosophy*, ed. R. E. Flathman (New York: Macmillan, 1973), p. 129.
7 In the first chapter of *The Authority of Law* (Oxford: Oxford University Press, 1979), I explained some of the formal features of preemptive reasons. My analysis has been criticized by Flathman in *The Practice of Political Authority*, among others. It is not possible to reply to the criticism here.
8 This would be a very wide interpretation indeed. It would, for example, count my instruction to my son to be back by midnight as legislative, and the policeman's order to move on when a driver stops in a prohibited zone as adjudicative. But this liberality does not affect the argument.
9 The no-difference thesis is about what happens if authorities reach the right decision. Since their directives are binding even when mistaken, they do then make a difference.
10 It would be a mistake to think of them as exactly tied options. All that is assumed here is that reasons are insufficient to establish the superiority of one option over the others.
11 On the role of authorities in prisoner's-dilemma type situations, see Ullman-Margalit, *The Emergence of Norms* (Oxford: Oxford University Press, 1980).
12 For an analysis of the way prisoner's dilemma problems arise within the bounds of various moral theories, see D. Parfit, *Reasons and Persons* (Oxford: Oxford University Press, 1984), chap. 4.
13 A. M. Honoré pointed out that even if an (informal) arbitration concluded in my favor, if I later become convinced that my original claim was mistaken, I should acknowledge the claim of the other litigant rather than rely on the arbitrator's decision. Here it seems as if, contrary to the premption thesis, the original reasons are not preempted by the arbitrator's decision. Nevertheless one's duty undergoes a complete change in such circumstances. I may rely on the arbitrator. I may say that we both agreed that our relations will be governed by his decision, that I would have gone along with it had he made a mistake which harmed me. I would be rather ungenerous and unfriendly but nevertheless formally correct. The situation is the same

as in cases of agreement. I buy a chest from you and a price is agreed. It then transpires that the chest is a valuable antique and the price I paid is ludicrously low. If I ought to pay a fair price for what I buy, then I ought to come back and add to the agreed price.

14 This objection was first put to me by R. M. Dworkin who is not responsible for the way it is treated here.

6
On the Source of the Authority of the State

G. E. M. ANSCOMBE

I

My question is: how the state, or again how government, can be justified.

The question may seem a silly one because, like it or not, we are stuck with the state. But it is after all not silly, because we can take up different attitudes to being governed. As Aristotle said about philosophy: if there isn't an enquiry to make, there *is* an enquiry. The conclusion that the pretensions of civil authority lack justification tells us not to look for a foundation, the thing is merely there. But that conclusion, if it is justified, is justified only by such an enquiry. A Marxist believes in the 'withering away of the state' after the dictatorship of the proletariat has exercised the powers of government in the last phase of the class war. He, therefore, has not got to tell us the theory of the state when its institutions, laws, courts, armies, police, prisons, systems of property, etc. are something other than weapons in the class war: for it will no longer be there. That should mean, not that he thinks he can show that there isn't a question, but that he has already decided that the state with its institutions is evil. If it is, then our attitude to it may be purely pragmatic, or may be determined by a revolutionary goal. But the question itself has not been rejected: however implicitly, it has been answered.

Whether one's attitude to 'legitimate government' should be always, ever, or just sometimes that of acknowledgment of authority is a potentially serious question for everyone. I suppose that will readily be granted. But to many, especially philosophers, at the present day, it will appear as a 'moral' question. Legal authority, legal validity, legal obligation: these are one thing; their presence or absence is to be ascertained by looking at certain institutions and their rules. It is another question altogether whether one should grant moral authority, moral validity, and moral obligation.

On the Source of the Authority of the State 143

Assuming no quarrel about whether the government is what is called 'legitimate', that is essentially a personal and private question. Now I suppose I understand as well as anyone the point of someone's saying: "This is what I am legally obliged to do, but it would be e.g. an act of horrid injustice, and so I refuse to go along with my legal obligation." But I am struck by the following: one might say the exactly corresponding thing about an obligation arising under the rules of some club that one belonged to. The difference between the two is that one can resign from the club and so escape the obligation arising under its rules, but one can't very well resign from being governed. This raises the question: suppose the club (something like the Jacobin Club) grew tremendously powerful, became able to control anything it wanted to in the society, to extort money and sequester property from whom it chose; to issue and enforce edicts affecting people at large, and suppose it forbade resignation of its members; what then would be the difference between the judgement: "This is what I am obliged to do by the rules of the club ..."? and that other judgement "This is what I am legally obliged to do ..."? I am not necessarily supposing that the two are made together in the same place, though I suppose they might be. Cf. what one hears about the Mafia and the government in Southern Italy. If we want to understand civil authority, we need too distinguish there being a government exercising civil authority from two contrasting things: on the one side, from large-scale voluntary cooperative associations, and on the other from a place's being quite under the control of a smooth sophisticated Mafia. It seems clear that this is not a private or personal question, not a question to be answered by consulting one's 'moral intuitions' or debating inwardly whether one thinks oneself 'morally' obliged to obey the exercisers of power.

Starting with the former, we shall see what distinguishes civil authority from the authority to be found in voluntary associations. For here too we find authority. It comes in two kinds. When courses of action are adopted, ends and means taken towards them aren't the only things looked to or implicitly invoked in determining what is done. Someone or some group (up to the whole membership) must make decisions. "Authority" may stand for a personal characteristic: what a certain person says or presses for is felt as weighty. This is the first kind. But authority is also vested in the various rules or customs used in determining matters; there is, say, a definite procedure for deciding, and appeal is made to rule or custom in doing so. Both these sorts of authority I call "weight relative to free decisions". People are allowed to pull out.

There is then not an unconditional demand for obedience (except the demand that one either comply or get out of the committee or the association, etc.). Authority here, then, is quite different from that of the state.

Not that such a demand is the peculiar mark of a state. Obviously it is made by parents, teachers, gangsters, slave-owners, employers of indentured labour, religious superiors. A further distinguishing mark of the authority of the state is the exercise, actual or threatened, of institutional violent coercive power. I say "institutional" to exclude its being personal, casual or sporadic. Calling it institutional signifies that it is a norm of a continuing organization for there to be this threat. And, in particular, that there are some people effectually ordered by others to make the threat and sometimes to exert the violence. But again, I don't use the word "norm" as it were to canonize or sanctify, to suggest validity of some sort. For I would call it institutional violent coercive power if a town were taken over and run in a systematic fashion by a bandit gang. Here would be organization in which there were different roles, and violence or the threat of it would be a norm. It would thus be institutional. The gang, we suppose, is supreme in power. But we shouldn't have civil authority as that is generally understood.

One might say, shortly: government is distinguished from authority in voluntary cooperative enterprises by 'bearing the sword', by its exercise, actual and threatened, of coercive force. And: *if* it is distinguished from the control of a place by a gang of bandits, it is so by its authority in the command of violence. This portmanteau phrase covers (a) authority to lay commands and prohibitions on people, which are backed up by the threat of coercion, and to lay down forms for doing and determining things in such a way that decisions can be enforced and (b) authority to order some people to use force on others.

Authority on the part of those who give orders and make regulations is: a right to be obeyed. More amply, we may say: authority is a regular right to be obeyed in a domain of decision.

It might be thought that the difference we are seeking could be stated, not as one of authority, but as one of the domain of concern. But that is not so. We may suppose that our gangsters want things orderly. And beyond that very superficial indication, how can we specify a domain of concern which is special to government, and of no interest to gangsters? It is indeed one of the troubles about government, that it is difficult to specify the 'things that are Caesar's'. If a government concerns itself with no matter what, then even to comment on the subject of its concern is to enter the domain of 'politics'.

On the Source of the Authority of the State   145

The picture of the problem that I am drawing may seem to be fantastic. Here in England, for example, a minister of the Crown cannot single me out and tell me what to do and what not, just because he would like to, using the police to back him up if I am recalcitrant. I and many others feel pretty safe from 'arbitrary' demands. That is surely very different from what we imagine of gangsters running a place. They can decide 'arbitrarily' that some individual must do or suffer what suits them.

But now, just what distinction have we in mind here? That the gangster decisions relate to an individual directly, rather than because he is a member of some class? This would suggest that in Acts of Attainder the English Parliament adopted the posture of gangsters. Perhaps they did. But it would be a bold legal theorist who would say that legislation, let alone governmental decision, could never refer directly to individuals.

Or is it the lack of procedure? Well, must a government, to be a government, always be non-arbitrary in its actions? And, may not a gang of bandits be all tied up with rules of procedure? Remember my imaginary jumped-up club. Our gangsters may be a large efficient organization, so institutional in character that men outside the organization are in general ordered to do this, prohibited from doing that, made the victims of extortion (of money and other things too), threatened with violence if they disobey, merely as each one falls under some general classification, and there may be formalities. May not the agents of our gang act much like 'officials'?

"But you can't imagine gangsters being so self-restrictive! Even if the common run of people are under their heel only as each falls into some classification, even if there are rules of procedure and a smooth organization, the gangsters will be a lawless lot at the top. Succession to positions of power will often be by acts of murder, for example." But the like has also often been heard of among what are counted as governments.

"But government is for the benefit of the governed, banditry for the profit of the bandits! Of course, a regime may not succeed in benefiting its people, it may do rather a lot of harm. But the general idea of government is the idea of something good for and necessary to 'men in multitudes'. The idea of banditry is of something whose point is to rob people. A bandit who enriches himself by the opportunities of his profession is doing the work and attaining the end of a bandit: a ruler or politician who does the same does it, we must earnestly say, only *per accidens*." This Aristotelian mode of thought helps us to see the distinction. But now is it because of *that* distinction that ordinary people under government can feel safe, unimpeded and unthreatened? Surely not! Not everyone feels safe under government; some may feel safe under a robber chief.

Suppose it were suggested that we were merely conditioned not to want to go through locked doors. It is an illusion that I am unimpeded. I submit to the impediments. I let the knowledge of the restrictions and the dangers I would incur in taking certain courses modify my will to act. I have much free play, like a joint in a socket: it is seldom that some definite thing is absolutely required of me, like paying a tax bill. If I lived in a place that was rather smoothly run by the Mafia, would I not then too let the conditions modify my will to act? Then I, together with many others, might feel as safe and unimpeded and unthreatened as people do under many governments.

So does the difference lie in the good purposes of government? The comparison with bandits was suggested just by the use and threat of physical coercion which mark the state. If good purposes are the distinction, then we shall want an answer to the following question: if some people want to do good, does that give them the right to threaten me and make rules about my behaviour? Or: does it give them such a right, if there is already a long established practice of the same kind, already a body of rules made by predecessors of theirs, an established organization within which they go about their work?

If so, it will no doubt be some improvement in the situation for me if they themselves proceed by rules and go through formalities. I shall know better what to expect. An Italian painter of the Renaissance did a 'Decollation of St John' for the Great Turk. The Sultan, looking at the picture, remarked that the painter did not know the anatomy of the neck, and at a flick of his fingers the head of a bystanding slave rolled on the floor for the instruction of the painter. That shows what one means by "arbitrary"! By contrast, the proceeding would not be 'arbitrary' if there were an already existing ministerial regulation or Parliamentary enactment providing for the instruction of visiting painters, and someone had to sign a formal order. But if there have to be victims, the non-arbitrariness seems not to be much mitigation of their wrongs. Indeed, neither the non-arbitrariness nor the beneficent intention seems to serve. Lest I seem to be speaking too exotically, recall that there are current movements of thought in the direction of a requirement to make some people's organs available for transplant into others.

Our brief statement, then, is vindicated, and the question that arises is: with what right may people, in various ways exercising

On the Source of the Authority of the State   147

the power of the state, lay violence and threats of violence on anyone? For the distinction between the Mafia and a government is first and foremost that a government has authority in its doings. I do not say that the doings can be all just the same, the government having authority to do these things and the Mafia not. But *some* of the doings of government and its officers are distinguished from very similar doings of gangsters by that fact, and that is crucial.

We ask what can be the source of such a right, if it exists. And at the present level of enquiry, the answer cannot be law, because – to put it crudely – we are asking for the source of a right to lay laws on people at all.

The notion of 'a right' is one that we have some idea how to operate with, but it is unsatisfactory not to have an account of it. Indeed, a clear derivation of the right we are considering won't be possible without some account. I will give one a little later. But first, I will sketch my account of the source.

There are three sources to consider. (I will not spend time here arguing this.) They are: prescription, contract and task.

In traditional language a 'prescriptive' right is a customary right, a right established purely by custom: prescription in this connexion is another word for custom. It is clear that to the extent that we can speak of property among men in a state of nature, i.e. without legal institutions, property rights are prescriptive. *If* a slave owner could ever be said to have a right to the obedience of his slaves, this must have been basically a prescriptive right, however fortified it may have been by laws. (The 'right of conquest' was a prescriptive right.)[1] If you say to a guest in your house: "Please do not go into my study", this has the force of a prohibition even though the form of a polite request, and your authority in the matter is prescriptive.

I will not immediately debate the rationale of, or the *a priori* limits on the possibility of prescriptive authority, though I will later offer a calculation by which the authority of government cannot be merely that. Here I mention prescriptive rights only to set them on one side, wanting to say something fairly general about the ground of authority. Namely, that the ground of authority is most often a task. Authority arises from the necessity of a task whose performance requires a certain sort and extent of obedience on the part of those for whom the task is supposed to be done. If I said that this was always the sole ground of authority, I should be wrong; for there is such a thing as prescriptive authority (as the case of the guest makes clear). There is also contractually conceded authority. But this must be voluntary, and it terminates when the contract does. The interesting cases of authority are those where *the subjects of authority are so willy-nilly*. Apart from prescriptions, these are always cases were the authority, if there *is* authority stems from the task. Parental authority, for example, and – as I shall argue – governmental authority. You find yourself the subject of these whether you like it or not. Parental authority diminishes and finally lapses as the task is accomplished – or the time for doing it is over. But government is always with us. In the present state of the planet one can hardly escape beyond the frontiers of government. (It is interesting that in the last century, when it still looked as if people could do just that, a legal maxim was invoked or invented: *Nemo potest exuere patriam* – no one can shuck off his country – to deny this. The Boers, pressing into hitherto ungoverned regions, were held merely to extend the domain of the government that claimed to rule them where they were before.)

Authority stemming from a task does not indeed relate only to obedience. I mean that obedience and disobedience are not the only correlative responses to it. We see this where we speak of parental authority in relations other than the obedience of their children. A small baby does not obey, but we may acknowledge the authority of a parent in decisions about what should be done with it. So authority might be thought to be a right to decide in some domain, and its correlate not to be obedience, but respect. For you can go against someone's authority not merely by being a disobedient subject of it, but also by being an interfering outsider. Nevertheless this is secondary. We would not speak of someone's authority in every case where we admit his right to decide for example, in matters of his own dress. Here "authority" would be a redundant notion. So obedience/disobedience are the (logically) primary correlates of authority, i.e. the correlates without which there would be no such distinctive thing as authority (in our present sense); and, following upon this, there are *also* the correlative responses of respect, non-impediment, and their opposites.

Not that we can define authority by its having obedience/disobedience as its correlative responses. For gangsters can command obedience. If we are to make the distinction we want, we have to speak of a right to obedience.

Since a distinctive thing about civil government, as opposed to people's having dominant positions in common enterprises, is actual or threatened violence, it is either an evil or a necessity based on evil. If we were not dangerous to one another, if humans could be trusted not to violate one another's persons and unjustly impede one another's activities, there could be no need of government involving coercive power.

On the Source of the Authority of the State

It is possible to hold that the human world is one in which some of the bandits have got on top, so that their claim to a right in exercising power is just a huge trick. Thus Alexander the Great once caught a pirate, and asked him to explain himself. The man replied, "I do in a small way what you do in a big way." This may be called the pure pacifist position. Alexander was somewhat taken by the man and made him a provincial governor, a task which I believe he executed competently.

Or it is possible to hold that because it will be that some men do not leave others in peace, though these are peaceable, but will attack them and violently impede their activities and enterprises, it is after all a human need that there should be government and laws backed by force: people legally making decisions which can impose on all those on whom they impinge, and standing forces providing the backing.

If someone holds in a sufficiently radical fashion that government is a refined and grandiose banditry, it is hardly possible to convince him of error. It is, he says, a system whereby some people, who are able and willing to command violence, have succeeded in getting on top, and these clothe themselves in the luxurious cloak of 'authority'. He is as it were blind to everything but the evil of violence, which he is unable to concede may ever be just. This is an axiom for him.

Anyone who does think this ought to be clear about it. He ought not to be selective. If he is willing to invoke the law, to take anyone to court, or to call on the police for protection, then he should regard himself as making use of some available members of a bandit gang.

That is to say, one shouldn't deceive oneself by failing to recognize that the civil power essentially 'bears the sword': that what we have here is canonized violence.

True, the more successful and better used civil authority is, the less will this be apparent; the less actual use of violence on the part of the civil authority there will be. But the threat of it, the readiness to be violent to the point of killing where there are violent law-breakers – that is always there. No political theory can be worth a jot, that does not acknowledge the violence of the state, or face the problem of distinguishing between states and syndicates. There is a famous saying of St Augustine's: "Remota justitia, quid sunt regna nisi magna latrocinia?" This was difficult to translate, but modern institutions have given us the word: "Take away justice, and what are States but big Syndicates?" Now this might suggest that you 'only' need to add justice to force – i.e. to postulate that what is enjoined or aimed at by those exercising the force is what would otherwise be just – to render the force just. But there is the question of what renders it just to exercise force in, say, requiring what is just. The parent may in effect say "Don't hit your little brother, or I will hit you." What is the difference – *is* there a difference – between his threat and the threat of the child he so threatens? After all, the little brother may have been doing something quite unfair. The same question arises about the violence of the state. I judge that this is the fundamental question of political theory.

It may be objected to this thesis and to resultant theses *that civil power is either an evil or is based on evil*:

> You have missed the real nub of the matter. It is true that human beings are malignantly dangerous to one another. But that (for so long as it remains so) merely gives the state one of its tasks. And if it were not so, government would still be needed. It is no evil, in the sense either of malice or of defect, that individuals cannot severally and separately calculate what enterprises to give prior place, what activities to limit for the sake of other ones. Cooperative enterprises and procedures are needed for the enhancement of life – without them it would be poor and often short, even though it were not entirely solitary, nasty and brutish. But, where you have 'men in multitudes', such enterprises will sometimes collide. A machinery of decision will be needed, which is above the special enterprises, and which perhaps initiates some of them too. And besides that there are many proceedings, such as getting married, forming various sorts of association, disposing of property, for which either custom or explicit rule must provide the forms, so that people can 'know where they are'. Only in very simple societies is custom sufficient. Here again we need a machinery for fixing the forms and determining what has been in accord with them; and it needs to be connected with the machinery for decision between colliding enterprises. 'Utopianly' this machinery, acknowledged by all (for we are supposing humans without vice, hence without that of stupidity) and never working contrary to wisdom and justice, nor needing any violence to support it, would be something like a government. It would indeed *be* government in the ideal situation. It is wrong to concentrate on an unfortunate incidental task which arises from man's disordered state, and say that *that* gives us the essential mark of civil authority.

On the Source of the Authority of the State

To this I reply: No, it is not wrong. For I raised the question: What distinguishes the state from a voluntary association? and the present objection says no more than: "If there were no malignancy among humans, there would be voluntary association in having something like government – a topmost authority fixing forms and adjudicating between colliding enterprises." That is to say that, were there no human malignity, my problem of finding that distinction would not arise. At most there would be a question of distinguishing civil society from other forms of voluntary association. I said that the interesting cases of authority are those where the subjects of authority are so willy-nilly. In the 'Utopian' conception, there is no 'nilly'. My imaginary opponent spoke of the unfortunate incidental task which arose from man's disordered state. But of two things one: either my thesis has already been conceded, or the need for the machinery of decision spoken of does not yet show us anything about a government's right to coerce resistant wills.

Here is the point at which we need to enquire: What is a right? We need to do so, that is, unless we are willing without more ado to accept the following as a valid *form* of argument: Men in multitudes need governments, need laws backed by force and people exercising the powers of government. Therefore it is possible that there should be people exercising these powers as of right. But the performance of the task of government is not possible unless there is extensive civic obedience, and unless there is also force at the command of those exercising its powers, which force they have a right to command. Therefore those who by right exercise the powers of government have authority in the sense which I have argued we need.

The next section, in which I explain what a right is at all, is addressed to the further needs of philosophy, especially at the present day, and to all besides who are beset by the feeling that 'this is a moral question, and morality is purely relative and cultural, or a matter of a person's prejudices.' Anyone without these needs can skip the next section and proceed to the third one. There I argue for the premises of the above argument and maintain that the authority of the state cannot arise by a transfer of individual rights, and that there is a certain instrinsic limit to it.

II

The notion of a right is very fundamental and philosophically very intractable. It seems absurd to introduce it as an unexplained primitive. But how to explain it? No one has succeeded in this. At best, thinkers have sorted out distinctions within and around the notion, have noted some of its logical features, and so on. They have noted, for example, that a right is a right of someone against someone else. My right not to be molested cannot be infringed by a lion that mauls me or a boulder that falls on me. Only persons can infringe rights, only persons can have them. We may also note the variations in rights in respect of waivability, transferability etc. and the opposites of these. Justice as a personal virtue is that character in a man which means that he has a settled determination not to infringe anyone's right. A wrong is an infringement of a right. What is wrong about an act that is wrong may be just this, that it is *a* wrong. All this we may understand, and we may wish also to say much about actual rights, but we are still nowhere near explaining the concept of a right.

A right is not a natural phenomenon that can be discerned and named as a feature found in some class of creatures by, say, a taxonomist. It is in this respect like a rule and a promise: that 'natural unintelligibility' which Hume attributed to promises is true of all three things. A promise is naturally unintelligible because when I promise I am supposed to create a necessity, say, for me to do something. This happens (in suitable circumstances) by my telling someone that I will; or, again, by some feature of the way I speak in doing so. The explanation of the feature is precisely that it signifies imposing the necessity! But what kind of necessity is it? Some kinds of necessity we may derive from observation of nature, perhaps, but not this one. Yet it is produced. But what is produced is not an independently describable effect, as it were magically brought about by signs. It does not exist at all except for the signs. It is as if words produced it by signalling it; but what do they signal except the future action? The extra thing remains unexplained.

The parallel for rights will become clear a little later. Meanwhile, we may note that no useful definition of a right can be given. But definition is not the only mode of explanation. The thing to consider is modals.

Modals come in related pairs, the necessity modal and the possibility modal. What is common to all types is that the two modals of a given pair are mutually interdefinable. The actual use of modals is rather wider than we usually take account of in philosophy. The first extension of consideration in modern philosophy beyond logical and natural necessity and possibility was made by the investigation of so-called 'deontic logic'. In ancient times, Aristotle in his *Metaphysica*, made the pregnant remark that one sense of "necessary" is *that without which some good will not be obtained or some evil averted*

There is in fact a huge array of uses of modals, of can, can't, need, need not, has to, doesn't have to, is free to, is not free to, must, must not, ought, need not, necessary, possible, together with the modal inflections of other words. In Latin and Greek there is a necessity inflection of verbs as well as a possibility inflection; in some modern languages only the latter. When it is said categorically that something must be, or has to be, or can't but be, sometimes it is important for the correctness of this that it *is* then; sometimes that it *is* later; sometimes neither matters for the correctness of the 'must'. Examples of the first: "John must be in the kitchen", "The prime minister has to live in Downing Street." Of the second: "All we humans alive now have to die", "Surely N must win (can't lose)!" Of the third: "She must be given plenty of fluids", "You have to move your king." These types are a tiny selection.

Among the many many uses of modals we notice a range of uses which may be brought under the heading: "stopping from doing something". One might mention ones that are used to make people do things too; but in approaching the topic of rights I am interested in what I will call "stopping modals" for example, "You can't move your king." Someone may want to say that the latter means "Moving your king in this situation is against the rules." So it does. But one may equally well say: "That's against the rules" is *a* special form of "You can't do that." Think how a child learns to play chess. It grasps the idea of a rule partly from this use of "You can't." After all what it 'can't' do, in another sense it perhaps plainly *can*, if you don't physically stop it. But these utterances first accompany other methods of preventing or stopping an action, and then by themselves they function to prevent or stop it. With one set of circumstances (including consequences) this business is part of the build-up of the concept of a rule; in another, of that of a piece of etiquette; in another, of that of a promise, in another of an act of sacrilege, etc. It is characteristic of human intelligence to be able to learn the response to a stopping modal without which it could not exist as a linguistic form.

Naturally stopping cannots are compatible with – i.e. are to be found unfaulted with – the actual occurrence of what 'cannot' be. Except in the following type of case: where what 'cannot' be is, say, some move in a game, then what is actually done if the person isn't stopped by "You can't . . ." is not *called* a move in the game.

Now in the practice of human language and life stopping modals are often used with special mention of persons. "You can't do that, it might hurt Mary", "You can't sit there, it's John's place"; "You can't eat that, it's for N"; "You can't do that, its for N to do"; "You can't go there, its N's field"; "You mustn't do that, it will help/damage N"; "You mustn't do that, N wouldn't like it"; and many others like them. They are extremely various. "You can't eat that, it's for N" stops you, perhaps, with the determination of the speaker that N is going to have it. "It's for N to do" might be connected with tones of contempt for a despised task, and remarks assigning N to a degraded class, or again with respect for N's competence – he knows how, and will do it properly.

But this expression "Its for N to do" might be connected with something different. Take this case: N does not 'have to' do it. No one uses such a formula or even tries to get him to do it. But he is among those who 'can': that is, there are no 'stopping cannots' for him here either way. But if *you* set out to do it, the utterance. "You can't, it's for N to do" is followed up with, say, affronted behaviour on N's part, or on his behalf; or fear of the same if you *do* do it. And you may 'have to' make it up to N for having done what was his, not yours, to do. The connexion with him is given, not only as a reason for the 'stopping cannot' about your doing it, but also and especially about stopping him from doing it. And it is something that one might very much want to do, either naturally or because it is invested with desirability and dignity by these practices.

Now we can see the similarity to Hume's problem about promises. For what *is* the connexion, which is given as a reason? It cannot be explained. This fact is obscured if, as often, there are also substantive connexions – such-and-such an object was produced by N, or is used by N, these are N's children, and so on. But they are not *this* connexion, and *it is itself nothing, except that it is linguistically MADE*.

Here is (at least in embryo) the idea of 'a right'. The reasons why it is at once so clear and so inexplicable are these: it is clear because we have learned to respond to these stopping cannots, to comply with them, to issue them ourselves, to infringe them. It is inexplicable because, look as we may, we cannot find an *interpretation* of this 'cannot', just as we couldn't find any interpretation of the peculiar 'necessity' (called "obligation") generated by promising. The truth is: there is no interpretation to give, in any of these cases. If we used the language with conviction we 'believed in' the cannots: but what were we believing? We say we are

On the Source of the Authority of the State 155

believing in rights – but what sort of thing was that? In the case of games the situation was easier to comprehend: except among the very young, passionate conviction doesn't come into "You can't move the king." Or, if it does, it is conviction about what the rules are. Not about a, so to speak, metaphysical existence of a rule. Questions are usually easily settled by looking in a book. We know it's a matter of convention.

It may seem surprising that I so describe rights: I may seem rather to be describing privileges. But it isn't so. Suppose that, as we say, every man has 'a right' of quiet possession (i.e. occupation) of his home, and suppose the happy situation that everyone *has* a home. Then those stopping cannots will apply to anyone else's use of N's home as N uses it. N alone is free from restriction by those stopping cannots addressed to others in respect of doing there what he 'can' do there. The stopping cannots addressed to everyone else surround and protect his 'can'. Again, my right not to be molested is not a privilege. What does it amount to? It's 'mine' to be where I happen to be in that you 'cannot' simply thrust me out of my path. This is my voting paper – you 'cannot' snatch and mark it. And so on.

The passionate conviction about these cans and cannots – is it based on illusion? Well, what really is the illusion? Let us remember that in many cases a question about just such modal statements is to be settled comparably to the way of settling a question about a rule in chess. For it may be a matter of law. However complex, tortuous and expensive the enquiry, from our present point of view that doesn't make it essentially different. Nor does the fact that opinions may be ambiguous in the end. Again, it may be a matter of prescription: what is the custom among our tribe? Must the juniors stand back and let the seniors go in first? That, let us say, *is* the custom. We may or may not want to erode it. We may want to extinguish a former right on the part of those people, to create a new right for these, by a new practice. And here someone may manifest superstition by insisting that the eroded right is really, so to speak, an invulnerable truth.

But we have not yet asked the serious question, I mean the *grave* question. Here, according to our account, is a concept created by certain linguistic practices. I don't mean by the practice merely of uttering words in a particular arrangement or of doing so in a particular context, but by *actions* (of stopping from doing something) into which words were inserted in such a way that the use of the words themselves became such an action. And not only is the concept created by these practices, these actions with language;

it is necessarily created for any particular set of people by a particular set of such practices. Those whose practices they are make or maintain just those rights as the customary rights in their society, only by their having just these practices. Where then are we ever going to be able to argue that what is counted as a right is no right, and something not counted as a right is after all a right? It seems that the question of the *rights of man* falls to the ground! Truth about rights seems to fall into two kinds: what we may call theoretical, scientific truth on the one hand, which will be sociological or anthropological, and on the other statements *within* the practice and the law of a certain society, statements in which we are going along with the language and continuing the practices which create the concept of a right and the particular rights together. A new statement of a right hitherto not acknowledged in the practice of the society can only be a proposal, and the idea of its really being a proposal which accords with an 'abstract truth' about rights must be the merest superstition.

Yet I said in speaking of authority in connexion, say, with government we must speak of a right. How do I stand in so speaking? Am I noticing a practice, or proposing one? If the first, the whole old style search for a justification has got lost; if the second, who am I to make proposals? Am I not merely manifesting my own feelings, perhaps my 'moral' feelings, while falsely pretending to be maintaining a truth, every time I say any such thing as: "Whatever the custom, such-and-such could not be by right" or "Government is distinguished from control by bandits, because government has a right"?

I have often experienced a painful feeling of weakness is offering detailed arguments that such-and-such could not but be unjust, such-and-such could not but be an infringement of rights, this other thing could not but be, say, an act of murder, such-and-such in turn could not be an exercise of authority. They have fallen dead to the ground.

Having reached the beginnings of an account of a right, I see what suggests the impossibility of justifying such statements. Nevertheless, the suggestion is false.

I have located the generation of the concept of a right in a certain kind of use of stopping modal with what appears to be a reason attached; the reason says that something is N's, or is 'of N', or 'for N'. Note that "being N's" does not signify property, which is merely one case among a host of others. We have here a very special use of the name of a person, or a very special way of relating something to a person, which explains (not is explained

On the Source of the Authority of the State

by) the general term "right". Something is N's to do, N's to receive (for example, a message) N's to kill — as an ancient Roman would say about N's children: the *patria potestas*. The general term "right" is constructed because, as it were, our language feels the need for it. As, for example, a general term "relation" was invented.

At the level of generation of the concept of a right, all rights are necessarily prescriptive and in this sense rights are wholly based upon custom. The existence of such a thing as rights consists in the regular existence of certain proceedings, certain reactions, an integral part of which is the use of certain linguistic forms.

The form of statement 'It's N's' has a peculiar role. It appears to be the form of a reason. Certainly a statement of this form is 'a reason' in the sense of a *logos*, a thought of some kind. But if we ask what the thought is, and for what it is a reason, in: "You can't ..., it's N's", we find that we cannot explain these independently. We can't explain the "You can't ..." on its own; in any independent sense it is simply not true that he can't. But neither does "it's N's" have its peculiar sense independent of its relation to this "You can't". That doesn't mean that, once there are these linguistic practices, we can't detach "It's N's" and put it in another context, where it appears distinctly as a reason: "I didn't ... because it's N's." Let me restrict the word "reason" in this subject matter to something independent which someone actually uses as his reason for an act or abstention. So "I didn't ... because it's N's to ..." contains a statement of a reason; the sense that the statement makes is independent of its being a reason. But in You can't ... it's N's to ..." I shall call the particular content of "It's N's to ..." the *special logos* of the "You can't ...". My reason for introducing this peculiar terminology is this: I call the second half of the utterance the *logos* of the first because, as I have explained, they are not independent of one another, and I call the particular content the *special logos* because we have a general *logos*-type, with many kinds — diverse particular contents (as: "It's N's to kill or bring up his own child"; "It's N's chair to sit in"). The general type of *logos* gives the formal character of the "You can't ...", and a general type is always exemplified in a special *logos* of that type. The general type here is the type: a right. But remember that that is not an explanation of the type, it is rather a label for it. Another general type of *logos* is: a rule of a game, which gives the formal character to the "You can't ..." of "You can't move the king." In "You can't move the king, he'd be in check", "he'd be in check" gives the *special logos* of the "You can't".

Now since a *logos*, thus explained, is a thought, it can be argued about, discussed, reason can be sought for it, reason can be offered against it. Let us take an example:

(a) You can't destroy that, it's a message for N, and he hasn't seen it yet (won't get it if you destroy it).

which is closely connected with:

(b) You can't destroy that, it's for N to get a message which has been sent to him.

In (a) of course, the "You can't" is not necessarily fixed as having the formal character of the stopping modal associated with infringement of rights. It might be the quite different stopping modal exemplified in "You can't move that, the shelf will fall down." In (b) it *is* fixed as the kind of stopping modal we are concerned with — and that *might* be the intent of (a). But on the face of it the difference between (a) and (b) exemplifies the difference between 'fact' and 'right' (as in '*de facto*' and '*de iure*').

Someone to whom (b) is addressed may of course just go ahead and destroy the message; he has, we may suppose, a contempt for the consideration. That is not to argue with it, but merely not to let it weigh with him. But, as I said it can be argued with. One argument might be that was stated in (a) was not true. That would not interest us much. Nor would an argument (say "Why should I care? I . . .") for disregarding the consideration in (b). What interests us is an argument against the consideration in (b). The mere facts that (as we will suppose) a use of some such particular stopping modal (about messages) is standard practice in the society, and that if there were no such thing as practices of this general character there would be no such thing as rights among humans at all — these facts do not show that someone cannot argue with the *logos* in (b). What form, then, might our man's argument take? Perhaps "No, it isn't: N is a prisoner", or "a lunatic" or "a child", "a woman" or "my wife" or "my enemy" or "N intends harm and will be helped by this." Or the same things about the sender of the message. If he reasons like this, he seems to be making an exception to some general rule of right. He may however merely be *pointing out* that N, or the particular message, does not fall under the actually current rule of right.

Certainly general rules of right seem to be implicit in this linguistic practice with stopping modals. It is so simply because there has to be a practice. Of course some general rule of right may relate to only one person as the bearer of the right, in

On the Source of the Authority of the State

connexion with whom the same matter often crops up. But it is natural that there should often be general terms in the *logos* which are used similarly in reference to other people besides N.

Our man may be proposing to create new exceptions or to modify the current general rule of right, and in support of this he may produce various arguments. These might be about the ill consequences of including such-and-such types of people in the general rule, or about the inner meaning of the rule (like the 'intent' of a statute) understanding of which will make us 'see' that these people don't fall under it. Or he may attack the whole rule root and branch as doing nothing but harm or as 'senseless'. "Why should mere ... mean that one can ...; that equally or more valuable people should have to yield place in ...?" Thus the qualification referred to in the *logos* may be rhetorically belittled; the disadvantages to those not so qualified rhetorically enlarged upon. Qualifications may obviously be of the most diverse kinds, as: that a man has made a certain journey; has received a special designation; has a particular origin; has had certain marks made on his body; or was born with them; is a sick person; is insane; is a child; is old; is married; is not married; is not a foreigner. It is evident that argument against a general rule of right which belongs to one's tribe's customs can so far hardly take the form of a *proof* of no-right, unless conceding a right to one involves infringing the right of another, and the latter is already of greater weight. That is to say, with the means so far considered, we cannot envisage any other style of proof that a prescriptive right is no right.

There is however one path here. If someone has a role or function which he 'must' perform, or anything that he 'has' to do, then you 'cannot' impede him. Where necessity does not imply actuality, then "necessity implies possibility" may acquire a rather rich significance. This has been noticed before, witness the discussions of "ought implies can". The interesting thing is the switch, as in that case *from one type of modal* for 'necessity' *to a different type* for 'possibility'. "Ought implies can" is true, if true, however, only in as much as physical impossibility lets one off the hook of blame for something.[2] The crossing of modals that we are considering is more interesting. For any modal, of course "necessarily" is equivalent to "not possibly not" within the same type of modality: hence we may have an interpretation of "must" as "having no right not to". But that case is not one to interest us, it gets us no forrader. One interesting case is, for example, the "must" that is said by someone who threatens someone else with penalties if something is not done. Now if he also does not allow something without which, it is well understood, what he demands cannot be done, his demands are against reason. That does not mean that they cannot in fact be made; his aim after all may be to push into an 'impossible position', to punish or humiliate. The unreason is not a proof of mistake or stupidity; it may be quite cynical. But it remains unreason.

If any conjunction of modals of different type can be shown to be against reason in this fashion, then we have the materials for a disproof of it, and so we may be able to disprove one of the conjuncts. And this gives us a way of arguing for a right without appeal to custom, law or contract; and similarly of arguing that some customary right is no right but is, rather, a customary wrong. If something is necessary, if it is for example a necessary task in human life, then a right arises in those whose task it is, to have what belongs to the performance of the task. "A right" is of course to be explained as I have explained right, by reference to a certain sort of stopping modal, a set of "you cannots" which surrounds, fixes and protects a 'can' on the part of the one who is thereby said to have a right. The interesting point is precisely that the notion of necessity involved is not the correlate of the 'can' which expresses a right; it is not the equivalent of "no right not to". On the contrary, the necessity takes us out of the circle it is so easy to get into. The necessity, for example, may be human need. As: those who have and carry out the task of bringing up children quite generally perform a necessary task. It cannot be done without children's obedience. So those people have a right to such obedience. My contention is that this is a correct argument, but that it can't be analytically understood without the considerations about modals that I have just put forward. Of course it can be very readily understood at an ordinary common-sense level, but that isn't good enough for us philosophers. This is not mere conceit on our part: the requisite forms of speech would not exist without the practice I have described, and anyone will be at a loss if asked to explain. He has to explain *that* modals are involved, and *how* there is such a use of them. Justification by necessity (of a goal, and of the means to it) is one of the most common – and most commonly abused – forms of justification offered. One might ask: what has 'necessity' got to do with justification? The 'necessity' of the goal is very likely the suspicious term of the argument. But in *form* it is sound enough, if I am right about the relation between 'a right' and certain modals.

One thing remains to be said about the notion of a 'task', because it may be a partly modal notion itself. A task, as it is sometimes spoken of, is work which it is in some sense necessary should be done. It may for example be necessary in the sense of being imposed. Or it may be necessary because of a general or particular human need that it should be done. Such a task may not be anyone's task. Someone's task is work which it is necessary that *he* should do or work which it is necessary that someone should do and which it is his right to do. Someone might perform a task which was not his task, which he had even no right to do. Therefore the mere fact that someone is performing a task does not suffice to prove that he has a right to what is needed for the performance of the task. It must either be necessary that he should perform the task or be his right to do it, before he can derive a right to certain things from the fact that they are necessary for the performance of the task. This is needed if we are to use our explanation of a right and yet to derive a right from the necessity of a task. For we shall not have the "You cannot ... it's N's to ..." simply from the fact that what N is doing is necessary for someone to do. Unless, indeed, by prescription they say that in N's society; that is, it might be customary to have this sort of stopping modal about impeding anyone who was performing a necessary task, and about trying to take the task from him. Otherwise, before we can argue from performance to right we shall need an argument for particular types of task, that whoever does perform these acquires a right to perform them, or produces a necessity that he should perform them. These considerations have an obvious bearing on situations where some people are performing the functions of government, but without right. That is, they do have such a bearing if there is such a right on the part of governments as we want to find. To that question we must now address ourselves.

III

Frame the Utopian picture if you will. But now add that some people will use violence against others, and will violently resist the decisions and rules. What follows about how this should be reacted to?

Anyone, it may be said, may justly intervene with violence to resist violence committed without right. That is; it can be no infringement of the right of one so resisted. Were it counted one, that would be conceding a right in his violence. Except on the assumption that any violence against anyone is *eo ipso* an infringement of a right of his.

So, it may be said, anyone may protect the top-decision-making authority, and it may protect itself with a regular force. Such a force may also ward off attack on other people and activities.

Even in respect of protection against violence, the state goes far beyond this. We have pictured something like a business employing guards for its own direct protection, and extending their services to the direct protection of others. But the civil authority investigates past actions; tries and punishes people, and forces rules on them.

This would be an insolent claim on the part of any 'private' corporation. When these things are done with the authority of government, it seems we have a transition to a new kind of thing.

In fact we went absurdly far with the right to protect oneself and others against violence, though even so it got us nowhere near civil authority. The regular force for protecting the offices, etc., of the authority – how are we to picture it intervening *ad hoc* to protect the unjustly attacked? On whose side do they intervene? The role of the civil power in using a standing force cannot be assimilated to that of a passer-by who sees someone set on by a thug.

This is one of the fundamental questions of political theory: are we to understand civil *authority* as arising by a transfer of rights already possessed by men without a state? Those who maintain this always assume a private right of punishment in a state of nature. We deny this and take the alternative view: civil society is the bearer of rights of coercion not possibly existent among men without government.

A standing force that systematically has the protective task must be an intervening force to stop or prevent violence, and bring the parties to a place of judgement, not itself the on-the-spot judge of issues. Judgement is needed; this requires procedures for determining which disputants shall succeed. The question 'with what right?' asked about the action of the intervening force could have the answer that it was a customary right: this office exists and is generally acknowledged in the society. *Now* our picture is that of violence being checked and quarrels turned into 'civil dispute'. We haven't envisaged any way of enforcing decisions. The method might work – because people commonly accepted the decision – in a rather special community. But in a large natural society it could hardly be enough.

Thus we approach the necessity of laws in connexion with the protective role of a standing force. The force is no longer neutral. There is trial and punishment. 'Law' here need not be statutory but must be positive: it is in this context the at least customary

On the Source of the Authority of the State

and also manifest prohibition of various wrongs – and so far we are considering only wrongs of violence. There needs to be place for complaint of one man against another in respect of prohibited wrongs.

The justification falls into two parts. First, are those who are punished wronged by it? To this the answer is: evidently not, in the sense of getting what they don't deserve, in respect of their primary affliction. That is if the victims are the intended ones. If the conceptions of guilt and responsibility that operate are correct ones, they are not wronged in what I'll call the primary way, namely by getting punished without desert. But there is a second question, which concerns the right to give deserved affliction. One may be wronged in a secondary way by getting one's deserts at the hands of someone who had no right so to inflict them.

This part of the justification of the institution of law, trial and punishment resides only in its necessity for the protection of people. It cannot reside in mere custom. Here I will offer the promised calculation, whereby the right of government itself cannot be merely a customary right. Wherever we have what purports to be a customary right, let us form the hypothesis that those who are directly disadvantaged or damaged by its exercise are thereby wronged. If, if the damage is a wrong it is a great wrong, then the purported customary right itself can be no right but is rather a customary wrong. Now someone who is punished for wrongs that he commits by one who has no right to punish him gets at least as great a wrong as the damage counts as, that he suffers.

Test this on wrongs which no one does have a customary or legal or contractual right to punish, and where a right to punish cannot be derived from need: assume that the damage inflicted is of a kind that does count as a wrong if inflicted without right.

The justification of the institution of trial and punishment thus has to be based on need, not on prescription. With this is settled the wearisome dispute about the different theories of punishment by public authority: retributive, deterrent and reformatory. A retributive theory of punishment is merely a punishment theory of punishment; therefore correct, in that it declares that nothing can be properly called punishment if it is not offered as affliction deserved by ill-doing; but incorrect, in that it says that punishment of wrong-doing is *eo ipso* justified and needs no further reason. The deterrent theory is often discussed – and berated – in quasi-forgetfulness that it is a theory of the justification of *punishment* by civil authority. To be that, it must be a theory of putting affliction on people for something they have done, and therefore, if it is to be just at all the 'something' must be a known offence and the punishment deserved. Granted that, the deterrent theory is the correct one. For even if (which one may doubt) there is something intrinsically good about an evildoer's suffering, what is one man or some set of men that they should bring this about? Are they so good themselves? and are they in charge of the order of things, to see to it that such a good is brought about? It is obvious nonsense. The justification of the institutions of law, charge, trial and sentence can only be the protection of people. This cannot be supposed to be its effect but by potential wrongdoers being restrained by the terror of the law. For this, we need the assumption that without the law there would be a lot more of that wrongdoing than there is with it. The reformatory theory assimilates the state to a parent. In itself this is a monstrous impertinence. For it means that purely in virtue of the position of holding civil power, some men may claim to dispose of others in this way against their wills for their own good. Upholders of the 'reformatory' idea, or the idea of 'rehabilitation' are probably confused about this, not noticing the actual character of the claim; but they may be motivated by a certain sweetness. The good in their idea is the good of the injunction: "Do not forget, even in punishing him, that the convict is your brother, now in your power: do not become callous about *his* good." They take it for granted that they — or 'we' — have a right to decide 'what to do with criminals'. The question is, how such a right can exist? By my calculation, it cannot be just a customary right.

A parallel argument for the right of punishment could not supply the defects in, for example, Locke's argument[3] and so show that men in a state of nature may — nay it is needful that they should — severally punish those who unjustly attack them and their neighbours. For action on such a principle will perforce be action against those whom a man believes so to deserve punishment. His formation of opinion then takes the place of trial in our account. In consequence of such formation of opinion he is going to do some attacking himself. But on the same principle those who think otherwise than he will then equally attack him. And so instead of procuring a peaceful normality, such a principle would promote a general warfare within which even the quietest (namely, those who failed in that duty of punishing unjust attackers) could hardly hope to go safely. Hence I denied that right of punishment.

Nor is the ground of necessity an unsafe one in that there are no limits to what can be 'justified' by necessity, if anything can. For the necessity of the arrangement was not the whole justification. It

On the Source of the Authority of the State   165

was assumed that the wronger of others suffered a *condign* punishment. In the primary way, then, he is not wronged but, if he is wronged he is wronged in the secondary way because the inflicter of desert had no right to inflict it. It is only at this point that necessity is invoked as a justification. Nor is necessity the justification in the particular case. *There* the justification is the particular law, the citation of which in justification is an aspect of the institution of law with its enforcement. So the institution is what is justified – and only at this point of the argument – by necessity.

The institution creates the character of an act as one of *doing justice on* the wronger of others, which character was not guaranteed by an act's being an act of afflicting the wrongdoer not contrary to desert.

In this way we have the genesis of a quite new kind of right, something new has emerged. If we have this institution, we have civil society with civil government and its authority, and if not, not.

To take stock, and see gaps, consider the following objections. First, we have concentrated too much on protection against violence. There is as much need of protection against fraud. Second, we are being unhistorical, and influenced by the characteristic claim of a modern state to a monopoly of violence.

Taking the second first: it is true that there may be a state with laws, none of which generally prohibit violence. Unrestricted violence is not tolerated in any society, but violence may be left to be partly restricted by social disapproval and by strong men; for the rest, it may be regarded as a sort of brawling which no one interferes with. The laws all concern, say, status and its obligations and rights, property, marriage, jurisdiction, contracts. You strike your neighbour and damage him: that's between him and you (or your families). If you move his landmark, fail in some due, usurp his function, he can complain of you before judges. Corporations also have many rights, and they will take you to court if they can claim you have infringed them. All this may strike us as strange, but it is possible: the people of such a society might regard us as obsessed with protection against violence: this is either unmanly concern or the matter is just the concern of heads of great households. Of course killing one man may be regarded as damage to another, and a claim for damages may lie, as among the Anglo-Saxons. But there is not a direct law against murder, mayhem and blows. Strong men are able to help themselves and their dependants! The protection of the law is needed for quite other purposes.

It is quite true: we cannot say that there is no state (no government), where there is not legal protection against personal violence. But I have not said this. We *can* say that one of the principal things that people in general need governments (governmental violence) for *is* protection against violence. If many must rely for this on 'strong men' whose clients or serfs they thus become, they are at the mercy of the strong men themselves. The need of systematic protection, I argued, involves a need for laws trials and punishment in the matter; a need, in short, for an administration of justice. And I further said that having 'this institution, i.e. an administration of justice, was involved in there being civil government and civil authority. But this does not imply that there is civil government and civil authority only where there are laws against murder and assault.

The other objection related to people's having as great a need to be protected against fraud as against violence. The claim is specious, I suspect, because "fraud" sounds like a clear-cut notion covering a large number of actions that one may need protection from. And this in turn is because "fraud" is a legal term of enormously wide application. Legally understood, it seems to be applied to pretty well any criminally or civilly wrongful act by which one person is prejudiced through the deception of another. But it is not applicable *unless* the act is legally wrongful. I might lyingly tell someone that Roman remains have been found in my neighbour's garden, and that I am not interested, but that if he cares to dig up my garden, he can have any that he finds. My garden is a mere section of field and I am much pleased when it gets thoroughly dug over. Would that be fraud? Not legally. Now, if one isn't relying on legal notions of fraud, how can one specify the need for protection against fraud? Is there a general need of protection against ruses? The idea is absurd.

What has to be said is: people need protection against some infringements of rights by deception. And: they need protection against being deceived in going through various transactions, usually though not always already legally characterized (conveyancing, for example). The protection here takes the form of allowing the invalidation of such transactions on grounds of fraud. But the relevance of the authority to use coercive force which is characteristic of the state lies far in the background in these cases, at least where there is no question of criminal prosecution. In a society with a legal system people want and need certain things for which there are legal forms, and in some cases the very things that they want are legal facts, such as entitlements, letters of administration, powers of attorney, discharges of various kinds. The protection from fraud that is in question is then not a protection by the force in the hand of the rulers, it is a protection by legal provision and practice from being entrapped through fraud in undesired legal states of affairs. These no doubt usually have solid material consequences. But the whole possibility of the fraud from which protection is needed in such cases is not one which could arise and threaten you in a state of nature. There is thus something confusing and misleading about putting force and fraud together as two equal things, the need of protection from which gives a foundation for civil authority. The scope for fraud, of kinds that laws directly protect one from, is relatively limited in a state of nature.

What should be said, rather, is that in any human society of many families, there will be institutional practices, conventions and customary rights. Of these latter, some may be quite simple to give an account of, as: a right to fish a certain stretch of river. Whereas others are connected with very complex practices, as: a right, perhaps unique to an individual, to wear something or to make a quite particular mark somewhere. The exercise of such rights may have considerable practical consequences, and their existence be important instruments in living. (Think for example of signing one's name.)

Now when this is so, and when there are great numbers of people, mostly not knowing one another but in fair proximity, customary rights will be protected by a system in which power (involving a threat of coercive force) is exercised over people; complaint of infringements may be made, issues decided by customary methods and according to customary principles, disputing parties have a solution laid down for them, accused people found guilty or not guilty, and the convicted punished. I say it will be so because it will be so if the people are to continue in the exercise of customary rights. Extinction of these by disorder, the 'war of everyone against everyone' or again by enslavement by conquerors, is of course also possible.

It is possible in a relatively small population that power and these judgements should be exercised by a general assembly operating by majority vote. That makes no difference to the point that concerns us. If such exercise of power and judgement is a regular institution of the society, then it has the essential mark of a civil society with laws. There we have civil authority. In the case just imagined the majority (severally) obey the majority (collectively). Since the orders and decisions may concern now one man now another, the majority may obey not only severally but for the most part piecemeal, in respect of different matters and at different times and in different places. As we have imagined the case, they obey under the implicit institutional threat of coercion, perhaps from a section of the population (whose office it is). This section acts against the few who choose not to obey. They have, it may be presumed, commanding officers, and there is some method by which they are formally cognisant of the decision of the assembly which they have to enforce.

It is of course true that the whole business rests on consent. But not much more so than any civil government does. Government always rests on consent in the sense that it could not exist without at least the passive consent of a large majority. Or (in very rare cases) the extremely active and lively consent of a large minority who keep the others down. I am thinking here of the Spartans and the Helots; each Spartan lad did active service in the field, living incognito among the Helots and murdering any who looked as if they might get uppity. *That* I do not call passive consent of the majority! In the case that I have imagined, if the whole or nearly the whole adult population go to the assembly, the consent of the majority (severally) to the decisions is perhaps not so passive as if they were not members of the assembly. What there is active consent to, and that simply by participation, is the procedure for deciding and judging. But we must not forget that "the" majority is not a particular set of people consenting severally to what they have all voted for. It is possible that, although every decision has been made by majority vote, the majority votes in the minority in a majority of cases. Let there be an assembly of ten voting (all of them) on a set of decisions, each of which especially affects one of them:

Decision on	A	B	C	D	E	F	G	H	I	J
A	0	0	0	1	1	0	1	1	1	1
B	0	0	0	1	1	1	1	1	1	0
C	0	1	0	1	1	1	1	1	0	0
D	1	1	1	0	1	0	1	1	0	0
E	0	0	0	1	0	1	1	1	1	1
F	0	0	0	1	1	0	1	1	1	1
G	1	1	1	1	1	0	0	1	0	0
H	1	0	1	1	1	0	1	0	0	1
I	1	1	0	1	1	0	1	1	0	0
J	0	0	1	1	1	1	1	1	0	0

Here A, B, C, F, I and J all vote in the majority only four times out of the ten. Everyone votes in the minority on the matter that

On the Source of the Authority of the State 169

especially affects himself. It doesn't seem reasonable to say that 'the majority', in going along with the decisions of 'the majority', is merely going along with itself. Although A, B, C, F, I and J have been active in voting one may still reasonably call their acceptance passive consent. The illusion of not being subject to an authority exercising power over one might prevail where one had voted with the majority, but it would be none the less an illusion.

Thus an assembly can be sovereign over all the members of a population, who are its subjects, even when it is constituted by all of them together. It can of course make law for its own action and methods of procedure, as well as for every member of itself. In the former case it is inappropriate to speak of 'it' as obeying itself; for in that case the law is made for its collective proceedings, and 'it' rather adheres to its law, which 'it' can change, than obeys it. But in respect of the individuals who are severally subject to the laws, decisions and verdicts, as also to the laws made for the actions and procedures of the assembly itself, the concept of obedience to commands promulgated by authority is perfectly applicable. Hart, who attacks the notions of 'sovereign' and 'subject' where we have a democracy,[4] has many reasonable things to say about rules. But he seems to think that his account of rules and of proceeding according to them is in competition with the conception of sovereign and subject. But how could it be? In a small and intimate group, there might be an autocratic father or leader giving direct orders *ad hoc* to everyone, and in consequence no institutional rules may be needed except those of language itself. But in a larger society, even with a single autocratic dictator there must be such rules as Hart discusses.

What counts as an order or permission from the dictator? Who are his agents and officers? What are the credentials by which they may be known?, etc.

This consideration of how the concepts of sovereign and subject still stand in the purest imaginable sort of democracy was something of a digression. I will take up the thread of my argument. There is no civil government except where there are laws, however these arise or are made. Laws entail an 'administration of justice' under which (a) there can be accusations of infringement of the laws themselves, or (b) there can be complaints (in respect of wrongs) and claims (in respect of rights). In either case the justification is the need for protection of the sort afforded by laws and the power of enforcing them.

The idea of civic authority, so far as it threatens coercion against *any* defiance of laws (no matter what they may be) seems to pull itself up by its bootstraps. The threatened violence cannot be just except against the man who is acting unjustly; he is acting unjustly if he is defying the law, but the sanction of force behind the laws is just only against the unjust. Which comes first, the injustice of the man the civic authority threatens, or the law? If the injustice of the man, how can he be threatened merely because he defies a law? If he is unjust *because* he defies the law, what gave the law this position, of something that could be sustained with the threat of force?

The answer to this is that we have to take two bites at the cherry. First, there is both a very general need of protection of life and limb against violence, *and* a need of protection of some customary rights. We have seen that there may be, indeed have been, legal systems that met the second need and not the first. We can then ask whether any of those over whom the civil power claims authority are without substantial rights which it protects? If so, then its claim to authority over them has no foundation at all. They are not among those whose needs are met.

Some much for our first bite. At this stage the answer to the question "Which comes first?" is "the injustice of the man the law threatens."[5] We will call the laws in question the 'primary' laws.

Now for the second bite. We saw and granted the need of a top decision-making machinery in a large complex society. Our *problem* concerned the right to coerce people who refused to accept the decisions. *The right could not derive directly from the need of this machinery for the general good.* For if for the sake of the general good it is proposed to damage my interests and erode or extinguish some of my customary rights, and I shall be subjected to force if I don't go along with this, the question arises: why should I respect the decision? It becomes a mere conflict of interests, with the more powerful clobbering the weaker, unless we can show an authority to impose the decisions on me. There has to have arisen a customary right to obedience, which customary right can then be protected by law. In our original construction we identified the top decision-makers with the people commanding protection of the whole top-decision-making machinery, who extended this protection to everyone's life and limb considered severally. This identified them with those responsible for the administration of justice, which was especially connected with the protection of people against violence. We have seen that the administration of justice *may* not be concerned with that. But the relevant identification will occur anyway. Those by whose authority the primary laws are enacted (a) acquire a customary right to obedience and (b) exercise, and therefore have,

On the Source of the Authority of the State

a good deal of power. It is thus very natural that they should extend their activities, perform the work of arbitration, make many decisions affecting now this now that section of the population, and promote as well as lending countenance to many large enterprises. If they *obtain* obedience in doing these things, such obedience is likely to become to some extent and in some contexts a customary right. That it does so is of course a result of the response of the people who accept the decisions. Then, either through more legal practice or through enactment, the right gets protected by laws. The right explicitly to make laws becomes a customary right — through being exercised without too much check or set-back. And here the answer to the question: which comes first, the injustice of the action of the man whom the law threatens, or the law? is: the law. The law creates the injustice of the man who breaks it.

We have to ask: how does the supposed customary right to obedience fare under the critical calculation which I offered? The answer is naturally not a simple failure or a simple success for custom. It evidently depends on what people are required to be obedient to. Thus though the law creates offences, authority to do so is not limitless. We have noted in passing that decisions may *destroy* customary rights. This fact produces a familiar sort of tension between the different functions of government (of the whole apparatus). It may be asked how, on my construction, law can ever extinguish a customary right without thereby committing a wrong. I suppose the answer is that a need can extinguish a right (see Section II for the logic of this) and that those who have the authority to make certain decisions about what is needed thereby acquire a right to extinguish such rights as are extinguishable by needs. This is the source of as many dangers as arguments from necessity are subject to abuses.

Our original question: what distinguishes the authority of government from control by bandits? has received an at least preliminary answer. The distinction lies in the association of government with a system of administration of justice. This, incidentally, shows how the original condition of being run by bandits could actually develop into a situation of having a government.

But there is a change in the reverse direction, which must give us pause. If bandits acquire control, they may after all keep the forms and machinery of the administration of justice in being, and utilize them (Huey Long). And what at one stage is a government, enjoying civic authority, may degenerate into a sort of banditry, equally keeping and utilizing those forms and that machinery. Again, foreign invaders usurping the powers of government will perhaps maintain and utilize those forms and cannot be said thereby straightaway to acquire the authority of legitimate government. It is clear that with the lapse of time, if their 'government' is not then such as to designate them rather as bandits, they do eventually acquire it. So the serious question for us is posed by the first cases.

There is one consideration here which has something like the position of absolute zero or the velocity of light in current physics. It cannot possibly be an exercise of civic authority deliberately to kill or mutilate innocent subjects. The steps are sufficiently obvious, by which we can arrive from the consideration of the questions involved in clarifying this proposition at this (rather academic) one: the enactment of a law by which it was an offence to go on living (though one had committed no *other* offence) is not a possibility for legitimate government. The proposition is academic because when governments take to murdering their subjects they seldom make positive law explicitly authorizing the killing. But the academic proposition is of interest to us. The reason for it should be clear from our whole investigation: authority in the command of violence (which was what we first saw as distinguishing government from a Mafia in control of a place) is based on its performance of a task which is a general human need. A way of treating someone which puts him outside the class of those for whom the task is performed puts him outside the class of those subject to the authority. It is arguable that the death penalty for crimes does itself do this, but also arguable (I think successfully) that it does not. But if one's only 'offence' is supposed to be that (being a Welshman, say, or a gypsy) one continues to exist, then it is clear beyond argument that one is put out of that class and so cannot be guilty under the law purporting to create the offence.

NOTES

Originally delivered at the Fifth Bristol Philosophy Conference, July 16–19, 1976.
1 We should distinguish between regular slavery and the condition of the Athenian prisoners in the quarry at Syracuse, or the prisoners regularly worked to death in the Krupps factories under the Nazis.
2 I mean that, in my opinion, its more interesting interpretation is a falsehood. Namely, that the proof that I 'ought' to do something is

On the Source of the Authority of the State   173

sufficient also to prove that I 'can', i.e. that my freedom of will is such that I can.

3 Locke's argument depends on assuming a Law of Nature; he argues that like any other law, it must have sanctions. But if the legislator does not speedily punish transgressions of the law, it is not clear why we may.
4 Hart, *The Concept of Law* (Oxford University Press 1971), p. 74.
5 Except in a special case, where there are people who have no customary rights which are infringed by casually killing them, though there is not supposed to be a customary right of killing them either. I will not go into this here for lack of space.

7
Authority

J. M. FINNIS

IX.1 THE NEED FOR AUTHORITY

Questions about the need and justification for authority can arise in different ways. Someone reflecting on the fact of human freedom in moral choosing, or on the basic values of authenticity and freedom in practical reasonableness, may be moved to ask how any man can have authority to require one to choose what one would not otherwise have chosen. Orders and rules may weigh with me because of accompanying threats, or because of my uncritical conformism or my careerism. But can they have for me the authority of a fully critical conclusion of authentic practical reason? Someone else may raise a question about authority in reflecting more speculatively on human community. Is authority in a group required only because of the stupidity and incompetence of its members, their infirmity of purpose and want of devotion to the group, their selfishness and malice, their readiness to exploit and to 'free ride'? In a community free from these vices, would authority be needed, or justified?

It will be helpful to respond first to this last question. The human weaknesses recited in the question do indeed give good reason for having authority. But, more interestingly, it is also true that the greater the intelligence and skill of a group's members, and the greater their commitment and dedication to common purposes and common good (VI.8), the *more* authority and regulation may be required, to enable that group to achieve its common purpose, common good.

For, as I hinted in relation to the fifth requirement of practical reasonableness (V.5), the dedicated member of the group will always be looking out for new and better ways of attaining the common good, of co-ordinating the action of members, of playing his own role. And the intelligent member will find such new and better ways, and perhaps not just one but many possible and

Authority

reasonable ways. Intelligence and dedication, skill and commitment thus multiply the problems of co-ordination, by giving the group more possible orientations, commitments, projects, 'priorities', and procedures to choose from. And until a particular choice is made, nothing will in fact be done. Moreover, in some forms of human community, that something be done is not just a matter of optional advantage, but is a matter of right, a requirement of justice. Somebody (e.g. parents) must decide how children are to be educated; in the political community, there must be decisions about the management and use of natural resources, about the use of force, about permitted forms or content of communication, and about the many other problems of reconciling aspects of justice with each other (VII.7), and of reconciling human rights with each other and with other 'conflicting' exercises of the same right and with public health, public order, and the like (VIII.4, 5). In the broad sense of 'co-ordination problem', these are all co-ordination problems which need a solution (VI.6). And for most though not all of these co-ordination problems there are, in each case, two or more available, reasonable, and appropriate solutions, none of which, however, would amount to a solution unless adopted to the exclusion of the other solutions available, reasonable, and appropriate for that problem.

There are, in the final analysis, only two ways of making a choice between alternative ways of co-ordinating action to the common purpose or common good of any group. There must be either unanimity, or authority. There are no other possibilities.

Exchange of promises (see XI.2) is not a third way; rather, it is a modality of the first way, unanimity. For there is no agreement without just that: some meeting of minds on what is to be done, or at least on what is the specific content of that promise. Even a unilateral promise is not binding unless accepted by the promisee. Moreover, the agreed co-ordination of action will occur only so long as the parties either retain their original unanimity, or acknowledge the authority of a rule requiring fulfilment of promises, or are held to their agreement by some authoritative person or body.

Now there is no need to labour the point that unanimity about the desirable solution to a specific co-ordination problem cannot in practice be achieved in any community with a complex common good and an intelligent and interested membership. Unanimity is particularly far beyond the bounds of practical possibility in the political community. For here we have the most complex common good, which (subject to the principle of subsidiarity) excludes no aspect of individual well-being and is potentially affected by every aspect of every life-plan (VI.8). And the principle of subsidiarity (VI.5, VII.3) has wide implications here. For experience suggests that individuals and particular groups (this family, this firm, this university, this government department ...) should have a certain autonomy, a certain prior concern and responsibility for their own particular good, their own particular interests or speciality. Yet this concern of particular persons and groups for individual goods, for particular common goods and for particular aspects of the overall common good, will enhance the overall common good only if the resulting particular options are subject to some degree of co-ordination. And if the particular individuals and groups have as their *prior* concern (as they should) their respective particular interests, such overall co-ordination can hardly be achieved save by some person or body of persons whose prior concern and responsibility is to care for the overall common good. Again, the life of the political community is open-ended; its ends are never fully achieved and few of its co-ordination problems are solved once and for all. Finally, it must not be forgotten that unanimity is not a practical possibility in a community in which intelligence and dedication to the common good are mixed with selfishness and folly.

IX.2 THE MEANINGS OF 'AUTHORITY'

A person treats something (for example, an opinion, a pronouncement, a map, an order, a rule ...) as authoritative if and only if he treats it as giving him sufficient reason for believing or acting in accordance with it *notwithstanding* that he himself cannot otherwise see good reason for so believing or acting, or cannot evaluate the reasons he can see, or sees some countervailing reason(s), or would himself otherwise (i.e. in the absence of what it is that he is treating as authoritative) have preferred not so to believe or act. In other words, a person treats something as authoritative when he treats it as, in Joseph Raz's useful terminology, an exclusionary reason, i.e. a reason for judging or acting in the absence of understood reasons, or for disregarding at least *some* reasons which are understood and relevant and would in the absence of the exclusionary reason have sufficed to justify proceeding in some other way.[1]

This is the focal meaning of authority, whether that authority be speculative (the authority of learning or genius) or practical

Authority

(the authority of good taste, or practical experience, or office ...), and whether the authority be ascribed to a man, or to his characteristics, or to his opinions or pronouncements, or to some opinion or prescription which has authority for reasons other than that its author(s) had authority (e.g., as we shall see, custom or convention). I need say no more here about speculative authority, beyond observing in passing that a man's theoretical knowledge is often a good reason for treating him as having practical authority, but is not a necessary condition for so regarding him.

Before going further, it is as well to face up to some linguistic complications which, when not clearly understood, cause serious confusion between 'positivists' and 'natural law theorists' in jurisprudence. The foregoing two paragraphs have treated as focal or primary the meaning which the proposition 'X has authority' has when that proposition is asserted by a speaker (S_1) who treats X (or X's pronouncements, etc.) as authoritative not merely for others but also *for himself* (S_1), i.e. as giving anyone [relevant] including *him* (S_1) exclusionary reason for action in accordance with X (or X's pronouncement, etc.). But 'X has authority' may be said, truthfully, by someone (S_2) who does *not* regard X as having authority over or in relation to himself (S_2); for S_2 the truth of his proposition is established by showing that some people (S_1 and his fellows) in fact treat X as authoritative. In short, S_2 speaks as a historian, a sociologist or, in general, an observer. (He may, of course, be S_1 speaking as an observer.) Finally, 'X has authority' may be asserted by someone (S_3) *neither* in recognition of X's authority or authoritativeness in relation to himself (S_3), *nor* by way of report about other people's attitudes to X, but rather by way of stating what is the case from the viewpoint of S_1 but without either endorsing or rejecting S_1's view. (S_3 may of course be S_1, speaking from a 'detached' or professional viewpoint.) Statements of this third type are very common in textbooks which explain the rules of a game, or of English or Russian or Roman law, and in professional opinions, advice, and arguments. In what follows I use the notation S_1, S_2, S_3 to refer to statements of the three types respectively, rather than, as above, to the speakers.

The difference between these three senses of 'X has authority' is found across the whole range of normative statements: for example, 'that is a binding promise', 'A has a legal duty to φ', and even (and above all) 'there is a rule that C must/may/has power to φ'. In all these cases one and the same grammatical form may be used to assert (S_1) what there is good reason to do, or what a sufficient reason is for doing φ, *or* it may assert (S_2) that a group considers that there is good reason to φ, *or* it may assert (S_3) what there is good reason to do from the viewpoint of a certain group or on the basis of certain rules or *if* certain rules give good reason for so acting (but without affirming or denying that that viewpoint is reasonable or correct or that those rules do provide good reason for acting). One and the same person may, even on one and the same occasion, make statements of all three types, switching his viewpoint without warning or grammatical indication. This is quite common in legal advocacy.

Joseph Raz has identified and explained these three types of statement. While stressing the importance of not trying to collapse S_3 into either S_1 or S_2, he clearly recognizes that S_1 and S_2 are 'basic' and 'primary'.[2] S_3, though widespread in discourse, is parasitic. And in discussing a closely related distinction between three 'properties or dimensions of norms' he says that 'beyond doubt the primary one' is the dimension or property of actually being a good reason (as distinct from being believed by some people to be a good reason, or being intended by some people to be taken as a good reason by others).[3] But to assert that something is or provides a good reason is to make an S_1 assertion. Thus, even for Raz's purposes, while lie within the 'formal part' of 'the philosophy of practical reason' (i.e. that part which is concerned with 'conceptual analysis', as distinct from the 'substantive or "evaluative" part'),[4] the primary and focal type of statement about authority and norms is the S_1 type. For our purposes in this book (which are sufficiently described by Raz's description of substantive practical philosophy),[5] this primacy of S_1 statements is even more evident. That is why the explanation of authority advanced in the first sentence of this section is an explanation of that form of recognition of authority which would be expressed by an S_1 statement.

But what is the importance of these technical distinctions between types of statement, or types of recognition of authority? It is this. As is already obvious from the opening section of this chapter, my explanation of the need and justification for authority, and of its limits and its proper modes of operation, is going to be an explanation by reference to the common good (including justice and human rights); see, for example, the account of the authority of custom in the next section. Now to all such explanations, some 'positivists' in jurisprudence have made the following sort of objection:

> You claim to be explaining what it is for an authority, an authoritative custom, or a rule, to exist. But at best you succeed in explaining only what it is to believe that such an

authority, custom or rule *ought* to exist. For on your explanation it would be *redundant* to say, for example, '(P_1) an authoritative custom exists and (P_2) it is for the common good that it should exist.' But it is odd and counter-intuitive to claim that P_2 is redundant when conjoined with P_1. Or again, on your explanation it would be *contradictory* to say '(P_1) an authoritative custom exists but (P_2) its existence is not for the common good'. But it is odd and counter-intuitive to claim that P_1 contradicts P_2. We conclude that your method of explaining authority and rules is itself unsatisfactory, since it yields results which are counter-intuitive and inconsistent with ordinary language and common sense.

To this 'positivist' objection the reply is now obvious. My programme of explanation does not commit me to condemning as either redundant or contradictory the conjunction of P_1 with P_2. Such a conjunction *does* entail redundancy or inconsistency if and only if P_1 is understood as an S_1 statement. But the positivist objection simply overlooks the fact that 'existential sentences about norms are used for a variety of purposes ...'.[6] The 'existential sentence' P_1 can perfectly well be understood as an S_2 or an S_3 statement, and someone who makes either of the conjunctive statements mentioned in the positivist's objection will of course intend the first half of his statement (i.e. P_1) in an S_2 or S_3 sense and the second half (i.e. P_2) in an S_1 sense. His meaning simply is: 'people treat this custom as justified, and indeed it is [or: is not]'; or perhaps, 'speaking from the lawyer's point of view, this is a legally authoritative custom; and, I may add, in my personal opinion it is [or: is not] for the common good that it be treated as such'; '"this is law; but it is too iniquitous to be applied or obeyed"'.[7] The fact that I systematically treat S_1 statements as primary, because the focus of my theoretical interest is in justificatory explanations, in no way requires me to regard any of those statements as objectionable (though the history of contemporary jurisprudence shows that they are open to misunderstanding): see II.2, XII.4. Hence this 'positivist' objection to my programme of explanation need not deflect us.

IX.3 FORMATION OF CONVENTIONS OR CUSTOMARY RULES

In this section I show how an authoritative rule can emerge (i.e. begin to regulate a community) without being made by anyone with authority to make it, and even without the benefit of any authorized way of generating rules. The discussion will enable us to deepen our understanding of the relation between acknowledging the authority of a rule and following the principles of practical reasonableness. It will also enable us to understand more adequately both the distinctions and the connections between unanimity and authority in a community. For in studying the formation of custom we are studying the emergence of a substitute for unanimity under conditions which require a substantial degree of unanimity.

It will be convenient to conduct our discussion of the formation of custom by reference to the international community and the formation of customary rules of international law. For this is the context in which the problem of custom arouses most interest today, has been most debated, and found most difficult to explain satisfactorily. In what follows, I use the term 'custom' as shorthand for 'authoritative customary rule', and by 'authoritative' in this context I mean 'legally authoritative'. I use the term 'state' as a short form of reference to any entity acting in the sphere of international law as a subject or potential subject thereof.

There is a vast and confused literature on custom as a source of international law. It is generally agreed that custom involves some concurrence or convergence or regularity of practice amongst states. It is further agreed that such concurrence, convergence, or regularity is not enough to constitute custom. There must be a concurrence of deliberate practice, not induced by force or fraud or mistake. And, more positively, the practice must be accompanied by a certain attitude, belief, intention, or disposition: in the literature this is called the *opinio juris*. It is this last condition for the formation of custom that causes difficulty. For the classical accounts of the required content of the *opinio juris* are openly question-begging or paradoxical (but alternative accounts have not been forthcoming). As Oppenheim's treatise says: 'International jurists speak of a custom when a clear and continuous habit of doing certain actions has grown up under the aegis of the conviction that these actions are, according to international law, obligatory or right.'[8] But this is paradoxical, for it proposes that a customary norm can come into existence (i.e. become authoritative) only by virtue of the necessarily erroneous belief that it is already in existence (i.e. authoritative).

The method of analysis and explanation which I have been developing in this Part of this book (and which is only completed in the final chapters of this Part) enables us to offer an analysis of the formation of custom which makes intelligible something like the classic position of international jurists, a position which they themselves, however, have been unable to free from the paradox just mentioned. Technically speaking, the key to a solution of the problem lies in the distinction (expressed in the preceding section as that between S_1 and S_2 statements) between, on the one hand, practical judgements and, on the other hand, empirical judgements about the existence and extent of practices. As throughout this book, 'practical judgement' here refers to judgements made by any person, whether privately or in some official capacity, which explicitly or implicitly state that some action (including always omissions or forbearances) by some (potential) agent should (not) be done, or could (not) appropriately or justifiably be done (in any of the various senses of 'should', 'appropriately', or 'justifiably'): I.4.

At the root of the formation of custom, and in particular at the core of that factor in the formation of custom which is usually labelled the *opinio juris*, are two different but related practical judgements:

(a) in this domain of human affairs (e.g. passage of warships through coastal waters), it would be appropriate to have *some* determinate, common, and stable pattern of conduct and, correspondingly, an authoritative rule requiring that pattern of conduct; to have this is more desirable than leaving conduct in this domain to the discretion of individual states;
(b) *this* particular pattern of conduct ϕ (e.g. innocent passage on the surface under flag to be permitted by coastal states)[9] is appropriate, or would be *if* generally adopted and acquiesced in, for adoption as an authoritative common rule of conduct.

These are both practical, not empirical, judgements, and they are not yet legal judgements. When the contents of a multilateral treaty, or the resolutions of an international body representative of states, are spoken of as sources or evidence of custom, what is really (or, at any rate, justifiably) being said is that the treaty or resolutions are evidence not of an opinion about what the law already is, but of *opinio juris* in the limited sense expressed in these two judgements. They are indeed judgements that might be made by anyone thinking about the relevant domain. They affirm that something is desirable (*a*) in general, (*b*) in particular. In a well-ordered international community, the frame of reference for assessing desirability would be primarily the common good of the whole community and its members (including considerations of justice and rights), and only secondarily the interests of the person or state making the judgements. Very commonly, of course, this ranking of the frames of reference is in fact reversed. This fact is an obstacle to the formation of custom, but only an obstacle, not insuperable.

The next step in the analysis is to observe that both the foregoing practical judgements are distinct from the empirical judgement that many (or few) states in fact subscribe to them. And this empirical judgement is, in turn, to be distinquished from two further empirical judgements: (1) that the practice of many (or few) states, in the relevant domain, is convergent in pattern and is of the pattern referred to in the second ((b)) of the aforementioned practical judgements; and (2) that other states do (or do not) acquiesce in that pattern of conduct.

Empirical judgements of the three sorts just mentioned are pre-requisites to the making of a new, practical judgement. This new practical judgement is a further aspect of the undifferentiated '*opinio juris*' of the classic treatises. (Indeed, it is the aspect which, by its undue or even exclusive emphasis, renders the whole doctrine of those treatises paradoxical). It affirms that the empirically widespread making of the two practical judgements ((a) and (b)), and the empirical concurrence of practice and generality (not necessarily universality) of acquiescence, together warrant the claim that a custom exists as an authoritative legal norm. Notice that the latter claim is a practical or S_1 statement; like S_2 statements it uses the indicative grammar of 'existence', but unlike S_2 statements it is not empirical. It expresses the view that the norm imposes *justified* requirements on all actors in the relevant domain. Even more obviously practical is the judgement that that claim is warranted in the circumstances. This judgement builds on the three empirical judgements mentioned above, but it relates the relevant empirical facts about state practice and opinion to some principle(s) about what is required for the common good of the international community. The action-guiding and requirement-imposing force of the legal norm which this judgement is affirming to be justified derives from some such meta-legal principle of practical reasonableness about the needs of international community. About this meta-legal principle I shall say more when I have completed and reviewed the analysis in outline.

The practical judgements identified in the preceding paragraph are to be distinguished from the empirical (S_2) judgement (often expressed in the same grammatical forms) that 'there is a legal norm requiring such-and-such', in the sense that states empirically do generally recognize such a norm, i.e that the norm is more or less 'effective'. Those practical judgements are also to be distinguished, of course, from the (S_3) statements which neutral jurists make. Although juristic statements are, quite properly, the ones most frequently on lawyers' lips, I say no more about them here, since they are parasitic upon the attitudes of, and corresponding statements open to, those persons who consider that the relevant body of norms ought to be adhered to in practice, i.e. who actually use those norms to guide their own conduct: IX.2. Our problem about the formation of custom is to explain how a course of international practice can become a legal rule imposing requirements that *those* persons should and would recognize.

The distinctions made in the preceding four paragraphs can now be summarized. For brevity and clarity we can use an *ad hoc* and elementary notation, merely as a shorthand: PJ signifies a practical (S_1) judgement, EJ an empirical (S_2) judgement, and JJ a juristic (S_3) judgement in the sense explained above:

PJ_0 (a) it is desirable that in this domain there be some determinate, common, and stable pattern of conduct and corresponding authoritative rule;
(b) this particular pattern of conduct, ϕ, is (or would be if generally adopted and acquiesced in) an appropriate pattern for adoption as an authoritative common rule.
EJ_1 there is widespread concurrence and acquiescence in this pattern of conduct, ϕ, by states.
EJ_2 the *opinio juris* (i.e. PJ_0) is widely subscribed to by states.
PJ_1 the widespread subscription to PJ_0, and the widespread concurrence or acquiescence in the pattern of conduct ϕ, are sufficient to warrant the judgement (PJ_2) that there is now an authoritative customary rule requiring (or permitting) ϕ ...
PJ_2 ϕ is required (or pemitted), by virtue of an authoritative customary rule of international law.
EJ_3 states generally accept the rule that ϕ is to be done (or may be done) ...
JJ_1 according to international law, ϕ is required (or permitted) ...

What are the virtues of this analysis? Firstly, by differentiating between PJ_0 and PJ_1, it enables us to see that there need be no paradox or circularity in the classic notion that, it order to amount to an authoritative custom, a course of practice must be accompanied by a particular sort of attitude or *opinio*. Secondly, by differentiating between PJ_0 and PJ_2, it enables us to see that the legal judgement PJ_2, while in various ways dependent upon prior political or moral judgements PJ_0 (not necessarily made by the person now making the legal judgement), is quite distinct and 'positive' (*de lege lata*, not merely *ferenda*). Thirdly, by separating out EJ_1, EJ_2, and EJ_3 from the other judgements, the relation of authoritative rules to facts is clarified: an authoritative rule can be said to be a fact, but it is more than the fact of concurrent practice, and more even than the fact of concurrence of opinion; and it is a fact only because it is treated as an exclusionary reason for action (i.e. as more than a fact).

Fourthly, the analysis enables us to see clearly the real problems involved in explaining (for practical reasonableness) the formation of custom. The main problem emerges clearly in PJ_1, the immediately proximate preliminary to the judgement that a norm is in force and authoritative. For PJ_1, if it is not to be a mere *non sequitur*, must have a suppressed practical premise; this premise, I think, is the meta-legal or framework principle PJ^m:

PJ^m the emergence and recognition of customary rules (by treating a certain degree of concurrence or acquiescence in a practice and a corresponding *opinio juris* as sufficient to create such a norm and to entitle that norm to recognition even by states not party to the practice or the *opinio juris*) is a desirable or appropriate method of solving interaction or co-ordination problems in the international community.

In turn, the clear identification of the meta-principle PJ^m enables us to see that the formation of custom is possible only because PJ^m enjoys wider favour among states than does the PJ_0 relating to almost any particular problem of conduct. Just as it is easier to get agreement that *some* rule would be desirable ($PJ_0(a)$) than to get agreement that *this* particular rule is desirable (PJ_0 (*b*)), so it is easier still to get agreement that the international community needs methods of solving its interaction and co-ordination problems and that custom, *if* there is sufficient acceptance that custom is an appropriate method, is an appropriate method (since it often is the only practicable method). And this way of expressing PJ^m shows that the desirability or appropriateness of accepting PJ^m is conditional upon a sufficient number of other states also accepting PJ^m. This is not a paradox or vicious circle!

Thus, although there are direct 'moral' arguments of justice for recognizing customs as authoritative (for example, arguments

Authority

against unfairly defeating reasonable expectations or squandering resources and structures erected on the basis of the expectations), the general authoritativeness of custom depends upon the fact that custom-formation has been *adopted* in the international community as an appropriate method of rule-creation. For, given this fact, recognition of the authoritativeness of particular customs affords all states an opportunity of furthering the common good of the international community by solving interaction and co-ordination problems otherwise insoluble. And this opportunity is the root of all legal authority, whether it be the authority of rulers or (as here) of rules.

In short, the 'framework' practice of treating custom-formation as a source of authoritative norms is itself one instance of the pattern-of-conduct 'φ' in the analysis. In other words, the requirements, pre-conditions, and forms of custom-formation are themselves determined, in large part, by custom (i.e. by a framework custom whose source is similar in form to the customs for the formation of which it itself provides the framework). The authoritativeness of this framework custom derives not from some yet further custom, but from the opportunity of advancing the common good, the opportunity which is afforded by widespread (not necessarily universal) recognition of the framework custom, and of the particular substantive customs, as authoritative. But it is also very important to see that the authoritativeness of particular customs should not be explained by saying that their formation was 'authorized' by the framework custom. The framework custom does indeed regulate the making of PJ_1 judgements by states, and thus to some extent controls the emergence of customs, and determines the range of their authoritativeness (e.g. by determining what degree, if any, of prior protest exempts a state from adhering to the emergent custom). But it is artificial and unnecessary to say that the framework custom 'authorizes' states to make customs, or that it is 'the source' of the authority of particular customs. Both the framework custom and the particular customs which become authoritative within its framework derive their authoritativeness directly from the fact that, if treated as authoritative, they enable states to solve their co-ordination problems – a fact that has normative significance because the common good requires that those co-ordination problems be solved.

Finally, the analysis reveals the further problems that must be solved if custom-formation is to work at all well as an instrument of international order and community. For if it is to work, there must be a sufficient degree of agreement in answering these questions, amongst others:

1 What actions of what persons in what contexts count as state practice?
2 What degree of practice counts as 'widespread' in a given domain, and for how long?
3 What expressions or silences, and whose, count as subscribing to the *opinio juris* ($PJ_0(a)$ and (b))?
4 To what extent can custom be localized geographically, granted that the interaction and co-ordination problems of the international community, in a given domain, are perhaps not peculiar to a particular geographical area (but perhaps have local variations)?

Answers to these and similar questions go to make up the content of the framework custom. Although they will reflect assessments of what is for the common good of the international community, they are none the less answers that have to be *adopted* by most members of the community if they are to *count as* answers. They therefore can change, i.e. be changed — not necessarily by the exercise of authority (custom is authoritative but not the result of anyone's exercise of international authority) but, authoritatively, by change in practice and opinion.

IX.4 THE AUTHORITY OF RULERS

The clumsiness of custom-formation as a method of generating authoritative solutions to co-ordination problems is obvious enough. Although the process does not require unanimity, it does require a substantial convergence of practices and of opinions, not merely on the desirability of *some* solution but on the desirability of a particular solution. And, as my analysis showed, there are numerous potential causes for doubt about whether an authoritative custom has emerged, whom it binds, and so on. The need for somebody, or some body, to settle co-ordination problems with greater speed and certainty is apparent in any community where people are energetic and inventive in pursuit of their own or of common goods, not to mention any community threatened with military, economic, or ecological disaster.

Authority (and thus the *responsibility* of governing) in a community is to be exercised by those who can in fact effectively settle co-ordination problems for that community. This principle is not the last word on the requirements of practical reasonableness in locating authority; but it is the first and most fundamental.

The *fact* that the say-so of a particular person or body or configuration of persons will in fact be, by and large, complied with and acted upon, has normative consequences for practical reasonableness; it affects the responsibilities of both ruler and ruled, by creating certain exclusionary reasons for action. These normative consequences derive from a normative principle – that authority is a good (because required for the realization of the common good) – when that principle is taken in conjunction with the fact that a particular person, body, or configuration of persons can, for a given community at a given time, do what authority is to do (i.e. secure and advance the common good).

Of course, this derivation of the relevant normative consequences is not indefeasible. That is to say, the conjunction of the principle with the opportunity is only presumptively sufficient to justify the claim to and recognition of authority. Someone who uses his empirical opportunity, or even his legally recognized authority, to promote schemes thoroughly opposed to practical reasonableness cannot then reasonably claim to have discharged his own responsibilities in reason, and may be unable to justify his claim to have created a good and sufficient exclusionary reason affecting the responsibilities of those whose compliance he is seeking or demanding. I take up the problem of unjust exercise of authority more fully in Chapter XII.

It is for political science to examine the empirical conditions under which particular persons, bodies, or configurations of persons can make stipulations for action, with empirical effectiveness. It will, for example, be pointed out immediately that the state of affairs I am calling simply 'acquiescence', 'compliance', and 'effectiveness' is in reality more complex: while the mass of a population may passively obey, each 'for his own part only' and out of fear of sanctions, there must also be a class of more active, willing, 'consenting' supporters including many if not most officials. But for present purposes it is quite sufficient to say, in simple terms, that the motives or reasons which people have for complying with and acting upon stipulations presented to them as authoritative (and for being willing to do so should occasion arise) vary widely – fear of force, hope for (perhaps fraudulently suggested) profit, respect for age or for wisdom or for numbers or for the fall of the lot, belief in divine designation (charisma) or world-historic mission, adherence to convention or custom (which in turn may designate blood-lineage, or lot, or age, or ...) ... Some of these motives are more reasonable than others, either absolutely or at least in given situations. Political science can say important things about this relative reasonableness, and thus about the legitimacy, for reasonable men, of various forms of constitution. But, for an understanding of the authoritativeness of rulers, as a concern of practical reasonableness, it is the sheer fact of effectiveness that is presumptively (not indefeasibly) decisive.

In fact, political theorists pondering the location of authority have frequently erred by carrying certain legal modes of thought beyond the origins of law. The lawyer (reasonably, as we shall see: X.3), when confronted by a claim to a certain status, title, power, or right, inquires after the root of the alleged title; he asks to be shown the conveyance or enactment or other transaction which gave rise to the title, and in turn he will want to be satisfied that those who made that conveyance or enactment had been given authority to do so by some further enactment or transaction which in turn ... From this train of thought arise the theories of governmental legitimacy and political obligation which tacitly assume that the present authority of particular rulers must rest on some prior authority (of custom; or of the community over itself, granted away to the ruler by transmission or alienation; or of the individual over himself, granted away by promise or implied contract or 'consent').

The legalistic theories which seek to justify the authority of rulers by reference to the prior authority of some presumably self-authorizing transaction such as a 'contract of subjection' or an act of 'consent', have often been reinforced by a train of reasoning which employs the quite correct premise that *all* the members of a community are entitled in justice to a certain concern and respect. An argument along these lines became popular amongst scholastic writers in the sixteenth century. At the beginning of the seventeenth century, Cardinal Bellarmine formulated this argument with precision: Natural reasonableness requires that there be governmental authority; But natural reasonableness does not identify any particular man or class as the bearer of governmental authority; Therefore natural reasonableness requires that the bearer of governmental authority be the multitude, the whole community itself. (And the multitude, or community, then *transmits* its authority to representatives, be they kings, councils, or assemblies.) Bellarmine's 'syllogism' is helpfully clear; it reveals the fallacy in his theory, and in all such 'transmission' theories (which secular writers later developed, of course, into theories that governmental authority rests for its legitimacy on 'the consent of the governed').[10] The argument's two premises are certainly correct; but the conclusion obviously does not follow from them.

Authority

Indeed, the conclusion is intrinsically implausible. For the need for authority is, precisely, to substitute for unanimity in determining the solution of practical co-ordination problems which involve or concern everyone in the community. To say 'the community has authority over itself' *either* amounts to saying that there is no authority in this community (so that co-ordination problems are solved by unanimity, or are dissolved by sheer force), *or* it amounts to saying something else, by way of a confusing legal fiction or ideological manner of speaking, about the location of authority in *some* communities; for example, that each member of such and such a community has an opportunity to participate in determining that location (though such acts of participation, while not devoid of significance, do not themselves amount to an exercise of authority, as every outvoted voter in a parliamentary election is well aware).

Consent, transmission, contract, custom — none of these is needed to constitute the state of affairs which (presumptively) justifies someone in claiming and others in acknowledging his authority to settle co-ordination problems for a whole community by creating authoritative rules or issuing authoritative orders and determinations. Rather, the required state of facts is this: that in the circumstances the say-so of this person or body or configuration of persons probably will be, by and large, complied with and acted upon, to the exclusion of any rival say-so and notwithstanding any differing preferences of individuals about what should be stipulated and done in the relevant fields of co-ordination problems.

This emergence of authority without benefit of prior authorization requires, of course, the definite solution of a vast preliminary or framework co-ordination problem: *Whose* say-so, if anyone's, are we all to act upon in solving our co-ordination problems? Necessarily the solution will require virtual unanimity; *here* there will be no solution unless the preferences of the individual members of the community are brought into line. Such unanimity of practical judgement is, obviously, not easy to come by. Individual motivations for concurring in the relevant judgement will vary, and very commonly those who aspire to benefit from the judgement (i.e. who aspire to authority) will be busy ensuring that anyone who is failing to appreciate their claims to intrinsic fitness to rule will be supplied with some extrinsic motive to concur — fear or favour. The effort to bring everyone to at least an acquiescence in this judgement is usually very taxing and exhausting for all concerned, and makes clear to all what is indeed the case: that those general needs of the common good which justify authority, certainly also justify and urgently demand that questions about the location of authority be answered, wherever possible, by authority. I have been stressing that there are situations where this is not practically possible, and that the emergence of particular bearers of authority in such situations is, nevertheless, neither impossible nor unduly mysterious. Now it is time to recall that, very commonly, the first authoritative act of unauthorized bearers of authority is to lay down directions for ensuring that in future the location of authority (whether in themselves or in their successors) shall be determined, not by the hazards of those processes of arriving at unanimity from which they have just emerged as the beneficiaries,[11] but by authoritative rules.

Of course, some rulers are content to rule charismatically, and to leave their succession to the movements of a spirit which blows where it listeth (not perhaps without some huffing and puffing by those who would like it to breathe on them). But Weber was well justified in his tendency (contrary, perhaps, to some of his own methodological notions) to speak of the 'legal' type-form of rulership as the 'rational' type-form.[12] Once the problems of social order, and of authority as a rational response to such problems, have become the object of practically reasonable reflection in a community, 'constitutional' provision for the location of authority becomes a first priority. If the ruler does not make it his business to determine the location of authority for later times (not to mention for lower levels), thoughtful members of such societies will commonly make it their business to try, as best they can, to reach some understandings about it. The tendency of political thinkers to utter legalistic fictions about the original location of authority has its excuse, and perhaps its occasion (but not a justification), in the urgent need to legalize the devolution of undevolved authority.

It remains true that the sheer fact that virtually everyone *will* acquiesce in somebody's say-so is the presumptively necessary and defeasibly sufficient condition for the normative judgement that that person has (i.e. is justified in exercising) authority in that community. But to this perhaps scandalously stark principle there are two significant riders. First: practical reasonableness requires (because of the self-same desirability of authority for the common good) that, faced with a purported ruler's say-so, the members of the community normally should acquiesce or *withhold* their acquiescence, comply or *withhold* their compliance, precisely as he is, or is not, designated as the lawful bearer of authority by the constitutional rules authoritative for that time, place, field, and function — *if*, by virtue of custom or authoritative stipulation, *there are such rules.* The second rider is this: while 'consent' as distinct from acquiescence is not needed to justify or legitimate the authority of rulers, the notion of consent may suggest a sound rule of thumb for deciding when someone should be obeyed even though general acquiescence is not likely, and for deciding when someone whose stipulation will be generally acquiesced in should nevertheless be treated as having no authority in practical reason. This rule of thumb is: a man's stipulations have authority when a practically reasonable subject, with the common good in view, would think he *ought* to consent to them.

The standing temptation of the lawyer, and of the political philosopher in a culture saturated with legal ideals and legalistic assumptions, is to treat these riders not as riders but as the fundamental principle – shutting his eyes to the fact which the lawyer and political philosopher, Sir John Fortescue, squarely faced during the turbulent emergence of nation-states in Europe: 'amongst *nearly all* peoples, realms have come into being by usurpation, just as the Romans usurped the government of the whole world'.[13] The fact that bad men happen to originate a government does not (Fortescue explained) affect the truth that governing power has its beginnings under, and by virtue of, the 'law of nature', and at all times was and remains regulated by that natural law. (Where Fortescue speaks of the law of nature, I have preferred to speak of the principles of practical reasonableness that call for co-operative life in the wide 'political' community, and for the authority that alone makes that life practicable.) In the very frequent case where bad men establish their rulership over a realm, there as elsewhere the law of nature itself (said Fortescue) operates to initiate the rulership, for the sake of human well-being: 'in one and the the same act both the force of justice and the malice of wrongfulness effect the operation of the law of nature' – one can say that men establish governing power through the law of nature, but in the last analysis it is better to say (he concluded forcefully) that it is the law of nature that establishes that power through men, be they good or bad.[14] In these formulations, his lawyers' jargon about powers being created by operation of (natural) law does not obscure this English judge's moral realism which refuses to trace the ultimate origin of authority to any fiction of transmission, contract, or actual consent, or to anything other than the principles of practical reasonableness and the basic values of the common good, generating practical conclusions ('I have the responsibility of ruling'; 'He has authority ...') from the sheer fact of ability to co-ordinate action for the common good.[15]

IX.5 'BOUND BY THEIR OWN RULES'?

The foregoing section was not a defence of the rule of the few over the many. For convenience, I referred often to 'the ruler'. But nothing turned on the number of persons entitled, in a given community, to participate in rulership. As the classics said, the ruler may be one, or few, or many ('the multitude', 'the masses'). There are social circumstances where the rule of one will be best, and other circumstances where the rule of a very narrow, or a very wide, class will be best. (The classical 'preference' for the rule of one − 'mon-archy' − was not a preference for life tenure of office, hereditary titles, or the paraphernalia of royal courts, but expressed a concern for effectiveness of co-ordination, for unity and consequently effectiveness in the pursuit of common good; and the preference was carefully qualified by the proviso that the conditions must be right − for where the conditions are wrong, the rule of one is the absolutely worst form of rule: tyranny.) The discussion of the best forms of rule under given conditions is for political science. My concern is with the distinction, which all social thought easily employs and recognizes and which legal thought formalizes with convenient fictions, between acting in the capacity of ruler and acting in the capacity of subject.

Nothing in the notion of authority which I have been expounding requires that authority rest in some permanently or even quasi-permanently distinct governing personnel. The axiom that authority is required as a substitute for unanimity in no way entails that authority cannot vest in an assembly of all the sane adults of a community, or even in such an assembly determining issues only by unanimous vote. Provided that the determinations of such an assembly are treated by the members as authoritative after the determination, and after its members have returned to their own private affairs, we have co-ordination of action in the community by authority rather than by unanimity of judgement (for minds can change; assemblymen can come to regret their vote, and yet comply, and be bound to comply, with the determination). Of course, any requirement of unanimity amongst those who exercise authority tends to render authority inefficient as a substitute for unanimity amongst the members of the community: hence some form of majority rule will ordinarily meet with general acquiescence, at least 'in principle', i.e. as a method of generating authoritative determinations. But the axiomatic distinction remains conceptually clear: as Yves Simon said, imagining a small farming community practising direct, non-representative government by participatory democracy: 'Between [a] few hundred farmers scattered in their fields, busy with their own private affairs, and the same farmers gathered in an assembly in charge of the community's affairs, the qualitative difference is just as great as between the President of the United States and any of us United States citizens.'[16]

There is nothing mysterious about this distinction between the assemblymen in their 'collegiate capacity' (as John Austin aptly put it)[17] and each assemblyman in his individual capacity as subject to 'the assembly's' stipulations (i.e. the stipulations which have met the approval of that number of assemblymen — and according to that manner and form of expressing such approval — which wins general acquiescence, either merely *de facto* or, more usually, because of rules so providing). The distinction simply corresponds to two distinct though related human excellences which Aristotle summed up when he said that a citizen, in the focal sense of that word, is one who shares in rulership (whether in the deliberative assemblies or in the courts of law), and added that 'the good citizen must possess the knowledge and capacity requisite both for ruling and for being ruled, and the excellence of a citizen may be defined as consisting in a practical knowledge of the governance of free men from *both* points of view'.[18]

Just as it is obvious that each and every member of a governing assembly is bound by its authoritative stipulations, in so far as these stipulate what he is (not) to do, so it is obvious that a ruler who rules alone may stipulate what he is himself (not) to do, and is then bound by this stipulation. If we are to call these stipulations 'laws', and their obligation 'legal', so far as they touch and bind any mere subject, why should we not call them laws and their obligation legal so far as they touch a person who also rules? It will not do to object that a monarch may have the authority to relieve himself of his obligations by amendment or dispensation — for the question relates to his position, in reason's contemplation of law, *while* the law which embraces him is not thus amended or dispensed from. Nor is it helpful to declare that such a monarch's obligations must be merely 'political' or 'moral', not legal — for commonly they are obligations deriving not from this or that political 'factor', nor (directly) from any general moral rule, but directly and precisely from that very manner and form of acting which, in that society at that time, counts as authoritative laying-down-of-law.

The elementary distinction needed for present purposes — made clearly in medieval terminology and only gradually slipping out of

English legal language during the two centuries dividing St German, through Hale, from Blackstone — is that between the 'directive' and the 'coercive' force of authority. But when we speak of the coercive force of rules, we are beginning to speak of law (which is not the same as saying that one cannot conceive of law without coercion).

* * *

IX.1

It works to the common good that particular goods be properly defended by particular persons ... For insistence on this, and a vivid illustration, see Aquinas, *S.T.* I–II, q. 19, a. 10c; also Yves Simon, *The Philosophy of Democratic Government* (Chicago: 1951), pp. 41, 55–8, 71. The first chapter of Simon's book also provides an excellent analysis of the reasons why, and differing ways in which, authority is natural to man, i.e. is required for his good but not (only) because of the deficiencies of individuals. Discount, however, his theory (taken from Maritain) of 'affective knowledge'.

Co-ordination problems ... The concept of co-ordination problem recently developed for analysis of games, strategies, and conventions is summarized by Edna Ullmann-Margalit, *The Emergence of Norms* (Oxford: 1977), p. 78. 'Co-ordination problems are interaction situations distinguished by their being situations of interdependent decision. That is, they are situations involving two or more persons, in which each has to choose one from among several alternative actions, and in which the outcome of any person's action depends upon the action chosen by each of the others ... The specific difference of co-ordination problems within this class is that in them the interests of the parties coincide.' Ullmann-Margalit rightly employs central case/focal meaning analysis here: 'When the coincidence of interests is perfect we speak of a *pure* co-ordination problem. In the non-pure co-ordination problems the convergence of the parties' interests is less than perfect, but still outweighs any possible clash of interests.' In my discussion, 'co-ordination problem' ranges from the pure to the very non-pure instances, approaching asymptotically the 'pure conflict case' where 'the parties' interests diverge completely and one person's gain is the other's loss' (Ibid.). For a legislator or judge, considering the problems of social order generically, the pure conflict situation cannot be conceded to exist as between the members of a community: A and B may be in a pure conflict situation here and now; but A might have been in B's position, and vice versa; so, in advance or generically (i.e. for the purpose of selecting rules and conventions), people of A's and B's sorts have a convergent interest in containing, modulating, and conditioning the possible loss (and gain).

IX.2

'*Exclusionary reasons*' ... Joseph Raz has developed the concept in his *Practical Reason and Norms* (Hutchinson, London: 1975). An exclusionary reason is a reason to exclude, or refrain from acting upon, a relevant reason for acting: see pp. 39, 42, 62; sometimes, as where someone is under orders, it is a reason for not acting on 'the merits of the case' at all — the order operates as a reason for not acting on an assessment of the pros and cons of the action ordered and alternative courses of action: see p. 42. As Raz rightly observes at p. 64: 'if authority is to be justified by the requirements of co-ordination [as he thinks it is: ibid.] we must regard authoritative utterances as exclusionary reasons. The proof is contained in the classical analysis of authority. Authority can secure co-ordination only if the individuals concerned defer to its judgement and do not act on the balance of reasons, but on the authority's instructions ...'. Raz, 'On Legitimate Authority', in R. Bronaugh (ed.), *Philosophical Law* (Westport: 1978), pp. 6–31, is a useful analysis of authority in terms of 'protected reasons', a protected reason being one that is both a reason to φ and an exclusionary reason for disregarding reasons against doing φ.

Distinction between S_1 and S_3 statements ... See also Raz, 'Kelsen's Theory of the Basic Norm' (1974) 19 *Am. J. Juris.* 94 at pp. 107–9. A similar point is made by, e.g., Winston Nesbitt, 'Categorical Imperatives' (1977) 86 *Phil. Rev.* 217 at p. 221: 'The judgment that from the point of view of etiquette one should do a certain thing is not "a 'should' statement based on rules of etiquette" ...; it is not a "should"-judgment at all, but a theoretical judgment about what etiquette requires, and is quite consistent with "But of course, it's nonsense that you should do any such thing". A "should" statement based on the rules of etiquette is not a judgment to the effect that one should from the point of view of etiquette do A, because the rules of etiquette require it ...'. See also Neil MacCormick, *Legal Reasoning and Legal Theory* (Oxford: 1978), p. 62.

IX.3

'Opinio juris' *as belief in obligatory character of the practice* ... Besides Oppenheim see (amongst countless other sources) Judge Manley Hudson's Working Paper (dated 3 March 1950) on Art. 24 of the Statute of the International Law Commission: 'The emergence of a principle or rule of customary international law would seem to require presence of the following elements: (a) concordant practice by a number of States with reference to a type of situation falling within the domain of international relations; (b) continuation or repetition of the practice over a considerable period of time; (c) conception that the practice is required by,' [surely too strong a requirement for the *opinio juris*] 'or consistent with' [surely too weak a requirement] 'prevailing international law; and (d) general acquiescence in the practice by other States': *International Law Commission Yearbook 1950*, II, p. 26. Hudson's element (b) is rejected (so far as concerns the modern world) by Tanaka J. (dissenting) in *Ethiopia v. South Africa, I. C. J. Rep.* 1966, at p. 291; already Suarez and the earlier jurists whom Suarez cites were clear that custom can be established in a short period provided that knowledge of the custom is quickly spread to all concerned (which is Tanaka J.'s point): *De Legibus*, VIII, xv, 8–9, reading '*princeps*' in the light of xiii, 1. Critical questions could also be raised about the sense in which Hudson intended his element (d). The International Court of Justice employed the classic doctrine of *opinio juris*, almost in Oppenheim's words, in the *North Sea Continental Shelf Cases, I. C. J. Rep.* 1969, at p. 44. But in the *North Sea Fisheries Case (Great Britain v. Iceland), I. C. J. Rep.* 1974, at pp. 23, 26, can be seen an understanding of custom-formation rather closer to that set out in our analysis.

'*Appropriateness' of a practice as a solution to a co-ordination problem* ... The text simplifies matters here. A rational judgement of appropriateness, which is made both as a component of the PJ_0 judgements and again (but now taking more facts into account) as a component of PJ_1 judgements, will consider not only the intrinsic features (so to speak) of the relevant co-ordination problem, but also the extent to which concurrent practice in the relevant sphere has created structures (whether physical, economic financial, or of habit, 'goodwill', etc.) the dismantling of which would involve sheer loss to many (for what gain? and to whom?). It will also consider whether (as is likely) many have benefited from the regularity and concurrence of practice and the consequent relative stability of expectations and predictions; and will ask whether it would be reasonable for those who have so benefited (or who had the free opportunity of so benefiting) to depart from the practice whenever they consider it burdensome to them. These considerations tend in practice to reduce somewhat the difficulty occasioned by the fact that, as D. K. Lewis stresses in his book *Convention: A Philosophical Study* (Ithaca: 1969), p. 24, 'co-ordination problems' are typically 'situations of inter-dependent decision ... in which there are two or more proper co-ordination equilibria'; for his account of the relation between practice, opinion (expectations and preferences), and convention, see ibid., p. 42. See also the analysis of 'conformative behaviour' in David Shwayder, *The Stratification of Behaviour* (London: 1965), pp. 233–43, 247–80.

'*Appropriateness' of custom as a method of settling both substantive and framework questions* ... This appropriateness does not derive from any abstract principle that what has always been done ought to continue to be done; or from any principle that what a majority of individuals or states want to be done (or to be authoritative) intrinsically ought to be done (or to be regarded as authoritative). (Majority rule is often a highly convenient, and therefore reasonable, principle of authority for a com-

Authority

munity to adopt — but it is not, *pace* Locke, a 'natural law' principle; it must be *adopted*, by unanimity or by authoritative, e.g. customary, rule: see Burke, *Appeal from the New to the Old Whigs* (1791) in *Works* (1826), vol. VI, pp. 212–16, summarized in J. W. Gough, *The Social Contract* (Oxford, 2nd ed.: 1957), pp. 194–5; contrast Locke, *Second Treatise of Government* (1689), para. 96, and see the tangle of opinions recorded by Otto Gierke, *Natural Law and the Theory of Society, 1500–1800* (trans. E. Barker [1934], Cambridge: 1950), pp. 110, 120, 127, 247, 315, 321, 372, 387.) This judgement of appropriateness rests not only on the considerations mentioned in the text and the preceding note on appropriateness (which apply not in all but in many particular cases), but also on the consideration (parasitic, but reinforcing) that where this method of creating authoritative rules is accepted, those who take the benefits of the resulting system of practice, restraints, etc., will normally be acting unreasonably (partially, or unfairly) if in particular cases they claim to be free from the products of the method.

Failure to disentangle PJ_0 from PJ_2 judgements ... Hart's notion of the 'internal viewpoint' and the 'internal aspect of rules' has a close relationship to the notion of *opinio juris*; certain problems in understanding and applying Hart's notion arise from his conflation of elements which I have here tried to disentangle. See *Concept of Law*, pp. 86–8, 54–7, 99–100.

Defeasibility, or only presumptive sufficiency, of effectiveness as the basis of authority ... For this use of 'defeasible' and, especially, 'presumptive', see MacCormick, 'Law as Institutional Fact' (1974) 90 Law Quarterly Review 102 at pp. 123–7.

IX.4

Empirical conditions for effective rulership ... An early study is Aristotle, *Pol.* V: 1301a–1316b27. Hart, *Concept of Law*, pp. 111–14, 59–60, 197–8, 226, 86–8, 242, 247, regularly and sharply distinguishes between 'the ordinary citizen's obedience' and 'acceptance on the part of officials of constitutional rules' (though he fails to reserve the word 'acceptance' exclusively for the latter attitude of voluntary, critical acceptance of the rules as common public standards of conduct); likewise Raz, *Practical Reason*, pp. 124–6. Classical political science also regularly distinguished between the two classes of persons likely to be found in any society: those who need to be compelled to keep the peace, and those who freely make the law their own — as Aquinas says, *S. T.* I–II, q. 96, a. 5c, these are the two principal ways of being 'subject to law' (or 'subject to authority'). On the empirical concerns of political science as conceived by Aristotle, see Eric Voegelin, *Plato and Aristotle* (Baton Rouge: 1957), ch. 9, esp. p. 357.

Differing motives for compliance ... See Hart, *Concept of Law*, pp. 198, 226; Rheinstein (ed.), *Max Weber on Law*, p. 328.

Bellarmine's transmission theory ... His syllogism (in fact, of course, an enthymeme) actually runs: '[Political] power is of divine right, but divine right did not give it to any particular man; therefore it gave it to the multitude'; or again: 'apart from positive law, there is no greater reason why, out of many equals, one rather than another should dominate; therefore power belongs to the whole multitude': *Controversiarum de membris ecclesiae* (1588), III, c. 6, trans. Simon, *Philosophy of Democratic Government*, p. 166. For an earlier formulation, see Francisco de Vitoria, *De Potestate Civili* (1528), c. 7: 'Nam cum de iure naturali et divino sit aliqua potestas gubernandi rempublicam, et sublato communi iure positivo et humano, non sit maior ratio ut potestas illa sit in uno quam in altero, necesse est ut ipsa communitas sit sibi sufficiens et habeat potestatem gubernandi se.' For Cajetan's looser formulation in 1512, see Simon, *Philosophy of Democratic Government*, pp. 160–5. All these theorists took encouragement from some ambiguous and unsatisfactory remarks of Aquinas, especially *S. T.* I–II, q. 90, a. 3; q. 97, a. 3 ad 3. For an elaborate discussion, which evasively recognizes that in the not infrequent case of a conquered people mere acquiescence suffices for 'transmission' of authority from the people to the new rulers, see Suarez, *De Legibus*, III, c. iv, para. 2; also paras. 3–5, 8; also c. ii, paras. 3, 4; c. iii, para. 6.

From transmission (or translation) theories to social contract theories ... See Otto Gierke, *Political Theories of the Middle Age* (trans. F. W. Maitland, Cambridge: 1900), notes 138–65, 305–8; for the distinction between the supposed contract of social union and the supposed contract of subjection to a ruler, see Gierke, *Natural Law and the Theory of Society, 1500–1800*, pp. 107–11 (sec. 16, para. iv). Generally, see Gough, *The Social Contract*, esp. ch. VI.

Usurpation and conquest as modes of acquiring authority ... The frequency with which authority (i.e., as always throughout this discussion, authority which ought to be respected by a reasonable citizen) is acquired by these methods is rightly stressed by David Hume, 'Of the Original Contract' [1748] (*Social Contract*, ed. E. Barker, Oxford: 1947, pp. 230–5). The US Dept. of the Army, *The Law of Land Warfare* (1956), para. 358, sums up the principle on which the International Regulations respecting the Laws and Customs of War on land, annexed to The Hague Convention IV (1907), implicitly proceed: '... military occupation ... does not transfer the sovereignty to the occupant, but simply the authority or power to exercise some of the *rights of sovereignty*. The exercise of these *rights results from the established power of the occupant and from the necessity of maintaining law and order, indispensable* both to the inhabitants and to the occupying force' (emphasis added). See also A. D. McNair, 'Municipal Effects of Belligerent Occupation' (1941) 57 *L.Q.R.* 33, stressing, at p. 36, that 'the morality or immorality of the occupation is irrelevant ...;' the occupying ruler acquires 'a right against inhabitants who remain that they should obey his lawful regulations for the administration of the territory ...' (p. 35). On the authority of usurpers, according to English law, see Honoré, 'Allegiance and the Usurper' [1967] *Camb. L. J.* 214; Finnis, 'Revolutions and Continuity of Law' in *Oxford Essays II*, 44 at pp. 46—7.

Fortescue on the origins of authority ... See also *De Laudibus Legum Anglie* (ed. S. B. Chrimes, Cambridge: 1942), cc. 12, 13, (and the analysis of c. 13 in Voegelin, *The New Science of Politics*, Chicago: 1952, pp. 41—5). The full title of Fortescue's treatise on natural law is significant: *De Natura Legis Naturae et de ejus Censura in Successione Regnorum Suprema* (i.e. ... and its judgement on the succession to supreme office in kingdoms). Despite the value of its teaching (aimed against a teaching of Cicero (*De Re Publica*, I, 25, 39) and Augustine (*De Civitate Dei*, XIX, 24) lying at the root of later social contract doctrine) that a people without authoritative rulership cannot be called a body, c. 13 of Fortescue's *De Laudibus* is not as wholly free from assumptions about transmission of authority as a reading of Voegelin's valuable analysis might suggest. By 1670, a similarly philosophically-inclined judge, Sir Matthew Hale C. J., is denying the frequency of conquest as an origin of authority and is looking assiduously for a 'consent of the governors and the governed': see his 'Reflections on Hobbes's Dialogue of the Common Law' in Holdsworth, *A History of English Law*, vol. V (London: 2nd ed., 1937), at p. 507.

IX.5

The ruler may be one, few or many (even 'all') ... Plato, *Statesman*, 291d—303d; Aristotle, *Pol.* III, 5: 1279a28; IV, 11: 1298a7—9; *Nic. Eth.* VIII, 10: 1160a32—35; 11: 1161a30; Aquinas, *De Regimine Principum*, c. 1, para. 11; Blackstone, I *Comm.*, p. 49.

Classical preference for monarchy ... The argument is simply from the need for efficiency (*not* to be contrasted here with justice) in co-ordination: Aquinas, *De Regimine Principum.* c. 2.; and the rule of one *bad* (self-interested) man ('tyrant') is the worst form of government, ibid., c. 3 (also Plato, *Statesman*, 302e—303b; Aristotle, *Nic. Eth.* VIII, 11: 1161a31—33). Plato particularly stresses that these questions about the form and number of the ruling authority are of little moment compared with questions of substance about what this authority *does*: ibid., and Voegelin, *Plato and Aristotle*, pp. 158—61.

Aristotle on citizenship as participation in government ... *Pol.* III, 1: 1275a22—24, a33, b17—22. (These pages of the *Politics* are the *locus classicus* on definition of terms in social science; and see I.3, above and XII.4, below.)

Single rulers may be bound by their own stipulations, just as members of governing assemblies are ... The argument in the text is that used by Vitoria, *De Potestate Civili*, 21.

Can laws made by a sovereign be binding upon him? ... This question is not of great practical moment in polities where governing powers are distributed amongst various persons and bodies, and the distribution is judicially supervised. Indeed, it has never been of great practical moment for lawyers, since sovereign monarchs of the sort supposed in the discussion will not lack powers of self-dispensation. But the question remains significant for uncovering basic assumptions and confusions about law and legal obligation – just as a critique of Austin's conception of law can most profitably begin by assessing the adequacy of his reason for asserting that a sovereign is legally illimitable; see *Province*, pp. 253–4. For the late scholastic ('voluntarist') view of obligation as a force whereby a *superior* by an act of will moves an *inferior* to the performance of a particular act, see Suarez, *De Legibus*, I, c. v, 24; c. iv, 7 (and see XI.8, below, and II.6, above). For the English legal doctrine that 'the King can do no wrong', see Blackstone, I *Comm.*, pp. 235–40, 243–4; esp. p. 237 'the King himself can do no wrong; since it would be a great weakness and absurdity in any system of positive law, to define any possible wrong, without any possible redress'; III *Comm.*, pp. 254–5; IV *Comm.*, p. 32.

The single ruler is under the 'directive' though not the 'coercive' obligation of the law ... The fundamental discussion is Aquinas, *S. T.* I–II, q. 96, a. 5 ('Is everybody subject to the law? Yes'), ad 3: 'A *princeps* is said to be "exempt from the law" in relation to the coercive power of law, for no-one is compelled, in the strict sense of the word, by himself (and the law only has its coercive force from the power of the *princeps*) ... But in relation to the directive authority of the law, the *princeps* is subject to the law made by his own will ... Before God's judgment, the *princeps* is not "exempt from law" in relation to its directive authority, and ought to fulfil the law freely, not under coercion (though he is above the law, in so far as he can change it if expedient, and grant dispensations from it adapted to place and season)'. The distinction is found in Bracton, *De Legibus Angliae* [*c.* 1250] I, 38 (and see Maitland, *The Constitutional History of England* [1888] (Cambridge: 1919), pp. 100–1); in Matthew Hale, *Pleas of the Crown* [*c.* 1670] (1st ed. 1736) I, 44; Hale, 'Reflections on Hobbes's Dialogue of the Common Law' [*c.* 1670], in Holdsworth, *A History of English Law*, vol. V, at pp. 507–8; and as a vestigial relic, in a discussion of 'the King can do no wrong', muddied with fiction and shifting rhetoric, in Blackstone, 1 *Comm.*, pp. 235, 237; and esp. IV *Comm.*, p. 33. For the undifferentiated proposition that the ruler should (save in extraordinary circumstances) be subject to the law, see already Plato, *Seventh Letter*, 337a, d; *Laws*, IV: 715b–d, 875d.

NOTES

1 J. Raz, *Practical Reason and Norms* (Hutchinson, London: 1975), pp. 35–48, 58–73.

2 J. Raz, *Practical Reason*, p. 172. For his account of the three types see pp. 171–7; see also his 'Promises and Obligations', in P. M. S. Hacker and J. Raz (eds), *Law, Morality and Society: Essays in Honour of H. L. A. Hart* (OUP: 1977), at p. 225.
3 J. Raz, *Practical Reason*, p. 84. 'Existential statements about norms are used for a variety of purposes, among which three are the most important. In saying that there is a norm one may state either that it is valid (that is, justified), or that it is practised, or that it has been prescribed by a certain person or body. These are the three dimensions of norms ...': p. 80.
4 Ibid., p. 10.
5 Ibid., p. 10: 'Substantive practical philosophy includes all the arguments designed to show which values we should pursue, what reasons for action should guide our behaviour, which norms are binding, etc.' See also p. 11 on 'the most important branches of practical philosophy'.
6 Ibid., p. 80.
7 Hart, *Concept of Law* (OUP: 1961), p. 203, where the 'positivist' objection here under discussion is deployed in a compact form.
8 Oppenheim, *International Law*, vol. I (8th ed., H. Lauterpacht, London: 1955), sec. 17. To like effect the International Court of Justice in the *North Sea Continental Shelf Cases, I. C. J. Rep.* 1969, p. 44.
9 Note that the relevant pattern of conduct φ may be procedural or 'framework' in nature: e.g. *negotiation of agreements*, as the appropriate and required method of settling disputed questions about (substantive) conduct in such-and-such a domain.
10 American Declaration of Independence, 1776.
11 'Beneficiaries': the *hereditas* can, however, be *damnosa*; in any event, authority is (in reason, as in modern British constitutional draftsmanship) responsibility.
12 Max Rheinstein (ed.), *Max Weber on Law in Economy and Society* (Cambridge Mass: 1954), pp. 336, xxxi: 'Indeed, the continued exercise of every domination (in our technical sense of the word) always has the strongest need of self-justification through appealing to the principles of its legitimation. Of such ultimate principles, there are only three ... (a) A domination can be legitimately valid because of its rational character: such *legal domination* rests upon the belief in the legality of a consciously created order and of the right to give commands vested in the person or persons designated by that order ...'
13 Fortescue, *De Laudibus Legum Angliae* (c. 1470), c. 12: 'Sic et Romani orbis imperium usurparunt, qualiter fere in omnibus gentibus regna inchoata sunt'.
14 Fortescue, *De Natura Legis Naturae* (c. 1463) I, c. 18 (entitled 'Lex naturae statum regium in eius initio operata est, licet iniqui eundem statum primordiarunt').

15 Thus there was sound philosophy behind the formula employed to claim jurisdiction for the Crown in British 'protectorates': 'Whereas by treaty, grant, usage, *sufferance* and other lawful means, Her Majesty has power [sc. authority] and jurisdiction in the said territories ...' (emphasis added).
16 Yves Simon, *Philosophy of Democratic Government* (Chicago: 1951), p. 151.
17 John Austin, *The Province of Jurisprudence Determined* (The Noonday Press, New York: 1954), pp. 254, 259, 279, etc.
18 *Pol.* III, 2: 1277b14–16; also III, 7: 1284a1–3.

8
Perspectives on Authority

S. LUKES

What is authority? It is an old question. Indeed, Hannah Arendt in the first *NOMOS* volume asked "what *was* authority?" somewhat nostalgically, fearing that even the answer might be lost in the mists of antiquity. But the question goes on being asked and has recently received much renewed attention from political and legal philosophers.

The question is, on the face of it, at least two questions. It could be the analytical question: what are the elements of the concept of authority and how are they structured? What are the criteria by which we may recognize the possession, exercise, and acceptance of authority? How is it to be distinguished from other forms of influence over persons and from, say, persuading, threatening, advising, and requesting? Or it could be the normative question: what is legitimate authority? What is it that renders authority legitimate? What justifies the claims of authority as being worthy of acceptance? When should utterances be treated as authoritative?

Discussions of authority divide over the issue of how the analytical question relates to the normative question. Some hold that the questions are quite distinct: that we can elucidate the concept of authority and as a separate matter ask when, if ever, submission to it is justified. They may well go on to say that this latter question is not a timeless one: that what is justified in one context and from one point of view may not be so in and from another. Others hold that the questions cannot be divorced in this way. They hold that to do so is to advance a "relativized" notion of authority, according to which "we simply state what authority is had by whom from a certain point of view"[1] and that this "severs the connection between authority and practical reason."[2] For them the nonrelativized notion is primary and is presupposed by the relativized notion. On this view of the matter, to analyze authority is to analyze legitimate or justified authority, to which different people in different times and places lay claim and submit, some rightly, some wrongly. It is on this view not a matter of meaning that a person can have authority, be an authority or in authority only if his authority is recognized by some people whose identity will vary with the nature of his authority (though in practice, especially in political contexts, it will be contingently true that such recognition will be a condition of his exercising his legitimate authority effectively). On this second approach, establishing the grounds on which an authoritative utterance should be recognized as such is prior to all empirical inquiry into beliefs and practices. On the first, it is not. Indeed, on the first view, what is authoritative will not, in any given case, be independent of a whole web of beliefs, some explicit and some implicit in practices. Of course, not anything can be a ground or reason for treating an utterance as authoritative (e.g., that it is loud – though that could be a sign that there is such a reason). But what counts as such a reason will be internal to a web of beliefs.

Both approaches, however, concur in the aim of enabling us to identify relations of authority and distinguish them from others. What I seek to suggest in this chapter is that such identification is an even more complex matter than is often supposed and always involves a process of interpretation. More particularly, I claim that every way of identifying authority is relative to one or more perspectives and is, indeed, inherently perspectival, and that there is no objective, in the sense of perspective-neutral, way of doing so. This feature of attributions of authority has, I think, been far too little attended to in the voluminous literature on the topic, including that compatible with its recognition.

Without analyzing or exploring the notion of "perspective" here,[3] I mean it to refer to a point of view, a more or less integrated set of ways of seeing and judging matters of fact and practical questions, not excluding basic moral and political questions, and incorporating beliefs about the possibilities and necessities of social life, and about how the self, its relation to society, and its manner of reasoning are to be conceived. In this domain, of course, the reality upon which perspectives bear is itself in part constituted by contending perspectives. To speak thus of perspectives is not in itself to embrace any deep form of relativism: some will be, for example, more perspicuous or comprehensive or consistent than others. Typically, different perspectives – and at what points and how much they differ will in turn be variously interpretable – are associated with different positions within a social relation (such as an authority relation), with different social and political roles (e.g., the judicial, the bureaucrat's and the citizen's perspectives) and with different activities (for example, the actor's and observer's perspectives). How to individuate perspectives is a complex question into which I can not go here. The question of whether differences of belief and judgment are variations within one perspective or demarcations between two cannot be answered in the abstract and in general. The answer will depend on the reasons for which perspectives are being discriminated. I do not of course mean to suggest that any one person ever adopts only one perspective. We all engage in multiple relations, roles, and activities and accordingly adopt and negotiate multiple perspectives.

For the purposes of what follows, I shall distinguish a number of potentially different perspectives. First, with respect to the authority relation itself, we can distinguish between the exerciser or holder of authority and those who accept or are subject to it. I shall, in the time-honored philosophical fashion, call the first A and the second B and thus speak of *perspective A* and *perspective B*. I shall call the observer (who may or may not be internal to the authority relation or to the society in which it occurs) C and his perspective *perspective C*. Authority relations generally occur within a wider framework of social norms and conventions, legal and customary. Some of these are officially and definitively interpreted by judges, courts, and representatives of the state. I will call this perspective society's official perspective or *perspective SO*. This is likely to diverge at various points from prevalent, unofficial, and informal understandings of such norms, rules, and conventions. I shall call such unofficial ways of understanding *perspective SU* — and, on the plausible assumption that these will be various and conflicting, $SU_1, SU_2 \ldots SU_n$. It is, however, often suggested that there is, in some or most societies, an underlying consensus that will be implicit in, though distinct from, SO and $SU_1 \ldots SU_n$, which may be elicited by a sensitive interpretation or reconstruction of a society's beliefs and practices. This notion of consensus has long played a role in contemporary sociology and has recently surfaced in political philosophy. It is what Michael Walzer relies on in order to determine the criteria that demarcate his "spheres of justice."[4] And it is what John Rawls supposes will result from the confrontation of a society's unreconstructed beliefs with theoretical criticism through "reflective equilibrium." Let us call this third, consensual social perspective *perspective SC*. (We can see it as an amalgam of perspectives SO and SU interpreted from perspective C.) Finally, we may postulate a putative impersonal, "objective and "archimedean" perspective from which all other perspectives may be assessed. Rawls calls it a stand-point that is "objective and also expresses our autonomy," which "enables us to be impartial, even between persons who are not contemporaries but who belong to many generations." To "see our place in society from the perspective of this position" is, he eloquently continues, "to see it *sub specie aeternitatis*: it is to regard the human situation not only from all social but from all temporal points of view." It is "the perspective of eternity" – not "a perspective from a certain place beyond the world, nor the point of view of a transcendent being; rather it is a certain form of thought and feeling that rational persons can adopt within the world."[5] Thomas Nagel calls it "a conception of the world which as far as possible is not the view from anywhere within it."[6] Let us call this perspective *perspective O*. One central question this chapter seeks to address is whether there is indeed any such perspective.

I now turn to consider some attempts to analyze the nature of authority. All mark out a distinctive mode of securing compliance which combines in a peculiar way power over others and the exercise of reason. On the one hand, authority appears to be part of that network of control concepts that includes power, coercion, force, manipulation, persuasion, etc. As Hobbes said, "command is a precept in which the cause of the obedience depends on the will of the commander" and "the will stands for the reason." Even authority over belief appears to involve an influence that bypasses rational argument. On the other hand, reason is plainly involved: authority offers a reason and operates through reasoning. Moreover, only rational agents are capable of claiming, recognizing and accepting authority. As Friedrich observed, it involves "a very particular kind of relationship to reason," namely "the potentiality of reasoned elaboration."[7]

I shall first consider three accounts exemplifying the first, "relativized" approach presented above, in order to illustrate the different perspectives that they exemplify. I shall then turn to a further account that illustrates the second approach in order to show that even an account that explicitly seeks to avoid perspective dependence fails and must fail to do so.

Consider first Max Weber's celebrated account of authority. Weber was, of course, concerned with *Herrschaft*, or domination, but he was interested specifically in "the authoritarian power of command," as against "domination by virtue of a constellation of interests (in particular by virtue of a position of monopoly)." Domination in Weber's preferred sense indicated the securing of compliance which occurs "as if the ruled had made the content of the command the maxim of their conduct for its very own sake."[8] He wrote,

> The merely external fact of the order being obeyed is not sufficient to signify domination in our sense; we cannot overlook the meaning of the fact that the command is accepted as a "valid" norm.[9]

Of course, Weber was well aware that commands may be obeyed for a wide variety of reasons: "the command may have achieved its effect upon the ruled either through empathy or through inspiration or through persuasion by rational argument or through some combination of these three principal types of influence of one person over another."[10] Indeed,

> In a concrete case the performance of a command may have been motivated by the ruled's own conviction of its propriety, or by his sense of duty, or by fear, or by "dull" custom, or by a desire to obtain some benefit for himself.[11]

Yet it is a striking fact that Weber's sociology of domination never explores these possibilities by investigating the question "When and why do men obey?" or looks at authority relations from below, that is, from perspective B. On the contrary, his classification of authority is exclusively from perspective A, in terms of prevailing rationales for obedience – claims typically made by those in command. As Parkin observes, Weber never asks "whether the legitimations put out by traditional, charismatic and legal-rational authorities differed in the degree to which they were actually endorsed by the masses."[12] On the contrary, he proceeds throughout "as though widespread endorsement of all three types of legitimation was typically found among all and sundry." It is "as if Weber simply assumed the correctness of Marx's dictum that the prevailing ideas in any society are the ideas of its ruling class."[13] I suspect this may be because Weber, as a cynical "realist" concerning power, and despite his talk of the "voluntary" acceptance of maxims, basically saw prevailing principles of legitimation (especially democratic ones) as "myths" injected into the masses by elites. At all events, the Weberian approach, while offering an illuminating classification of authority claims, succeeds in identifying authority relations by only taking account of perspective A. Authority on this view is the securing of compliance by command on the basis of claims, of the three indicated types, assumed to be accepted by the commanded.

Consider next the illuminating analysis of the authority relation offered by Richard Friedman, as consisting in two tiers: first, "that special and distinctive kind of dependence on the will or judgment of another so well conveyed by the notion of a 'surrender of private judgment'"; and second, "the recognition and acceptance of certain criteria for designating who is to possess this kind of influence."[14] This analysis is intended to cover both the cases of "an authority" and "in authority."

In both cases, "we have to see the notion of authority in connection with the idea of a very special sort of reason for action (or belief)"; one difference being that "belief in authority calls for internal assent, whereas the notion of acting in conformity to the commands of authority allows for the dissociation of thought and action."[15]

A claim to the former, Friedman suggests, rests on the ground of "superior knowledge or insight, that makes belief, and not merely external conformity, the appropriate response to authority."[16] It presupposes an inequality of knowledge, insight, or wisdom prior to the authority relation itself; and it presupposes the epistemological claim that such superior knowledge, insight or wisdom is in principle available. It presupposes, in short, "a world of common beliefs and the recognition of inequality in the capacity of men to understand those beliefs."[17]

By contrast, the relation of those "in authority" to those who defer to them presupposes a world in which there is "a complex *recognition* of dissensus and equality at the substantive level over against which men are prepared to step up to the procedural level and abide by the decisions of the person designated as being 'in authority,' whether or not those decisions happen to coincide with their 'private' opinions."[18] Indeed, authority serves to mark off the distinction between private and public in this sense. Such authority is a response to a "predicament" in which "a collection of individuals wish to engage in some common activity requiring a certain degree of coordinated action but they are unable to agree on what the substance of their common behavior should be."[19]

In general, according to Friedman, both forms of authority imply "some mutually recognized relationship giving the one the right to command or speak and the other the duty to obey. Authority thus involves a form of influence that can only be exercised from within a certain kind of normative arrangement accepted by both parties."[20]

Friedman's account is decidedly an improvement on Weber's. It hinges on the notion of mutual recognition: what is essential is that perspectives A and B agree in "a certain kind of 'recognition' that the person to whom one defers is entitled to this sort of submission."[21] Legitimation claimed and the according of legitimacy coincide in a shared recognition of entitlement. That recognition may be based on a very wide range of possible "marks" or credentials of authority – "office, social station, property, 'great' power, pedigree, religious claims, 'miracles' (Augustine) etc."[22]

A number of problems are raised by this account. Less seriously, it seems obvious that many cases of "an authority" over belief need not involve mutual recognition of that authority; such authorities can go unrecognized and they can be seen as authorities unwittingly or posthumously. Similarly, persons "in authority" may sometimes properly be said to have it even if those subject to it fail to endorse it, as parents and teachers know well. Second, Friedman's discussion of the "marks" of authority does not successfully distinguish between *signs* and *grounds*: the crown and scepter are the former, the regal office they betoken the latter. But two more serious problems arise. First, what are the criteria by which these "marks" are recognized as marks of authority? Is it just up to the parties in an authority relationship to fix on anyone they wish to recognize as authoritative? And second, what is the nature of that recognition? Is it like a "cue" triggering off "blind obedience" and the "surrender of judgment?" Or is a process of rational judgment involved?

These last two questions are addressed by the third account we will consider, namely that of Richard Flathman. He answers the first by placing the authority relation within a wider "practice" of authority in which shared values and beliefs prevalent in a community play a constitutive part. And he answers the second by firmly resisting the notion of a "surrender of private judgment," maintaining this notion to be "at the very least, seriously misleading."[23]

For Flathman, both "in authority" and "an authority" relations are "grounded in shared values and beliefs to which we are referring as the authoritative":[24] the "partly constitutive character of the values, beliefs, actions and so forth of subscribers ... to a set of rules, institutions, etc." is "a central feature of our entire theory of authority."[25] But how are these to be identified and just how do they bear on the authority relation? Sometimes, Flathman seems to be referring to perspective SO, as when he, rather oddly, assumes that "the values and beliefs which make up Marxism-Leninism are now among the constitutive features" of the practice of authority in the Soviet Union.[26] Sometimes, he seems to be referring to SU, without any real sensitivity to the systematic divergences it embraces – as when, rather baldly, he remarks that "if we are trying to determine whether Ivan had authority in sixteenth-century Russia we must ascertain the criteria that had standing among sixteenth-century Russians and we must determine whether sixteenth-century Russians thought those criteria were satisfied."[27] Sometimes, as when discussing the shared values and beliefs of modern liberal democracies, as allowing for disagreement and the practice of civil disobedience, he seems to be embracing a version of perspective SC.

But a further and deeper problem is raised by his rejection of the notion of the surrender of private judgment and his insistence that participants in the practice of authority are making "judgments grounded in evidence and reason," that there is within the authoritative "a basis both for grounded, reasoned judgments concerning it and for grounded reasoned disagreements concerning those judgments"[28] and his call for a "critical justificatory theory of authority."[29] Do such judgments transcend the confines of prevailing authoritative beliefs and values? Or, to make the same point conversely, does the "authoritative" in part determine what counts as convincing "evidence or a good reason? What kind of a constraint does "evidence and reason" place upon the constitutive character of the "authoritative?" Flathman rejects what he calls "collectivistic subjectivism" but we need to know more about why he does so.

So I turn finally to an account of authority that fearlessly avoids such dangers and temptations by offering a straightforwardly rationalist "critical justificatory theory of authority" on the assumption that this can be done independently of and prior to any "relativized" way of conceiving it, while acknowledging that "the relativized notion is useful because it reveals the views of people or societies concerning non-relativized authority."[30] The account in question is that developed in a number of writings by Joseph Raz. I shall refer here to his 1979 book *The Authority of Law* and to his 1985 article "The Justification of Authority"[31] in which the relation between authority and reason and the justification of authority are systematically explored.

Raz, starting from the "basic insight" that "authority is ability to change reasons for action,"[32] sees authority as "a species of normative power" which changes such reasons by exclusion. Thus, orders are both first-order reasons (for acting) and "exclusionary reasons" which "exclude by kind and not by weight": their impact is "not to change the balance of reasons but to exclude action on the balance of reasons."[33] Accepting authority involves "giving up one's right to act on one's judgment on the balance of reasons";[34] the authority is legitimate if such exclusionary reasons are valid.

When, then, is authority legitimate? What renders its exclusionary reasons valid? Raz advances what he calls the "dependence thesis," namely that *"All authoritative directives should be based, in the main, on reasons which already independently apply to the subjects of the directives and are relevant to their action in the circumstances covered by the directive."*[35] The "normal" and "primary" way to show that one person should be acknowledged to have authority over another is given by what he calls the "normal justification thesis": it is to show *"that the alleged subject is likely better to comply with reasons which apply to him (other than the alleged authoritative directives) if he accepts the directives of the alleged authority as authoritatively binding and tries to follow them, rather than by trying to follow the reasons which apply to him directly."*[36] These reasons need not be confined to the furthering of his interests (as when a military officer orders soldiers to defend their country, against their personal interests). Other justifications for accepting authority — such as consent, or respect for the law, or identification with a community — are merely secondary. They are valid only if they accompany the primary reason. Typical of situations where the normal justification holds are those presenting coordination problems, including prisoner's dilemma type situations. Indeed, Raz argues, solving coordination problems is one of the important tasks of political and many other practical authorities. The key idea (especially in relation to politics) is what Raz calls "the service conception of the function of authorities" — namely, that "their role and primary normal function is to serve the governed," which they do when they "help them act on reasons which bind them."[37]

Raz's attempt is to "explain the notion of legitimate authority through describing what one might call an ideal exercise of authority." It is through their "ideal functioning" that the practice of authorities must be understood. This is given by how they publicly claim that they attempt to function, which is "the normal way to justify their authority."[38]

This is an unwarrantably rapid summary of Raz's complex account, which is the most perspicuous analysis of the concept to date and the most systematic attempt I know of to escape the problems we have been investigating, by presenting an analysis of authority relations that purports explicitly not to be an account of "what authority is had by whom from a certain point of view."[39] Does it do so?

I doubt it. For Raz, "the normal and primary way of justifying the legitimacy of an authority is that it is more likely to act successfully on the reasons which apply to its subjects",[40] accepting legitimate authority offers the advantage of having found "a more reliable and successful guide to right reason."[41] But how are we to ascertain what the reasons that apply to authority's subjects are and in what "success" in acting on them or guiding us to them consists?

There is a whole range of cases where the answers to these questions seem obvious and uncontroversial. The traffic policeman, the tax authorities, legislators, judges, military officers, parents can all be seen as "in the main," at least in certain areas, directing us to act on reasons that independently apply to us, so that we may properly see them as having the right to replace people's own judgment on the merits of the case. Of course the legitimacy of such authorities is (in perhaps ascending order of frequency) questioned, on particular occasions, over whole ranges of cases, and (as with anarchists, pacifists, and revolutionaries) in general. It may be questioned in various ways. They may be held to have a false or misconceived idea of the "reasons which apply to [their] subjects." Lawmakers and judges may be denounced for being out of touch with the interests and needs of those they purport or are claimed to protect and guide (as they have been by blacks in the US or opponents of abortion). Military leaders may appeal to duties and commitments that both soldiers and citizens reject (as in the US during the Vietnam War or Israel during the later stages of the invasion of Lebanon). Secondly, the legitimacy of authorities may be questioned on grounds of "reliability" and "success," the reasons applying to their subjects being taken as given. Corrupt policemen and incompetent military regimes (rarely) lose their legitimacy in this way. But either way, Raz would probably argue, questioning the legitimacy of particular authorities, even in general, in these ways does not show that they would not be legitimate if the conditions set by the normal justification thesis were to be met.

I fail to see how the reasons that apply to authority's subjects, on which authoritative directives should be based, are to be ascertained in a perspective-neutral manner. The objectives an authority is to further are not determinable a priori and are often matters of intense controversy. On the other hand, it is plausible to suggest that, once such objectives are agreed, the question of a given authority's "reliability" and "success" (like that of an investment consultant) could be seen as a matter of fact. Yet even this is not obvious. What is being judged: the institution or its agents, and over what period of time? Raz's phrase "in the main" leaves leeway here too for judgment and interpretive dispute.

The sorts of cases we have considered are plainly those on which this account of legitimate authority is centrally based and to which it is most obviously applicable. The most obviously applicable cases are those in which authority establishes or helps sustain conventions, seen as solutions to coordination problems, or enables people to escape prisoner's dilemma type situations. More generally, this account works best for all those cases where there is what we might call an extrinsic relation between authoritative directives and reasons they depend on and replace. Authority on this view is an invaluable device to achieve, more reliably and successfully, independently given and agreed objectives that would otherwise be less easy or impossible to attain. Even here, as we have seen, there is much room for interpretive dispute as to which objectives are relevant and what constitutes success.

But what of cases where the relation between authority and reason is intrinsic: where the objectives authority serves are internal to, that is shaped and sustained by, the authority relation itself. The examples that come most naturally to mind here are religious, though the point is far wider than that. The role of the priesthood is, in part, to lead men along the path of righteousness or truth, as it is interpreted by the priesthood — to show the way to destinations that people might not have conceived apart from it (that is, apart from the institution and tradition it embodies) — and may not even be characterizable without presupposing it (e.g., living according to the Torah). The fundamentalist preacher, say, and his congregation are in a relationship of self-reinforcing authority, in which the word of God (as he interprets its expression in the Bible) gives them reasons for actions concerning which he is, in turn, the authoritative guide.

Religious examples demonstrate this intrinsic relation with clarity. Here the "primary normal function" of authority is not always best described as "serving the governed." Of course, religions often do have instrumental functions, promising (as magic typically does) to bring benefits in the here and now or (more probably) in the hereafter. But they also have soteriological functions and Durkheimian social functions, both of which involved *transforming* rather than serving their adherents — by leading them to salvation, imbuing them with faith, giving meaning to their lives, and so on. In such cases, the legitimacy of authority does not lie in its reliability and success in securing independently given objectives, as measured against some objective standard, since it itself defines the objectives and sets the standard. And this applies, beyond religious cases, to all cases of intrinsic authority, where Raz's picture of an exclusionary reason justifiably preempting the balance of reasons does not really fit. A better picture might be that of a dominant reason that reduces the significance of other reasons that would otherwise prevail, and removes the point of weighing them. Thus (to take disparate examples at random): charismatic leaders define their followers' goals, their legitimacy resting on "the belief in and devotion to the extraordinary, which is valued because it goes beyond the normal human qualities" and "transvalues everything";[42] the Party prescribes certain objectives as primary; psychoanalysts (on one view of what they do) transform their patient's self-understanding; women exhibit patriarchal attitudes. In all these cases, it seems that if authority is justified, it is justified from a point of view, namely that of the authority itself, which becomes that of the subject.

It may, of course, be replied that only extrinsic authority is legitimate: only if putative authorities guide their subjects extrinsically to "right reasons" can their claims be justified. In this case, we are owed a doctrine of "right reason," indicating which *are* the "reasons which bind them." Moreover, it is not clear why, on principle, this reply should be given. Are there no cases of legitimate intrinsic authority? More generally, it may be suggested that the analysis proposed is, in principle, neutral between different perspective-dependent accounts within which different reasons, or sorts of reasons, can be judged to be "right reasons." This suggestion would bring Raz's analysis much closer to the position this paper seeks to advocate, since it leaves the answer to the question. When is authority legitimate? perspective-dependent. However, for the reason indicated in the previous paragraph, it is not clear that the analysis itself, with its "service conception" of authority's function, successfully captures the nature of authority as understood in all contexts and cultures.

We are, it is clear, back to the problem with which we began. We are offered a test by which claims to authority that are imposed (à la Weber), mutually recognized (à la Friedman) or culturally given (à la Flathman) are to be judged genuine or spurious. Could such a test be perspective-neutral?

The very idea of such a test is central to our cultural tradition. Since the Enlightenment, we have believed that some such test should be available, distinguishing "right" from spurious reasons, autonomy from heteronomy, self- from other-directedness, and providing a bedrock for practical judgment. This strand of our tradition is deeply hostile to priestly power, paternalism, and mystifying ideologies of all kinds. Basic to it is the image of an autonomous rational individual. Consider now the metaphor at the heart of Raz's account. "Exclusionary reasons," excluding by kind rather than changing the balance of reasons, conjure up the old image of the scales of justice, and therewith an underlying and specific conception of the subject of authority. It suggests, in a word, a distinctly judicial conception of the individual, weighing and balancing, in an impartial spirit, the reasons that present themselves, in order to reach an independent judgment as to what to do or think "all things considered" – but on occasion allowing "binding" reasons to prevail. Yet this picture of the individual is not unique. Other pictures exist to which other styles of reasoning are central[43] – Talmudic, Confucian, Buddhist, etc. – whose relevance to the testing of authority claims merits investigation. Indeed, the thought suggests itself that Raz's aspiration to perspective-neutrality shapes his very notion of the subject, and that this aspiration and notion are no less perspective-dependent than any other.

Indeed, Raz freely admits that his argument is "inescapably a normative argument," "part of an attempt to make explicit elements of our common traditions," a "partisan" account "furthering the cause of certain strands in the common tradition by developing new or newly recast arguments in their favor."[44] The critical justificatory theory of authority he develops is true to "our" concept of authority and behind it to "our" notion of the reasoning subject. It offers a test for legitimacy that is tailor-made for Friedman's "second world," riven by conflicting interests and opinions but with a shared interest in the procedural resolution of coordination problems. It is, unquestionably, worth defending and propagating, in a world in which authoritarian and obscurantist notions of authority are rife and growing. But it is, while compelling, "our" view, gaining its plausibility from the web of beliefs in which it is embedded. For this reason, I agree with Flathman's suggestion that "caution is appropriate in positing – as for example Joseph Raz does – a 'non-relativized' notion of authority that is a presupposition of the 'relativized' notions we in fact find among this or that historical people."[45]

NOTES

1 J. Raz, *The Authority of Law* (Oxford: Oxford University Press, 1979), p. 11.

2 Ibid. Cf. Hannah Pitkin, *Wittgenstein and Justice* (Berkeley: University of California Press, 1972), pp. 280 ff.
3 See my "Relativism in Its Place," in M. Hollis and S. Lukes, eds, *Rationality and Relativism* (Cambridge: MIT Press, 1982).
4 M. Walzer, *Spheres of Justice* (New York: Basic Books, 1983).
5 J. Rawls, *A Theory of Justice* (Cambridge: Harvard University Press, 1972), p. 587.
6 T. Nagel, *Mortal Questions* (Cambridge: Cambridge University Press, 1979), p. 208.
7 C. J. Friedrich, "Authority, Reason and Discretion," in C. J. Friedrich, ed., *NOMOS I: Authority* (Cambridge: Harvard University Press, 1958). p. 35
8 Max Weber, *Economy and Society*, ed. G. Roth and C. Wittich, 2 vols. (Berkeley: University of California Press, 1978), pp. 943, 946.
9 Ibid., p. 946.
10 Ibid.
11 Ibid., pp. 946–7.
12 F. Parkin, *Max Weber* (London: Methuen, 1982), p. 78.
13 Ibid.
14 Richard B. Friedman, "On the Concept of Authority in Political Philosophy," in R. Flathman, ed., *Concepts in Social and Political Philosophy* (New York: Macmillan, 1973), pp. 131, 134.
15 Ibid., p. 135.
16 Ibid., p. 143.
17 Ibid., p. 146.
18 Ibid., pp. 145–6.
19 Ibid., p. 140.
20 Ibid., p. 134.
21 Ibid., p. 131.
22 Ibid., p. 133.
23 Richard E. Flathman, *The Practice of Political Authority* (Chicago: University of Chicago Press, 1980), p. 124.
24 Ibid., p. 26.
25 Ibid., p. 231–2.
26 Ibid., p. 87.
27 Ibid., p. 228.
28 Ibid., p. 234.
29 Ibid., p. 232.
30 J. Raz, *The Authority of Law*, p. 11.
31 J. Raz, "The Justification of Authority," in *Philosophy and Public Affairs* 14 (Winter 1985): 2–29.
32 J. Raz, *The Authority of Law*, p. 16.
33 Ibid., pp. 22, 23.
34 Ibid., p. 26. However, "there is no reason for anyone to restrain their thoughts or their reflections on the reasons which apply to the case" ("The Justification of Authority," p. 10) and one may always challenge a putatively authoritative directive on jurisdictional grounds by questioning whether it has violated the conditions of its rightful power.

35 J. Raz, "The Justification of Authority," p. 14.
36 Ibid., p. 19.
37 Ibid., p. 21.
38 Ibid., p. 27.
39 J. Raz, *The Authority of Law*, p. 11.
40 J. Raz, "The Justification of Authority," p. 20.
41 Ibid., p. 25.
42 H. H. Gerth and C. Wright Mills, *From Max Weber: Essays in Sociology* (New York: Oxford University Press, 1948), pp. 296, 250.
43 See M. Carrithers, S. Collins and S. Lukes, eds, *The Category of the Person: Anthropology, Philosophy, History* (New York: Cambridge University Press, 1985).
44 J. Raz, "The Justification of Authority," p. 27.
45 R. Flathman, *The Practice of Political Authority*, p. 77.

9
Obligations of Community

R. M. DWORKIN

THE PUZZLE OF LEGITIMACY

We now turn to the direct connection between integrity and the moral authority of the law. The concept of law – the plateau where argument among conceptions is most useful – connects law with the justification of official coercion. A conception of law must explain how what it takes to be law provides a general justification for the exercise of coercive power by the state, a justification that holds except in special cases when some competing argument is specially powerful. Each conception's organizing center is the explanation it offers of this justifying force. Every conception therefore faces the same threshold problem. How can *anything* provide even that general form of justification for coercion in ordinary politics? What can ever give anyone the kind of authorized power over another that politics supposes governors have over the governed? Why does the fact that a majority elects a particular regime, for example, give that regime legitimate power over those who voted against it?

This is the classical problem of the legitimacy of coercive power. It rides on the back of another classical problem: that of political obligation. Do citizens have genuine moral obligations just in virtue of law? Does the fact that a legislature has enacted some requirement in itself give citizens a moral as well as a practical reason to obey? Does that moral reason hold even for those citizens who disapprove of the legislation or think it wrong in principle? If citizens do not have moral obligations of that character, then the state's warrant for coercion is seriously, perhaps fatally, undermined. These two issues – whether the state is morally legitimate, in the sense that it is justified in using force against its citizens, and whether the state's decisions impose genuine obligations on them – are not identical. No state should enforce all of a citizen's obligations. But though obligation is not a sufficient condition for coercion, it is close to a necessary one. A state may have good grounds in some special circumstances for coercing those who have no duty to obey. But no general policy of upholding the law with steel could be justified if the law were not, in general, a source of genuine obligations.

A state is legitimate if its constitutional structure and practices are such that its citizens have a general obligation to obey political decisions that purport to impose duties on them. An argument for legitimacy need only provide reasons for that general situation. It need not show that a government, legitimate in that sense, therefore has moral authority to do anything it wants to its citizens, or that they are obligated to obey every decision it makes. I shall argue that a state that accepts integrity as a political ideal has a better case for legitimacy than one that does not. If that is so, it provides a strong reason of the sort we have just now been seeking, a reason why we would do well to see our political practices as grounded in that virtue. It provides, in particular, a strong argument for a conception of law that takes integrity to be fundamental, because any conception must explain why law is legitimate authority for coercion. Our claims for integrity are thus tied into our main project of finding an attractive conception of law.

Tacit Consent

Philosophers make several kinds of arguments for the legitimacy of modern democracies. One argument uses the idea of a social contract, but we must not confuse it with arguments that use that idea to establish the character or content of justice. John Rawls, for example, proposes an imaginary social contract as a device for selecting the best conception of justice in the circumstances of utopian political theory. He argues that under specified conditions of uncertainty everyone would choose certain principles of justice as in his interests, properly understood, and he says that these principles are therefore the right principles for us.[1] Whatever we may think of his suggestion, it has no direct connection to our present problem of legitimacy in the circumstances of ordinary politics where Rawls's principles of justice are very far from dominion. It would be very different, of course, if every citizen were a party to an actual, historical agreement to accept and obey political decisions taken in the way his community's political decisions are in fact taken. Then the historical fact of agreement would provide at least a good prima facie case for coercion even in ordinary politics. So some political philosophers have been tempted to say that we have in fact agreed to a social contract of that kind tacitly, by just not emigrating when we reach the age of consent. But no one can argue that very long with a straight face. Consent cannot be binding on people, in the way this argument requires, unless it is given more freely, and with more genuine alternate choice, than just by declining to build a life from nothing under a foreign flag. And even if the consent were genuine, the argument would fail as an argument for legitimacy, because a person leaves one sovereign only to join another; he has no choice to be free from sovereigns altogether.

The Duty to Be Just

Rawls argues that people in his original position would recognize a natural duty to support institutions that meet the tests of abstract justice and that they would extend this duty to the support of institutions not perfectly just, at least when the sporadic injustice lay in decisions reached by fair, majoritarian institutions.[2] Even those who reject Rawls's general method might accept the duty to support just or nearly just institutions. That duty, however, does not provide a good explanation of legitimacy, because it does not tie political obligation sufficiently tightly to the particular community to which those who have the obligation belong; it does not show why Britons have any special duty to support the institutions of Britain. We can construct a practical, contingent argument for the special duty. Britons have more opportunity to aid British institutions than those of other nations whose institutions they also think mainly just. But this practical argument fails to capture the intimacy of the special duty. It fails to show how legitimacy flows from and defines citizenship. This objection points away from justice, which is conceptually universalistic, and toward integrity, which is already more personal in its different demands on different communities, as the parent of legitimacy.

Fair Play

The most popular defense of legitimacy is the argument from fair play:[3] if someone has received benefits under a standing political organization, then he has an obligation to bear the burdens of that organization as well, including an obligation to accept its political decisions, whether or not he has solicited these benefits or has in any more active way consented to these burdens. This argument avoids the fantasy of the argument from consent and the universality and other defects of the argument from a natural duty of justice and might therefore seem a stronger rival to my suggestion that legitimacy is best grounded in integrity. But it is vulnerable to two counterarguments that have frequently been noticed. First, the fair play argument assumes that people can incur obligations simply by receiving what they do not seek and would reject if they had the chance. This seems unreasonable. Suppose a philosopher broadcasts a stunning and valuable lecture from a sound truck. Do all those who hear it — even all those who enjoy and profit by it — owe him a lecture fee?[4]

Second, the fair play argument is ambiguous in a crucial respect. In what sense does it suppose that people benefit from political organization? The most natural answer is this: someone benefits from a political organization if his overall situation — his "welfare" in the way economists use that phrase — is superior under that organization to what it would otherwise be. But everything then turns on the benchmark to be used, on what "otherwise" means, and when we try to specify the benchmark we reach a dead end. The principle is plainly too strong — it justifies nothing — if it requires showing that each citizen is better off under the standing political system than he would be under any other system that might have developed in its place. For that can never be shown for all the citizens the principle is meant to embrace. And it is plainly too weak — it is too easy to satisfy and therefore justifies too much — if it requires showing only that each citizen is better off under the standing organization than he would be with no social or political organization at all, that is, under a Hobbesian state of nature.

We can deflect this second objection if we reject the "natural" interpretation I described of the crucial idea of benefit. Suppose we understand the argument in a different way: it assumes not that each citizen's welfare, judged in some politically neutral way, has been improved *by* a particular social or political organization, but that each has received the benefits *of* that organization. That is, that he has actually received what is due him according to the standards of justice and fairness on which it is constructed. The principle of fair play, understood that way, states at least a condition necessary to legitimacy. If a community does not aim to treat someone as an equal, even according to its own lights, then its claim to his political obligation is fatally compromised. But it remains unclear how the negative fact that society has not discriminated against someone in this way, according to its own standards, could supply any positive reason why he should accept its laws as obligations. Indeed, the first objection I described becomes more powerful yet if we make this response to the second. For now the argument from fair play must be understood as claiming, not that someone incurs an obligation when his welfare is improved in a way he did not seek, but that he incurs an obligation by being treated in a way that might not even improve his welfare over any appropriate benchmark. For there is nothing in the fact that some individual has been treated fairly by his community according to its own standards that guarantees him any further, more material advantage.

OBLIGATIONS OF COMMUNITY

Circumstances and Conditions

Is it true that no one can be morally affected by being given what he does not ask for or choose to have? We will think so if we consider only cases of benefits thrust upon us by strangers like philosophers in sound trucks. Our convictions are quite different, however, when we have in mind obligations that are often called obligations of role but that I shall call, generically, associative or communal obligations. I mean the special responsibilities social practice attaches to membership in some biological or social group, like the responsibilities of family or friends or neighbors. Most people think that they have associative obligations just by belonging to groups defined by social practice, which is not necessarily a matter of choice or consent, but that they can lose these obligations if other members of the group do not extend them the benefits of belonging to the group. These common assumptions about associative responsibilities suggest that political obligation might be counted among them, in which case the two objections to the argument from fair play would no longer be pertinent. On the whole, however, philosophers have ignored this possibility, I believe for two reasons. First, communal obligations are widely thought to depend upon emotional bonds that presuppose that each member of the group has personal acquaintance of all others, which of course cannot be true in large political communities. Second, the idea of special communal responsibilities holding within a large, anonymous community smacks of nationalism, or even racism, both of which have been sources of very great suffering and injustice.

We should therefore reflect on the character of familiar associative obligations to see how far these apparent objections actually hold. Associative obligations are complex, and much less studied by philosophers than the kinds of personal obligations we incur through discrete promises and other deliberate acts. But they are an important part of the moral landscape: for most people, responsibilities to family and lovers and friends and union or office colleagues are the most important, the most consequential obligations of all. The history of social practice defines the communal groups to which we belong and the obligations that attach to these. It defines what a family or a neighborhood or a professional colleague is, and what one member of these groups or holder of these titles owes to another. But social practice defines groups and obligations not by the fiat of ritual, not through the explicit extension of conventions, but in the more complex way brought in with the interpretive attitude. The concepts we use to describe these groups and to claim or reject these obligations are interpretive concepts; people can sensibly argue in the interpretive way about what friendship really is and about what children really owe their parents in old age. The raw data of how friends typically treat one another are no more conclusive of an argument about the obligations of friendship than raw data were conclusive for arguments about courtesy in the community I imagined or for arguments about law for us.

Suppose we tried to compose, not just an interpretation of a single associative practice, like family or friendship or neighborhood, but a more abstract interpretation of the yet more general practice of associative obligation itself. I cannot carry that project very far here or develop any deep and thorough study of that abstract practice. But even a quick survey shows that we cannot account for the general practice if we accept the principle many philosophers have found so appealing, that no one can have special obligations to particular people except by choosing to accept these. The connection we recognize between communal obligation and choice is much more complex and more a matter of degree that varies from one form of communal association to another. Even associations we consider mainly consensual, like friendship, are not formed in one act of deliberate contractual commitment, the way one joins a club, but instead develop through a series of choices and events that are never seen, one by one, as carrying a commitment of that kind.

We have friends to whom we owe obligations in virtue of a shared history, but it would be perverse to describe this as a history of *assuming* obligations. On the contrary, it is a history of events and acts that *attract* obligations, and we are rarely even aware that we are entering upon any special status as the story unfolds. People become self-conscious about the obligations of friendship in the normal case only when some situation requires them to honor these obligations, or when they have grown weary of or embarrassed by the friendship, and then it is too late to reject them without betrayal. Other forms of association that carry special responsibilities – of academic colleagueship, for example – are even less a matter of free choice: someone can become my colleague even though I voted against his appointment. And the obligations some members of a family owe to others, which many people count among the strongest fraternal obligations of all, are matters of the least choice.[5]

We must therefore account for associative obligations, if we accept these at all, in the different way I suggested a moment ago in describing how most people think of them. We have a duty to honor our responsibilities under social practices that define groups and attach special responsibilities to membership, but this natural duty holds only when certain other conditions are met or sustained. Reciprocity is prominent among these other conditions. I have special responsibilities to my brother in virtue of our brotherhood, but these are sensitive to the degree to which he accepts such responsibilities toward me; my responsibilities to those who claim that we are friends or lovers or neighbors or colleagues or countrymen are equally contingent on reciprocity. But we must be careful here: if associative concepts are interpretive – if it can be an open question among friends what friendship requires – then the reciprocity we demand cannot be a matter of each doing for the other what the latter thinks friendship concretely requires. Then friendship would be possible only between people who shared a detailed conception of friendship and would become automatically more contractual and deliberative than it is, more a matter of people checking in advance to see whether their conceptions matched well enough to allow them to be friends.[6]

The reciprocity we require for associative obligations must be more abstract, more a question of accepting a kind of responsibility we need the companion ideas of integrity and interpretation to explain. Friends have a responsibility to treat one another as friends, and that means, put subjectively, that each must act out of a conception of friendship he is ready to recognize as vulnerable to an interpretive test, as open to the objection that this is not a plausible account of what friendship means in our culture. Friends or family or neighbors need not agree in detail about the responsibilities attached to these forms of organization. Associative obligations can be sustained among people who share a general and diffuse sense of members' special rights and responsibilities from or toward one another, a sense of what sort and level of sacrifice one may be expected to make for another. I may think friendship, properly understood, requires that I break promises to others to help a friend in need, and I will not refuse to do this for a friend just because he does not share this conviction and would not do it for me. But I will count him a friend and feel this obligation only if I believe he has roughly the same concern for me as I thereby show for him, that he would make important sacrifices for me of some other sort.

Nevertheless, the members of a group must by and large hold certain attitudes about the responsibilities they owe one another if these responsibilities are to count as genuine fraternal obligations. First, they must regard the group's obligations as *special*, holding distinctly within the group, rather than as general duties its members owe equally to persons outside it. Second, they must accept that these responsibilities are *personal*: that they run directly from each member to each other member, not just to the group as a whole in some collective sense. My brother or my colleague may think he has responsibilities to the reputation of the family or the university he best acquits by concentrating on his own career and thus denying me help when I need it or company when I want it. He may be right about the best use of his time overall from the standpoint of the general good of these particular communities. But his conduct does not form the necessary basis for my continuing to recognize fraternal obligations toward him.

Third, members must see these responsibilities as flowing from a more general responsibility each has of *concern* for the well-being of others in the group; they must treat discrete obligations that arise only under special circumstances, like the obligation to help a friend who is in great financial need, as derivative from and expressing a more general responsibility active throughout the association in different ways. A commercial partnership or joint enterprise, conceived as a fraternal association, is in that way different from even a long-standing contractual relationship. The former has a life of its own: each partner is concerned not just to keep explicit agreements hammered out at arm's length but to approach each issue that arises in their joint commercial life in a manner reflecting special concern for his partner as partner. Different forms of association presuppose different kinds of general concern each member is assumed to have for others. The level of concern is different — I need not act toward my partner as if I thought his welfare as important as my son's — and also its range: my concern for my union "brother" is general across the economic and productive life we share but does not extend to his success in social life, as my concern for my biological brother does. (Of course my union colleague may be my friend as well, in which case my overall responsibilities to him will be aggregative and complex.) But within the form or mode of life constituted by a communal practice, the concern must be general and must provide the foundation for the more discrete responsibilities.

Fourth, members must suppose that the group's practices show not only concern but an *equal* concern for all members. Fraternal associations are in that sense conceptually egalitarian. They may be structured, even hierarchical, in the way a family is, but the structure and hierarchy must reflect the group's assumption that its roles and rules are equally in the interests of all, that no one's life is more important than anyone else's. Armies may be fraternal organizations if that condition is met. But caste systems that count some members as inherently less worthy than others are not fraternal and yield no communal responsibilities.

We must be careful to distinguish, then, between a "bare" community, a community that meets the genetic or geographical or other historical conditions identified by social practice as capable of constituting a fraternal community, and a "true" community, a bare community whose practices of group responsibility meet the four conditions just identified. The responsibilities a true community deploys are special and individualized and display a pervasive mutual concern that fits a plausible conception of equal concern. These are not psychological conditions. Though a group will rarely meet or long sustain them unless its members by and large actually feel some emotional bond with one another, the conditions do not themselves demand this. The concern they require is an interpretive property of the group's practices of asserting and acknowledging responsibilities — these must be practices that people with the right level of concern would adopt — not a psychological property of some fixed number of the actual members. So, contrary to the assumption that seemed to argue against assimilating political to associative obligations, associative communities can be larger and more anonymous than they could be if it were a necessary condition that each member love all others, or even that they know them or know who they are.

Nor does anything in the four conditions contradict our initial premise that obligations of fraternity need not be fully voluntary.

If the conditions are met, people in the bare community have the obligations of a true community whether or not they want them, though of course the conditions will not be met unless most members recognize and honor these obligations. It is therefore essential to insist that true communities must be bare communities as well. People cannot be made involuntary "honorary" members of a community to which they do not even "barely" belong just because other members are disposed to treat them as such. I would not become a citizen of Fiji if people there decided for some reason to treat me as one of them. Nor am I the friend of a stranger sitting next to me on a plane just because he decides he is a friend of mine.

Conflicts with Justice

An important reservation must be made to the argument so far. Even genuine communities that meet the several conditions just described may be unjust or promote injustice and so produce the conflict we have already noticed in different ways, between the integrity and justice of an institution. Genuine communal obligations may be unjust in two ways. First, they may be unjust to the members of the group: the conception of equal concern they reflect, though sincere, may be defective. It may be a firm tradition of family organization in some community, for example, that equal concern for daughters and sons requires parents to exercise a kind of dominion over one relaxed for the other.[7] Second, they may be unjust to people who are not members of the group. Social practice may define a racial or religious group as associative, and that group may require its members to discriminate against non-members socially or in employment or generally. If the consequences for strangers to the group are grave, as they will be if the discriminating group is large or powerful within a larger community, this will be unjust.[8] In many cases, requiring that sort of discrimination will conflict, not just with duties of abstract justice the group's members owe everyone else, but also with associative obligations they have because they belong to larger or different associative communities. For if those who do not belong to my race or religion are my neighbors or colleagues or (now I anticipate the argument to follow) my fellow citizens, the question arises whether I do not have responsibilities to them, flowing from those associations, that I ignore in deferring to the responsibilities claimed by my racial or religious group.

We must not forget, in puzzling about these various conflicts, that associative responsibilities are subject to interpretation, and that justice will play its normal interpretive role in deciding for any person what his associative responsibilities, properly understood, really are. If the bare facts of social practice are indecisive, my belief that it is unjust for parents to exercise absolute dominion over their children will influence my convictions about whether the institution of family really has that feature. Even if the practice of dominion is settled and unquestioned, the interpretive attitude may isolate it as a mistake because it is condemned by principles necessary to justify the rest of the institution. There is no guarantee, however, that the interpretive attitude will always justify reading some apparently unjust feature of an associative institution out of it. We may have to concede that unjust dominion lies at the heart of some culture's practices of family, or that indefensible discrimination is at the heart of its practices of racial or religious cohesion. Then we will be aware of another possibility we have also noticed before, in other contexts. The best interpretation may be a deeply skeptical one: that no competent account of the institution can fail to show it as thoroughly and pervasively unjust, and that it should therefore be abandoned. Someone who reaches that conclusion will deny that the practice can impose genuine obligations at all. He thinks the obligations it purports to impose are wholly canceled by competing moral principle.

So our account of associative obligation now has the following rather complex structure. It combines matters of social practice and matters of critical interpretation in the following way. The question of communal obligation does not arise except for groups defined by practice as carrying such obligations: associative communities must be bare communities first. But not every group established by social practice counts as associative: a bare community must meet the four conditions of a true community before the responsibilities it declares become genuine. Interpretation is needed at this stage, because the question whether the practice meets the conditions of genuine community depends on how the practice is properly understood, and that is an interpretive question. Since interpretation is in part a matter of justice, this stage may show that apparently unjust responsibilities are not really part of the practice after all, because they are condemned by principles needed to justify other responsibilities the practice imposes. But we cannot count on this: the best interpretation available may show that its unjust features are compatible with the rest of its structure. Then, though the obligations it imposes are prima facie genuine, the question arises whether the injustice is so severe and deep that these obligations are canceled. That is one possibility, and practices of racial unity and discrimination seem likely examples. But sometimes the injustice will not be that great; dilemmas are then posed because the unjust obligations the practice creates are not entirely erased.

I can illustrate this complex structure by expanding an example already used. Does a daughter have an obligation to defer to her father's wishes in cultures that give parents power to choose spouses for daughters but not sons? We ask first whether the four conditions are met that transform the bare institution of family, in the form this has taken there, into a true community, and that raises a nest of interpretive questions in which our convictions about justice will figure. Does the culture genuinely accept that women are as important as men? Does it see the special parental power over daughters as genuinely in the daughters' interest? If not, if the discriminatory treatment of daughters is grounded in some more general assumption that they are less worthy than sons, the association is not genuine, and no distinctly associative responsibilities, of any character, arise from it. If the culture does accept the equality of the sexes, on the other hand, the discrimination against daughters may be so inconsistent with the rest of the institution of family that it may be seen as a mistake within it and so not a real requirement even if the institution is accepted. Then the conflict disappears for that reason.

But suppose the culture accepts the equality of sexes but in good faith thinks that equality of concern requires paternalistic protection for women in all aspects of family life, and that parental control over a daughter's marriage is consistent with the rest of the institution of family. If that institution is otherwise seriously unjust – if it forces family members to commit crimes in the interest of the family, for example – we will think it cannot be justified in any way that recommends continuing it. Our attitude is fully skeptical, and again we deny any genuine associative responsibilities and so deny any conflict. Suppose, on the other hand, that the institution's paternalism is the only feature we are disposed to regard as unjust. Now the conflict is genuine. The other responsibilities of family membership thrive as genuine responsibilities. So does the responsibility of a daughter to defer to parental choice in marriage, but this may be overridden by appeal to freedom or some other ground of rights. The difference is important: a daughter who marries against her father's wishes, in this version of the story, has something to regret. She owes him at least an accounting, and perhaps an apology, and should in other ways strive to continue her standing as a member of the community she otherwise has a duty to honor.

I have paid such great attention to the structure of associative obligation, and to the character and occasions of its conflict with other responsibilities and rights, because my aim is to show how political obligation can be seen as associative, and this can be plausible only if the general structure of associative obligations allows us to account for the conditions we feel must be met before political obligation arises, and the circumstances we believe must either defeat it or show it in conflict with other kinds of obligations. The discussion just concluded echoes my discussion, in chapter 3 of my *Law's Empire*, about the kinds of conflict citizens and judges might discover between the law of their community and more abstract justice. We used, there, much the same structure and many of the same distinctions to disentangle the moral and legal issues posed by law in wicked places. That echo supports our present hypothesis that political obligation — including an obligation to obey the law — is a form of associative obligation. Our study of conflict within associative obligation is important, too, in responding to an objection to that hypothesis I noticed briefly earlier. The objection complains that treating political obligation as associative supports the more unattractive aspects of nationalism, including its strident approval of war for national self-interest. We can now reply that the best interpretation of our own political practices disavows that feature, which is anyway no longer explicitly endorsed even by bare practice. When and where it is endorsed, any conflict between militant nationalism and standards of justice must be resolved in favor of the latter. Neither of these claims threatens the more wholesome ideals of national community and the special responsibilities these support, which we are about to consider.

FRATERNITY AND POLITICAL COMMUNITY

We are at last able to consider our hypothesis directly: that the best defense of political legitimacy — the right of a political community to treat its members as having obligations in virtue of collective community decisions — is to be found not in the hard terrain of contracts or duties of justice or obligations of fair play that might hold among strangers, where philosophers have hoped to find it, but in the more fertile ground of fraternity, community, and their attendant obligations. Political association, like family and friendship and other forms of association more local and intimate, is in itself pregnant of obligation. It is no objection to that claim that most people do not choose their political communities but are born into them or brought there in childhood. If we arrange familiar fraternal communities along a spectrum ranging from full choice to no choice in membership, political communities fall somewhere in the center. Political obligations are less involuntary than many obligations of family, because political communities do allow people to emigrate, and though the practical value of this choice is often very small the choice itself is important, as we know when we contemplate tyrannies that deny it. So people who are members of bare political communities have political obligations, provided the other conditions necessary to obligations of fraternity, appropriately defined for a political community, are met.

We must therefore ask what account of these conditions is appropriate for a political community, but first we should pause to consider the following complaint about this "solution" of the problem of legitimacy. "It does not solve the problem but evades it by denying there is any problem at all." There is some justice in this complaint, but not enough to be damaging here. The new approach, it is true, relocates the problem of legitimacy and so hopes to change the character of the argument. It asks those who challenge the very possibility of political legitimacy to broaden their attack and either deny all associative obligations or show why political obligation cannot be associative. It asks those who defend legitimacy to test their claims on a new and expanded field of argument. It invites political philosophers of either disposition to consider what a bare political community must be like before it can claim to be a true community where communal obligations flourish.

We have no difficulty finding in political practice the conditions of bare community. People disagree about the boundaries of political communities, particularly in colonial circumstances or when standing divisions among nations ignore important historical or ethnic or religious identities. But these can be treated as problems of interpretation, and anyway they do not arise in the countries of our present main concern. Practice defines the boundaries of Great Britain[9] and of the several states of the United States well enough for these to be eligible as bare political communities. Our most widespread political convictions suppose the officials of these communities to have special responsibilities within and toward their distinct communities.[10] We also have no difficulty in describing the main obligations associated with political communities. The central obligation is that of general fidelity to law, the obligation political philosophy has found so problematic. So our main interest lies in the four conditions we identified. What form would these take in a political community? What must politics be like for a bare political society to become a true fraternal mode of association?

Three Models of Community

We are able to imagine political society as associative only because our ordinary political attitudes seem to satisfy the first of our four conditions. We suppose that we have special interests in and obligations toward other members of our own nation. Americans address their political appeals, their demands, visions, and ideals, in the first instance to other Americans; Britons to other Britons; and so forth. We treat community as prior to justice and fairness in the sense that questions of justice and fairness are regarded as questions of what would be fair or just within a particular political group. In that way we treat political communities as true associative communities. What further assumptions about the obligations and responsibilities that flow from citizenship could justify that attitude by satisfying its other conditions? This is not a question of descriptive sociology, though that discipline may have a part to play in answering it. We are not concerned, that is, with the empirical question of which attitudes or institutions or traditions are needed to create and protect political stability, but with the interpretive question of what character of mutual concern and responsibility our political practices must express in order to justify the assumption of true community we seem to make.

A community's political practices might aim to express one of three general models of political association. Each model describes the attitudes members of a political community would self-consciously take toward one another if they held the view of community the model expresses. The first supposes that members of a community treat their association as only a de facto accident of history and geography, among other things, and so as not a true associative community at all. People who think of their community this way will not necessarily treat others only as means to their own personal ends. That is one possibility: imagine two strangers from nations that despite each other's morals and religion are washed up on a desert island after a naval battle between the two countries. The strangers are thrown together initially by circumstance and nothing more. Each may need the other and may refrain from killing him for that reason. They may work out some division of labor, and each may hold to the agreement so long as he thinks it is to his advantage to do so, but not beyond that point or for any other reason. But there are other possibilities for de facto association. People might regard their political community as merely de facto, not because they are selfish but because they are driven by a passion for justice in the world as a whole and see no distinction between their community and others. A political official who takes that view will think of his constituents as people he is in a position to help because he has special means — those of his office — for helping them that are not, regrettably, available for helping other groups. He will think his responsibilities to his own community special in no other way, and therefore no greater in principle. So when he can improve justice overall by subordinating the interests of his own constituents, he will think it right to do so.

I call the second model of community the "rulebook" model. It supposes that members of a political community accept a general commitment to obey rules established in a certain way that is special to that community. Imagine self-interested but wholly honest people who are competitors in a game with fixed rules or who are parties to a limited and transient commercial arrangement. They obey the rules they have accepted or negotiated as a matter of obligation and not merely strategy, but they assume that the content of these rules exhausts their obligation. They have no sense that the rules were negotiated out of common commitment to underlying principles that are themselves a source of further obligation; on the contrary, they take these rules to represent a compromise between antagonistic interests or points of view. If the rules are the product of special negotiation, as in the contract case, each side has tried to give up as little in return for as much as possible, and it would therefore be unfair and not merely mistaken for either to claim that their agreement embraces anything not explicitly agreed.

The conventionalist's conception of law considered in chapter 4 of *Law's Empire* is a natural mate to this rulebook model of community. Conventionalism suits people each trying to advance his or her own conception of justice and fairness in the right relation through negotiation and compromise, subject only to the single overriding stipulation that once a compromise has been reached in the appropriate way, the rules that form its content will be respected until they are changed by a fresh compromise. A conventionalist philosophy coupled to a rulebook model of community would accept the internal compromises of our checkerboard statutes, as compromises reached through negotiation that ought to be respected as much as any other bargain. The first two models of community – community as a matter of circumstance and as a matter of rules – agree in rejecting the only basis we might have for opposing checkerboard compromises, which is the idea of integrity, that the community must respect principles necessary to justify one part of the law in other parts as well.

The third model of community is the model of principle. It agrees with the rulebook model that political community requires a shared understanding, but it takes a more generous and comprehensive view of what that understanding is. It insists that people are members of a genuine political community only when they accept that their fates are linked in the following strong way: they accept that they are governed by common principles, not just by rules hammered out in political compromise. Politics has a different character for such people. It is a theater of debate about which principles the community should adopt as a system, which view it should take of justice, fairness, and due process, not the different story, appropriate to the other models, in which each person tries to plant the flag of his convictions over as large a domain of power or rules as possible. Members of a society of principle accept that their political rights and duties are not exhausted by the particular decisions their political institutions have reached, but depend, more generally, on the scheme of principles those decisions presuppose and endorse. So each member accepts that others have rights and that he has duties flowing from that scheme, even though these have never been formally identified or declared. Nor does he suppose that these further rights and duties are conditional on his wholehearted approval of that scheme; these obligations arise from the historical fact that his community has adopted that scheme, which is then special to it, not the assumption that he would have chosen it were the choice entirely his. In short, each accepts political integrity as a distinct political ideal and treats the general acceptance of that ideal, even among people who otherwise disagree about political morality, as constitutive of political community.

Now our stage is properly set (or rather managed) for the crucial question. Each of these three models of community describes a general attitude that members of a political community take toward one another. Would political practices expressing one or another of these attitudes satisfy the conditions of true associative community we identified? We need not pause long over the de facto model of circumstance. It violates even the first condition: it adds nothing, by way of any special attitudes of concern, to the circumstances that define a bare political community. It admits community among people who have no interest in one another except as means to their own selfish ends. Even when this form of community holds among selfless people who act only to secure justice and fairness in the world as they understand these virtues, they have no special concern for justice and fairness toward fellow members of their own community. (Indeed, since their only concern is abstract justice, which is universalistic in its character, they can have no basis for special concern.)

The rulebook model of community might seem more promising. For its members do show a special concern for one another beyond each person's general concern that justice be done according to his lights, a special concern that each other person receive the full benefit of whatever political decisions have in fact been taken under the standing political arrangements. That concern has the necessary individualized character to satisfy the second condition: it runs separately from each person directly to everyone else. But it cannot satisfy the third, for the concern it displays is too shallow and attenuated to count as pervasive, indeed to count as genuine concern at all. People in a rulebook community are free to act in politics almost as selfishly as people in a community of circumstances can. Each one can use the standing political machinery to advance his own interests or ideals. True, once that machinery has generated a discrete decision in the form of a rule of law or a judicial decision, they will accept a special obligation to secure the enforcement of that decision for everyone whom it happens to benefit. But that commitment is too formal, too disconnected from the actual circumstances it will promote, to count as expressing much by way of genuine concern, and that is why it rings hollow as an expression of fraternity. It takes hold too late in the political process; it permits someone to act at the crucial legislative stage with no sense of responsibility or concern for those whom he pretends, once very possible advantage has been secured at their expense, to count as brothers. The familiar version of the argument from fair play – these are the rules under which you have benefited and you must play by them – is particularly appropriate to a rulebook community, which takes politics, as I said, to be a kind of game. But that is the version of the argument most vulnerable to all the objections we began by noticing.

The model of principle satisfies all our conditions, at least as well as any model could in a morally pluralistic society. It makes the responsibilities of citizenship special: each citizen respects the principles of fairness and justice instinct in the standing political arrangement of his particular community, which may be different from those of other communities, whether or not he thinks these the best principles from a utopian standpoint. It makes these responsibilities fully personal: it commands that no one be left out, that we are all in politics together for better or worse, that no one may be sacrificed, like wounded left on the battlefield, to the crusade for justice overall. The concern it expresses is not shallow, like the crocodile concern of the rulebook model, but genuine and pervasive. It takes hold immediately politics begins and is sustained through legislation to adjudication and enforcement. Everyone's political acts express on every occasion, in arguing about what the rules should be as well as how they should be enforced, a deep and constant commitment commanding sacrifice, not just by losers but also by the powerful who would gain by the kind of logrolling and checkerboard solutions integrity forbids. Its rationale tends toward equality in the way our fourth condition requires: its command of integrity assumes that each person is as worthy as any other, that each must be treated with equal concern according to some coherent conception of what that means. An association of principle is not automatically a just community; its conception of equal concern may be defective or it may violate rights of its citizens or citizens of other nations in the way we just saw any true associative community might. But the model of principle satisfies the conditions of true community better than any other model of community that it is possible for people who disagree about justice and fairness to adopt.

Here, then, is our case for integrity, our reason for striving to see, so far as we can, both its legislative and adjudicative principles vivid in our political life. A community of principle accepts integrity. It condemns checkerboard statutes and less dramatic violations of that ideal as violating the associative character of its deep organization. Internally compromised statutes cannot be seen as flowing from any single coherent scheme of principle; on the contrary, they serve the incompatible aim of a rulebook community, which is to compromise convictions along lines of power. They contradict rather than confirm the commitment necessary to make a large and diverse political society a genuine rather than a bare community: the promise that law will be chosen, changed, developed, and interpreted in an overall principled way. A community of principle, faithful to that promise, can claim the authority of a genuine associative community and can therefore claim moral legitimacy — that its collective decisions are matters of obligation and not bare power — in the name of fraternity. These claims may be defeated, for even genuine associative obligations may conflict with, and must sometimes yield to, demands of justice. But any other form of community, whose officials rejected that commitment, would from the outset forfeit any claim to legitimacy under a fraternal ideal.

The models of community used in this argument are ideal in several ways. We cannot suppose that most people in our own political societies self-consciously accept the attitudes of any of them. I constructed them so that we could decide which attitudes we should try to interpret our political practices to express, which is a different matter, and the exercise warrants the following conclusion. If we can understand our practices as appropriate to the model of principle, we can support the legitimacy of our institutions, and the political obligations they assume, as a matter of fraternity, and we should therefore strive to improve our institutions in that direction. It bears repeating that nothing in this argument suggests that the citizens of a nation state, or even a smaller political community, either do or should feel for one another any emotion that can usefully be called love. Some theories of ideal community hold out that possibility: they yearn for each citizen to embrace all others in emotions as profound, and with an equivalent merger of personality, as those of lovers or the most intimate friends or the members of an intensely devoted family.[11] Of course we could not interpret the politics of any political community as expressing that level of mutual concern, nor is this ideal attractive. The general surrender of personality and autonomy it contemplates would leave people too little room for leading their own lives rather than being led along them; it would destroy the very emotions it celebrates. Our lives are rich because they are complex in the layers and character of the communities we inhabit. If we felt nothing more for lovers or friends or colleagues than the most intense concern we could possibly feel for all fellow citizens, this would mean the extinction not the universality of love.

Summary

It is time to collect the strands of a long argument. This chapter claims that any successful constructive interpretation of our political practices as a whole recognizes integrity as a distinct political ideal that sometimes calls for compromise with other ideals. Since this is an interpretive claim, it must be measured along two dimensions. Integrity as a political ideal fits and explains features of our constitutional structure and practice that are otherwise puzzling. So its standing as part of an overall successful interpretation of these practices hinges on whether interpreting them in this way helps show them in a better light. We noticed various reasons, both practical and expressive, a community might have for accepting integrity as a political virtue. I emphasized one of these by constructing and contrasting three models of community. I argued that a community of principle, which takes integrity to be central to politics, provides a better defense of political legitimacy than the other models. It assimilates political obligations to the general class of associative obligations and supports them in that way. This defense is possible in such a community because a general commitment to integrity expresses a concern by each for all that is sufficiently special, personal, pervasive, and egalitarian to ground communal obligations according to standards for communal obligation we elsewhere accept.

Neither this argument nor the others we noticed more briefly provides any conclusive argument for integrity on first principles of political morality. I began by conceding that integrity would have no distinct role to play in a community that was understood by all its members to be perfectly just and fair. I am defending an interpretation of our own political culture, not an abstract and timeless political morality; I claim only that the case for integrity is powerful on the second, political dimension of interpretation, which reinforces its strong claims on the first dimension of fit.

NOTES

1 See Rawls, *Theory of Justice* (Harvard University Press, 1971), at 11–12, 118–92.
2 Ibid. at 333–62. See also his "Kantian Constructivism in Moral Theory", *Journal of Philosophy* 77 (1980) 515 at 569.
3 Though this name for the argument is in wide use, Rawls (and Nozick and others following them) call it the argument from the principle of fairness. I do not use the latter name because I use "fairness" in the different way described in this chapter.
4 This is an adaptation of Robert Nozick's argument against the fair play principle as the basis of political authority. See his *Anarchy, State and Utopia* 93–5 (New York, 1974).
5 Family shows that different fraternal relations are matters of choice not only to different degrees but also in different senses of choice. It

also shows that fraternal reasons can be differently mixed with other sorts of reasons for recognizing various forms of obligation. Parents choose to have children but do not, in the present state of technology at least, choose the children they have. Children do not choose their parents but often have grounds for obligations to them they do not have to siblings, whom they do not choose any more than they do parents. It is therefore interesting that the class of obligations we are considering is named after the bond between siblings taken as a paradigm for the class.

6 Can we solve this puzzle about fixing the right level of concreteness for the demands of reciprocity by separating the question of when people are members of a fraternal community from the question of what each then owes others within that community? If so, it would be one question when someone is my friend, and another how I must treat him in virtue of our friendship. If this separation were sensible, we might answer the latter question by insisting that I owe him nothing more than he thinks he owes me. But that is an incoherent solution, among its other difficulties, because he would not know what he owes me until I had decided what I owe him, and I began by not knowing this.

7 I owe this example to Donald Davidson.

8 Large questions about justice, including questions about how far justice extends beyond human beings to at least some other animals, are raised by this hasty observation, which I do not pursue.

9 I ignore the special problem of Northern Ireland here.

10 See the discussion of personification in my *Law's Empire*, chapter 5.

11 This kind of concern is sometimes called "altruism." See Duncan Kennedy, "Form and Substance in Private Law Adjudication," 89 *Harvard Law Review* 1685 (1976).

10
Commitment and Community

L. GREEN

To this point, we have rejected two and given qualified acceptance to one of the popular justifications for political authority. Neither the power of government to create conventions serving the common good, nor its capacity to solve certain problems of collective action warrants citizens taking its directives as binding. These are, indeed, among the important functions of government and they do contribute to its value. But they do not justify its authority. To do that we must find principles which recommend regarding the state as a duty-imposer, as having the power to create binding, content-independent reasons to act. The traditional theory of consent succeeds here. But it is equally true that its scope is limited: not many of us have, in fact, consented. It follows then that the state has legitimate authority only over some of its citizens.

Some may feel that the modesty of our conclusions to this point is a consequence of a particular philosophical perspective which underlies the three families of theories we have been considering. To be sure, there are profound differences among them: the two instrumental theories of social order offer very different pictures of the ills which authority is alleged to cure — different pictures of the state of nature. And consent theory is unlike each of these in offering an argument which does not represent authority as a necessary or desirable means of securing a valued form of social order, but rather as a product of another form of social relation. Yet despite these differences all three share one important feature. They are in a perfectly obvious sense *individualistic* theories, for central to their fundamental explanatory and justificatory apparatus are individual human beings and their interests.

Is it perhaps this individualism which puts political authority beyond their reach? The contrary view is, however, a popular one. Only Leviathan, it is claimed, can tame Hobbes's warriors: the more demanding the id, the more repressive the superego. Perhaps for this reason radicals of many persuasions (including Rousseau and Marx) have felt that it is only through self-transformation and the rejection of individualism that the problem of domination can be solved. But it is a consequence of the argument thus far that a social theory can accommodate a very large measure of individualism without conceding the authority of the state. So far from providing the ground for authority, individualism militates against it. Would it perhaps follow that, in relaxing individualism, we would provide a context in which authority is more justifiable? This chapter investigates one such way of enlarging the scope of legitimate authority.

MODES OF INDIVIDUALISM

Non-individualistic theories of authority have often emerged in reaction to the perceived weakness of classical contractarian and consent-based doctrines, and that is how I shall approach them here. In chapter 6 of my book, *The Authority of the State*, I discussed a number of possible general objections to consent theory, objections which centred on doubts about whether consent is ever given, and if so, whether it is ever free and informed. The result was a qualified defence of consent. But even if that argument were unsound, the damage to consent theory would have been minimal. At best, it would have shown that the state has legitimate authority over few if any, and not that consent theory misrepresents what it would be for such authority to exist. Hence, these objections are perfectly compatible with the view that consent theory is the correct account of our relation to the state: an anarchist can be a consent theorist. For this reason, the arguments to which we now turn are more radical. They seek to establish that, even when the validity conditions for consent *are* fulfilled, the theory presents a misleading picture of the forms of commitment at stake.

Reacting against that strand of western political theory which regards political and sometimes even social life as artificial, some writers emphasize the social dimension of human existence and see the atomic individual as an artificial abstraction. The recent popularity of such views is not unprecedented; they echo an earlier line of criticism of market society found in thinkers as varied as Carlyle, Marx, and Durkheim, one which urges us to begin with the community and attempt to understand individual lives as necessarily constructed in that context. The uses to which such theories have been put are diverse. Here, I wish to consider only whether some such view might offer an alternative to the justifications for political authority which we have already discussed. More exactly, I shall examine some communitarian approaches to the problem of political obligation, namely, the thesis that everyone has an obligation to obey all the laws of his of her own state.

A communitarian may begin with the correct observation that not all obligations are assumed voluntarily. (The obligation to keep promises, as Hume saw, obviously cannot be.) Consent theory, however, attempts to assimilate duties to one's state to commitments to a voluntary organization. A radically individualistic approach, it sets the threshold for rational commitment too high; it makes our attachment to a reasonably just state look weaker than it is by supposing that we must intentionally do something in order to become attached, something which has attachment as part of its aim. But underlying all this, the objector continues, is a suspect social metaphysics according to which the only morally significant relations between abstract individuals are external ones created by acts of will. Only in this peculiar context does the question of political obligation even arise. As one writer puts it: 'political obligation is an important concept for certain theorists only – in general, liberals, individualists, believers in the artificiality of society.'[1] Similarly, it is sometimes said that the plausibility of Socrates' very strong view of the duty to submit to the laws is tied to a classical conception of the person as much less individualistic and independent than the modern one; the questions that rive our public and private commitments just do not arise for the polis-animal. And in a related vein, Hegel's distaste for contractarianism lies in the fact that it attempts to reduce the deeper unities of the state to a mundane mechanical combination of wills. As in marriage, the social relations between individual and state should be seen as internal and constitutive, not as external and instrumental. This family of objections poses a radical critique of the whole social theory underlying consent-based arguments. Rejecting individualism, it offers a counter-image of our moral predicament. Just what is at issue here?

When it is objected that individualistic assumptions render some accounts of political authority unsound and perhaps unintelligible, the acceptability of several different theses may be at issue, for individualism in a social theory may be manifest in different forms.[2] At the deepest, metaphysical level, one could be an *ontological* individualist, regarding only individual human beings as ultimately real. This would not preclude talk of societies, nations, groups, classes, and so on, although it would require a reductionist interpretation of them. Similarly, social relations could be retained, provided they were understood as external relations between independently existing and uniquely real persons.[3]

Individualism in that sense is to be distinguished from the family of views which go under the name of *methodological* individualism, that is, the doctrine that the only acceptable ultimate explanations of social phenomena are those couched wholly in terms of facts about individuals. The boundaries of this second theory are somewhat vague. As Lukes has persuasively argued, there is actually a continuum of so-called individual facts, ranging from purely physical descriptions to those richly detailed accounts which make reference to 'institutional facts' (such as 'casting a vote', or 'obeying a law'). So far, explanations of social phenomena only seem to work if they admit at least some facts well along towards the institutional end of the scale: we can explain election results in terms of votes cast but not in terms of neurophysiology, and nothing on the horizon suggests that this is about to change.[4]

Although sometimes confused, the methodological and ontological theses are logically independent. It may be that only individuals are ultimately real in some favoured metaphysical sense, but also that reductive explanations of social phenomena are untrue, unavailable, or not worth pursuing. This might be the case if social phenomena are systemically or functionally organized. An analogy may help clarify here. Arguably, the only ultimately real components of a computer are the hardware (under a purely physical description); however, any adequate theory of its operation will also need to make reference to the program and the rest of the software. Moreover, how we ought to study some subject matter depends not only on the inherent nature of that thing, but also on our natures, including our limited capacities for receiving, interpreting, and processing data. A predictive model which could not be calculated in real time, for example, would be useless. This means that the sort of considerations supporting methodological individualism will need to be quite different from those supporting ontological individualism.

Finally – and this may be more obvious – both of these are logically independent of the third, and for our purposes most important, mode of individualism. Lukes divides *ethical* individualism into two variants:[5] the view that individual human beings are the object of all value, and the view that they are the source of all value in the sense that what is of value depends entirely on the nature of their choices, desires, and commitments. Here, I shall regard the latter thesis as more properly a theory of moral epistemology and not of first-order, or substantive, value theory at all. As to the former, it extends well beyond ethical egoism, the case considered by Lukes. It includes everything covered by McTaggart's view that only conscious beings and their mental states can be of ultimate value, i.e. of value as an end in themselves and not merely as a means.[6]

For anyone accepting a strong version of the fact–value distinction, the independence of ethical from ontological or methodological individualism follows immediately. Naturally, there are historical, ideological, and other affinities among these views. But the relation is no stronger than that. One can view social classes as ultimately real features of the social world and deplore their existence, and one can regard the nation state as non-instrumentally valuable while subscribing to a reductivist explanatory account of it. Even if values must supervene on natural facts, it does not follow that these must be ultimate ones, such as matter and motion, rather than secondary ones. Thus, one can reject ethical individualism without adopting anti-individualistic ontologies or methods. And if the main objection to this sort of theory is (as it is often thought) that we must at all costs avoid the ontological slum of general wills and group minds, then we can reduce the domain of contention by providing a theory which admits ultimate values other than individual persons and their mental states, but which is compatible with a fairly sparse social ontology. There is therefore no need to reject non-individualistic theories a priori, in the way that certain philosophers still do, by supposing that methodological or ontological considerations rule them out from the beginning. The relative independence of the different modes of individualism frees up some space for a serious assessment of the alternatives.

THE CONCEPT OF MEMBERSHIP

One sort of anti-individualism reacts against consent theory with various conceptual claims about obligation and authority, including the argument that authority relations are transmitted through the very terms of political discourse. Hanna Pitkin, for example, says that it is a 'symptom of philosophical disorder',[7] to ask for the ground of our obligation to obey. There is, she claims, no theoretical explanation superior to the following point of 'grammar': 'It is part of the concept, the meaning of "authority" that those subject to it are required to obey, that it has a right to command. It is part of the concept, the meaning of "law", that those to whom it is applicable are obligated to obey it.'⁸ Those, like the traditional consent theorists, who fail to see this are in the grips of what she calls 'a peculiar picture of man and society', an abstractly individualistic one which ignores that, 'It is only as a result of [society's] influence that he becomes the particular person he does become, with his particular interests, values, desires, language and obligations.'⁹

Pursuing a similar line of thought still further, Thomas McPherson comes to conclude that it is literally meaningless to ask for a general justification for political obligation:

'Why should I (a member) accept the rules of the club?' is an absurd question. Accepting the rules is part of what it *means* to be a member. Similarly, 'Why should I obey the government?' is an absurd question. We have not understood what it *means* to be a member of political society if we suppose that political obligation is something we might not have had and that therefore needs to be *justified*.¹⁰

These arguments simply shift the line of dispute in a way which highlights the inherent weakness of the linguistic approach to political theory. Even if the justification of authority can only be answered by reference to the fact of membership, we can still coherently ask whether it is justifiable to be a member of an association like the state, knowing that it brings with it the obligations that it does. Moreover, the options facing the conscientious citizen are not simply the acceptance of authority or revolt; she may choose to comply peacefully with the state, obeying often or always, though never for the reason that her obedience is required. Peaceful compliance is possible without membership, and thus without its obligations.

It is implausible that the normative issues can be resolved by lexicography, or even by appeals to philosophical grammar. Which are the words whose meaning establishes that peaceful compliance is not the appropriate relationship between the conscientious citizen and the state: 'member'? 'citizen'? One would naturally have thought that the political dispute between those who affirm and those who deny the state's claim to authority simply includes a dispute about what those words mean. And suppose there were some term whose use was universally recognized as implying that one was obliged to obey; could we not then just refuse to play that language game, everything else remaining the same? So long as the concept of good citizenship remains a complex and contested one, political argument will infect every level of inquiry and the normative issues will have to be joined at some level. Chasing them along the road of grammar delays but does not eliminate the meeting point.

NO ARCHIMEDEAN POINT

Although unacceptable, the above argument can be restated in non-linguistic terms, as in the common idealist thesis, made notorious by T. H. Green, that, 'To ask why I am to submit to the power of the state, is to ask why I am to allow my life to be regulated by that complex of institutions without which I literally should not have a life to call my own.'[11] The argument is that there is no neutral, uncommitted point to which we might retreat and assess our obligations, as the consent theorist would have us do. One's very existence — and even more, the concept of one's existence as an independent individual with a life of one's *own* — depends on political institutions. And if individual lives are in this way deeply social, so is morality. To think of moral duties as self-imposed laws in the Kantian fashion is incoherent; laws, properly so called, are always imposed by others. Similarly, consent-based duties are purely abstract and not socially situated, and hence we can explain neither their content nor their motivating power. In contrast, the idealists direct our attention to a certain kind of community which, in its positive morality, expresses our duties as inherently social demands that are not merely products of our wills. Under certain conditions, which Hegel and Bradley among others purport to describe, the state can be understood as such a community. When it is, the duty of obedience becomes morally unproblematic.

A related way of bringing in the social dimension is the neo-Wittgensteinian view that, as a normative institution, political authority depends upon social practices and rules which provide the criteria for right and wrong ways of acting. Peter Winch once promoted a very strong version of this thesis. Beginning with the sound premise that authority is not a causal relation between wills but an internal and normative one, he argued that the very idea of a right and wrong way of doing things essentially involves shared concepts of value. But one can have no such concepts unless one follows certain criterial social rules which constitute them. It is to these normative judgements that authoritative requests therefore appeal and, because they are so imbricated in the fabric of social life, we are unable to view our situation without them. It therefore makes no sense, he held, to suppose that we 'choose' to accept authority. Rather, 'the fact that one is a human social being, engaged in rule-governed activities and on that account able to deliberate and to choose, is in itself sufficient to commit one to the acceptance of legitimate political authority. For the exercise of such authority is a precondition of rule-governed activities. There would, therefore be a sort of inconsistency in "choosing to reject" all such authority.'[12]

What are we to make of such claims? Suppose it were true that our most central moral notions need public criteria for their application and intelligibility, and that there can be no Archimedean point from which we can at once judge all of these criteria. Surely some room for critical reflection would remain, however, for we could call into question some of the criteria without calling into question all of them; we could repair our ship at sea. What then licenses the final inference in the argument, from 'we must accept some social rules' to 'we must accept political authority'? Could we not use the inherently social criteria of, for example, religion or customary morality to evaluate political order? The leap from the necessity for a rule-governed outlook to the necessity for political regulation is unsupported, as Winch later came to accept.[13] In rejecting his earlier argument, however, Winch none the less maintained that social life would be impossible without some kind of authority, although not necessarily the authority of a specialized institution like the state. Yet even this does not follow. We must insist on a still finer analysis, and distinguish the necessity for a normative framework of rules and practices from the necessity for that special sort of normative framework which characterizes authority. That cannot be established by the sort of considerations to which Winch appeals.

These arguments, like those which purport to show that ethics must be socially situated, all fall to a fundamental objection: they fail to distinguish global and local criteria for the intelligibility of evaluation. If they are correct they apply globally, to all obligations, to all other moral concepts, and indeed to the possibility of all practical judgements. They do not apply in a distinctive and local way to the problem of political authority. In this respect they are, like meta-ethical claims, independent of the substantive issues and cannot therefore function as a critique of individualistic accounts like consent theory. At best they show that both consensual obligations and non-consensual obligations are intelligible only in a social context, that consent itself has constitutive criteria which are inherently social, and so on. Even if all that is true, however, it goes no way to establishing that consent is inferior to other socially constituted concepts as an account of the relation in question. More generally, no philosophical theory about the *status* of concepts like 'consent' or 'individual' is going to support or weaken the plausibility of any normative position, any more than the falsity of methodological individualism would entail the rejection of ethical individualism.

ATOMISM AND THE SOCIAL THESIS

The failure of the above versions of the communitarian thesis points to a significant, if sometimes neglected, truth about what sort of argument is needed here. If it is to be at all persuasive, communitarianism must isolate some value or first-order normative consideration which individualistic theories miss. If it attempts to remain above the political fray in the lofty realm of methodology or meta-ethics, it can too easily be neutralized by an individualist willing to concede that people are essentially social creatures and that moral and political life is a social achievement, while maintaining that the best life for these social creatures is one which best serves their socially constructed individualities. To block this, we must bring community back down to earth.

Charles Taylor begins to move in the right direction in an insightful essay which locates the errors of consent theory in a general philosophical stance he calls 'atomism'.[14] This doctrine is a complex network of ontological, methodological, and ethical positions. In political theory, Taylor takes its distinctive symptoms to be talk of a state of nature, the view that people can flourish outside society, that individual rights have primacy over other moral considerations, and that the only ultimately valuable goods are divisible ones. Although ideologically harmonious, these positions are logically distinct and it is a little difficult to find representatives of the atomist tradition in political thought who consistently held to all of them. This itself need pose no objection, however, for Taylor is not really offering a definition of 'atomism' but just seeking to describe a related family, or perhaps syndrome, of attitudes. In fact, his main concern is only with one particularly influential member of that family: the doctrine of the primacy of individual rights. A moral theory based solely on natural rights is indeed an individualistic one in the serious sense, for it counts as intrinsically valuable goods only the interests of individuals, and explains other moral concepts by their logical or justificatory relationship to individual rights. On a rights-based theory, moral obligations must be explained and justified in terms of rights and are thus of secondary importance. The state therefore has legitimate authority only as a correlate of individuals' obligations to obey which must in turn be derived from their exercising or taking measures designed to protect the exercise of their rights. Taylor presents an attractive argument against that view by investigating the ground of individual rights. Rights exist to protect and express respect for certain fundamental human capacities. But if these capacities are the ultimate foundation of rights then one cannot exclude the possibility that they may directly give rise to moral obligations, including the obligation to belong to a community, if they are instrumentally necessary to, or a constitutive part of, a society which respects and promotes these capacities.

The idea of an obligation to 'belong' is, one must admit, a bit hazy. It presents a real challenge to individualists only if it is or includes an obligation to obey. Moreover, it is possible to conceive of human capacities in such a way as to bring them under the umbrella of individual interests and this suggests that Taylor's theory may not be as anti-individualistic as he thinks. But let that pass. Even under a favourable interpretation, the argument does not support the desired conclusion.

A communitarian political theory must show not merely that people are naturally *social* animals and can only flourish in a social context — what Taylor calls the 'social thesis' — but also that they are naturally political. Interpreted in its broadest form, it is not clear that any political theorist apart from Hobbes has ever rejected the social thesis. The battle between individualists like Kant and Mill and their critics like Hegel and Marx was never fought over that piece of territory but rather over what sort of social conditions encourage individual flourishing. One way of putting this point is to say that communitarians must either respect or give reasons for rejecting the common distinction between state and society. It is true that any form of social order from the family and tribe onwards is a theatre of conflicts of interest, exercises of power, legitimating ideologies, and so forth. In this weak sense all forms of human society are political. To concede this does not show, however, that any form of human society must incorporate those particular relations of subordination which we recognize as authority nor does it show that there is no difference in kind between, say, the family and the modern state. What then is the power of the social thesis? If sound, it creates a strong case for thinking that there are some moral obligations which are primary and not merely derived from rights. But it does nothing to prove that no moral obligations are secondary. The possibility therefore remains that while some obligations are not dependent on consent for their validity, others are and political obligations fall in the latter category. The crucial step for our purposes therefore remains to be taken. We need to establish, not just that the free individual is a product of a certain kind of society and therefore must support the social conditions of such freedom, but also that such support is not possible, or not complete, without conceding the moral authority of the state. This argument cannot proceed conceptually. As Taylor notes, anarchism is a possible account of the relation between a free citizen and the culture of freedom. For two reasons, however, he thinks that the odds are against it. First, 'it seems much more likely from the historical record that we need rather some species of political society. And if this is so then we must acknowledge an obligation to belong to this kind of society in affirming freedom.'[15] Secondly, 'men's deliberating together about what will be binding on all of them is an essential part of the exercise of freedom. It is only in this way that they can come to grips with certain basic issues in a way which will actually have an effect in their lives.'[16] Neither claim is sound as it stands. To concede that the conditions of human development require society is not to concede that they require authority, unless we repeat Hume's error of holding that the former is impossible without general recognition of the latter. Nor is the value of public deliberation essentially tied to deliberating about what our duties will be. We can conceive of a public order of mutual coercion which relies only on sanctions to promote the common good and in which sanctions are regarded merely as threats and not as duties.[17] In those circumstances, debate about which sanctions should be imposed would bring home in a lively way our common fate – but it would not be debate about duties. A gang of robbers can argue about their own policies without for a moment supposing that they are disputing their moral obligations. Hence, the social thesis does not provide sufficient reply to the consent theorist's objection that even if the conditions for human flourishing are social, they are not political in any sense that presupposes authority relations.

CONSENSUAL COMMUNITIES

Thus far we have found nothing to dislodge the conclusion that only if individuals consent are they bound to obey the state and thus nothing to mitigate the individualistic rigours of that theory. But perhaps we have been looking in the wrong place. There is much more to the communitarian picture than the arguments for obedience which have just been criticized. Indeed, on two substantive points I think that communitarian objections are decisive. First, it is wrong to think of political life as purely instrumental in the way many consent theorists, contractarians, and conventionalists tend to do, to see it as the public means for securing essentially private ends. If there is anything worth preserving of the civic republican tradition it is the view that political life may have intrinsic value. Secondly, the consent theorist does tend to overestimate the role of the will at the expense of communal traditions in establishing those moral relations which are constitutive of political life. And these two faults in consent theory are not merely incidental; they are intimately connected with its main feature, the analogy between life in a state and a voluntary association. Descriptively, states are not like that for the scope of their authority is maximal and their jurisdiction compulsory. Normatively, the bonds of commitment appropriate to purely voluntary associations are qualitatively different from those in a flourishing political community. One's tennis club very rarely generates the same deep feelings of belonging combined with relative externality that one experiences in the state. Ideally, we would like to amend the individualist picture in such a way as to capture these truths while retaining the normative function of consent.

Consent theory is not only wrong but incoherent if it supposes that all obligations are self-assumed (the duty to keep promises cannot be the result of a promise). And it is wrong if it supposes that all self-assumed obligations are wholly creatures of consent. Fortunately, an acceptable version of it need make neither error. There are two reasons why the range of legitimate authority seems so limited according to consent theory. First, some people perform no actions that can be counted as consent of any sort. Secondly, the scope of the state's authority is so wide that some who do consent will not be thought to consent to *that*. They may intend, for example, to bind themselves to just laws only, and to reserve their own right to judge about cases of moral necessity or civil disobedience. But this ignores that the state purports to regulate such defences as well. To expand the range of the state's authority many have tried to weaken the nature of consent by extending it to cover notions of tacit or hypothetical consent. For reasons already given, that cannot succeed. A distinct possibility, however, is to expand the scope of the state's authority by widening the implications of consensual acts. If it could be shown that people need not consent to every detail of the state's jurisdiction, but only to a general social role of citizenship which includes an obligation to obey, then the consent-based argument will have been widened without undermining the normative foundations of consent. I approach the issue by considering some recent reflections on the most important of classical consent theorists.

With increasing frequency it is argued that Locke is not a consent theorist in the sense of chapter 6 of *The Authority of the State* at all. Pitkin challenges the traditional view by examining those limits which Locke imposes on the validity of consent.[18] The difficulties in Locke's argument about 'tacit consent', she argues, do not go so far as to obliterate the distinction between legitimate authority and coercion, for the terms of the original contract are dictated, not by the will of the parties, but by the law of nature. The only intention we need impute to contractors is the aim for self-preservation; the law of nature guarantees that in pursuing that aim they cannot voluntarily become the slave of another. We lack absolute arbitrary power over our own lives and so cannot transfer such power to another. Pitkin thus reasons that for Locke, 'you are obligated to obey not really because you have consented; your consent is virtually automatic. Rather you are obligated to obey because of certain characteristics of the government – that it is acting within the bounds of trusteeship based on an original contract.'[19] Thus, consent appears to cast only the faintest hypothetical shadow over Locke's theory: political authority is a matter of what rational people could be supposed to agree to, not what duties they have created for themselves. 'For now the Lockean doctrine becomes this: your personal consent is essentially irrelevant to your obligation to obey, or its absence. Your obligation to obey depends on the character of the government – whether it is acting within the bounds of *the* (only possible) contract.'[20] Similarly in John Dunn's influential work on Locke, consent is demoted from the status of a duty-generating practice to a mere limiting condition on legitimacy. In an important article, he argues that Locke means by consent little more than uncoerced acceptance of some practice: 'where a practice is legitimate and a role involves participation in the practice, consent to do so and hence consent to its responsibilities is axiomatic – all potential doubts are resolved in favour of the practice.'[21] But the legitimacy of the practice does not itself flow from consent. Locke was too much a theist to think of human consent as generating moral duties *ex nihilo*. Often, 'men's psychological reach exceeds their juristic grasp';[22] they freely and deliberately form the intention to undertake duties which violate the law of nature. But that law is independent of our will and cannot be amended or repealed by our consensual acts. Thus slavery contracts are void *ab initio*. Now, this is not the view of one who celebrates the unfettered human will as a mode of creating duties. To suppose that it is, is to substitute our concerns and our metaphysics for Locke's. The *Two Treatises* should therefore properly be read, not as an account of how such obligations can be generated by a sheer act of will, but as an argument for limitations on the possible scope of political obligation.[23] As might be expected from a moralist who has a fundamentally theological world view, Locke's theme is human dependence, not independence.

These powerful arguments have a common strength and a common weakness. They usefully remind us of the historical and theoretical limitations of the view that consent is essentially a duty-creating act. Why would people wish to create duties out of nothing; and how could they do it? Consent theory should not be seen as a celebration of the value-creating power of the human will. It is in order to express or secure certain values that we have the practice of consent. The limitation of these arguments is their assumption that if consent is not a duty-creating act it is irrelevant, at best a limiting condition on the legitimacy of a practice established in some other way. This ignores other important alternatives. Consent can also be seen as a device not for generating duties out of nothing but the will of the parties, but for determining the conditions of application or varying the content of pre-existing, socially (or for Locke, divinely) constituted duties.

Consider again the institution of marriage and the duties it entails. Here, I am not thinking of cohabitation contracts, or other devices by which couples desiring to enter a relationship of legally recognized and enforceable monogamy can do so without getting married, but of the standard case where they avail themselves of an independently existing institution which is partly constituted by a set of publicly recognized rights and duties. Now, whether one thinks of the form of that institution as being set by social convention or divine sanction, it is certainly not a product of the agreement of the parties. In this respect, it is very unlike a contract which creates duties in a morally empty universe. The content of the duties is external to the will of the parties, but they apply to particular couples only through their own consent. In these circumstances, consent is something less than a duty-generating device or an expression of an omnipotent individual will which alone is competent to bind itself. The sovereignty of the will is hedged in by social convention over which it has applicative but not creative power. This is plainly the case in the traditional institution of marriage, for this feature often attracts radical criticism. Yet although marriage is not fully responsive to the will of the parties, it would be equally wrong to characterize it as a situation in which consent is 'essentially irrelevant' or 'axiomatic', a mere limiting condition on a practice whose validity is independently established. For the institution of marriage would have little value if consent were not essential to its application to a particular couple; not merely for the obvious reason that monogamy would go less well among pairs who do not agree to it, but more importantly because consent is a constitutive feature of the relationship they seek to establish. And yet at the same time, their consent does not go all the way down to ground level: the normative contours of the institution are relatively external to their wills, although its application and value for them is not. This suggests that one may have a two-part explanation of consent-based duties: an account of their structure and content, subject to the social thesis, and an independent account of their validity and application subject to consent.

We should, I think, accept the communitarian critique in so far as it suggests that much of contemporary consent theory is in the grips of an odd, strangely individualistic picture of human nature and its moral powers. It is wrong to think of our most important duties as being consequences only of our own wills; this is to drain them of the social dimension which explains their form and content. In this respect, our duties will be subject to the social thesis. The duties incumbent on the good citizen, then, are those which constitute citizenship in his community. To attempt to step back from these, and ask, from the point of view of nowhere at all, whether they are really his duties is perhaps to ask the unaskable. They are constitutive of his identity as a citizen and in this sense, but only in this sense, are prior to his particularities. The scope of consent may therefore be extended somewhat, to cover those individuals who willingly assume the role of citizen and thus its constitutive duties, but in whose psychological history we can locate no acts or intentions which create those duties. If we can explain the value of such role-bound consent, we may be able legitimately to extend the doctrine without relying on the fiction of tacit consent or on the unacceptable theories of hypothetical consent. But as we have seen, calling attention to this fact cannot itself explain how the duties constitutive of our roles come to bind. At this point the normative force of consent must still take over, not as a device to explain the structure of our moral worlds, but to explain our own positions within them. The fact that the duties of a citizen are my duties is still a question which depends inherently on whether I have consented to occupying the role which they constitute.

SHARED GOODS AND CIVIC LIFE

This revision of consent theory has certain affinities with Bradley's view that the realm of obligation cannot adequately be understood in either purely consequentialist or Kantian terms but only as 'the objective world of my station and its duties'. It adds to that theory the provision that at least political stations, including citizenship, are to be occupied only by consent.[24] Such a hybrid view is vulnerable to attack from both sides. In this section I defend it from the radical consent theorist who argues that consent should go all the way down to the ground floor and include the nature of stations. In the next section I defend it against the communitarian who holds that the objectivity of duties must extend all the way up, and include an immediate obligation to belong.

If we value consent as a means of acquiring obligations then why not extend it to the nature of the obligations themselves? Even if the so-called natural duties of fidelity, charity, and so on resist an account as being will-constituted, the duty to obey may none the less seem a likely candidate. One might reconsider the earlier analogy with marriage. If we value consenting as a means of making monogamy go well, or expressing mutual trust, would a more perfect expression of that not be a monogamy contract whose terms were exhaustively set by the parties involved? Why should a socially given cluster of rights and duties be treated as any more than a default option, available to those unable to or uninterested in designing their own, in the way that intestacy laws bind only those who do not create a will? To establish the difference one must show that there is some intrinsic value in a common public status, such as being married, which value would not be realizable, or would only be realized to a lesser degree, under a regime of individualized private contracts.

One might be tempted to pursue an instrumental explanation for this, to understand it as a means of economizing on the time and effort needed to tailor social relations precisely to one's individual circumstances or as a means of providing a standard form of relationship in order to simplify and stabilize interactions with others by creating reasonably reliable grounds for social expectations. No doubt this is part of the story. But it is unlikely to be fully satisfactory in the present context. In recognizing the authority of the state as a set of standard, boiler-plate terms of a social contract, too much is at risk over interests that are too vital, and the security of expectations can be attained in too many other ways. Moreover, this is not how such common social forms are understood by their members; those who approve of our familiar system of monogamous marriage do not regard its general framework of rights and duties as second-best to an ideal individually negotiated contract. They regard it as essentially constitutive of the relation itself. This suggests that the instrumental explanation is too simple and that we should search for an alternative.

Let us consider the distinction between an ordinary private good and a public good in the economist's sense. In its pure form, the latter is jointly supplied and inexcludable – co-operation is needed to produce it, but once the good is available for some then all can benefit from it. This causes well-known problems because such goods are difficult to price, and markets for them are not generally efficient. Typical institutional solutions to such problems include enforcement mechanisms to ensure supply and exclusion devices to control consumption. But these are imperfect and work, when they do, by partially transforming the good into a private one, such as when we sell gas masks to allocate clean air, or charge admission to a public beach. And yet those who value public goods prefer the presence of these imperfect devices to their absence. This shows that the public nature of such goods is not part of their value, but rather an obstacle to be overcome. Now, not all goods with a communal aspect are public goods in this sense. In some cases, to privatize a good is to transform it in a way which changes its value. There can be no market in friendship so it is not a private good, but neither are its external effects (reciprocity, mutual respect, trust, etc.) mere externalities whose presence confounds its production: they are essential to it. Thus, friendship is not a public good in the above sense. Rather, it is a *shared* good which can be enjoyed only in a form of association which itself partly constitutes the good shared.[25]

It seems likely that, for some people anyway, the pleasures of civic life are shared goods. In a reasonably just society the status of citizen is something of value in part because it is a common one. All those who value social solidarity for its own sake are likely, in the context of the modern state, to see civic ties as providing a common nexus linking those who share little else. The status of citizenship is in part constituted by our political obligations and to assume it is to assume them, not as a matter of linguistic propriety or as a tool instrumental to securing the public good, but as an element of an inherently valuable relationship. Now we are on the threshold of a more acceptable version of the organic view discussed in chapter 6 of *The Authority of the State*. It is not so much that consenting to obey expresses a valuable feeling of belonging to one's society, but that it concretely instantiates a form of association which may be regarded as a shared good. But a final step is needed to explain the role of authority relations in such an association.

Most valuable things are good in different respects or, as we might say, contain goods of different sorts. One can value an unspoiled forest as a resource for the pulp and paper industry, as a recreational area, or as intrinsically valuable for its natural beauty. This is equally true of human associations. Some of them have public aspects — inexcludable and non-rival dimensions of instrumental value, as well as shared aspects — inherently valuable relationships. A racially tolerant society, for example, promotes the public goods of security and the efficient use of human capital, but it also expresses valuable associations among people. We might say that it is a good with at least two very different aspects. These can on occasion give rise to practical conflicts: on the one hand, in its guise as a public good it provides a justification for free-riding (a general atmosphere of tolerance does not depend on my contribution), while on the other its shared aspect gives reason for participation (one cannot share in the valued relationship if one is a free-rider). From one point of view, the communal aspect of the good is a burden, from another it is a benefit. In some cases, this conflict can be resolved in the standard way: one weighs the benefit against the burden and decides whether, on balance, it is worth it. In other cases, the shared aspect of the relationship is jeopardized by this very calculation. Close friendships, for example, are unavailable to those who treat all conflicting reasons as potentially negotiable against the value of the relationship. For that reason, friendship is often recognized as a paradigm of the sort of commitment shared goods can generate. The natural expression of the attraction of such goods is to regard the relationship as obligation-imposing, as putting at least certain competing claims out of consideration at all. Many organic theories of the state have suggested that political relations can sometimes be understood in this way, as *philia politike*, civic friendship. No doubt this is extremely idealistic. And civic friendship may conflict with other loyalties. But where it exists it is of value, and it survives because its norms are regarded as binding. They provide a common framework or structure for a shared good.

This is the primary reason why some would value a system of many different private contractual arrangements less than a common social contract. Only the latter would express civic friendship. Note that this argument does not seek to establish that one must view political life in this way, that it is impossible, immoral, or inherently unfulfilling to reject it. Nor is it claimed that this view is common in the modern state; on the contrary, the decline of the public realm is well documented. It only seeks to show that such a view is intelligible and that it can figure in a sound argument extending the scope of legitimate authority to those who consent to the social role of citizenship even if they have not created the set of duties which are constitutive of it.

SOCIAL ROLES AND IDENTITY

In that way the communitarian thesis can and should modify consent theory. But most modern communitarians would not be satisfied with the concession that the social thesis applies to the nature and content of our duties because they feature in the shared goods of citizenship, but not to their incidence. They would see this as half-hearted, giving up the social thesis just where it begins to have bite and would argue, not merely that individual consent is not sufficient to be bound, but that it is not necessary either. In this, they tend to share Hegel's view,[26] that when we understand our political obligations as socially situated in the realm of objective ethics, we can no longer see them as optional in the way that the consent theorist does. The concession that they are not optional all the way to ground level is not for them adequate, for it still admits the possibility that the subject of a reasonably just state may lack the duty of obedience. Indeed, if taken seriously, such obligations must bind few citizens of modern states who usually view citizenship as a private or public good or as a shared good to which they do not themselves subscribe (just as one can see the value of friendship which one does not share). A full-blooded communitarian will want to argue that the social reality of obligation requires that it be, fundamentally, non-optional.

To establish this the communitarian characteristically appeals to the social thesis. As argued above, that cannot succeed: even if our moral nature depends on institutions which nurture our essential capacities, that does not show that we cannot support such institutions without accepting their claim to create duties for us, and thus without acknowledging the authority of the state. Other avenues remain open, however. The communitarian might instead try to weaken the role of consent by reminding us that some social roles generate duties even when they are not voluntarily assumed.

In some cases, it is unclear to what extent the assumption of a given role is voluntary. It seems reasonable to suppose that, if one agrees to assume a certain risk of occupying a role, then one's occupying it is voluntary if the risk materializes. Someone who agrees to draw straws for a dangerous mission cannot be said to have been selected non-voluntarily. Perhaps that analysis can be extended to cover a number of other social roles commonly thought to be non-voluntary (e.g., juror, army draftee, etc.). There remains, however, a range of cases which is less easily accommodated. For example, a famous athlete who becomes a role-model for children may acquire certain duties of good conduct which he neither voluntarily assumed nor willingly undertook the risk of; a woman who becomes pregnant as a result of a rape and who could not terminate the pregnancy without serious risk to her health is an involuntary mother and may yet have some duties towards her infant. Now, in such non-voluntary roles, it is not the occupancy of the role itself which justifies holding their incumbents to be under the duty. Such institutions have an identificatory function in showing which duties their incumbent has, but they have no justificatory function in grounding those duties.[27] For every role-based duty it is possible to give a role-independent explanation of why the duty binds. But that explanation need not rest on the claim that the role was voluntarily assumed. It is a matter of controversy which non-voluntary roles do generate valid duties, and also what the ground of their validity is. There are, however, two conditions which make it more likely that the duties are binding. First, the attendant duties may not be very onerous. One rarely becomes an uncle or aunt voluntarily, but the minor obligations which that role brings generally require little beyond the demands of natural duty. Secondly, the duties, although more substantial, may secure a very great benefit for those who are themselves non-voluntarily dependent on their performance. Non-voluntary parenthood, for example, plausibly brings at least the duty to ensure that the child is cared for. Now, when it is true both that obligations are slight and the benefits great, as in the duty of an athlete to set a good example for children, the case in favour looks quite powerful.

To what extent can a communitarian follow this route in attempting to disestablish consent? Not, I think, very far at all. Consider the social role of citizenship. It cannot be said that the duties it brings are slight. The state claims supreme authority over vital concerns; at the very least it includes the liability to taxation and military service. These alone may at times require substantial sacrifice of what would otherwise be one's legitimate interests. What about the benefits which result from holding people non-voluntarily to be under such duties? Concede for the sake of argument that they are substantial. But what needs to be shown, and what this approach cannot show, is that unless occupiers of the role of citizen recognize that they are duty-bound to act in these desirable ways, they cannot be relied on to do so. Once again, the proposal founders on the fact that peaceful compliance with the law will be sufficient to protect the interests of other citizens. No one except the officials of the state will be harmed if people fail to regard it as authoritative.

It seems then that we cannot abandon consent as a validating condition of the political role. But instead of defending role-bound duties, the communitarian may attack the assumptions about moral personality which underpin the whole idea of consenting to occupy a role. Who is it that does the consenting? Michael Sandel's criticisms of Rawls register a sceptical note. He says that the individualism of modern deontological liberals, whose moral theory assigns priority to the right over the good, incorporates an incoherent view of the self as prior to all of its merely contingent ends.[28] Not only is this said to be a philosophically unsatisfactory position, but it is also held to promote a morally undesirable form of individualism by devaluing the rich communal – but merely contingent – fabric of our lives. It is not clear to what extent this last charge holds good. Rawls could reply that the mutual disinterestedness of parties to the social contract does not prejudice life in actual societies in favour of individualistic habits in which people pursue their own plans of life without valuing the good of others (although respecting their rights and liberties). Rawls foresees a diversity of actual motivation and levels of concern and his political theory seeks to describe a framework within which free communal association is a possible value. Sandel believes that this misses the point. Of course the abstract self can accommodate community in this diminished form. What it cannot accommodate, he says, is a form of community constitutive of the very bounds of the self. One consequence of always standing at a distance from those interests and concerns which are only contingently its own is to 'put the self beyond the reach of experience, to make it invulnerable, to fix its identity once and for all. No commitment could grip me so deeply that I could not understand myself without it.'[29] The Rawlsian metaphysics is thus alleged to support a politics of interests, not a politics of identities: 'It rules out the possibility of a public life in which, for good or ill, the identity as well as the interests of the participants could be at stake.'[30] The same charge can be brought against the present proposal. In accepting the social thesis with respect to the content of our obligations but rejecting it with respect to their incidence, I have presupposed that we can coherently talk of a self which gives or withholds its consent to these arrangements and I have excluded the crucial claim that these commitments are not merely constitutive of the station of citizenship, but also of the identity of the citizen. And that is simply to ignore the charge that Hegel, Green, and the other idealists bring. Thus we return to the objection that there is no Archimedean point from which to assess our obligations.

Is this view about the constitution of our identities really a coherent one? There can be no doubt that as a matter of fact they are socially constituted in the way the thesis suggests. Of course, not all of one's projects are constitutive of one's identity; it may not even be true of such vitally important concerns as one's vocation. (It is a sure sign of middle-class professionalism to think that most people have no conception of themselves as persons which does not include their jobs.) Yet there is no doubt that many people cannot conceive of themselves apart from at least some of their merely contingent, 'morally arbitrary', social characteristics, such as gender, religion, ethnicity, fundamental moral values, and so on. However, what we regard as identity-constituting characteristics tends to change over time: religion was once so treated in the political sphere and hence conflicts between religious groups were seen, not as conflicts among interests, but as conflicts among identities. To compromise an interest was seen as selling out one's essential personhood, to secure a right as establishing it. In some modern states, ethnic nationalism continues to play a similar role. Whether or not we should welcome the politics of identity or not is a very complicated issue. Here I merely wish to suggest why it poses no threat to this compromise between consent and community.

To challenge the thesis that consent is necessary for justified authority it is not sufficient to prove that *some* of our morally arbitrary, accidental characteristics are identity-constituting. For suppose that gender has this role. That would not weaken the claim that men and women have an obligation to obey only if they agree to do so. For it to do the work expected of it, we would have to show that *political obligation* is constitutive of one's identity as a person. If that were true it would indeed make no sense to ask whether we are bound by our consent, because if we were not so bound we would be different people. Now, political obligation involves the acceptance of authority relations, that is, acceptance that the requirements of one's state create moral duties. Can these be identity-constituting? It is not impossible that this should be so, although it does seem much less plausible than the claims of religion, values, or ethnicity. It is important to note that a consent theorist is not committed to the unlikely position that one's nationality is not part of one's identity. In so far as such questions are intelligible at all, perhaps it does make sense to say that if one had been Italian rather than Scots one would have been a different person. But this has little to do with the authority states claim. After all, what would it mean to say that outside authority relations one had no conception of oneself as a person? It would mean that at the core of one's very self-understanding lie the commands of another. This is much more than the normal surrender of judgement characteristic of any obedience to authority. There, an independently constituted subject surrenders his judgement, usually for limited time and purposes. In the political communitarian view, however, the person has lost any conception of himself apart from what others tell him to do. I do not know how common that attitude is, but it is hard to imagine why it should be thought to have any moral value. The great obstacle for modern communitarians is finding some way to give the theory critical edge, of allowing for evaluation of the identity-constituting communities to which people belong (some way of approving Bruderhof while denouncing Salem Massachusetts), and of allowing for the competing commitments which each person feels.[31] It is, of course, possible to follow the classical idealist route and posit some transcendental or historical standpoint from which to adjudge communities as good or bad, say by the extent to which they help realize the idea of the state, or freedom, or human perfection. But that move, common to thinkers like Hegel and Green, finds little favour among modern communitarians, who are drawn to the warmth and local colour of community precisely because they are sceptical of any transcendental standpoint. They may propose instead that all criticism begin internally, as must the criticism of a social practice, in Alasdair MacIntyre's view.[32] But if the community's authority relations are constitutive of our very identities, even this edge gets dulled. To begin to transform one's community would not simply be an exercise in self-discovery or the first tentative kick at the ladder upon which we have ascended; it would be a violation of duty. An identity constituted by authority relations is communitarianism at its least appealing. It is no accident that many communitarians have seen the ideal social order as being non-authoritarian and that some have found the appeal of anarchism hard to resist. One may perfectly well hold that ethics must be socially situated and reject the view that there can be no coherent self-understanding apart from authority relations. Moreover, both the transcendental and the internal critical stances misunderstand what is at issue. To show that good communities can be distinguished from bad ones is not sufficient to the task at hand. It does not establish the authority of good communities any more than being able to distinguish good parents from bad ones secures their authority. No one can have legitimate authority if they use it unjustly; but some just people and institutions can none the less lack it.

THE COMMUNITY OF COMMUNITIES?

Underlying much of modern communitarianism are certain classical doctrines which have found their way into the civic republican tradition. These have coalesced around the rejection of political instrumentalism. The original text puts the point as well as any of its modern supporters:

> a polis is not a mere society, having a common territory, established for the prevention of wrong-doing and for the sake of exchange. These are conditions without which a polis cannot exist; but all of them together do not constitute a polis, which is a community of families and aggregations of families in well-being, for the sake of a perfect and self-sufficing life.[33]

The polis is thus a community of communities and, because it is uniquely self-sufficient, it provides the paramount forum for human development. The instrumental justifications for association, such as those offered by conventionalists and contractarians, at most touch the necessary infrastructure for political life.

The weaker thesis, that political life has non-instrumental value, has been accepted here. The common status of citizenship may indeed have intrinsic value. But the above passage also suggests a stronger and less attractive thesis that political life is the highest form of social existence. Whatever the truth concerning the polis, it is difficult to accept that the modern state is a complete community, sufficient for its members' material and moral needs. Not even the largest and most wealthy of our states can be self-sufficient. Ecological interdependency has become a real constraint on their actions; citizens' wants have expanded to include goods which their own states do not or cannot profitably produce, leading to economic interdependency; and, most important of all, the changes in the technology of warfare have irreversibly altered almost every state's capacity to guarantee the security of its own citizens. In view of such changed circumstances, it would be very odd to continue to insist that the state is a complete form of community. Nor can its status be underwritten by appeal to that other famous Aristotelian argument: 'If all communities aim at some good, the polis, which is the highest of all, and which embraces all the rest, aims, and in a greater degree than any other, at the highest good.'[34] That is to confuse the common good with the highest good. It may be that the all-embracing goods which civic association provides are in fact merely the lowest common denominators amongst a wide range of diverse values. The claim that these common goods have non-instrumental value does not establish that they are goods of the highest value.

The relevance of these strands of traditional civic republicanism to the moral situation of modern citizens is therefore somewhat limited and, despite their prominence in communitarian thought, they do not advance the present argument. The rejection of political instrumentalism need not incline us to accept that the state is the unique or paramount arena for pursuing the common good. Indeed, those communal forms of association which are now felt to have the greatest importance are narrower ones like families, trade unions, and ethnic and religious groups. These do tend to be identity-constituting and they impose serious obligations on their members. Indeed, when the political order is viewed as external and anonymous, their demands will be felt to be particularly important and will often give rise to conflicts of duty. There is nothing in the nature of the state which guarantees that these conflicts will always be resolved in its favour. Here, at least, the pluralists' picture seems the most plausible: 'no man's allegiance is, in fact, unique. He is a point towards which a thousand associations converge; what then we ask is that where conflict comes we have assurance that he follows the path of his instructed conscience.'[35]

None of this means that commitment to civic life as one's primary locus of loyalty must be irrational. Far from it: there remain many contingent factors which make political community and its shared goods reasonable as primary commitments. It might be, for example, that people have a yearning for middle-range attachments, broader than most other associations in the political system but stopping short of the human race or the Kingdom of Ends, which help them partly transcend the claims of their particular ethnic, religious, or partisan group, but which are more intelligible and easily accommodated than the requirements of complete community. Simply as a decision problem, it is often easier to obey the law than the moral law: its requirements are often (though not necessarily) clearer and thus provide a publicly recognized standard of aspiration. In a reasonably just state they will normally coincide with the requirements of morality and will thus tend to produce the same ends by other means. And to this mundane thesis we might join a more speculative claim. T. H. Green suggests that, 'the love of mankind ... needs to be particularized in order to have any power over life and action. Just as there can be no true friendship except towards this or that individual, so there can be no true public spirit which is not localized in some way.'[36] The human condition being a finite one of limited intelligence and sympathies, it may be that we can only participate in the ideal of complete community in partial and incomplete ways. A reasonably just state may provide a realistic and reachable forum for the wider forms of friendship. But none of these considerations is powerful enough to sustain the conclusion that rational persons *must* have as their primary locus of loyalty the civic order, for they cannot show that the shared goods of civic life are always dominant. At best, they show that such commitments may be rational and justified, and that they can figure in a sound theory of legitimate authority. Perhaps we cannot fairly expect a stronger conclusion from arguments at this level of generality.

Thus it appears that the radical consent theorist and the radical communitarian both offer inadequate conceptions of what is at stake in the problem of political authority. The radical consent theorist is wrong to think that consent can only function to create duties *ex nihilo* and wrong to think that there are no indivisible goods which are intrinsically valuable. The radical communitarian is wrong to think that the social thesis justifies treating the state's requirements as authoritative, and wrong to think that authority relations partly constitute our identities. The truth of the matter is best understood by seeing that each of these addresses a different aspect of our problem: the communitarian the structure and content of our duties, the consent theorist their incumbency. A suitably socialized extension of consent theory will therefore provide an adequate justification of political authority, one superior to the classical conventionalist, contractarian, and consent-based accounts, and without the unattractive features of full-blooded communitarianism. It is clear, however, that its scope will still be narrower than any of those theories, for it is unlikely to be able to deliver the conclusion that everyone is so bound. It offers a picture of the state in which authority is justified over some perhaps, but not over all.

NOTES

1 T. McPherson, *Political Obligation* (London: Routledge and Kegan Paul, 1967), 63.
2 Following S. Lukes, *Individualism* (Oxford: Basil Blackwell, 1973).
3 Cf. C. C. Gould, *Marx's Social Ontology* (Cambridge, Mass.: MIT Press, 1978), ch. 1.
4 For some interesting reflections on why not, see H. Putnam, *Meaning and the Moral Sciences* (London: Routledge and Kegan Paul, 1978), 66–77.
5 S. Lukes, *Individualism*, 99–106.
6 J. McT. E. McTaggart, 'The Individualism of Value', in *Philosophical Studies* ed. E. V. Keeling (London: Edward Arnold, 1934), 109.
7 H. F. Pitkin, 'Obligation and Consent', *American Political Science Review* 59 (1965) and 60 (1966), repr. in P. Laslett, W. G. Runciman, and Q. Skinner, eds., *Philosophy, Politics and Society*, 4th ser. (Oxford: Blackwell, 1972), 75.
8 Ibid. 78.
9 Ibid. 75.
10 T. McPherson, *Political Obligation*, 64. Cf. T. D. Weldon, *The Vocabulary of Politics* (London: John Murray, 1946) 57 for what may be the original source of these arguments.
11 T. H. Green, *Lectures on the Principles of Political Obligation* (London: Longmans, Green and Co., 1950), 122.
12 P. Winch, 'Authority', in Quinton, ed., *Political Philosophy* (Oxford, 1967), 105.
13 Ibid. 110. And compare H. F. Pitkin, 'Obligation and Consent' with her *Wittgenstein and Justice*, (Berkeley: University of California Press, 1972), 199–204.
14 C. Taylor, 'Atomism', in A. Kontos, ed., *Powers, Possessions and Freedom* (Toronto: University of Toronto Press, 1979), 39–61.
15 Ibid. 58–9.
16 Ibid. 59.

17 On the difference between liability to sanctions and recognition of duties see, H. L. A. Hart, *The Concept of Law* (Oxford: Oxford University Press, 1961), 79–88; and P. M. S. Hacker, 'Sanction Theories of Duty', in A. W. B. Simpson, ed., *Oxford Essays in Jurisprudence*, 2nd ser. (Oxford: Clarendon Press, 1973), 131–70.
18 H. F. Pitkin, 'Obligation and Consent'.
19 Ibid. 56.
20 Ibid. 57.
21 J. Dunn, 'Consent in the Political Theory of John Locke', in his *Political Obligation in its Historical Context* (Cambridge: Cambridge University Press, 1980), 52.
22 Ibid. 33.
23 J. Dunn, *The Political Thought of John Locke* (Cambridge: Cambridge University Press, 1969), 143.
24 '[A]lthough within certain limits I may choose my station according to my own liking, yet I and everyone else must have some station with duties pertaining to it, and those duties do not depend on our opinion or liking.' F. H. Bradley, *Ethical Studies*, 2nd edn. (Oxford: Oxford University Press, 1962), 176.
25 Cf. D. Réaume, 'Individuals, Groups and Rights to Public Goods', *University of Toronto Law Journal* 38 (1988), 1–27.
26 G. W. F. Hegel, *The Philosophy of Right*, trans. T. M. Knox (Oxford: Oxford University Press, 1958), §§ 75, 75A (pp. 58–9, 242).
27 The distinction is due to M. Stocker, 'Moral Duties, Institutions, and Natural Facts', *Monist* 54 (1970), 605.
28 M. J. Sandel, *Liberalism and the Limits of Justice* (Cambridge: Cambridge University Press, 1982), esp. 59–65.
29 Ibid. 62.
30 Ibid.
31 For an excellent introduction to these problems, see A. Gutmann, 'Communitarian Critics of Liberalism', *Philosophy and Public Affairs* 14 (1985), 308–22.
32 A. MacIntyre, *After Virtue* (Notre Dame: University of Notre Dame Press, 1981), 175–89.
33 Aristotle, *Politics*, 1280^b 30–5, trans. B. Jowett (amended) (New York: Modern Library, 1943).
34 Aristotle, *Politics*, 1252^a 1–5, trans. B. Jowett. See the discussion in S. I. Benn and R. S. Peters, *Social Principles and the Democratic State* (London: George Allen and Unwin, 1965), 268–77, and in M. Walzer, *Obligations* (Cambridge, Mass.: Harvard University Press, 1970), 19–20.
35 H. J. Laski, *Authority in the Modern State* (New Haven: Yale University Press, 1919), 92.
36 T. H. Green, *Lectures on the Principles of Political Obligation*, 175.

11
Promissory Obligation: The Theme of Social Contract

K. GREENAWALT

For most of the history of liberal democracies, the dominant theory about why citizens are obligated to obey the law has been social contract. According to a traditional version of that theory, a person is obligated to obey the law because he has consented to the government in a manner that includes a promise to abide by its decisions. In English-speaking countries, including the United States, it is John Locke's account of social contract[1] that has been most influential; as recently as 1970 a leading academic lawyer could speak of his theory as "the only modern rival for the doctrine that power proceeds from the barrel of a gun."[2]

This chapter deals with social contract theory insofar as it stands for genuine claims about consent and promise. The aim of the chapter is to outline the present and potential place of promise as a source of obligation to obey the law. That effort requires pursuit of a number of different but related topics. I first sketch the basic social contract theory and its tie to political liberalism. After exploring varieties of consent and promise, I conclude that many persons do apparently have promissory obligations to obey laws and other rules but that on no plausible account have all or nearly all citizens or residents of liberal democracies promised to obey. I next try to identify more carefully the persons who have undertaken to obey in a promiselike way and inquire whether their apparent obligations are vitiated by some defect. Finally, I discuss the possibility of liberal democracies consciously making greater use of promise as a source of obligation.

SOCIAL CONTRACT THEORY AND PROMISES TO OBEY

The main question that traditional social contract theory tries to answer is how a government can justly have coercive powers over free individuals. The answer, in familiar words, is that governments derive their just powers from the consent of the governed. People agree to the authority of government because the alternative of life without government would be much worse. This consent to government most directly involves acquiescence in actions of the government that are within the sphere of the authority conferred. Although the last chapter shows that such consent need not logically carry an undertaking to comply with what the government demands, the traditional social contract view is that acceptance of the government's authority does involve a corollary agreement to obey.[3] Thus, the thrust of social contract theory is to make a person's relationship to the state, or to fellow citizens, like that of a promisor: he has made something like a promise to obey the law.

This view conceives a person's obligation to obey as based on an autonomous commitment to act in accordance with the law; the limitation on what one can do is self-chosen. A promissory theory of why one should obey the law, therefore, involves moral obligation not only in the broader sense generally employed in this essay, but also in the narrower sense of moral constraints that are voluntarily undertaken.

Social contract theory connects to liberalism in two important ways. Although Hobbes's endorsement of authoritarian rule[4] and Jean Jacques Rousseau's proposal of what might be called democratic totalitarianism[5] show that social contract accounts of political legitimacy need not invariably support liberal democracy, the prevailing Anglo-American theory, drawn from Locke, has contemplated a government limited in its authority to the purposes that underlie its existence and constituted according to the periodic expression of wishes by its citizens. In this conception, a promise to obey is not unqualified; its force depends on continuance of democratic processes and on the government not exceeding its proper powers. In a deeper sense, social contract theory is a reflection of a liberal conception of human nature that emphasizes freedom and autonomy.

Although theories differ on exactly why promises carry moral force, promise is widely regarded as the clearest way in which people voluntarily assume moral obligations. By promising to perform an act, a person may generate a moral requirement that did not previously exist or may (as when one promises to do what is already a moral duty) supplement independent moral reasons for doing the act. The moral force of promise is sometimes thought to depend on the existence of a social convention of promise keeping, but mutual understanding of the significance of promise language, which could exist between two people aware of conventions of promise in another society, is sufficient to create moral obligation.[6] In any event, since both the apposite linguistic conventions and the social practice of promise keeping exist in modern society, the power of promises to generate moral obligations is undisputed.

That conclusion does not settle whether promises to do morally wrong acts carry any force, a problem I discuss later, nor does it tell us how great the moral force of promises is. On the latter subject, I shall accept the common assumptions that any undefective serious promise does carry substantial moral force and that breach of even the most clearly unconditional promise can sometimes be morally appropriate. If I foolishly say, "On absolutely no account will I fail to be there," and then find myself in the unexpected position of having to choose between showing up and saving ten lives, I should save the ten lives.[7]

EXPRESS, TACIT, AND IMPLIED PROMISES

One can be obligated in the way promissory theory assumes if one has made a promise or engaged in a promise-like act, and the promise is not undercut by duress or some other vitiating condition. Assessment of the idea that citizens have promised to obey the law demands a careful appraisal of the ways in which promissory obligations can arise.

Instances of express and tacit consent are fairly straightforward. Suppose a law school dean tells Faith, a prospective teacher, "Our practice is that faculty members teach whatever subjects the dean assigns." If Faith responds, "That's all right with me," she has explicitly agreed to comply with the practice. But promise are not always express. If the dean explains the practice and says, "If I don't hear to the contrary, I'll assume you have no objections," Faith has tacitly agreed by remaining silent and accepting a faculty position. When a person expressly or tacitly promises, he has actually signified commitment. As long as no misunderstanding exists about the nature of his words or acts,[8] the force of the commitment is plain.

Beyond clear instances of tacit promise, we move to murkier waters, where both the proper terminology and the force of one's actions become more troublesome.

Illustration 1:
The dean simply describes the practices of the law school to

Faith without asking for any indication of her agreement to them. Two years later, Faith objects vociferously when the dean asks her to teach Torts. Although not denying that, given her background and the school's needs, Torts would be a reasonable course for her to teach, Faith objects that she does not want to teach Torts. The dean responds, "You impliedly agreed to follow our practice of dean assignment when you accepted the job."

What would the dean's statement about implied agreement mean? The dean might mean that both he and Faith understood that when a job applicant is told conditions of employment and does not object, the acceptance of the job really *signifies* agreement to the conditions. In this view, the dean would be claiming that Faith had tacitly promised to comply. But the dean might mean something different — that even though Faith's accepting the position did not signify agreement to the condition of dean assignment, her course of action committed her in some way to comply with it.

One claim of this sort is that a person's actual agreement to one thing represents a logical or moral commitment to something else.

Illustration 2:
A mother tells her twelve-year-old son he can attend a local college basketball game. She remarks on the evening of the game, "Be home by 10:00." He responds, "You said I could go to the game; it won't be over until 10:45 and it takes fifteen minutes to get home; so you've already agreed I can stay out until 11:00."

Assuming that leaving in midgame is not a serious option, the mother's original permission committed her logically to the 11:00 hour, even if she did not realize that at the time.[9] The moral connection between what someone did agree to and what it is claimed he impliedly agreed to may be represented by a person's sharing an apartment with a friend. In the absence of an explicit disclaimer before the friend moves in, the original tenant may impliedly have consented to the friend's having visitors, since it would be morally wrong to deny that liberty to a friend with whom one shares an apartment.

Whether Faith was committed logically or morally would depend on the circumstances. If Faith, without reading the stated rules governing the school, had signified acceptance of them, and these rules included the practice of dean assignment, she would logically have committed herself to accept the practice though not consciously agreeing to it. If she had initially expressed a willingness to do whatever was in the school's interest, the dean might argue that she was morally committed to accept dean assignment. Since some fortunate law school teachers are not subject to the dean's discretion about teaching assignments, Faith's acceptance of the job alone probably would not represent either a logical or a moral commitment to accept the practice.

The dean's assertion about implied consent might instead amount to a more complex claim that Faith's failure to raise any objection when she could have and her acceptance of the job bind her morally to accept his assignment. The dean's position would be strongest if three factors coalesced. The first involves Faith's state of mind up to the time she accepted the job. Faith may have acquiesced in the stated conditions even if she never agreed to observe them. (Exactly what state of mind a person need have in this respect is sometimes a tricky question, since some matters are so routine they are not explicitly considered. If a tennis player's actions presuppose the relevance of the usual rules – serving behind the baseline, attempting to hit the ball in court, and so on – we might say he intends to play by the rules even if he has not addressed his thoughts to the question.) The second factor is the reasonable belief of others about Faith's intent. If others at the law school believed and had good reason to believe that Faith acquiesced in dean assignment, the dean's claim of implied consent is strengthened. Reasonable belief depends substantially on factual likelihood, but the moral relationship between teaching law in a faculty and having the dean assign one's courses is also relevant. The closely related third factor involves the locus of responsibility for clarifying matters. If accepted conventions would require Faith to express a nonacquiescent state of mind, then her silent acceptance of the job can have a significance it might not have if everyone understood that no one is bound to a practice like dean assignment unless he signifies consent. When all three factors are present – subjective unexpressed acquiescence, reasonable belief in acquiescence by others, and conventions placing the burden of expressing nonacquiescence on the individual applicant – then implied consent is clearly present.

None of the factors, alone, appears sufficient to generate implied consent. If the conventional burden was on the dean to elicit an expression of consent and others did not reasonably think Faith had acquiesced, the fact that her unexpressed state of mind was acquiescent would not amount to implied consent. If others reasonably supposed she was acquiescent, but she in fact was not and the dean had failed to carry his burden of finding out, she would not have impliedly consented. And if the conventional burden was on Faith, but she had neither acquiesced nor been reasonably thought to do so, she would not have impliedly consented.

When two of the factors are present, the outcome is more debatable. Suppose, first, that Faith did acquiesce and others reasonably thought she did, although the dean failed to discharge his burden of finding out. The dean would have a strong argument that since she and others were proceeding on the assumption that she acquiesced, she was bound to comply. Similarly, if her state of mind was acquiescent and she had failed to indicate to the contrary, and conventions were quite clear that it was her responsibility to do so, she may be bound although others, knowing her character, doubted she was really willing to go along.

The most interesting case may be one in which Faith never intended to acquiesce but others reasonably supposed she had and conventions placed on her the burden of indicating nonacquiescence. This case raises the question of whether one can ever impliedly consent without being willing to acquiesce.[10] Plainly, if Faith assumed the burden was on her to indicate nonacquiescence and remained silent only because she thought she would not be offered the job is she said she was unwilling to accept assignment by the dean, she has intentionally misled others about her state of mind, and that is enough for implied consent. If she was negligent about her responsibilities, at fault for her unawareness of the relevant convention, she may also be bound to act as if she had consented, although here it becomes somewhat arbitrary whether one says "she did impliedly consent" or "she is bound to act as if she impliedly consented." Her present obligations may at this point be partly determined by a fourth factor – the degree to which others have detrimentally relied on her acquiescence. If the school's hiring of her or taking other steps depended on the assumption that she accepted dean assignment, it is evident that she is bound.

Detrimental reliance, an essential element in the legal doctrine of promissory estoppel, plays a particularly critical role if Faith's failure to follow the convention is innocent and not her fault, for example, because she comes from another culture where it is always up to the dean to ask about acquiesence to practices. If the school has not relied on her acquiescence, she can fairly resist being bound on the basis of an innocent mistake that has caused no harm; but if the school has reasonably relied, she may be bound not to shift the damage for her innocent failure onto the school. Although some of these variations leave uncertainty about the precise boundaries of implied promise, this uncertainty is warranted both by our loose understanding of the concept and, more important, by genuine doubts about what is necessary at the edges to trigger normative obligations like those accompanying promise.

At the outer boundaries of implied promise, notions of fair play may figure more importantly than promise; and it may not matter greatly in which vein some situations are described. But we need to be aware of the possibility that as one moves from express to tacit to implied consent, not only do opportunities for misunderstanding about what conduct signifies increase, but the *force* of obligations undertaken may diminish somewhat. If Faith accepts the dean's claim that she impliedly consented, she might still say, "That's not the same as actually promising." Some people who knowingly mislead others into thinking they agree to do something may nonetheless balk at saying so explicitly. Although such hesitation might reflect a wish not to lie about one's present state of mind, it may also indicate a sense that explicit promises carry more force.

Even claims of implied promise rest on some act of Faith that is asserted to be the basis of her obligation to comply; these claims are thus distinguishable from claims based on hypothetical consent or agreement. Some versions of social contract theory purport to describe what institutions *would be* agreed to by people: actual people, people rationally pursuing their own self-interests, or imaginary people denuded of some human characteristics.[11] These theories, of which John Rawls's original position is best known,[12] do not depend on the special moral force of promises or consent; rather, they reveal independent reasons why an institutional scheme is morally supportable, showing that it is fair or promotes the interests of all or most people.[13] The fact that I might have agreed to some practice under certain circumstances does not itself establish that I have actually undertaken any obligation to comply,[14] and claims based on hypothetical agreement are thus outside the scope of this discussion.

ARE PROMISSORY UNDERTAKINGS A GENERAL SOURCE OF OBLIGATION TO OBEY THE LAW?

For a promissory theory of political obligation to be persuasive, people must have undertaken a promissory obligation to obey the law. I now turn to examine whether some or all people have

Promissory Obligation: The Theme of Social Contract 275

undertaken to obey some or all laws through actions that amount to a promise in one of the senses examined in the previous section.

Typical social contract theories envision some stage at which people agree to set up a government with a certain form. Room for disagreement exists over whether historical events like the Mayflower Compact or the adoption and ratification of the federal Constitution represent a voluntary creation of government consented to by the governed. In the case of the Mayflower Compact, the government created by agreement was ultimately subsidiary to the British government; in the case of the Constitution not all citizens participated in the representative processes by which the new government was created and not all those who did participate acquiesced. In any event, for a genuine promissory theory of obligation, the status of these historical events is largely beside the point. A particular person, right now, can be obligated only if that person has undertaken to obey. Our ancestors do not have the capacity to agree and promise for us, even if they have acted with the welfare of succeeding generations in mind. Their voluntary agreements may be some evidence that had we been in their shoes we would have agreed to the same things, but the argument based on such evidence is one of hypothetical consent and promise. It concerns what we would have promised in hypothetical conditions, not what we have actually undertaken to do.

The crucial question for any promissory theory is whether people now alive have promised to obey the law. For this purpose, whether a government was actually created by a process involving consent or originated through an exercise of force is not central. What counts for an individual is whether he or she has promised to obey; neither the unanimous agreement of those originally subject to the legal order nor the agreement of most of one's fellow citizens can obligate an individual who has not agreed.

Some people do expressly promise to obey at least some laws. Many elected officials and some appointed officials take oaths of office; and some professionals, including lawyers, take oaths when they enter their professions. These oaths, I suggest below, concern official or professional performance; they do not directly commit one to general law-abidingness. Naturalized citizens take oaths with more inclusive import. They promise to "defend the Constitution and the laws of the United States" and to "bear true faith and allegiance to the same."[15]

Most citizens make no such express promise. True, the large majority of Americans have said the Pledge of Allegiance, but that is vague in content,[16] usually said as matter of rote, and recited mainly in childhood. Whatever force a pledge like this *might be given*, presently it does not constitute a serious promise to obey. A Law Day speaker who swears faithfulness to the law may have promised his listeners that he will obey; and more informal remarks may have a similar effect, but relatively few members of liberal societies go about telling others of their generalized commitment to be law-abiding.

If most citizens have agreed to obey the law, the agreement must be tacit or implied; but the grounds for such agreement are very hard to find.

The most frequent assertion about consent in liberal democracies is that by participating in the government, citizens acknowledge its legitimacy and agree to obey its laws.[17] Participating directly in the deliberations and voting of small groups, such as faculties or student councils, may be understood in this manner. A person who was not willing to comply with the outcome would be expected to withdraw or at least state an unwillingness to be bound. Someone who participates without any disclaimer may reasonably be understood to be bound by the result in the same manner as someone who explicitly agrees to accept the majority's decision.

The application of this approach to citizens of liberal democratic states faces substantial obstacles. We may note, first of all, that voting could not amount to consent in states such as Australia, where people are actually required to vote. More significantly, in states where voting is optional a good many citizens never exercise their privilege, so a theory of obligation based on voting (or any other form of active participation in government) will omit substantial numbers of citizens, as well as alien residents who are not allowed to vote.[18] Thus, voting or other forms of voluntary political participation cannot underlie a fully general theory of obligation that would reach all residents or even all citizens. Despite these obvious limitations of the theory, if uncompelled voters have implicitly promised to obey the law, a powerful and broad ground of obligation exists. Unfortunately, the argument for such an obligation fails.

Certainly voting in an ordinary election does not involve any explicit promise; the voter engages in no undertaking. Nor is it plausible to suppose that voting amounts to tacit consent, in the sense of a clear, though nonverbal, indication of an accepting attitude toward the government and its laws. In the United States and many other countries, avowed revolutionaries are permitted to vote; no one takes their efforts to manipulate the political processes as showing their approval of the government. Ordinary citizens are not told authoritatively that voting, by which means they express preferences for some candidates over others,[19] counts as approval of the government and a promise to obey its laws; no established social convention treats voting in political elections as a signification of agreement.

What remains is a possible argument about implied consent and promise – that although voting does not actually signify agreement to comply with law, it puts an individual in the normative posture of one who has agreed. Although any attempt to evaluate this argument fully is plagued by uncertainties concerning the boundaries of implied promise, I will outline and criticize two of the forms in which it might be developed.

The first form relies heavily on the mental attitude of the person who votes, claiming that if the voter believes the privilege of voting carries duties of compliance, then voting constitutes an implied promise to comply.[20] Assuming, as I have suggested, that voting does not actually signify consent, it may be asked how voting itself figures in this form of the argument. Unless the claim is that voting generates justifiable expectations in others, a possibility that lies at the heart of what I will treat as the second form of the argument for implied promise, the role of voting must be to focus the voter's mental attitude. Were this its exclusive significance, presumably everyone with the requisite mental attitude would be bound whether he or she had voted or not. This conclusion fits well with the idea expressed by some political scientists that for many poeple *not* voting reflects acquiescence with the present state of affairs, and that such people will choose to vote only when they become disturbed with existing or prospective government officials. A mental attitude alone, however, is not enough on which to ground a promise-like obligation to obey, as I have already suggested.

A further difficulty with this argument concerns the mental attitude most voters are likely to have. Until relevant empirical evidence is obtained, we must rely on our intuitions and informal sources of information. These lead me to conclude that most voters do not think very precisely about what obligations the privilege of voting carries.[21] Many may have some vague sense that they owe, in return, some duty to acquiesce in the results of the political process; but this sense typically falls far short of a perceived obligation to comply with every law, or even every just law, that eventuates from the officials elected.

Building on the notion of promissory estoppel, the second form of the argument from implied consent asserts that, since a person would act unfairly by voting and declining to be bound, others are justified in assuming that voters who are silent are willing to be bound and the act of voting alone is enough to obligate.[22] This version of the argument also has powerful difficulties. The direct argument that fairness requires obedience to law is considered in chapter 7 of my book *Conflicts of Law and Morality*, but I shall here assume an element of unfairness in someone's voting and not submitting to responsibilities of citizenship. The steps from this premise to a conclusion about implied consent, however, are strained.

One problem concerns what others might reasonably assume about the voter's willingness to be bound. The kinds of acquiescent attitudes that different people have toward their governments vary greatly, as do their ideas of what sort of behavior is unfair. When the act of voting is so far removed from the decisive deliberations and decisions that yield legal norms, an assumption that a voter is willing to comply with all laws would not be warranted.

Other difficulties inhere in the supposed mechanisms through which a promise to obey is implied. In the ordinary situation of implied promise, the person who is bound acts in a manner known to those toward whom he is obligated, he has forfeited an opportunity to disclaim the obligation, and others have relied on his behavior. In modern urban settings, a person's decision to vote may or may not be known to those outside his family, depending on how much he talks about his political behavior. At the polling place, he meets mostly strangers, though a few acquaintances may be voting at the same time. The fact of his voting is recorded, of course, and some unfamiliar local election official has checked off his name; but no significant government official is aware that he has voted.

Occasionally people do make statements about what their actions regarding voting signify. As Peter Singer notes, radical American opponents of the Vietnam War publicized their refusal to vote in the 1968 presidential election.[23] They said they did not wish to confer legitimacy on the political process and urged others to follow their example. We can certainly imagine other groups publicizing the fact that their participation in an election does connote acceptance of the results. But what can be done by the ordinary person who is not politically active but is highly alienated or wishes to qualify any commitment otherwise implied by voting? Is he supposed to tell his friends and neighbors exactly what his vote means or write a letter to the government? No one in the government is expected to deal with such matters and many friends and neighbors simply would not care precisely what one's attitudes about voting are. Thus, although anyone is *free* to make a disclaimer, it is not a serious option for many people. And the absence of that a serious option severely compromises what can reasonably be inferred from the failure to disclaim.

The government's actions are not affected by what individual voters conceive as their obligations of citizenship; and it is highly doubtful that any individual's attitudes toward government and the law are altered by the simple fact that someone else has voted. Whether or not others loosely assume that a voter is willing to be bound, they do not rely on that assumption in their own lives. No one else is worse off because a person has failed to disclaim a possible implication of his vote. Detrimental reliance is not a necessary condition of implied consent; but when it and any subjective acquiescence are absent, a failure to disclaim could generate an obligation only if the chance to disclaim and its significance were readily apparent in the society. Neither condition is met in the context of voting.

The strongest argument for obligation deriving from voting is one that combines what I have treated as the first and second forms of the argument. If *both* the voter and others aware of his act of voting understand his vote to carry a duty to comply, then voting may have that effect even if it does not actually *signify* an undertaking to comply. Even in the cases meeting these requisites, however, it is probably unusual to have anything as precise as an implied promise to obey all laws.

The other familiar arguments about tacit and implied consent rely on residence and receipt of benefits. Remaining in a country certainly does not amount, as Locke supposed,[24] to tacit agreement to obey the laws.[25] People stay in homelands because of language, culture,[26] job, friends, and family; their inertia hardly indicates approval or acceptance of government and laws.[27] Nor is this, alone, enough to lead others to suppose any commitment to obey has been undertaken. The old bumper sticker message "America: Love It or Leave It" is an appeal; it does not reflect common understanding of what remaining in the United States means.

Although apparently conceding this much, Harry Beran has urged that continuing in residence after one reaches majority does generate an obligation to obey the law.[28] He argues that by remaining in the state people do understand that they "accept full membership" in the community; that acceptance is taken by Beran to imply an obligation to obey because such an obligation is an aspect of the moral significance of full membership and one would fail to realize this only through negligence. Beran's theory can be understood as a variant of the idea that consent to one thing logically or morally implies a commitment to something else of a sort that one initially does not recognize. To establish that an adult resident was negligent in not recognizing that full membership carries a duty to obey, Beran would need to show that full membership does carry this significance. Much of chapters 6–8 of my book *Conflicts of Law and Morality* casts serious doubt on the proposition that being a good citizen necessarily means conceiving oneself as under a duty to obey all laws. But there are more straightforward objections to Beran's approach.[29] As people continue in residence, neither they nor their neighbors assume that their doing so is accepting full membership; and, as with the case of voting, they are presented with no realistic way to disclaim such an understanding. Failing to leave the country does not usually amount to tacit or implied consent to any obligations of citizenship.

Any conclusion about agreement to obey based on receipt of government benefits would be similarly misfounded. Residents have no choice about many benefits; for example, they cannot refuse the general security afforded by police and military protection. Even as to benefits voluntarily taken, the claim of tacit or implied agreement has a fatal flaw. People continue to receive benefits from the state that they could refuse even when their preferred government is overturned by domestic revolution or foreign invasion. Receiving benefits from the state does not indicate acceptance of a regime and its laws, as starting a game of tennis indicates acceptance of the standard rules, nor is it understood to do so by others.

The arguments about implied promise based on residence and receipt of benefits are less plausible than the argument based on voting. We must conclude that most citizens do not have a promise-like obligation to comply with all laws that issue from the government.

WHO HAS UNDERTAKEN TO OBEY THE LAW?

Though promise is not a general source of obligation to obey the law, it is a source for some people at least with respect to some laws. In the next section, I will examine the significance and force of explicit and formal undertakings such as oaths. Here I consider what other acts and attitudes may generate promissory or related obligations to obey.

Even if they do not take oaths of office, people who voluntarily

Promissory Obligation: The Theme of Social Contract

assume positions of official responsibility have tacitly or impliedly promised to perform their duties in accordance with the rules that govern the exercise of those duties. If taking office does not itself amount to signifying one's willingness to comply, then the new office holder's silence is the basis for legitimate expectations on the part of others that he will perform the duties of the office.

May promise-like obligations exist when neither an oath nor a definite acceptance of official position is involved? The claim that they may is strongest when someone, such as a Law Day speaker, publicly pledges himself to observe the law. A pledge of this sort may not be accepted by particular individuals in the manner that most promises are accepted,[30] but because it is designed to influence those who hear it and may be relied upon in some remote way,[31] the promise carries moral force. More informal comments that express or imply a commitment to obey laws could also carry some force. For this purpose, a statement about the obligations one already conceives oneself to be under — "I think every citizen is bound to obey the law" — would not suffice; but an actual undertaking — "I commit myself to obey" — would create a binding obligation to those who have received the communication.

Can a mental attitude alone be the source of some obligation to obey the law, if not an obligation based on promise? In the starkest case, one might simply determine that he will obey every law or assign a substantial moral weight in favor of obedience. A more typical attitude would be somewhat less precise, involving respect for one's government and a disposition to obey its laws. Joseph Raz has argued that this attitude of "practical respect" for the law can unlerlie an obligation to obey.[32]

We need to begin by inquiring what the basis for such an attitude might be. If the attitude represents nothing more than the recognition of all the valid arguments for obeying the law, then the attitude itself would seem to add nothing to the force of these arguments. Suppose, instead, the attitude reflected only a mistaken assessment of the force of reasons for obeying the law. Again, the attitude would not constitute an independent obligation to obey the law (except in the general sense that people should do what they *think* is morally right); and once the person understood that his assessment of reasons to obey the law was mistaken, he should feel free to abandon his prior attitude and its practical consequences.

The claim that the attitude can have force is strongest when the attitude is freely chosen, that is, when it is adopted by a person who does not think he is morally compelled to take that point of view. Raz has in mind just such a conscious choice to give to the government more obedience than independent moral principles require. He draws an interesting analogy to friendship. A person is not morally obligated to have friends, but if he does have them, he has obligations to act toward them in certain ways. Raz suggests that similar obligations to comply with law can arise from an attitude of practical respect for law.

Scrutiny of the proposed analogy creates doubt that one's attitude alone is enough to underlie an obligation to obey. The force of moral obligations of friendship derives largely from the mutuality of expectations that arise as people become friends. Sometimes, before a relationship has developed very far, one person may *regard* another as a friend, though neither person has yet treated the other as a friend.[33] Does that attitude alone give rise to obligations? Perhaps a person's free choice of character and commitments does affect what he really ought to do. There may be some virtue, perhaps moral virtue, in sticking to certain choices once they have been made even if choices could have been made differently and even if no one else is relying on them. This position is probably unsound for discrete choices of action: a woman who makes an uncommunicated New Year's resolution to donate money to one charity and ends up donating the money to another is probably not less praiseworthy than a similar woman who carries out the initial resolution. But deeper choices of character and commitment may carry moral force even when freely entered into in the first instance.

If some moral ought does lie behind freely chosen uncommunicated commitments, it is a much weaker ought than derives from communicated commitments and mutual expectations. When a person with the attitude of practical respect for the law has acted toward others in a way that communicates his attitude, the expectations he creates may well be a source of obligation, though reliance on those expectations will be much weaker and more diffuse then the mutual reliance of friends. In this form, implied consent becomes the basis for obligation that derives from the attitude of practical respect.

Any moral force that derives directly from an attitude of practical respect or its communication to others will be limited in scope to its actual coverage. Persons who perceive no independent obligation to obey the law may be unlikely to adopt an undifferentiating attitude of practical respect. Rather, they may identify areas of blindess, invasion of personal domain, overregulation, and so on in which they do not respect the government and would not freely choose to put themselves under an obligation to obey that does

Promissory Obligation: The Theme of Social Contract 283

not already exist. In short, their approval of the government may be selective, much as many older children give considerable respect to elder authority figures in some domains and virtually none in other domains. Thus, even for those who make free choices and communicate them, attitudes of compliance may not constitute the general source of obligation toward all laws that social contract theory has traditionally posited.

THE FORCE AND SIGNIFICANCE OF PROMISES TO OBEY

The conclusions that most citizens have not undertaken to obey the law generally but that some citizens have undertaken to obey at least some laws leave us with two important questions. What is the force and scope of the promises that officials, professionals, and some citizens have made? Should consensual bases of obligation be more widely employed? These questions are explored in this and the succeeding section.

Not everything that looks like a promise creates a binding obligation. As the law of contracts suggests, a promise may lack moral force because of the conditions in which it is given or because of some defect in its terms. As far as the law is concerned, a promise either has force or it does not;[34] moral judgments can be more subtle, recognizing the possibility that conditions may diminish the force of a promise without eliminating it altogether.

Conditions

I will look first at the circumstances of the promise. If the person making a promise is not able to understand its significance, or is incapable of rational judgement, or is forced by a very unpleasant and unfair alternative, the promise is without effect.

None of these conditions vitiates the typical oath of office, or the tacit promise to perform that officials make simply by taking their offices. No one has to hold public office and office holders understand the duties they are undertaking. Society is justified in trying to obligate officials to perform responsibly, and the demand that one who chooses such a position agrees to perform its duties does not amount to anything like duress.

Matters may be a little less clear-cut when we turn to the prospective lawyer. He or she has invested a lot of time and money in preparing for that career. A refusal to take an oath to support the law may mean loss of an opportunity to practice.

Here, the alternative is much more forbidding than in the case of the office holder. Yet, society has a strong interest in the responsible performance of professional duties, and the practice of a profession is a kind of privilege. One has ample warning what is expected when one embarks on training of it. Conditioning the privilege on a stated willingness to perform professional duties is not duress.

The same conclusion applies to the oath of naturalized citizens. A country is undoubtedly under some moral constraints in how it chooses who to permit to be residents and citizens. Strong reasons support the admission of some prospective residents, such as spouses of citizens and those who have cooperated with war efforts of the government; and it may be, as Michael Walzer suggests, that a healthy political order should permit most permanent alien residents to become citizens.[35] In the United States citizenship makes one eligible for a limited number of jobs that aliens may not occupy and gives additional security against deportation, but most legal rights of citizens are also enjoyed by alien residents. Even if the government is morally required to offer resident aliens the chance to become citizens, its decision to extend that opportunity only to those who agree to comply with law does not amount to duress toward those who would like to become citizens.

The situation may be different when persons reasonably fear they will suffer serious harm if they do not agree to obey. Conscripted soldiers in the United States have traditionally taken a "step forward" that represents a promise of allegiance, conscripted jurors take an oath to perform conscientiously, and subpoenaed witnesses must swear to tell the truth. A soldier may rightly perceive that a determined refusal to assent may lead to jail; and some jurors and witnesses fear similar consequences if they refuse to promise. What is the status of promises made in such circumstances?

Putting aside the possible religious significance of an oath to God, the answer will depend on the state of mind of the oath taker and the fairness of the conditions under which the oath is extracted. I shall assume that the choice facing a soldier or prospective juror or witness is not so disturbing that he is rendered incapable of rational choice; the person deliberately chooses to take the oath. That the alternative itself is forbidding is not by itself enough to deprive a promise of its force; a person's consent to an operation and the accompanying implied promise to pay for it carry force, even if they are given in response to a diagnosis that imminent death is the likely alternative.[36] But the threat facing the soldier is different; it has been created by the very institution that seeks his promise. Granting that a government can morally conscript citizens and penalize them for failing to fulfill duties, can it use of vastly unequal bargaining power to compel a person to promise to fulfill the duties actually increase the force of the person's obligations to do so?

I shall attack this complex and troublesome question by initially addressing the less difficult variations. Let us first imagine a soldier or subpoenaed witness who thinks the government's compulsion is fair and who freely gives the requisite oath. When I say he freely gives the requisite oath, I mean he would be willing to promise to perform his duties even if no negative consequence attached to his refusal to promise. Such a person might not have served without the government's compulsion, but finding himself conscripted, he thinks he should perform the role as demanded and is willing to promise to do so. His promise is not extracted under duress because he gives it without regard to the sanctions for refusal. At the other extreme we can imagine someone who correctly thinks that his government's compulsion is unfair and its demanded performance immoral and who would be unwilling to promise to perform the duties were not a serious sanction the only alternative. In that circumstance the requisites of duress – that is, strong and improper pressure producing an unfree choice – are present and the promise is without force.[37]

The intermediate situations are more debatable. Suppose the promisor rightly understands that the government's original compulsion and the demand for a promise are fair, but he would be unwilling to promise unless the demand for his promise was also backed by compulsion. In this case the government has done nothing wrong, yet the promise is offered only to avoid an unpleasant alternative that the government has created to extract the promise. We might initially be inclined to think the government could never justifiably extract a promise under this sort of compulsion; but its doing so generally may lead to a somewhat higher level of performance of important public duties and allow a greater degree of trust between actors and government officials regarding the performance of compelled duties. Given the longstanding swearing of compelled witnesses and the generally accepted use of affirmations of truthfulness on tax forms, we should hesitate to conclude that all forced undertakings are of no effect, especially since our social life is probably somewhat enhanced if people assume they do have force. Quite possibly, however, compelled undertakings have *less* effect than undertakings given under freer conditions.

Does the promise have force if the promisor wrongly thinks government compulsion to promise is unfair? We can imagine the circumstance under which the promisor commits himself, only because of compulsion he regards as wrongful and later is persuaded that the compulsion was appropriate. Such a person should probably regard himself as bound, having consciously given a promise that he recognizes would have had force if he had understood more fully the conditions of its utterance. This conclusion, however, does not determine what view an outsider should take at the time the promise is given. Unless others have relied on the promise to their detriment, the fact that the promisor believes he is promising only under pressing and unfair conditions is probably enough to deprive the promise of moral force.

I have implicitly assumed in all this discussion that whether or not one intends at the time to keep a promise is not critical to its force. Certainly this is true in ordinary settings, and I see no reason it should be different here.

This lengthy discussion shows just how difficult it is to identify instances of duress when government compulsion leads to promises to obey; but I have suggested that the critical elements are the presence of compulsion that is, or is perceived to be, unfair and the fact that a promise would not have been given without the compulsion. Deciding what amounts to unfair compulsion, of course, leaves great latitude for disagreement.

Terms

A second basis for believing a promise to be without force is some defect in its substance: the terms may be part of an unfair exchange, require more than can reasonably be expected, or demand the commission of immoral acts.

Not every binding promise need involve an exchange at all. If someone freely decides to commit himself to perform an act benefiting others, his promise has force even if he expects nothing in return. But when promises to do something are given in return for benefits to be received, a gross unfairness in the exchange may undermine the force of the promise. In some circumstances, the question of fairness of terms may be hard to distinguish from the question of duress, but the basic inquiry concerning terms is whether or not the promisor gets a fair return for what he gives, not whether the promisee acted fairly in trying to elicit a promise.[38]

If one looks at the exchange of benefits and burdens, the oaths of officials, lawyers, and naturalized citizens are fair; those who take the oath receive as much as they promise to give.[39] From the standpoint of almost all prospective witnesses, telling the truth and promising to tell the truth are preferable to going to jail, so the concern about these compelled promises goes to the legitimacy of the government's establishing the grounds of exchange, not to the balance of benefit and burden. A similar conclusion applies to the compelled oath of conscripted soldiers.

Different aspects of the terms of many oaths are troubling and bear on both their force and their reasonable interpretation. These aspects are breadth and duration. John Simmons has suggested that the promise of naturalized citizens may be understood as one "to obey all valid laws."[40] If so, the promise covers all of a society's laws for the rest of a citizen's life. That is quite a promise. Certainly the citizen will not fully keep his promise, because everyone breaks the law on occasion; very likely, the citizen will face at least some circumstances in which the force of the promise will conflict with his sense of moral duty.

Rolf Sartorius has made the claim that people cannot reasonably be held to a promise that covers a vast variety of laws for a long period of time.[41] Before we swallow that claim too readily we should note that in its overall impact on people's lives, a promise to obey laws is, as Sartorius recognizes, not more constraining than the marriage contract; most of us subscribe to that at least once, and we think it has force. The single promise to take someone "in sickness and in health" covers unforeseeable contingencies whose effect those making the promise can scarcely comprehend. Sweeping promises do have force, but the analogy to marriage promises helps illustrate the truth that lies behind the objection to such promises. External conditions and one's own attitudes and beliefs can change drastically over time. People are much less to blame for abandoning commitments when circumstances have altered radically.[42] An *irrevocable* sweeping promise may well lose moral force slowly over time,[43] and it carries more force for expected situations than for unexpected ones.

Another way of dealing with this problem is to suggest that long-term promises carry implied exceptions for changed circumstances. We can certainly imagine circumstances in which the answer to a claim that one is bound by a promise is that the situation at hand simply was not conceived at the time of the promise. A person asked to obey a very wicked law might respond that when he promised to obey a country's laws he never imagined a law of this sort could ever be adopted. The possibility of implied exceptions is important and will often aid in giving a reasonable construction to apparently unqualified promises. Sometimes, though it may often be hard to say just when, the correct analysis is that the promise, properly understood, does not apply rather than that its force is diminished or is outweighed by stronger countervailing reasons.

Implied exceptions, however, do not cover all the difficulties of changed circumstances. Often when one makes a promise, one is consciously aware of the possibility of variant circumstances and promises to be faithful regardless of their dimensions. The marriage contract is a striking example; one whose spouse suffers a debilitating physical illness that drastically alters a relationship cannot plausibly say the marriage promise did not cover this contingency. One of the purposes of many promises is to commit one against a possible change in one's present perspectives and desires. For this reason, the implied exception approach works particularly badly if all that is involved is a change in the outlook of the promisor, not in the external circumstances he faces. Yet people do change over time, and their undertakings of times long past should not exercise too great a restraint on their development. The idea of diminishing force often better captures this normative judgment than the idea of an implied exception.

Even if we put aside the problem of unforeseen circumstances, a promise to obey all laws will certainly be broken. Could a conscientious person subscribe to such a promise? People recognize that the obligation of a promise may be overridden, so when they make one they implicitly acknowledge that something may require them to break it. But honest people do not make unqualified promises if they are sure they will break them.[44] A thoughtful person cannot sincerely promise to obey all valid laws on all occasions.[45] That in itself is strong reason to construe the vague oath of naturalized citizens in some weaker sense, as a promise to support the legal order generally and comport oneself as a law-abiding citizen, or conceivably as a promise always to assign some moral weight to one's legal duty.

The oath of an office holder is less sweeping than the oath of a naturalized citizen. It concerns obedience to the laws that control performance of official duty and only while the official is in office. The oath may not be explicitly limited in these ways, but a present or past official who engages in illegal acts of prostitution or overreports charitable deductions on his income tax is not thought to have violated his oath of office.

Although an official may not have a chance to retract the oath, he may resign if his legal duties conflict with conscience. For those reasons, the power of the oath does not lessen over the term of office; and the oath should reasonably be understood as covering

Promissory Obligation: The Theme of Social Contract 289

compliance with all official legal duties. These conclusions do not settle two very important matters — how one's legal duties are to be understood and whether or not an official is ever justified in violating his oath while staying in office; these subjects are dealt with in Part IV of my book *Conflict of Law and Morality*.

The lawyer's oath is limited like that of the official but extends in time like the oath of the naturalized citizen. Like the resigning official, the lawyer may stop practice if he finds that performing his role conflicts with moral duty; but for most lawyers such a choice has momentous consequences. With respect to lawyers, I will illustrate the problems regarding the force and meaning of an oath with a specific example.

Illustration 3:
Larry is approached by a group of people who plan to demonstrate against the use of civilian nuclear power at a local facility. They want to make sure that no one gets hurt, but they also want to commit a crime for which they will be arrested. Larry is a former member of the county attorney's office who is well versed in the criminal code and police department practices during demonstrations. He is not himself opposed to the use of nulcear power but respects the conviction of the demonstrators and believes their actions are proper in a democratic society. He also thinks he has it in his power to minimize the possibility of violence by carefully planning with them a trespass that will remain peaceable but will result in arrest. Larry believes that if he does engage himself to this degree, he will be guilty, under the state's criminal law, of aiding and abetting the trespass, and he fears he will also run afoul of standards of professional ethics.[46] He wonders whether he will also violate his oath as a lawyer if he helps plan to trespass.

The answer may well depend on the precise language of the oath or preliminary undertakings.[47] If Larry has promised to comply with the law and with rules of professional ethics, his having taken the oath will constitute a substantial moral reason against giving the advice. In some jurisdictions, however, what an applicant has promised may be subject to a more flexible interpretation. In Georgia, for example, one taking the oath swears that he will "justly and uprightly demean [himself] according to the laws, as an Attorney, Counsellor and Solicitor."[4] Though the oath might be read as barring every conscious illegal act in one's role as a lawyer,[49] Larry, by his own lights, would be acting justly and uprightly, technically breaking the criminal law in order to prevent violence and serve the broader aims of the legal order. Perhaps this oath is flexible enough to permit his behavior.[50]

One possible defect in a promise to obey the law is that it may require the commission of immoral acts. It has often been suggested that a promise to do what is morally wrong is not binding.[51] Unless a regime were so wicked that obeying the law would be wrong a high proportion of the time, the claimed lack of force of promises to do wrong would not infect one's whole undertaking; a general promise to obey would ordinarily be binding but would lack force on those occasions when obeying the law would be wrong. I will consider the claim on this assumption, suggesting that a promise to do an individual wrong is not always without force and that, in any event, promises to obey are quite different from promises to do individual wrongs.

In typical examples illustrating the lack of force of promises to do wrong, the initial promise is an obviously unjustified promise to perform a very bad act. If Pat promises to help Frank kill an innocent person, then obviously Pat should not carry out her promise; and such an example inclines one to suppose that the promise has no force at all. But we would be mistaken to conclude quickly that promises to do wrongful acts never have force.

Illustration 4:
Frank is a lifelong friend of Pat. Frank has been deeply hurt by Gloria's breaking up with him. Frank pleads with Pat to lie to Gloria that Frank is really interested in someone else. Pat tries to dissuade Frank from his plan to deceive Gloria, but Frank is insistent. Pat finally promises that if Frank does not change his mind she will tell the lie. All along Pat has regarded Frank's course of action as morally wrong and she subsequently concludes that despite the claims of friendship she should not have agreed to help him. But she feels a hesitancy to desist now that she has promised.

In this illustration Pat faces a difficult choice at two stages. Although Frank's wish to deceive Gloria is not morally justified, the moral bonds of friendship may be strong enough that Pat should assist Frank if she cannot deflect him from his plan. Whatever the proper initial choice, at the second stage Pat's promise is in place. I am not sure how much can be provided in the way of defense, but my own sense is that in this context, given the relative nonseriousness of the wrong and the close ties between Pat and Frank, the promise carries normative force.[52] How this conclusion bears on analysis of the promise to kill is difficult. One might suppose that the promise to kill has some slight force that is simply far outweighed by the moral reasons not to kill. But we might say that promises to do wrong can have force only if reliance on them by the promisee is reasonable; in this respect the promise to kill and the promise to tell a minor lie are qualitatively different.

The promise to obey the law is different from both these examples in important respects. The promise covers a class of actions most of which are morally required, or at least morally appropriate, and a small minority of which may be morally wrong; often the promisor will lack acquaintance of facts that would make possible confident assessment of the morality of a particular act of obeying the law. Given the value of a consistent pattern of behavior that does not demand close assessment of individual instances, a promise to follow such a pattern may have force in its occasional immoral applications even if a separate promise to conform to the law on a single occasion when it would be immoral might not have force. When the promise is not sufficient to justify doing what would otherwise be wrong, it may still be enough to require the actor to pursue an alternative course that does not require breaking the promise. The oath of office, for example, might affect whether an official should resign rather than breach a legal duty that requires a wrongful act.

This discussion is hardly dispositive on the force of promises to do what is wrong; however, it shows both that if a regime is generally just, the problem of wrongful applications does not undermine the force of the promise for other applications and that a promise to obey may well have a normative force on some occasions when the act of obedience would be wrong in the absence of the promise.

POSSIBLE EXTENSION OF PROMISSORY OBLIGATIONS TO OBEY

Having suggested that many citizens make no promise-like undertaking to obey the law, I have also argued that some do engage to obey in a general way and others promise to comply with laws relating to special duties. I have concluded that such promises ordinarily have moral force and constitute a substantial moral reason for obedience. The degree to which obligations in any society depend on voluntary promises is subject to change, and promises to obey the law could loom as more or less important in the future than they are now.

Given their present relative unimportance, I will ask whether expansion of their significance would be warranted. An expansion in promise-like undertakings could occur over time as informal conventions shift, establishing tacit or implied promises where none existed before; but I shall focus on the more straightforward courses of the government's demanding or requesting people to make explicit promises to obey or its clearly stating that certain acts will be construed as amounting to such a promise.

Whether or not the government could elicit a greater number of explicit or tacit promises with moral force depends on the conditions under which they would be given and the fairness of their terms. Suppose the government either expelled native-born citizens who refused to promise to obey or deprived such persons of all benefits of government that are capable of being taken away. The severity and unfairness of these sanctions would render promises to obey without force for persons who gave the promise to avoid these harms. The same conclusion would also be reached if the government, instead, announced that continued residence or acceptance of benefits would be *taken* as a promise to obey.[53] But if the government conditioned the privilege of voting on a promise to obey, or announced that voting would be so understood, neither duress nor unconscionability of terms would infect the result. People can live comfortably without voting, and a promise to obey is reasonably connected to the privilege of voting. If the government simply requested people to make periodic affirmations of continued willingness to obey, without conditioning any benefit on the affirmation, anyone who voluntarily offered the promise would also be bound. Many might, of course, be influenced by subtle and not-so-subtle social pressures to go along, but unless these were extreme, they would not undermine the force of the promise. In sum, there are steps a government might reasonably take to make promise a more important source of obligation than it now is. What effect such steps might have on the actual level of law-abidingness is highly uncertain, but many people might hesitate more to break the law if they thought they had promised not to do so.

Yet, there are very powerful reasons to oppose such a program. We have seen that an unqualified oath to obey all laws on all occasions is not one that can sincerely be given by thoughtful persons. Finding language that is less absolute but clear in its significance and comprehensible to ordinary persons is virtually impossible. We would be left with some vague undertaking to be law-abiding. Although such an oath might lead some people to take law observance more seriously, others would be offended by having to subscribe to it. Reliance on oaths of this breadth trenches on values of free belief and expression, and the pressures toward social conformity of which it smacks have unpleasant symbolic overtones. Further, extensive use of oaths and promises risks devaluing the currency. A child whose parents continually demand promises of conscientiousness – "Will you promise to do your homework and not watch TV while we are out?" – will begin to take promises less seriously. The same is undoubtedly true for adults. Insistence on promises can also have the undesirable effect of underemphasizing the significance of other bases of duty to obey the law. It is unfortunate if people begin to think all or most moral duties are matters of promise.[54] The benefits and costs of more extensive promises to obey are certainly subject to debate; however, my own conclusion is that outside the context of an alien's shifting his basic political loyalty, such promises should not be elicited from ordinary adults in a liberal democracy.

PROMISES TO PRIVATE INDIVIDUALS AND GROUPS THAT CONFLICT WITH PATTERNS OF OBEDIENCE

A chapter on promise and obligations to obey the law should not close without brief mention of the two-edged character of promise. Just as promises can create substantial moral reasons to obey, they can also create substantial moral reasons to disobey. Except in the context of cooperative criminal endeavors and large-scale political and social protests that involve lawbreaking, explicit promises to disobey the law on particular occasions are relatively rare, but undertakings of personal and group loyalty are not.[55] Some such undertakings never require action that violates the law, and with others the promisor may reasonably claim he never intended his broad promise to cover illegal acts. But this will not always be the case. Some organizations face predictable conflicts with the law; one need only think of the history of many religious sects. People who promise to support such organizations are aware that their group loyalty may require violations of law. Promises of assistance to family members or friends may have similar import when the promisor knows that the person to whom he promises has been breaking the law. Promises of group and personal loyalty are, of course, subject to the same sorts of qualifications and limitations as promises to obey the law, but there is no good reason to suppose that such promises will always be without moral force on every occasion when they require violation of law.

NOTES

1 J. Locke, *Two Treatises of Civil Government*.
2 E. Rostow, *The Rightful Limits of Freedom in a Liberal Democratic State: Of Civil Disobedience*, in Rostow, ed., Is Law Dead? 39, 48 (1970).
3 On the conceptual distinction between consent and promise, see A. J. Simmons, Moral Principles and Political Obligations 75–7 (1979); and Raz, Authority and Consent, 67 *Virginia Law Review* 103, 120–2 (1981). Although Raz recognizes that in certain situations consent need not involve the undertaking of an obligation, he says (mistakenly, in light of the analysis in the previous chapter) that "consent to a political authority is the same as a promise to obey it." Ibid. at 121.
4 T. Hobbes, *The Leviathan*.
5 J. J. Rousseau, *The Social Contract*.
6 As long as the promisee understood the kind of commitment the promisor was making, that would be a sufficient basis to give the promise force. Defeat of the justified expectations of the promisee without any good reason would come close to the kind of moral wrong done by telling a lie. See G. J. Warnock, *The Object of Morality* 105–10 (1971), who asserts a tighter connection between veracity and keeping promises.
7 The promise may leave me with some residual moral responsibility to apologize or try to make up the promisee's loss in some way, but I should not carry out its initial terms.
8 When the person to whom a promise has purportedly been given misunderstands the actor's intent, determining whether or not a promise exists is more troublesome. This problem is discussed later in connection with implied promises, but it is worth saying a few words about mistakes over actual significations of commitment. If the "promisor" has not intended to promise and could not reasonably have been thought to do so, no promise exists, whatever the "promisee" may suppose. When the "promisor" has intended to promise but the "promisee," though "receiving" the communication, does not realize its significance, the promise does exist and the "promisee" can take advantage of it when he comes to realize its significance. The difficult cases are those in which the "promisee" reasonably understands a promise to exist, but the promisor has not so intended his words or actions. Here, neither the idea that promises must be voluntarily given (see J. Rawls, *A Theory of Justice* 345 [1971]) nor the idea that promises can arise through negligence (see P. Soper, *A Theory of Law* 65 [1984]) is quite right as far as moral responsibility is concerned. Without doubt, the objective significance of one's words or acts can

bind at law just as if one intended to promise. No doubt, also, if one's negligence caused another reasonably to rely on one's apparent commitment, one would have a moral duty to rectify the situation in some way. But the person who can honestly say, "I'm terribly sorry; I really didn't intend my words to be taken in the way you did, though I can see the misunderstanding was entirely my fault," may well not have a moral obligation to do exactly what the "promisee" understood the commitment to be, especially if the promisee has not relied on the commitment to his detriment. Even then the "promisor" may owe the "promisee" *something* because of the latter's disappointment, but what he owes need not be identical with the scope of the apparent commitment.

9 Of course, her retraction of the original permission in light of what she now knows would not be illogical.
10 John Simmons addresses this question in Consent, Free Choice and Democratic Government, 18 *Georgia Law Review* 791, 802–7 (1984). See note 8 above for an analogous discussion in the context of express and tacit promises.
11 In attempting to draw a sharp analytical distinction between theories of genuine consent and theories of hypothetical consent, I do not mean to suggest that all traditional theorists fall clearly into one category or the other or that a theory resting on genuine consent cannot be profitably reinterpreted in terms of hypothetical consent.
12 John Rawls, *A Theory of Justice* (1971).
13 The point is forcefully made in R. Dworkin, *Taking Rights Seriously* 150–3 (1977).
14 A conceivable exception to this principle may occur when there was an actual occasion, say a meeting, at which I would have consented and actually planned to consent but for some fortuitous reasons that disturbed the ordinary course of events – say my car failing to start – I did not consent. Then, the fact that I would have consented may possibly put me in a position similar to that of those who did consent.

More broadly, what I as an individual would have agreed to may affect what it is fair now to do. Imagine that some parents agree with Phyllis that she will give physical instruction to their children for twenty dollars a day each over a period of three weeks. No mention is made of missed days. A child misses a day because of a family visit. His parents and Phyllis agree that neither payment or nonpayment is indicated by the original agreement and that neither resolution is *intrinsically* more fair than the other. Phyllis, however, says she would not have agreed to the arrangement if this possibility had been considered and missed days were to be unpaid, and the parents acknowledge that they would have agreed to pay for missed days if the subject had arisen. What these parties would have agreed to if the subject had come up has a bearing on what is now fair even if it establishes nothing about what *generally* would be fair for persons in this sort of arrangement.
15 8 *United States Constitution* § 1448 (1976).

16 "I pledge allegiance to the flag of the United States of America, and to the Republic for which it stands, one nation, under God, indivisible, with liberty and justice for all." Apart from the question of what attitudes toward law are consistent with allegiance, a point briefly considered below in connection with the naturalization oath, there is the further question of how far one's undertaking is qualified if one thinks disobedience will promote liberty and justice.
17 See, e.g., J. Tussman, *Obligation and the Body Politic* (1960); and J. Plamenatz, *Consent, Freedom and Political Obligation* (2d ed., 1968).
18 Professor Tussman recognizes this difficulty and suggests that some adult citizens will remain "political childbrides," governed, like minors, without their own consent. Tussman, ibid. at 37.
19 See Cohen, Liberalism and Disobedience, 1 Philosophy and Public Affairs 283, 311–12 (1972); Simmons, note 10 above at 800.
20 Speaking of what he calls tacit consent, Tussman says that an "act can only be properly taken as 'consent' if it is done 'knowingly,' if it is understood by the one performing the act that his action involves his acceptance of the obligations of membership." *Obligation and the Body Politic* at 36.
21 Compare Simmons, note 10 above at 801.
22 See P. Singer, *Democracy and Disobedience* 51–6 (1973).
23 Ibid. at 54.
24 J. Locke, *Second Treatise of Civil Government* at 98–9 (1960).
25 This ground, of course, has conceivable application to residents only if they are able to emigrate.
26 The plausibility of Socrates' claim that remaining in Athens created an obligation to submit to the punishment of that city-state (see Plato, *The Crito*) rests largely on the existence of other city-states nearby with the same language and similar cultures.
27 As Jeffrie G. Murphy has pointed out, the question whether continued residence can be taken as tacit consent is not the same as whether explicit consent given in order to continue residence would have moral force. Murphy, Consent, Coercion and Hard Choices, 67 Va. L. Rev. 79, 92 (1981). Murphy suggests that Hume's famous response to Locke that a poor peasant or artisan has no free choice to leave his country (D. Hume, Of the Original Contract, C. W. Hendel, ed., *David Hume's Political Essays* 43, 51 [1953]) may be understood either as an answer to the claim about tacit consent or as a claim that even explicit consent would not be binding.
28 See Beran, 'In Defense of the Consent Theory of Political Obligation and Authority', 87 Ethics 260 (1977).
29 A more expansive critique is provided in Simmons, note 10 above at 802–9.
30 See C. Fried, *Contract as Promise* (1981).
31 Philip Soper, *A Theory of Law* at 69, suggests that others will not rely to their detriment on a person's undertaking to be law-abiding, because they have ample prudential grounds, based on sanctions, to comply.

But a person may be confident he can break the law with impunity; if he complies because a respected friend has promised to obey the law, he has relied to the apparent detriment of his selfish interests.
32 J. Raz, *The Authority of Law* 250–61 (1979).
33 What I have in mind are situations in which someone feels a personal bond toward another met in professional situations or at parties, although the actual relationship between the two has not yet proceeded beyond the purely professional or social. The person may *feel* like a friend toward the other while recognizing that the relationship is not yet a friendship.
34 The law does distinguish between contracts that are totally void and those that are voidable at the option of a party. Also, available remedies may be regarded as reflecting some judgment about whether a certain class of promises has greater or lesser force.
35 See M. Walzer, *Spheres of Justice* 31–61 (1983).

Since some aliens have much more pressing reasons to become residents, than to become citizens once they are residents, the argument that to condition their residence on an oath to obey would constitute duress would be more powerful than the analogous argument about the grant of citizenship.
36 See generally Murphy, *Consent, Coercion and Hard Choices* at 83–8.
37 Even this point is debatable. One might argue that the best moral practice is one that always attaches some moral weight to a promise. J. L. Mackie has suggested that, in some contexts at least, even promises of hostages to pay money to their criminal captors have force, because the practice of keeping such promises leads to better treatment for hostages. J. L. Mackie, *Hume's Moral Theory* 104 (1980).
38 The sentence in text glosses over some complicated problems. If individuals are really autonomous and aware of the relevant facts, who but each individual is most competent to assess the balance of an exchange? How could a rational and fully informed individual agree to an exchange that would (*ex ante*) give him less than he receives? And even if actual individuals do not always make rational decisions about exchanges, in a liberal society should there not be a strong presumption in favor in their capacity to do so? On such premises as these, worry about the fairness of terms can be translated into worry either about the adequacy of the promisor's information and the rationality of his choice or over the fairness of the promisee's eliciting the promise in the way he did. A faltering swimmer who promises to give $100,000 to the only person capable of saving him gets as much as he promises to give, but the promisee has imposed unfair conditions of choice. It is a genuine question, therefore, whether the fairness of an exchange of benefits and burdens is relevant to the force of a promise except insofar as it indicates something about the appropriateness of the conditions under which the choice was made; an agreement like that made by the drowning swimmer can be understood as defective

in either respect. In contracts law, many "unconscionable" terms are subject to a similar analysis.
39 Jeffrie Murphy suggests that the monopolistic position of the government, its unequal bargaining power, and the vagueness of terms of a contract with citizens might undermine the force of an undertaking to obey (*Murphy, Consent, Coercion and Hard Choices* at 91–2). But he fails to note that the government has no means of penalizing someone for a faulty interpretation or indeed of enforcing the contract at all. A breach of law may be penalized but it is not penalized more seriously because one has promised to obey. The citizen's effective freedom to disregard the terms of the "contract" makes it seem a good bit less "unconscionable."
40 Simmons, Voluntarism and Political Associations, 67 Va. L. Rev. 19, 34, n. 28 (1981).
41 Sartorius, Political Authority and Political Obligation, 67 Va. L. Rev. 3, 13 (1981).
42 The doctrines of frustration of purposes and impossibility allow relief from contractual obligations when circumstances turn out very differently from what the parties expected. Of course, in contract law a change in attitudes and beliefs by one of the parties is not a basis for relief.
43 This point is tricky regarding the marriage contract. Although the original promise may lose force over time, duties based on detrimental reliance may increase in force.
44 One might argue that it is all right to make an unqualified promise if you know you are going to break it only in a small percentage of the instances it covers. At least in circumstances when one has some control over the scope of the promise, that does not seem correct. If I am asked to promise never to drink alcohol again, and I know I plan to drink on rare occasions, I should say: "Well, I am willing to promise to drink only rarely."
45 Perhaps if one has no control over the language of a promise and must simply choose between promising or not, one is morally justified in promising to do more than one is willing to do if one is willing to do most of what the promise encompasses. The *force* of the promise, which represents a commitment made to someone else, is probably not affected by this mental reservation.
46 *The Model Rules of the American Bar Association*, Rule 1.2, and the *Code of Professional Responsibility*, Disciplinary Rule 7–102(A)(7), forbid assisting a client in conduct that the lawyer knows is criminal.
47 In some jurisdictions, applicants for the bar answer questions about their willingness to comply with professional rules.
48 *Georgia Rules Governing Admission to the Practice of Law* B-19 (1984).
49 Whether this oath itself reaches the standards of professional ethics depends on whether they are understood to be laws. That question would be critical if what Larry considered doing was a violation of professional ethics but not of any ordinary law.

50 If the oath is so understood, someone who expects to give such assistance after becoming a member of the bar could sincerely take it.
51 E.g., A. J. Simmons, Voluntarism and Political Associations, 67 Va. L. Rev. 19, 36 (1981).
52 See generally Warnock, *The Object of Morality* at 109, 116.
53 Simmons, note 10 above at 809–18, has a much more extensive discussion leading to this conclusion.
54 Jonathan Bennett has made this point in correspondence with me.
55 See, generally, M. Walzer, *Obligations: Essays on Disobedience, War, and Citizenship* 7–16 (1970).

12
Moral Conflict and Political Legitimacy

T. NAGEL

I

Robert Frost defined a liberal as someone who can't take his own side in an argument. A bit harsh, but there is something paradoxical about liberalism, at least on the surface, and something obscure about the foundations of the sort of impartiality that liberalism professes. That is what I want to discuss.

Ethics always has to deal with the conflict between the personal standpoint of the individual and some requirement of impartiality. The personal standpoint will bring in motives derived not only from the individual's interests but also from his attachments and commitments to people, projects, and particular things. The requirement of impartiality can take various forms, but it usually involves treating or counting everyone equally in some respect – according them all the same rights, or counting their good or their welfare or some aspect of it the same in determining what would be a desirable result or a permissible course of action. Since personal motives and impartiality can conflict, an ethical theory has to say something about how such conflicts are to be resolved. It may do this by according total victory to the impartial side in case of conflict, but that is only one solution.

The clash between impartiality and the viewpoint of the individual is compounded when we move from personal ethics to political theory. The reason is that in politics, where we are all competing to get the coercive power of the state behind the institutions we favor – institutions under which all of us will have to live – it is not only our personal interests, attachments, and commitments that bring us into conflict, but our different moral conceptions. Political competitors differ as to both the form and the content of the impartial component of morality. They differ over what is good and bad in human life, and what kind of equal respect or consideration we owe each other. Their political disagreements therefore reflect not only conflicts of interest but conflicts over the values that public institutions should serve, impartially, for everyone.

Is there a higher-order impartiality that can permit us to come to some understanding about how such disagreements should be settled? Or have we already gone as far as necessary (and perhaps even as far as possible) in taking up other people's point of view when we have accepted the impartial component of our own moral position? I believe that liberalism depends on the acceptance of a higher-order impartiality, and that this raises serious problems about how the different orders of impartiality are to be integrated. To some extent this parallels the familiar problem in moral theory of integrating impartiality with personal motives; but the problem here is more complicated, and the motive for higher-order impartiality is more obscure.[1]

It is so obscure that critics of liberalism often doubt that its professions of impartiality are made in good faith. Part of the problem is that liberals ask of everyone a certain restraint in calling for the use of state power to further specific, controversial moral or religious conceptions — but the results of that restraint appear with suspicious frequency to favor precisely the controversial moral conceptions that liberals usually hold.

For example, those who argue against the restriction of pornography or homosexuality or contraception on the ground that the state should not attempt to enforce contested personal standards of morality often don't think there is anything wrong with pornography, homosexuality, or contraception. They would be against such restrictions even if they believed it *was* the state's business to enforce personal morality, or if they believed that the state could legitimately be asked to prohibit anything simply on the ground that it was wrong.

More generally, liberals tend to place a high value on individual freedom, and limitations on state interference based on a higher-order impartiality among values tends to promote the individual freedom to which liberals are partial. This leads to the suspicion that the escalation to a higher level of impartiality is a sham, and that all the pleas for toleration and restraint really disguise a campaign to put the state behind a secular, individualistic, and libertine morality — against religion and in favor of sex, roughly.

Yet liberalism purports to be a view that justifies religious toleration not only to religious skeptics but to the devout, and sexual toleration not only to libertines but to those who believe extramarital sex is sinful. Its good faith is to some degree attested in the somewhat different area of free expression, for there liberals in the United States have long defended the rights of those they detest. The American Civil Liberties Union is usually glad of the chance to defend the Nazis when they want to demonstrate somewhere. It shows that liberals are willing to restrain the state from stopping something that they think is wrong – for we can assume most supporters of the ACLU think both that it is wrong to be a Nazi and that it is wrong for the Nazis to demonstrate in Skokie.

Another current example is that of abortion. At least some who oppose its legal prohibition believe that it is morally wrong, but that their reasons for this belief cannot justify the use of state power against those who are convinced otherwise. This is a difficult case, to which I shall refer again.

Of course liberalism is not merely a doctrine of toleration, and liberals all have more specific interests and values, some of which they will seek to support through the agency of the state. But the question of what kind of impartiality is appropriate arises there as well. Both in the prohibition of what is wrong and in the promotion of what is good, the point of view from which state action and its institutional framework are supposed to be justified is complex and in some respects obscure. I shall concentrate on the issue of toleration, and shall often use the example of religious toleration. But the problem also arises in the context of distributive justice and promotion of the general welfare – for we have to use some conception of what is good for people in deciding what to distribute and what to promote, and the choice of that conception raises similar questions of impartiality.[2]

II

This question is part of the wider issue of political legitimacy – the history of attempts to discover a way of justifying coercively imposed political and social institutions to the people who have to live under them, and at the same time to discover what those institutions must be like if such justification is to be possible. "Justification" here does not mean "persuasion." It is a normative concept: arguments that justify may fail to persuade, if addressed to an unreasonable audience; and arguments that persuade may fail to justify. Nevertheless, justifications hope to persuade the reasonable, so these attempts have a practical point: political stability is helped by wide agreement to the principles underlying a political order. But that is not all: for some, the possibility of justifying the system to as many participants as possible is of independent moral importance. Of course this is an ideal. Given the actual range of values, interests, and motives in a society, and depending on one's standards of justification, there may not be a legitimate solution, and then one will have to choose between illegitimate government and no government.

The practical and the moral issues of political motivation are intertwined. On the one hand, the motivations that are morally required of us must be practically and psychologically possible, otherwise our political theory will be utopian in the bad sense. On the other hand, moral argument and insight can reveal and explain the possibility of political motivations which cannot be assumed in advance of moral discussion. In this way, political theory may have an effect on what motives are practically available to ground legitimacy, and therefore stability.

Defenses of political legitimacy are of two kinds: those which discover a possible *convergence* of rational support for certain institutions from the separate motivational standpoints of distinct individuals; and those which seek a *common standpoint* that everyone can occupy, which guarantees agreement on what is acceptable. There are also political arguments that mix the convergence and common standpoint methods.

A convergence theory may begin from motives that differ widely from person to person, or it may begin from a single type of motive, like self-interest, which differs from person to person only because it is self-referential. In either case, the difference of starting points means that the motivational base itself does not guarantee that there is a social result which everyone will find desirable. A common standpoint theory, by contrast, starts from a single desire that is not self-referential, and this guarantees a common social aim, provided people can agree on the facts.

Hobbes, the founder of modern political theory, is a convergence theorist par excellence. Starting from a premoral motive that each individual has, the concern for his own survival and security, Hobbes argues that it is rational for all of us to converge from this self-referential starting point on the desirability of a system in which general obedience to certain rules of conduct is enforced by a sovereign of unlimited power. This is a convergence theory because the motive from which each of us begins refers only to his own survival and security, and it is entirely contingent that there should be any outcome that all of us can accept equally on those grounds: our personal motives could in principle fail to point us toward a common goal. And as is generally true of convergence theories, the political result is thought to be right because it is rationally acceptable to all, rather than being rationally acceptable to all because it is by some independent standard right.

Utilitarianism, on the other hand, is an example of a common standpoint theory. It asks each person to evaluate political institutions on the basis of a common moral motive which makes no reference to himself.[3] If all do take up this point of view of impartial benevolence, it will automatically follow that they have reason to accept the same solutions – since they are judging in light of a common desire for everyone's happiness. A political result is then rationally acceptable to everyone because by the utilitarian standard it is right; it is not right because it is universally acceptable.

There are other types of convergence theories – notably those which find political legitimacy in a compromise among conflicting economic, social, and religious interests, acceptable to all as an alternative to social breakdown. And common standpoint theories can be based on motives other than general benevolence – commitment to the protection of certain individual rights, rejection of severe social and economic inequalities, even nationalism or a shared religious commitment.

But what I want to concentrate on is a type of mixed theory that is characteristic of contemporary liberalism. Recent political philosophy has seen the development of a new type of liberal theory, exemplified by the work of Rawls and others, whose distinctive feature is that it bases the legitimacy of institutions on their conformity to principles which it would be reasonable for disparate individuals to agree on, where the standard of individual reasonableness is not merely a premoral rationality, but rather a form of reasoning that includes moral motives. In contrast with Hobbesian convergence, reasonable agreement is in these theories sought by each person as an end and not merely as a means, necessary for social stability. At the same time, the moral motives which contribute to convergence are not sufficient by themselves to pick out an acceptable result: more individual motives also enter into the process. So the principles converged on are right because they are acceptable – not generally acceptable because they are by independent standards morally right.

With regard to Rawls, I am referring here not to the reasoning inside the Original Position (from which moral motives are excluded), but to the wider argument within which the Original Position plays a subsidiary role, the argument that we should regulate our claims on our common institutions by the principles that *would* be chosen in the Original Position.

It may seem surprising to characterize Rawls's theory as a mixed theory, for in asking us all to enter the Original Position to choose principles of justice, he seems simply to be proposing a common standpoint of impartiality which guarantees that we will all approve of the same thing. But an important element of Rawls's argument is his reference to the strains of commitment: even in the Original Position, not knowing his own conception of the good, each person can choose only such principles of justice as he believes he will be able to live under and continue to affirm in actual life, when he knows the things about himself and his position in society that are concealed by the Veil of Ignorance.[4] This introduces an element of convergence.[5]

True principles of justice are those which can be affirmed by individuals motivated both by the impartial sense of justice as fairness and by their fundamental personal interests, commitments, and conceptions of the good. As with other convergence theories, it is not logically guaranteed that there are such principles, but if there are, they will be shaped by the requirement of such convergence, and their rightness will not be demonstrable independent of that possibility. That is what Rawls means by describing the theory as a form of constructivism.

The other position I would like to mention is T. M. Scanlon's. The criterion of moral wrongness he proposes in "Contractualism and Utilitarianism" employs the notion of a rule which no one could reasonably reject, provided he had among his motives a desire to live under rules which no one who also had that motive could reasonably reject. This notion can be used to construct a mixed theory of political legitimacy, where the common standpoint is represented by the said harmonious desire and convergence enters because what people can and cannot reasonably reject is determined in part by their other, divergent motives as well.

Note that the standard is not what principles or institutions people will *actually accept*, but what it would be unreasonable for them not to accept, given a certain common moral motivation in addition to their more personal, private, and communal ends. As with Rawls, there would be no standard of political legitimacy or rightness independent of this possibility of convergence.

It is a distinctive feature of both these theories that they set moral limits to the use of political power to further not only familiar social and economic interests, but also moral convictions.

They are mixed theories based not just on a mixture of benevolence and self-concern, but on limits to the *content* of benevolence. They distinguish between the values a person can appeal to in conducting his own life and those he can appeal to in justifying the exercise of political power.

III

What I want to know is whether a position of this type is coherent and defensible. I am concerned less with the specific views of Rawls or Scanlon than with the fundamental moral idea behind such a position, which is that we should not impose arrangements, institutions, or requirements on other people on grounds that they could reasonably reject (where reasonableness is not simply a function of the independent rightness or wrongness of the arrangements in question, but genuinely depends on the point of view of the individual to some extent). The question is whether an interpretation of this condition, or something like it, can be found which makes it plausible, despite an initial appearance of paradox.

It is not clear why the possibility of this kind of convergence should be the standard of political legitimacy at all. Why should I care whether others with whom I disagree can accept or reject the grounds on which state power is exercised? Why shouldn't I discount their rejection if it is based on religious or moral or cultural values that I believe to be mistaken? Why allow my views of the legitimate use of state power to become hostage to what it would be reasonable for *them* to accept or reject? Can't I instead base those views on the values that I believe to be correct?

An antiliberal critic of Rawls could put the point by asking why he should agree to be governed by principles that he would choose if he did not know his own religious beliefs, or his conception of the good. Isn't that being *too* impartial, giving too much authority to those whose values conflict with yours — betraying your own values, in fact? If I believe something, I believe it to be *true*, yet here I am asked to refrain from acting on that belief in deference to beliefs I think are false. What possible moral motivation could I have for doing that? Impartiality among persons is one thing, but impartiality among conceptions of the good is quite another. Why isn't true justice giving everyone the best possible chance of salvation, for example, or of a good life? In other words, don't we have to start from the values that we ourselves accept in deciding how state power may legitimately be used?

And it might be added, are we not doing that anyway if we adopt the liberal standard of impartiality? Not everyone believes that political legitimacy depends on this condition, and if we forcibly impose political institutions because they do meet it (and block the imposition of institutions that do not), why are we not being just as partial to our own values as someone who imposes a state religion? It has to be explained why this is a form of impartiality at all.

To answer these questions we have to identify the moral conception involved and see whether it has the authority to override those more particular moral conceptions that divide us — and if so, to what extent or in what respects. Rawls has said in a recent article that if liberalism had to depend on a commitment to comprehensive moral ideals of autonomy and individuality, it would become just "another sectarian doctrine."[6] The question is whether its claim to be something else has any foundation.

IV

If liberalism is to be defended as a higher-order theory rather than just another sectarian doctrine, it must be shown to result from an interpretation of impartiality itself, rather than from a particular conception of the good that is to be made impartially available. Of course any interpretation of impartiality will be morally controversial — it is not a question of rising to a vantage point above all moral disputes — but the controversy will be at a different level.

In the versions of liberalism formulated by Rawls, Ronald Dworkin, and Bruce Ackerman, exclusion of appeal to particular conceptions of the good at the most basic level of political argument is one of the ways in which it is required that social institutions should treat people equally or impartially. But since this is much less obvious than the requirements of impartiality with respect to race, sex, social class, or even natural endowments, it requires a special explanation by reference to more fundamental moral ideas. The requirement itself may be modified as a result of the explanation: the proposal I end up with does not correspond perfectly to the views from which I begin.[7]

What form should impartiality take, in the special conditions which are the province of political theory? The specialness of the conditions is important. We have to be impartial not just in the conferring of benefits, but in the imposition of burdens, the exercise of coercion to ensure compliance with a uniform set of requirements, and the demand for support of the institutions that impose those requirements and exercise that coercion. (Even if the support is not voluntarily given, it will to some degree be exacted, if only through payment of taxes and passive conformity to certain institutional arrangements.) I suggest that this element of coercion imposes an especially stringent requirement of objectivity in justification.[8]

If someone wishes simply to benefit others, there can in my view be no objection if he gives them what is good by his own lights (so long as he does them no harm by theirs). If someone wants to pray for the salvation of my soul, I can't really complain on the ground that I would rather he gave me a subscription to *Playboy*. The problem arises when he wants to force me to attend church or pay for its upkeep instead of staying home and reading *Playboy*. The real problem is how to justify making people do things against their will.

We can leave aside the familiar and unproblematic Hobbesian basis for coercion: I may want to be forced to do something as part of a practice whereby everyone else is forced to do the same, with results that benefit us all in a way that would not be possible unless we could be assured of widespread compliance. This is not really forcing people to do what they don't want to do, but rather enabling them to do what they want to do by forcing them to do it.

There are two other types of coercion whose justification seems clear: prevention of harm to others and certain very basic forms of paternalism. In both these types of case, we can make an impersonal appeal to values that are generally shared: people don't want to be injured, robbed, or killed, and they don't want to get sick. The nature of those harms and the impersonal value of avoiding them are uncontroversial, and can be appealed to justify forcibly preventing their infliction. From an impersonal standpoint I can agree that anyone, myself included, should be prevented from harming others in those ways.

I can also agree that under some conditions I should be prevented from harming myself in those ways, as should anyone else. The clear conditions include my being crazy or seriously demented, or radically misinformed about the likely results of what I am doing. Paternalism is justified in such cases because when we look at them from outside, we find no impersonal value competing with the values of health, life, and safety. If I say I would want to be prevented from drinking lye during a psychotic episode, it is not because the dangers of internal corrosion outweigh the value of self-expression. We are not faced here with a conflict of impartialities.

But in other cases we are. I have gone over these familiar examples for the sake of contrast. There are cases where forcing someone to do what he doesn't want to do is problematic – not just because he doesn't want to do it, but because of his reasons for not wanting to do it. The problematic cases are those in which either the impersonal value to which I appeal to justify coercion would not be acknowledged by the one coerced, or else it conflicts with another impersonal value to which he subscribes but which I do not acknowledge, though I would if I were he. In such a case it seems that I shall have failed in some respect to be impartial whether I coerce him or not.

An example may help. I am not a Christian Scientist. If I ask myself whether, thinking of it from outside, I would want to be forced to undergo medical treatment if I *were* a Christian Scientist and had a treatable illness, it is hard to know what to say. On the one hand, given my beliefs, I am inclined to give no impersonal weight to the reasons I would offer for refusing treatment if I were a Christian Scientist, and substantial weight to the medical reasons in favor of treatment. After all, if I believe Christian Science is false, I believe it would be false even if I believed it was true. On the other hand, I am inclined to give considerable impersonal weight to the broader consideration of not wanting others to ride roughshod over my beliefs on the subject of religion, whatever they may be.

Or suppose a Roman Catholic who believes that outside the Church there is no salvation asks himself whether if he were not a Catholic he would want to be given strong incentives to accept the Catholic faith, perhaps by state support of the Church and legal discouragement of other religions.[9] He may be torn between the impartial application of his actual religious values and the impartial application of a more general value that he also holds, of not wanting other people's religious convictions to be imposed on him.

Which of these should dominate? It is really a problem about the interpretation of the familiar role-reversal argument in ethics: "How would you like it if someone did that to you?" The answer that has to be dealt with is "How would I like it if someone did *what* to me?" There is often more than one way of describing a proposed course of action, and much depends on which description is regarded as relevant for the purpose of moral argument.

V

This general problem is familiar in the context of interpreting universalizability conditions in ethics, but I am thinking of a particular version of it. Should a Catholic, considering restriction of freedom of worship and religious education for Protestants from an impersonal standpoint, think of it as:

1 preventing them from putting themselves and others in danger of eternal damnation;
2 promoting adherence to the true faith;
3 promoting adherence to the Catholic faith;
4 preventing them from practicing their religion; or
5 preventing them from doing something they want to do?

For the purpose of argument, let me suppose that as far as he is concerned, he would be doing all of these things. The question then is, which of them determines how he should judge the proposed restriction from an impersonal standpoint?

The defense of liberalism depends on rejecting 5 as the relevant description, and then stopping with 4 rather than going on to 2 or 1. Roughly, the liberal position avoids two contrary errors. To accept as an authoritative impersonal value everyone's interest in doing what he wants to do, for whatever reason (that is, to rely on description 5), is to give too much authority to other people's preferences in determining their claims on us. To accord impersonal weight to our own values, whatever they are (that is, to rely on descriptions 1 and 2), is on the other hand not to give others enough authority over what we may require of them.

The characteristic of description 4 that the others lack is that it has some chance of both (a), being accepted by all parties concerned as a true description of what is going on (something it shares with 3 and 5), and (b), being accorded the same kind of impersonal value by all parties concerned (something it shares, more or less, with 1 and 2).

This makes 4 a natural choice for the morally relevant description which provides a basis for impartial assessment. However several objections have to be dealt with.

First, why isn't 5 at least as impartial as 4? No one wants to be prevented from doing what he wants to do. Why can't we all agree that impersonal value should be assigned to people's doing or getting what they want, rather than to something more restricted like freedom of worship?

But the fact is that we cannot. To assign impersonal value to the satisfaction of all preferences is to accept a particular view of the good — a component of one form of utilitarianism — which many would find clearly unacceptable and which they would not be unreasonable to reject.[10] The objection to making it the basis of political legitimacy parallels the objection to making any other comprehensive individual conception of the good the basis of political and social institutions. A liberal who is a utilitarian should no more impose his conception of the good on others than should a liberal who is a Roman Catholic or a devotee of aesthetic perfection — that is, he should pursue the good so conceived for himself and others only within the limits imposed by a higher-order impartiality.

This reply, however, leads to another objection: If 5 is ruled out, why shouldn't 4 be ruled out for parallel reasons? The value of liberty seems more neutral than the value of preference-satisfaction, but perhaps it is not. The problem with assigning impersonal value to the satisfaction of preferences per se (description 5) is that if a nonutilitarian is asked, "How would you like to be prevented from doing something you want to do?" he can reply, "That depends on what it is, and why I want to do it." A similar move might be made against assigning uniform impersonal value to religious toleration (description 4). If a Catholic is asked, "How would you like to be prevented from practicing your religion?" why can't he reply, "That depends on whether it's the true religion or not"?

But in that case we are left with no version of what is going on that permits a common description resulting in a common impersonal assessment. If the description can be agreed on the assessment cannot be, and vice versa. Impartiality has been ruled out.

VI

A solution to this impasse requires that we find a way of being impartial not only in the allocation of benefits or harms but in their identification. The defense of liberalism requires that a limit somehow be drawn to appeals to *the truth* in political argument, and that a standpoint be found from which to draw that limit. It may seem paradoxical that a general condition of impartiality should claim greater authority than more special conceptions which one believes to be, simply, true — and that it should lead us to defer to conceptions which we believe to be false – but that is the position.

Gerald Dworkin discusses this issue in an essay called "Nonneutral Principles." He means principles like "The true religion should be taught in the public schools" – whose application to particular cases "is a matter of controversy for the parties whose conduct is supposed to be regulated by the principle in question."[11]

Dworkin argues that the liberal position has to rest on a skeptical epistemological premise – "that one cannot arrive at justified beliefs in religious matters."[12] That, he claims, is the only possible justification for suppressing knowledge of the parties' religious beliefs in Rawls's Original Position – a condition essential to Rawls's argument for tolerance. "If there were a truth and it could be ascertained," asks Dworkin, "would those in the original position who contemplated the possibility that they would be holders of false views regard their integrity as harmed by choosing that it [sic] should be suppressed?"[13]

Rawls, however, claims that his position depends on no such skepticism.[14] "We may observe," he says, "that men's having an equal liberty of conscience is consistent with the idea that all men ought to obey God and accept the truth. The problem of liberty is that of choosing a principle by which the claims men make on one another in the name of their religion are to be regulated. Granting that God's will should be followed and the truth recognized does not as yet define a principle of adjudication."[15]

He intends to put forward not a skeptical position about religious knowledge but a restriction on the sorts of convictions that can be appealed to in political argument. In his recent discussion he says: "It is important to stress that from other points of view, for example, from the point of view of personal morality, or from the point of view of members of an association, or of one's religious or philosophical doctrine, various aspects of the world and one's relation to it, may be regarded in a different way. But these other points of view are not to be introduced into political discussion."[16]

I believe that true liberalism requires that something like Rawls's view be correct, that is, that exclusion of the appeal to religious convictions not rely on a skeptical premise about individual belief. Rather it must depend on a distinction between what justifies individual belief and what justifies appealing to that belief in support of the exercise of political power. As I have said, liberalism should provide the devout with a reason for tolerance.

But is Rawls right? It is not sufficient to exclude knowledge of one's religious beliefs from the Original Position on the ground

Moral Conflict and Political Legitimacy

that this is needed to make agreement possible. The question is whether there is a viable form of impartiality that makes it possible to exclude such factors from the basis of one's acceptance of political institutions, or whether, alternatively, we have to give up the hope of liberal legitimacy.

I believe that the demand for agreement, and its priority in these cases over a direct appeal to the truth, must be grounded in something more basic. Though it has to do with epistemology, it is not skepticism but a kind of epistemological restraint: the distinction between what is needed to justify belief and what is needed to justify the employment of political power depends on a higher standard of objectivity, which is ethically based.

The distinction results, I believe, if we apply the general form of moral thought that underlies liberalism to the familiar fact that while I cannot maintain a belief without implying that what I believe is true, I still have to acknowledge that there is a big difference, looking at it from the outside, between my believing something and its being true.

On the view I would defend, there is a highest-order framework of moral reasoning (not the whole of morality) which takes us outside ourselves to a standpoint that is independent of who we are. It cannot derive its basic premises from aspects of our particular and contingent starting points within the world, though it may authorize reliance on such specialized points of view if this is justified from the more universal perspective. Since individuals are very different from one another and must lead complex individual lives, the universal standpoint cannot reasonably withhold this authorization lightly. But it is most likely to be withheld from attempts to claim the authority of the impersonal standpoint for a point of view that is in fact that of a particular individual or party, against that of other individuals or parties who reject that point of view. This happens especially in the political or social imposition of institutions that control our lives, that we cannot escape, and that are maintained by force.

Morality can take us outside ourselves in different ways or to different degrees. The first and most familiar step is to recognize that what we want should not depend only on our own interests and desires – that from outside, other people's interests matter as much as ours do, and we should want to reconcile our interests with theirs as far as possible. But liberal impartiality goes beyond this, by trying to make the epistemological standpoint of morality impersonal as well.

The idea is that when we look at certain of our convictions

from outside, however justified they may be from within, the appeal to their truth must be seen merely as an appeal to our beliefs, and should be treated as such unless those beliefs can be shown to be justifiable from a more impersonal standpoint. If not, they have to remain, for the purpose of a certain kind of moral argument, features of a personal perspective – to be respected as such but no more than that.

This does not mean we have to stop believing them – that is, believing them to be *true*. Considered as beliefs they may be adequately grounded, or at least not unreasonable: the standards of individual rationality are different from the standards of epistemological ethics. It means only that from the perspective of political argument we may have to regard certain of our beliefs, whether moral or religious or even historical or scientific, simply as someone's beliefs, rather than as truths – unless they can be given the kind of impersonal justification appropriate to that perspective, in which case they may be appealed to as truths without qualification.

We accept a kind of epistemological division between the private and the public domains: in certain contexts I am constrained to consider my beliefs merely as beliefs rather than as truths, however convinced I may be that they are true, and that I know it. This is not the same thing as skepticism. Of course if I believe something I believe it to be true. I can recognize the possibility that what I believe may be false, but I cannot with respect to any particular present belief of mine think that possibility is realized. Nevertheless, it is possible to separate my attitude toward my belief from my attitude toward the thing believed, and to refer to my belief alone rather than to its truth in certain contexts of justification.

The reason is that unless there is some way of applying from an impersonal standpoint the distinction between my believing something and its being true, an appeal to its truth is equivalent to an appeal to my belief in its truth. To show that the two are not equivalent I would have to show how the distinction could be applied, in political argument, in a way that did not surreptitiously assume my personal starting point – by, for example, defining objective truth in terms of the religion to which I adhere, or the beliefs I now hold. I have to be able to admit that I might turn out to be wrong, by some standards that those who disagree with me but are also committed to the impersonal standpoint can also acknowledge. The appeal to truth as opposed to belief is compatible with disagreement among the parties – but it must imply the possibility of some standard to which an impersonal appeal can be made, even if it cannot settle our disagreement at the moment.

VII

The real difficulty is to make sense of this idea, the idea of something which is neither an appeal to my own beliefs nor an appeal to beliefs that we all share. It cannot be the latter because it is intended precisely to justify the forcible imposition in some cases of measures that are not universally accepted. We need a distinction between two kinds of disagreement – one whose grounds make it all right for the majority to use political power in the service of their opinion, and another whose grounds are such that it would be wrong for the majority to do so.

For this purpose we cannot appeal directly to the distinction between reasonable and unreasonable beliefs. It would be an impossibly restrictive condition on political power to say that its exercise may be justified only by appeal to premises that others could not reasonably reject (though less restrictive than the condition that the premises be *actually* accepted by all). If the impossibility of reasonable rejection comes in at all, it must come in at a higher level, in justifying some less stringent standard for the justification of particular employments of political power.

Reasonable persons can disagree not only over religious doctrines and ultimate conceptions of the good life, but over levels of public provision of education and health care, social security, defense policy, environmental preservation, and a host of other things that liberal societies determine by legislative action. What distinguishes those disagreements from the ones where liberalism rejects majority rule? When can I regard the grounds for a belief as objective in a way that permits me to appeal to it in political argument, and to rely on it even though others do not in fact accept it and even though they may not be unreasonable not to accept it? What kinds of grounds must those be, if I am not to be guilty of appealing simply to my belief, rather than to a common ground of justification?

By a common ground I do not mean submerged agreement on a set of premises by which the claim could in principle be settled in a way that all parties would recognize as correct. Public justification in a context of actual disagreement requires, first, preparedness to submit one's reasons to the criticism of others, and to find that the exercise of a common critical rationality and consideration of evidence that can be shared will reveal that one is mistaken. This means that it must be possible to present to others the basis of your own beliefs, so that once you have done so, *they have what you have*, and can arrive at a judgment on the same basis. That is not possible if part of the source of your conviction is personal faith or revelation – because to report your faith or revelation to someone else is not to give him what you have, as you do when you show him your evidence or give him your arguments.

Public justification requires, second, an expectation that if others who do not share your belief are wrong, there is probably an explanation of their error which is not circular. That is, the explanation should not come down to the mere assertion that they do not believe the truth (what you believe), but should explain their false belief in terms of errors in their evidence, or identifiable errors in drawing conclusions from it, or in argument, judgment, and so forth. One may not always have the information necessary to give such an account, but one must believe there is one, and that the justifiability of one's own belief would survive a full examination of the reasons behind theirs. These two points may be combined in the idea that a disagreement which falls on objective common ground must be open-ended in the possibility of its investigation and pursuit, and not come down finally to a bare confrontation between incompatible personal points of view. I suggest that conflicts of religious faith fail this test, and most empirical and many moral disagreements do not.

The large question I have not addressed is whether there are significant differences of fundamental moral opinion which also fail the test – and if so, how the line is to be drawn between those cases and others, which fall into the public domain. My sense is that the sort of liberal restraint I have been describing should apply, in the present state of moral debate, to certain matters besides the enforcement of religious views. I would include abortion, sexual conduct, and the killing of animals for food, for example. Admittedly, if we refrain from enforcing any moral position on these matters, it has the same effect as we would get if the law were based on the positive position that whatever people choose to do in these areas is permissible. But the two justifications for restraint are very different, and if I am right, the first is available to those who may not accept the second.

To defend this claim would require serious analysis of the issues. I would try to argue that such disagreements come down finally to a pure confrontation between personal moral convictions, and that this is perceptibly different from a disagreement in judgment over the preponderant weight of reasons bearing on an issue. Of course there are reasons and arguments on both sides, but they come to an end in a different and more personal way than arguments about welfare payments or affirmative action, for example. This does not mean that such disagreements cannot move into the public category through further development of common grounds of argument. But at any given stage, the justifications on opposite sides of an issue may come to an end with moral instincts which are simply internal to the points of view of the opposed parties – and this makes them more like conflicts of personal religious conviction.

I realize that this is vague. It also raises a further problem: Why can't the same be said of some fundamental issues that clearly fall within the public domain? Aren't people's disagreements about the morality of nuclear deterrence and the death penalty just as ultimate and personal as their disagreements over abortion?

The question requires much more discussion than I can give it here. Briefly, these issues are poor candidates for liberal toleration because they are not matters of individual conduct, which the state may or may not decide to regulate. So no conclusion about what the state should do can be derived from the refusal to justify the use of state power by reference to any particular position on the moral issue. The application of the death penalty or the possession by the military of nuclear weapons cannot be left to the private conscience of each individual citizen: the state *must* decide.[17]

The same question might also be raised about fundamental issues of social justice – the conflicts of economic liberals with radical libertarians, or with radical collectivists who regard individualism as an evil. Here I would give a more complex answer. I do not believe these moral oppositions are as "personal" as the others: even radical disagreements about freedom and distributive justice are usually part of some recognizable public argument. On the other hand, social provision is not so essentially the function of the state as is warfare: voluntary collective action is certainly possible. So to the extent that some of these disagreements are like religious disagreements, there would be a place for liberal toleration in the economic sphere – for example, toleration of private ownership even by those who think it is an evil.

VIII

It is important to stress that the nondogmatic moral disagreements which fall within the public domain may nevertheless be irresolvable in fact. That there is common ground does not mean that people will actually reach agreement, nor does it mean that only one belief is reasonable on the evidence. I may hold a belief on grounds that I am willing to offer in objective justification, suitable for the public domain, while acknowledging that others who consider that justification and yet reject the belief are not being irrational or unreasonable, though I think they are wrong.

The idea is that in such a case there is a common reason in which both parties share, but from which they get different results because they cannot, being limited creatures, be expected to exercise it perfectly.[18] Differences in evidence result from the different experiences people have had and the different testimony and arguments to which they have been exposed. Even more important are differences in assessment of the evidence and the arguments, and these inevitably involve differences of judgment. In most significant cases reasonable belief is not strictly determined by the grounds that can be explicitly offered: that is why there can be reasonable disagreement – disagreement in judgment – even among those who are in general agreement about what kinds of grounds are relevant to the matter at hand, and what the evidence and arguments in the case are. (In some cases they may agree more precisely on what evidence not now available would demonstrate decisively which of them is right; but this need not be so – either in factual matters, if they are sufficiently general, or in questions of value.)

I believe – though I wish I could express it more clearly than this – that the parties to such a disagreement can think of themselves as appealing to a common, objective method of reasoning which each of them interprets and applies imperfectly. They can therefore legitimately claim to be appealing not merely to their personal, subjective beliefs but to a common reason which is available to everyone and which can be invoked on behalf of everyone even though not everyone interprets its results in the same way.

There is something of a paradox here: How can I believe something if I think others presented with the same grounds could reasonably refuse to believe it? Doesn't this mean I believe it but think also that it would be reasonable for *me* not to believe it – and is that possible?

Well, perhaps if I actually think that as things are and as I am, it would be reasonable for me not to believe p, I cannot believe it. But I may think it would be reasonable for someone else either to believe or not to believe p on the evidence available to me that I can specifically identify, yet find that I do believe it. Perhaps in that case I must also judge that it would not be reasonable for *me*, as I am, not to believe it on that evidence – though I don't know why. This would be true whether my grounds are highly personal, or impersonal and objective. There may be people enough like me in whatever determines judgment so that if I judge that they could reasonably disbelieve p, I cannot reasonably believe it. But if there is such a class of persons, it is not coextensive with my political community, and cannot determine the standard of public justification.

We therefore have to recognize that there can be enough considerations on more than one side of a question in the public domain so that reasonable belief is partly a matter of judgment, and is not uniquely determined by the publicly available arguments. But I do not believe this makes the distinction between a disagreement in the common, public domain and a clash between irreconcilable subjective convictions too rarefied to be of political significance. Judgment is not the same as faith, or pure moral intuition.

Admittedly it will be controversial in many cases whether an appeal to truth collapses into an appeal to belief — some people might try to deny objective, public status to scientific methods that most of us would take as clear cases of impersonal verification, whereas others might claim objective status for certain theological arguments or forms of revelation. Religious believers no doubt vary in this respect: some would deny that belief is a matter of reasonable judgment; but others would presumably claim that the truth of their doctrines is supported by objective reasons and evidence of a kind available to all. These issues have to be argued out one by one; I do not have a general test of public epistemological justification — which is not, I repeat, the same as intersubjective agreement. But I believe that the basic idea remains intelligible even if its application is problematic.[19] The appeal to truth in political argument requires an objective distinction between belief and truth that can be applied or at least understood from the public standpoint appropriate to the argument in question. Disagreements over the truth must be interpreted as resulting from differences of judgment in the exercise of a common reason.

Otherwise the appeal to truth collapses into an appeal to what I believe, and belief carries a very different kind of weight in political arguments. The fact that someone has certain religious or moral convictions has its own considerable importance, from an impersonal standpoint, in determining how he should be treated and what he should do, but it is not the same as the importance that the truth of those convictions would have, if it could be admitted as a premise in political argument. There would be no inclination to accept impersonally a general right to try to use state power to limit the liberty of others in order to force them to live as I *believe* they should live. None of us would be willing to have our liberty limited by others on such grounds. But if I am right, the appeal to the truth of a certain religion to justify enforcement collapses into just such an appeal to belief.

We can now return to the distinction between 4 and 5, which was left hanging at the end of section V. Why is liberty a more neutral standard of evaluation than preference-satisfaction? I have tried to explain why a believer, if asked, "How would you like to be prevented from practicing your religion?" cannot legitimately reply, "That depends on whether it's the true religion or not." But why doesn't the same argument rule out the corresponding reply to the question "How would you like to be prevented from doing something you want to do?" – namely, the reply "That depends on what it is, and why I want to do it"?

I believe this reply is not in general ruled out, because the judgments appealed to in following it up need not be pure personal beliefs, but may claim the kind of objectivity and admit the kind of public justification which allows them to be used in political argument. Of course sometimes they will turn out to be inadmissibly private or parochial, but they need not be: it can be argued that the satisfaction of some desires is valueless or harmful, by public and objective standards. The resistance to preference-satisfaction as a public measure of value can be objective in a way in which the resistance to religious liberty cannot be.

IX

Even if some form of liberal impartiality can be defended in this way, it has to contend with the persistence of those personal convictions which it excludes from political argument, or admits only under strict constraints. This is a general problem in ethics: the impersonal standpoint does not make personal motives go away, and in restricting their operation it may put itself under great strain.

It is difficult to decide how much weight the liberal version of impartiality can bear when it comes into conflict not only with purely personal interests but with the impartial application of more particular values that cannot be generally acknowledged. From an impersonal standpoint, how strongly is my commitment to religious toleration prepared to resist the value of health, when applied to the case of a Christian Scientist? And how strongly can the impersonal value of not being prevented from practicing one's religion resist the less impartial but still impersonal interest of a Catholic in the salvation of souls?

In such cases, the condition of public justification reverses the relative importance possessed by different values in the private domain. To a believer, salvation is more important than liberty, yet in political justification he may not appeal to the importance of salvation to justify the restriction of liberty, because liberty is a publicly admissible value and salvation is not.

One might ask whether the standard of liberal impartiality itself meets the condition of impersonal justifiability necessary for admission to the public domain. I believe that it does, because it is defendable, and attackable, by arguments of the right type, some of which I have tried to formulate. And I would add that its claim to objective status is not undermined by the fact that some people may not accept it because they reject the requirement of impersonal justifiability itself. Even those who accept the requirement may disagree about how it is to be applied, but that is another matter.

Liberalism is a demanding doctrine. Still, it is qualified somewhat by a division of the moral territory. Its relatively stringent impartiality applies only to uniform and involuntary social and political institutions. One might ask why. Why doesn't the same standard apply to the justification of all action that has an effect, even indirectly, on the interests of others? Part of the answer, already referred to above, is that when we force people to serve an end that they cannot share, and that we cannot justify to them in objective terms, it is a particularly serious violation of the Kantian requirement that we treat humanity not merely as a means, but also as an end. The justification of coercion must meet especially stringent standards.

The other answer I would give is that we have here an instance of the moral division of labor between society and the individual, corresponding to the division of standpoints in each of us.[20] We literally externalize the demands of the impersonal standpoint by placing in the hands of social and political institutions the task of enforcing the most general claims for assistance and restraint of our fellow human beings. Subject to our contribution to the support of those institutions, this ideally should leave us free to lead our individual lives in obedience to more personal attachments, commitments, and crotchets. It would be for most of us intolerably intrusive to have to live by a morality that required us to justify everything we did, insofar as it affected others, in terms that could be defended from an impersonal standpoint.

The liberal restriction on what kind of thing we may appeal to does not apply to the justification of action generally. It leaves individuals free to regulate their own personal lives (and to a lesser extent, though this is a problematic intermediate case, the lives of their children) according to their full personal conceptions of how life should be lived. And it also, importantly, leaves them free to refer to their own conceptions in determining how they will benefit others or help them avoid harm or misfortune, so far as this goes beyond what is morally or legally obligatory.

Most importantly of all, this extends to the domain of political activity which in a democracy is left open to the pursuit by individuals of their goals and interests — the large range of legislative and communal issues that are put under the control of the preferences of the majority, or of coalitions among minorities. In these cases it is not that we give the authority of the impersonal standpoint to the point of view of the winning side. Rather, on a certain range of questions, we regard the balancing of all sorts of personal preferences or opinions against one another as impersonally acceptable.

Liberalism certainly does not require us to run our lives, even our lives as political beings, on radically impartial principles. But it does require that the imposed framework within which we pursue our more individual values and subject ourselves to the possibility of control by the values of others be in a strong sense impartially justifiable. That means it must bear up under substantial moral and motivational strain.

The real issue is not just relative strength but relative priority. Liberal impartiality is not in competition with more specific values as one conception of the good among others. If it were, it would be unintelligible, for it would have to advocate impartiality between itself and alternative conceptions, and that would generate a meaningless regress of higher-order standpoints in search of common ground between liberalism and more sectarian views. But liberalism does not require its adherents to step outside liberalism itself to compromise with antiliberal positions. It purports to provide a maximally impartial standard of right which has priority over more specialized conceptions in determining what may be imposed on us by our fellow humans, and vice versa. (This is not just the familiar doctrine of the priority of the right over the good, since some of the specialized views that are subordinated by liberalism may themselves be conceptions of right.)

The real problems with the position arise in its interpretation, not from the fact that it is controversial. It must distinguish two types of grounds for belief, neither of which shows that those who reject the belief are necessarily unreasonable, but one of which justifies the exercise of political power and the other not — and it must explain why the distinction has this consequence, and how it is to be applied. Of course liberal impartiality claims for itself an authority that will not in fact be universally accepted, and therefore the justifications it offers for resisting the imposition of more particular values in certain cases will not secure actual universal agreement. But since it is a substantive moral position, that is not surprising.

NOTES

I am grateful to a number of people for comments, particularly T. H. Irwin, John Rawls, Lawrence Sager, Bernard Williams, and the editors of *Philosophy and Public Affairs*.

1 Leading contemporary examples of philosophical liberalism are: John Rawls, *A Theory of Justice* (Cambridge: Harvard University Press, 1971); Ronald Dworkin, "Liberalism," in *Public and Private Morality*, ed. Stuart Hampshire (Cambridge: Cambridge University Press, 1978); Bruce Ackerman, *Social Justice in the Liberal State* (New Haven: Yale University Press, 1980); T. M. Scanlon, "Contractualism and Utilitarianism," in *Utilitarianism and Beyond*, ed. Amartya Sen and Bernard Williams (Cambridge: Cambridge University Press, 1982).
2 See T. M. Scanlon, "Preference and Urgency," *Journal of Philosophy* 72 (1975) — an essay to which I am much indebted.
3 I am thinking of utilitarianism in a modern version, associated with Sidgwick. In Bentham and Mill, the motives that lead to compliance with the principle of utility are various, and not related to its truth.
4 Rawls, *A Theory of Justice*, p. 176.
5 This observation comes from Scanlon, "Contractualism and Utilitarianism," p. 126. Another interpretation has been suggested to me, however, by Warren Quinn. Perhaps the strains of commitment are simply strains it is unfair to impose on people, and this is shown by our unwillingness, in the Original Position, to choose principles which carry the risk of subjecting us to those strains. This would restore Rawls to the common standpoint category.
6 Rawls, "Justice as Fairness: Political not Metaphysical," *Philosophy and Public Affairs*, vol. 14, no. 3 (Summer 1985): 246.
7 Rawls himself treats these issues from a somewhat different point of view in the article just mentioned and in his H. L. A. Hart Lecture, "The Idea of an Overlapping Consensus," *Oxford Journal of Legal Studies*, 7(1987)1. I shall not try to compare our approaches here, except to say that mine seems to depend less on actual consensus, and

seeks an independent moral argument that can be offered to those holding widely divergent values.

8 This would be implied, on one reading, by the second formulation of Kant's categorical imperative — that one should treat humanity never merely as a means, but always also as an end. If you force someone to serve an end that he cannot share, you are treating him as a mere means — even if the end is his own good, as you see it (*Foundations of the Metaphysics of Morals*, Prussian Academy edition, pp. 429–30). See Onora O'Neill, "Between Consenting Adults," *Philosophy and Public Affairs*, vol. 14, no. 3 (Summer 1985): 261–3; and Christine M. Korsgaard, "The Right to Lie: Kant on Dealing with Evil," *Philosophy and Public Affairs*, vol. 15, no. 4 (Fall 1986): 330–4.

9 "He would want," in these examples, is not a conditional prediction of what his desires would be in those circumstances; rather, it refers to what he *now* wants to happen should those counterfactual circumstances obtain — as in the statement "I would want to be restrained if I tried to drink lye during a psychotic episode." The "want" goes outside rather than inside the conditional.

10 See Scanlon, "Preference and Urgency."

11 Gerald Dworkin, "Non-neutral Principles," *Journal of Philosophy* 71 (1974): 492.

12 Ibid., p. 505.

13 Ibid., pp. 503–4.

14 Rawls, *A Theory of Justice*, pp. 214–15.

15 Ibid., pp. 217–18.

16 Rawls, "Justice as Fairness: Political not Metaphysical," p. 231.

17 Conscientious objection is another matter: its legal acceptance can probably be explained by the liberal principle I am defending.

18 This resembles the conception of "free public reason" that Rawls introduces in section II of "The Idea of an Overlapping Consensus."

19 It may be that further development of this idea would also exclude disagreements based on exceptionally subtle and difficult forms of reasoning, whose results are not testable in any other way. But I shall not try to pursue the suggestion here.

20 See T. Nagel, *The View from Nowhere* (New York: Oxford University Press, 1986), pp. 188, 206–7.

Index

Ackerman, Bruce 307
adjudicative authorities 122–3
Alexander the Great 149
allegiance 37, 275, 296
anarchism 3–6, 13, 29–30, 133, 241, 250, 263
Anscombe, G.E.M. 5, 16, 142–73
apathy 28–9
Aquinas, Saint Thomas 67, 199
arbitration 121–2, 140–1
Arendt, Hannah 63–4, 72, 118, 203
Aristotle 25, 142, 193, 264; *Metaphysics*, 153
assertive style of discourse 96
associative obligations 222–7, 228–30, 232, 235
atomism, and the social thesis 248–50
auctor 74–7, 89
auctoritas 74–7, 80
Augustine, Saint 70, 149
Austin, John 30, 33–4, 75–6, 106, 193
author 74–5, 89
authority: analytical and normative questions 203; concept of being "an authority", 66, 76, 77, 80–5, 107, 108, 132; concept of being "in authority", 69, 76, 77–80; concept of (Wolff), 20–5; conflict with autonomy, 20–31; defining the issue, 1–3; descriptive and normative senses, 21–5; Finnis, 174–202; "having authority", 69; institutionalization of, 104, 112–13; meanings of, 176–9; nature of, 206–10; OED definition, 57; perspectives on, 203–17; scope of the concept, 57–9; socially accepted criteria for, 71; uses of, 2; *see also* political authority, practical authority, theoretical authority
autonomy, 176; abdication of, 4, 6, 11, 27; concept of, 25–9; conflict with authority, 20–31

Bagehot, Walter *The English Constitution*, 70
belief: and action 57–9; authoritative, 66–7; and authority, 80–3; authority over, 66; double system of, 83; and surrender to authority, 208–9; and truth, 314–23; types of, as to right, 68; unnecessary, 79–80
beliefs and reasons for authority 204–15; shared, 58, 84
Bell, John 138
Bellarmine, Cardinal 188
benefits, receipt of and consent 279–80
Bentham, Jeremy 70, 323; *A Fragment on Government*, 93; *Logic of the Will*, 93; *Of Laws in General*, 94; theory of law, 92–102
Beran, Harry 279–80
Bergson, Henri 72
Blackstone, Sir William 194
Bradley, Francis Herbert 246, 255
Brougham, Henry 61
bureaucracy, 22–3, 28, 29, 127, 132

Carlyle, Thomas 241
categorical imperative (Kant) 324
charismatic authority (Weber) 61, 80, 81, 190
citizenship 34, 193, 236, 245; intrinsic value of, 263–4; and legitimacy, 220; oaths of naturalized, 275–6, 284, 288, 296; rights and duties of, 123–4; social role of, 252–5, 260, 263–6
civic life, shared goods and 255–8
civil authority 143, 162
civil disobedience 88
civil power, evil of 150
claim-rights 3, 35, 116
coercion 14–16, 60, 116–17, 162, 194; justification and standards, 321–3; legitimacy of state, 218–22; relationship between political authority and, 37–40, 60–3; types justified, 308
commands 21–2, 28, 92–114; Bentham, 93–102; Hobbes, 65–6, 93, 100, 206; Weber, 206–7
commitment: and community 240–67; and promises, 270–4; uncommunicated, 282
commitments, competing 262–3
common good 174–6, 178, 185, 191, 264
common ground 315–17
common idealist thesis 246–8
communitarianism, and consent theory 14, 242–66

communities, consensual 250–5
community, commitment and 240–7; of communities, 263–6; models of, 232–8; obligations of, 218–39; political, 174, 175–6; "true", 226–7
compliance 6, 37, 187–8
concepts, legitimacy of 23
concern 144, 225–6
conquest 191, 198
conscientious objection 88, 324
conscription 124, 284–5, 287
consensual communities 250–5
consensus 15, 78, 82, 205
consent 168, 187–91; hypothetical, 18, 251–2, 274; and the limits of authority, 11–17, 252–3; and promises, 268–9; role-bound, 252–5; tacit, 219–20, 251–2, 296; and voting, 276–80
consent theory 240, 241–2: socialized extension of, 266
constitution 45–9
constructivism 305
contract 147–8; *see also* social contract
conventions 128, 233–4; formation of, 179–86
coordination problems 6–11, 15, 175–6, 185, 194, 196, 211
courts 46, 104, 110
covenants 93
custom, appropriateness of 181, 183, 196–7
customary rights 167, 170–1, 171
customary rules, *see* conventions

de facto authority, 3, 21, 23–5, 61, 117–18, 124, 126, 132
de Gaulle, Charles 61
de jure authority 24–5, 30, 60–1
death penalty 172, 317
decision, domain of 144
deduction 23
democracy 3, 28, 169, 219–20, 268, 276, 322; indirect, 11
democratic accountability 16
deontic logic 152
dependence thesis 122–9, 211; and justification of authority, 129–33; objections, 137–9
deterrence 163–4
detrimental reliance 273, 279, 298
directives 6, 10, 117, 118, 125, 127–8, 133: extrinsic relation to, reasons, 212–14; mediating role of, 134–5
disagreements, types of 315–20
divine right 42, 198
domination 201, 241: Weber, 206–7
Dunn, John 252
Durkheim, Emile 241
duties, imposition of 123–4

duty, conflicts of 264
duty to be just 220
duty to obey, *see* obedience
Dworkin, Gerald 312
Dworkin, Ronald 13, 33, 51, 110, 141, 218–39, 307

Easton, David 88
electorate, and sovereignty 45, 49
equality 25, 90–1
exclusionary reasons (Raz), *see* reasons, exclusionary
expectations, mutual, 282
expertise 2, 10, 27, 29, 80, 108, 129, 139

fact–value distinctions 244
facts, institutional, 243; and rights, 158–60
fairness 220–2, 278
family 238
Finnis, J.M. 5, 16, 174–202
Flathman, Richard 118, 209–10, 215
forced undertakings 285–6
Fortescue, Sir John 191
Frankfurter, Justice 60
fraternity, and political community 230–8
fraud, protection against 165, 166–7
free-riding 257
freedom 25–7, 250; of expression, 301–2; *see alos* liberty
Friedman, Richard 5, 56–91, 119, 208–9, 215
Friedrich, C.J. 206
friendship 244–5, 256; and advice, 129–30; civic, 257–8; and obligations, 282
Frost, Robert 300

game theory, and coordination 6–8
gender, and political obligation 261–2
Gert, Bernard 36
Gladstone, William 75
Godwin, William 118
government, doctrine of limited 12–14
governmental authority, and Hobbesian theory of law 32–40
governmental institutions, relations with 16–17
governmental power and acquiescence 116–18; common sense view, 38–9
governmental powers, seperation of 46–9, 55
Green, L. 14, 240–67
Green, T.H. 246, 261, 262, 265
Greenawalt, K. 268–99

Hale, Sir Matthew 194

Index

'Harm to Others' principle 14–15
Hart, H.L.A. 5, 15, 17, 69, 92–114, 118–19, 169; critique of Hobbesian conception of law, 32–49; *Essarys on Bentham*, 97–8, 109–10; *The Concept of Law*, 32–3, 40–2, 45–6, 49–50
Hegel, G.W.F. 73, 242, 246, 249, 258, 261, 262
hierarchy in authority relations 82
Hobbes, Thomas 30, 59, 70, 72, 78, 84, 118, 240, 249, 269, 303; commands, 65–6, 93, 100, 206; on law, 32–55; *Leviathan*, 37, 55, 60–1, 100; social contract, 100
Honoré, A.M. 140
Hudson, Manley 195
Hume, David 97, 152, 242, 250

identity 130–1: and interests, 260–1; social roles and, 258–63
immoral acts 290–1
impartiality 306–9: identification of, 311–23; and personal standpoint, 300–24; standard of liberal, 320–3
imperative style 96–7, 98–9
individualism 79, 88, 240–4, 260–1; ethical, 243–4; methodological, 243; ontological, 242–3
inequality 3, 81–3
influence 60, 61, 63–8, 71, 208
instrumentalism 13–14, 240, 263
integrity 218–22, 220, 227, 234, 236, 237–8
interests 5
internal assent 72, 79–80, 197, 208
international law 180–6, 195–6

judgement, differences of, 318–19; surrender of private, 11, 63–8, 64–7, 72–4, 118–22, 139, 208–9
judges 104, 110–12
justice 305; and obligations of community, 227–30; and social contract, 219–20; social and the state, 317
justification: of authority 1, 129–33, 210–15; authority and, 115–41; of government, 142–51; and political legitimacy, 302–6
justification-rights, 35–9, 42, 116–17

Kant, Immanuel 23, 25–6, 249, 324
Kelsen, H. 15
Kierkegaard, Søren 57, 68

Ladenson, Robert 4, 6, 32–55, 115–18, 140

language 152–60, 244–5
law: coercive nature of the 15; and conflict between authority and autonomy, 29–30; Hobbesian conception of, 32–55, moral authority of the, 218–22; normativity of, 103–13; obedience to the, and promissory undertakings, 274–83; sources of, 106–7; and sovereignty, 40–9
laws: necessity of 162–72; primary, 170
legal issues, relations with moral issues 17–18, 108–13, 218–22, 288–90
legal systems, persistence and continuity 40–4
legal-rational authority (Weber) 61, 81, 190
legislative authority 108–13, 122–3
legislature: moral legitimacy of 109–13; and sovereignty, 45–9
legitimacy, 3, 9–10, 60, 218–22, 231, 238; of an authority, 129–33; *see also* political legitimacy
legitimate authority: denial of possibility of 3–4, 11–12, 29–30; Raz, 211–12
legitimate government 142–73
"legitimate power", authority and 59–63
Lewis, D.K. 196
Lewis, G.C. *Essay on the Influence of Authority in Matters of Opinion* 66–7
liberalism 79, 138, 268, 269, 300–2, 321–3; defence of, 310–11; as a higher-order theory, 307–9
liberty 311, 320; *see also freedom*
limited government, doctrine of 12–14
limits of authority 1, 136–7, 305–6, consent and the, 11–17
Locke, John 21, 164, 173, 252–3, 268, 269, 279
logos, 157–8
Long, Huey 171
Lukes, S. 203–17, 243

MacIntyre, Alasdair 262: *Secularization and Moral Change*, 83–4
Mackie, J.L. 297
McPherson, Thomas 245
McTaggart, J.McT.E. 244
majority vote 167–9, 192
"mark" of authority 68–71, 209
marriage contract 253–4, 255, 287–8, 298
Marx, Karl 207, 241, 249
Marxism 142
membership 17, 244–6, 279–80
mental slavery 87
metaphors 120
Mill, James 61, 64
Mill, John Stuart 82, 249, *On Liberty*, 73
mistakes 136–7, 139

modals 152–60
modern state, and self-sufficiency 264
monarchy 192–3, 199
moral authority 142; dissolution of, 83–4; of the law, 218–22
moral conflict, and political legitimacy, 300–24
moral issues, relations with legal issues, 17–18, 108–13, 230, 288–90
moral obligation, and obedience 24, 269–70
moral personality 260
moral philosophy 25
morality 313–17, 321; self-conscious, 73–4
Murphy, Jeffrie G. 296, 298

Nagel, Thomas 13, 206, 300–24
nationalism 230, 261
natural law (Locke) 52, 173, 177
necessity 152–3
need, for authority 5, 160, 163, 171–2, 174–6
Nesbitt, Winston 195
no-difference thesis (Raz), 126–8, 140
NOMOS 203
normal justification thesis (Raz) 129–33, 211
normative concepts 23, 71, 137–9, 210–15
normativity of law 103–13
norms, existential sentences about 178–9, 201

Oakeshott, Michael 72, 118
oaths 275, 280–1, 283–4, 286–7, 288–90, 292–3; naturalization, 275–6, 284, 288, 296
obedience 148; blind, 72–4, 208–9; coerced or deferential, 62; and moral obligation, 4, 24, 115, 269–70
objectivity 9, 68, 73, 205–6, 308, 313
obligation 101–2: legal and moral unconnected, 109–13; promissory, 268–99; and obedience to the law, 274–80; possible extension of, 291–3
obligations of community 218–39: circumstances and conditions, 222–7; conflicts with justice, 227–30
opinio juris, 180–6, 195
Oppenheim, F. 180
Oxford English Dictionary 57

papal authority 80, 83, 90
parental authority 148
Parkin, F. 207
parliaments 122

participation 17, 257, 276
peremptory forms of address 100–2
permission 2, 95, 97
personality 22, 67, 260
perspectives 204–5: objective, 205–6; society's official, 205, 209; unofficial, 205
persuasion 60, 67
Peters, R.S. 63, 64, 74
Pitkin, Hanna 244–5, 252
Plato 28, 199
pluralism 134, 236, 264
polis 263
political authority 2–3
political community, fraternity and 230–8
political legitimacy: common standpoint theory 303, 304–6, convergence theory, 303–4; moral conflict and, 300–24
political obligation 218–22
political philosophy 20–30, 56–91
political power, moral limits to 305–6
politics, casuistical 25
positivism 108, 177, 178–9
power 20; and authority, 34, 115–16; institutional, 144; legitimized, 60, 62–3; *see also* governmental power
practical authority 104, 115–20; *see also* legislative authority
practical reasonableness 174, 178, 182, 187–8, 191
preemptive thesis 124–5, 133–7; objections, 135–6, 137–9
preference satisfaction 311, 320
prisoner's dilemma, and dependence thesis 128
private/public domains 78–9, 208–9, 314, 315, 319, 321
professions 275, 284
prohibition 95, 97
promises 102, 175, 242, 268–99; in conflict with patterns of obedience, 293–4; express, tacit and implied, 270–4; Hume, 152, 154; implied exceptions, 287–90; to obey, 283–91: conditions, 283–6; terms, 286–91
promissory estoppel 273, 277–8
public/private domains 78–9, 208–9, 314, 315, 319, 321
punishment, theories of 163–4

Quinn, Warren 323

Rawls, John 118, 138, 205–6, 219, 220, 260–1, 274; critique of, 306–7; Original Position, 304–5, 312; Rational Contractor Theory of Morality, 36; Veil of Ignorance, 37, 305
Raz, Joseph 1–19, 93, 110, 111, 115–41,

176, 201, 281–2; *The Authority of Law*, 210–15
reason 63–8; authority and, 1, 115–22
reasons: authoritative legal 102–7; and commands, 92–114; content-independent peremptory, 101–13; dependent (Raz), 121–9; exclusionary (Raz), 93, 176, 184, 195, 210–15; preemptive, 121–2, 124–5, 133–7
reciprocity 224
recognition principle 63–4, 68–71, 132, 208
regimes, evil 38, 38–9, 53
rehabilitation 164
relations of authority identification of 204–17
religious authority 80, 83, 213–14
religious convictions 261, 309, 312, 319–20
religious toleration 301–2, 311
residence, and consent 279–80, 296
responsibility 11, 25–7; taking or forfeiting, 12, 27–9
retribution 163
revolution 44, 54
Rheinstein, Max 201
right: maximally impartial standard 322; prescriptive, 147–8
right to rule 2, 3–6, 35–40, 42–4, 115
rights 151–61: citizenship, 123; primacy of individual, 248–50; transfer of, 162; *see also* claim-right; justification-rights
Rokeach, Milton 70
Rousseau, Jean-Jacques 17, 21, 27, 240, 269
rulership 186–94
rules 190–4; bound by their own, 192–4; of a game, 177; and orders, 33; primary and secondary (Hart), 49–50, 169; of recognition (Hart), 50, 69; role of, 134; social context of, 246–7; as stopping modals, 153–60

sanctions 94, 250
Sandel, Michael 260–1
Sartorius, Rolf 287
Scanlon, T.M. 305
self 260–1
self-defence 35–6, 39
service conception 131–2, 135, 137, 138, 211
shared goods, and civic life 255–8
shared values 209, 246
Sidgwick, Henry 323
Simmons, John 287
Simon, Yves 192
Singer, Peter 278
skepticism 312
social contract 11, 100, 219, 268–99; and promises to obey, 268–70
social control 60
social relations 241–2
social roles, and identity 258–63
social rules 104–5
social science 59–60, 88
social thesis 249, 254, 258; atomism and the, 248–50
Socrates 242, 296
Soper, Philip 296–7
sovereignty 20–1, 32–3, 37–40; divided, 43; Hobbes, 34, 37–8; legal limitations on, 45–9
speech acts 93
Spinoza, Baruch 72, 78
standpoints 311–14: impersonal, 320–3
state: authority of the 58–9; concept of the (Wolff), 20; de *facto*, 21, 23–5; legitimacy, 218–22; monopoly of violence, 165; moral authority of, 29–30, 250; necessity of the, 37; neutrality re good, 13; power of the, 3; and social justice, 317; source of authority of, 142–73
subjectivism, collective 210
subjectivity 8, 9, 68
submission to the will of others 4, 16–17
subsidiarity, principle of 176
succession, rule of 42–4, 49

task 148, 160–1
tax laws 122, 124, 127
Taylor, Charles 248–50
theoretical authority 2, 4–6, 108–13, 129
Thompson, Judith 35–6
Tocqueville, Alexis de 58, 64
toleration 257, 301–2, 309, 312, 317
traditional authority 72–4
traditions 22, 28, 137–8
transmission theories 188, 191
truth, belief and 314–23
Tussman, J. 296
tyranny 192

Ullmann, Walter 80, 83
Ullmann-Margalit, Edna 194
unanimity 175–6, 180, 189, 192
unfair exchange 286–7
universality conditions in ethics 307–9, 310–11
usurpation 191, 198
utilitarianism 5–6, 25, 304, 311

values 244
violence: evil as canonized 148–9; legitimate, 60; protection against, 162–72, 165–6; resistance to, 161–72; of

the state, 144, 147, 148–50
volition (Bentham) 94–102
voluntary associations 143, 151, 251
voting, and consent 276–80

Walzer, Michael 205, 284
Weber, Max 22–3, 30, 56, 60, 61, 190, 206–7; charismatic authority, 61, 80, 81, 190
will, 251, 253–4; Bentham's, 94–102; of commander, 65–6; not to will, 72; submission to another's, 4, 16–17
Winch, Peter 91, 246, 247
witness 75, 284, 286–7
Wittgenstein, Ludwig 246
Wolff, Robert Paul, 11, 20–31, 118: *In Defence of Anarchy*, 3–4

www.ingramcontent.com/pod-product-compliance
Ingram Content Group UK Ltd.
Pitfield, Milton Keynes, MK11 3LW, UK
UKHW041303180426
11947UKWH00009B/657